Books in

THE IRWIN SERIES IN INDUSTRIAL
ENGINEERING AND MANAGEMENT

THE WRITINGS OF THE GILBRETHS
Edited by WILLIAM R. SPRIEGEL *and* CLARK E. MYERS,
both of the University of Texas

PRINCIPLES OF MANAGEMENT
By GEORGE R. TERRY, *Northwestern University*

MANUFACTURING MANAGEMENT
By FRANKLIN G. MOORE, *Northwestern University*

THE WRITINGS

OF

THE GILBRETHS

The Writings

OF THE

GILBRETHS

Edited by

WILLIAM R. SPRIEGEL, *Dean*
College of Business Administration

and

CLARK E. MYERS, *Chairman*
Department of Management
College of Business Administration

BOTH OF THE UNIVERSITY OF TEXAS

1953

RICHARD D. IRWIN, INC.

HOMEWOOD, ILLINOIS

First Printing, May, 1953

Foreword

•••

It is a real service to bring the writings of the pioneers in Scientific Management back into print. Many of the younger group in the field of Industrial Management do not know these works; more hear them misinterpreted. All may well read for themselves what was said and evaluate for themselves the principles and practices described.

Dean Spriegel and Professor Myers have done a workmanlike job. They have sensed the compelling interest in human beings that inspired the invention and use of techniques. And they have woven the material in several books into a fabric which shows the pattern of the principles and practice of motion study. Not only the design but the color has been conserved.

The members of the Gilbreth family are grateful to Dean Spriegel, to Professor Myers, and to the Publisher. We believe that the larger family who use and develop Motion Study material will be grateful also.

LILLIAN M. GILBRETH

Introduction

●●

This volume pays tribute to two great American pioneers in the field of management, Frank B. and Lillian M. Gilbreth. The writings of the Gilbreths, based on the practical application of scientific management principles to their own business as well as the numerous other business concerns where they were called in consultation, merit publication in a single volume. Students and teachers in the field continue to seek and study their concepts and principles. The original books are out of print and are difficult to obtain.

It has not been easy to decide what to include and what to omit in editing the writings. The following general rules were followed:

1. To include all evidences of principles and problems which seem of a permanent and lasting nature.

2. To exclude those things which were of technological significance only at the time of the early writings. This has resulted in omitting many charts, tables, and photographs. Such omissions are usually noted.

3. To avoid repetition and duplication of concepts which were inevitable in such a series of writings.

4. To avoid as much as possible the duplication of their contemporaries' works which are found in detail in other writings. There are many references to Frederick W. Taylor's earlier writings. The early volumes are now out of print; but *Shop Management, The Principles of Scientific Management,* and *Taylor's Testimony before the Special House Committee* were combined into one volume and published by Harper and Brothers in 1947.

5. To retain the original wording except for minor editing and correction of words currently used or spelled differently from the time of the original writing, and where minor changes were necessary for continuity and readability.

Throughout the process of reading and studying the writings there has developed a growing appreciation of the recognition by the Gilbreths of basic concepts concerning (1) the joint relationship of the employer-employee, (2) the importance of feelings, sentiments, and emotions in the motivation of individual workers, and (3) the appropriate emphasis on methods improvement, that is, the search for "the best way" to perform a task as a means of greater production. Further, we have been increasingly impressed with the fact that in many more recent writings there has been too great a shift from some of these fundamental concepts to details and techniques.

The permanent contribution of the Gilbreths warrants the republication of parts of their major writings.

WILLIAM R. SPRIEGEL
CLARK E. MYERS

UNIVERSITY OF TEXAS
April, 1953

Table of Contents

1

•••

FIELD
*SYSTEM**

* *Field System,* by Frank B. Gilbreth, was published by the Myron C. Clark Publishing Co., New York and Chicago, in 1908.

Introduction [1]

●●

Organization in the contracting field presents two phases which often seem to diverge greatly. One, the possibilities in theory, and the other, the possibilities in practice. It is in the application of theory, in its reduction to an ultimate working basis, that its proof lies. The proof of the pudding lies in the eating no less truly than the proof of theory in the result of its application. The factor which varies, and which often brings apparently logical theories to an unfortunate conclusion, is the difference between working conditions which obtain in actuality, and ideal conditions which unfortunately exist only in theory.

The direction of a large body of men of various degrees of intelligence, working in different localities, some perhaps far removed from headquarters, is an assignment requiring experience, brains, and a highly specialized training in the art of handling men. The large contractor executing many contracts simultaneously has this proposition to face, and the problems which must be solved are many and puzzling.

The manufacturer as a rule groups his men, machines, and facilities at one location, possibly under one roof, in any case in one plant. His forces, under effective direction, may work as a unit; one branch of the industry is within sound of the whir of machinery incident to the next step in the process of manufacture. Such contact makes for unity, and system may more nearly follow the points of least resistance. A contractor has no such grouping of his forces by location to aid him. One structure is erected in one state and another perhaps a thousand miles distant. The one building may be a factory, the other a city sky-scraper. Both are structures, but further than this the analogy may cease. Such conditions, peculiar as they are to the in-

[1] From an article in "Business World" for November, 1907, in which John P. Slack outlines the dependence of Gilbreth's office system upon his "Field System." It shows how the loose-leaf reports from the field are made to serve the place of an elaborate set of books, and how it becomes unnecessary to employ high-priced bookkeepers.

3

dustry, must be met by a completeness of organization, and by an effectiveness and comprehensiveness of systematization, which will make for results in the strenuous competition which obtains in the building trade.

A notable instance of the application of a working system through which field work may be executed from beginning to end is found in the organization of Frank B. Gilbreth of New York. His "Field System" has become almost a by-word in the building trades, since its completeness and effectiveness have been excelled by no contractor's working system which has yet been devised. It is by no means the work of one man, or any few men. Many of the suggestions contained therein have emanated from the lips of the humblest workmen, and none of its effectiveness is lost through the fact that such suggestions are expressed in the terse, significant language of the workmen themselves.

For several years previous to its recent publication the Gilbreth "Field System" was open to the inspection only of the men in the employ of that organization. Only a limited number of copies of the volume were in existence, each being numbered, and the possessor of each being accountable for its return even to the extent of being bonded for a small sum to cover its loss. Notwithstanding such precautions, unscrupulous competitors sought in many ways to obtain the information contained in this volume. Office boys were bribed, certain pages were photographed, and discharged superintendents in one or two instances carried the book with them. However, its publication makes such attempts no longer necessary, and shows a most broad-minded and generous spirit on the part of the contractor as well.

A feature of the Gilbreth "Field System" which is worthy of comment, is the system of accounting without books, which it outlines and which has been in practical use by this organization for some little time. The idea is sufficiently broad in scope to make it adaptable to other than the needs of contractors alone, and is so economical that a number of owners of buildings erected by Frank B. Gilbreth, have adopted it for use in their factories as well. As an illustration of its effectiveness in large contracts, there may be cited three complete industrial towns which the Gilbreth organization erected, each in the phenomenal time of a few months; one at Sprague's Falls, Maine, one at Piercefield, N.Y., and another at Canton, N.C. On each of these contracts the system of accounting without books, fully described below, was used, and the size of the contracts alone furnishes eloquent testimony to the excellence of the system. It has been the execution of such contracts as the three above noted which has associated with the Gilbreth name the phase of "towns to order" and which amply justifies its use.

.   .   .   .

The Gilbreth system of accounting without books accomplishes, then, six things:

1. It does away with experienced or high-priced bookkeepers.

2. It shows the cost of the job each Saturday up to the previous Thursday night.

3. It shows the owner the cost of the materials before they are bought.

4. It shows constantly the comparative cost of the work with the contractor's estimate book.

5. It is a system of bookkeeping without books. It files the original memorandum and saves cost of copying and errors of copying.

6. It saves the cost of expert bookkeeping.

General Outlines
of Field System

•••

This system contains the written ideas of the most successful men in our employ.

In printing it we have in view the following aims:

1. To HAVE THE BEST PRACTICE in all departments put in writing for the benefit of all employees.

2. To AVOID REPEATING ORALLY, by putting in writing, all those instructions from which there are no exceptions.

3. To MAINTAIN THE POLICY OF THIS FIRM, namely—that the best work will in the long run bring us the most profit, success and satisfaction.

Maintaining this system has contributed to our success. It has en-

abled us to make a specialty of "speed work," because our superintendents, foremen and timekeepers are trained on the "duplicate
part" system.

As our organization is built thus, like a machine, we can supply
additional foremen, who, being already trained to their duties, know
what is expected of them and can take charge of the work immediately at any point.

Nothing in this system hinders progress. Improvements will be
incorporated as approved. These rules in their present condition
have been proved good by the great increase in our business during
their use.

All employees must follow these rules to the letter unless they receive written permission to suspend certain rules.

Employees who fail to abide by the spirit of these rules will not
receive promotion.

We shall appreciate and will pay money for suggestions that will
improve this system.

Under Our "Cost-Plus-A-Fixed-Sum" Contract

••

We furnish all superintendence, labor and materials, and complete
the project for actual cost plus a fixed sum. To owners desiring speed
combined with economy, this form of contract has the following advantages:

The owner's and the contractor's interests are made identical.

The owner knows in advance exactly how much the contractor's
profit will be.

The owner's interests require that the work be executed in the
shortest possible time at the lowest possible cost and with the best
quality of workmanship.

The owner's interests are absolutely identical with those of the
contractor in every one of these particulars, because his profit or

salary being assured, the contractor's only interest is to perform the work in such a manner as to retain the Owner's patronage.

The owner is relieved of the menace of "extras"—all the work is done at cost. The contractor's fixed sum is in no way affected by the changes in the plans.

The owner has the benefit of all cash discounts for materials.

The owner knows what all materials will cost before they are purchased.

The owner gets the benefit of the lists of materials we have on file which the various dealers have in stock ready for immediate delivery.

The owner has the advantages derived from accurate schedules and shop drawings made for our purchasing department.

The owner has the use of our purchasing department, which is constantly in touch with the best class of sub-contractors and material dealers in several cities.

The owner can purchase the materials if he so desires.

The owner can have his excavation and foundations completed while plans for the superstructure are being drawn.

The owner, Engineer or Architect can make changes and alterations at any time without delaying the work.

The owner has the benefit of the saving occasioned by special designs for all kinds of labor saving devices.

The owner can have any number of skilled and carefully trained mechanics massed on his contract at a moment's notice.

The owner has at his command our mechanical and steam engineers, and riggers for unloading and setting all kinds of engines, boilers, pumps, machinery, shafting, piping, generators, conveyors, etc.

The owner, Engineer and Architect have at their command the services of our specially trained staff of civil, mechanical and concrete engineers.

The owner knows what the contractor's profit is to be, from the very outset of the work. It is the same amount irrespective of the cost of the work, and there is, therefore, no incentive for the contractor to produce anything but substantial and economical work.

The owner has his building at a minimum cost.

The owner has his building completed as rapidly as is consistent with good workmanship.

The owner, or his authorized representative, has access at all times to all matters pertaining to the work.

Every superintendent and foreman should use special efforts at all times to secure the greatest speed and at the same time be economical.

Speed is more often secured by organization than by crowding the work with a large number of men.

There is no way that speed can be obtained so easily, with so little confusion, and with so little trouble to the superintendent and foreman as by dividing the job into several portions and then by dividing any one kind of work into several similar portions, placing a working foreman and the same number of men on each portion.

Workmen like athletic contests and will enter into the spirit of them quite as quickly and with the same spirit of rivalry as a college trained team. Therefore, the men will be interested in their work to a larger extent if it is understood at the time that the several gangs start on the several pieces of work that there is to be an athletic contest.

Contests of this kind not only give great speed and reduce cost, but they also enable the superintendent to recognize foremen and mechanics of ability and promote them to higher positions.

In carrying out this scheme, careful attention must be given to the following points:

(a) The work should be divided into similar portions and conducted under approximately the same conditions.
(b) The same number of men should be on each portion.
(c) The same amount and kind of plant should be utilized on each portion.
(d) It has been found advisable in some cases to arrange the men in accordance with their nationality or other bonds of sympathy.
(e) Recognition in the form of promotion or increase of pay to the working foreman whose men do the most and best work.

An increase of 20 per cent in the total day's work was the result on one of our jobs because the superintendent permitted the pile driver gang that drove the most piles one day to float their country's flag from the top of the machine all the next day.

When contests cannot be forced by pride of victory alone, the reward of an extra half hour or hour to each member of the winning gang has been found very effective. On one of our jobs it was found that an extra hour to the winning gang unloading cars of brick cut down the total labor expense nearly 50 per cent.

Example No. 1: If two brick walls can be started at the same time with the same number of bricklayers and laborers, the men will undoubtedly lay more brick than they would if no athletic contest were taking place. It is advisable also to place an even number of men on each wall so that the same number will be on each side of the team, and there can then be made a contest to see which side lays out its line first.

Example No. 2: If a concrete wall is to be constructed, it can generally be divided up into rows of columns and bays, and if the same number of rows of columns be given to the same number of men and careful statistics kept as to which one can set up the most columns in a given time, there is no doubt but that more work can be accomplished in competition than otherwise.

Example No. 3: If brick piers are to be constructed in a basement, there should be at least as many bricklayers start as there are rows of piers. They should all start at the same time and the piers should be divided up preferably by rows, so that when a bricklayer has finished his pier, instead of taking the first pier that comes along he takes the next pier in his row, so that the extent of the contest should be one entire row of piers for each man.

By careful study a superintendent can divide up nearly every part of his work on this basis. By so doing, there will be less trouble for the foreman in charge. Money will be saved for the Owner. More speed will be obtained, all of which will tend to increase if possible the popularity of "Cost-Plus-a-Fixed-Sum" method of contracting.

General Rules

•••

1   A copy of this *Field System* must be kept in the office on each job.

2   Address all communications to *Frank B. Gilbreth,* and not to any other name. They will then be attended to promptly and not treated as personal mail.

3   Notify office of *accidents* at once by telephone or telegraph if accident is serious. Accident blanks must be filled out, the original mailed to insurance company's agent, and the duplicate to New York Office at once.

4   Sign *"received,"* with name and date on the back of all plans, details, drawings or sketches (stamp in the middle of the plan if possible), regardless of where or from whom the plans are received. This will prevent the substitution of blueprints from altered tracings.

5   Provide every convenience for Owners or Officials who inspect your work.

6   To prevent confusion, Superintendents must do business through the Architect or Engineer—*not* with the Owner direct.

7   Estimates are not to be given by anyone, at any time, without first consulting the Office.

8   Foremen, Superintendents and Timekeepers should ask the Office for schedules of lumber, hardware, iron, etc., to assist in checking up the material when it is received.

9   Dimension stone, window and door frames, and steel, should be checked for dimensions upon arrival at the job. Make full report of material received in damaged condition.

10   Notify Office of shortages of windows, doors, steel, stone, etc., as early as possible, to avoid *waiting* later.

11   Get receipts for all money paid and stock delivered.

12   When buying brick, remember that for every 1/8″ that one make of brick is longer than another it is worth about 10 cents more per 1,000. For every 1-16″ that one make of brick is thicker than another it is worth about 20 cents more per 1,000.

13   Consult Office about itemizing workmen's time so that costs may be compared with similar jobs and with our estimate book.

14   Every Superintendent starting a job shall write to the Office for definite instructions as to just what action to take in regard to accidents to our employees.

15   When men are wanted, ask the Office. We have men calling at the Office every day, and can sometimes send them to a job at once. Do not, however, depend upon the Office—get the men yourself if possible.

16   Do not bother the Office unnecessarily.

17   Get from foremen and workmen the names and addresses of men in other trades who would be good men for us.

18   *Union* laborers are to be given preference at all times, but no nonsense is to be taken from them.

19   *Business agents of unions* are to have full opportunity to consult job stewards. See that they confine themselves strictly to business.

20   Any one of our employees found guilty of disobeying any Rule in the *Field System* must render an explanation in writing. This explanation will be filed, so that we may find out those who make the least mistakes and those who do not understand the Rules.

21   Ignorance of the Rules in this *system* excuses no employee.

22   No employee is to sign any agreement with any *labor union* without written permission from F. B. G.

23   *Blow one blast of whistle* at 5 minutes before starting time.
      Two blasts at starting time.
      One blast at quitting time.
      Blasts of whistle to be not over *4 seconds long.*

24   All men are expected to quit work at quitting time as promptly as they began work.

25   Keep duplicate engine bells on the job to avoid delay in case of a breakdown.

26   No smoking is allowed on the job except to finish noon smoke —not over one half hour—and no refilling of pipes. All steady pay men must see that this rule is fully enforced.

27   On all jobs where there is a temporary privy or a permanent closet, there should be kept a small can of chloride of lime. This can best be handled in one pound cans. Common lime is often used as a disinfectant, but is less effective and costs more.

28   *No employee is to sign an agreement* with anyone which will place upon this firm any legal liability. By this is meant rights-of-way across land, use of buildings, etc.

29   When placing *builders' risk fire insurance* be sure that our plant is covered, as well as the building. Also see that the fire insurance policies include lightning and earthquake clauses.

30   Superintendents, foremen and timekeepers are to provide themselves with transit, steel tape, plumb bob, and Sargent steel square graduated in twelfths and sixteenths.

31   Our *office force* of *civil, mechanical,* and *concrete engineers* can be had to lay out work or assemble machinery.

32   When a job is completed, superintendent and timekeeper must see that all plans, letters, papers, manifold books, etc., are returned to Office, and that all White List cards have been made out.

33   Take advantage of *average freight service* wherever possible. This system, which is in force on most railroads, is as follows:—If the usual time allowed for unloading cars before demurrage is charged is 72 hours, we are allowed an average of 72 hours for all cars (under this system). That is, if we save 24 hours by unloading one car in 48 hours, we can have this time credited to us on some other car and thereby have 96 hours to unload that car before demurrage charges commence.

34   When piling lumber:

Leave wide spaces between the boards or planks, so that they may dry more quickly.

Give the top layer considerable pitch, so that water will drain off.

Turn the top layer over frequently to prevent curling.

Rules for Suggestions and Reports

Monthly reports are requested from everybody in our organization desiring promotion. The reports are to contain suggestions on work improvement, rendering better service to customers, and securing additional jobs, as well as any other suggestions that will tend to promote our business.

[EDITORS' NOTE: Recently much attention has been given to stimulating the initiative and creative imagination of workers. Gilbreth early recognized that his subordinates were capable of making valu-

---

PRIZES FOR
SUGGESTIONS

We desire to secure improvement in all departments of our business, and to this end have adopted a plan whereby employees and others may have an incentive to make suggestions with the assurance that all such suggestions will have careful and impartial consideration. Should such suggestions prove of value, the suggester will thereby qualify to compete for a series of prizes to be awarded monthly to employees offering the best suggestions.

Suggestions are invited from all classes of employees. No suggestion need be held back because it appears to be of little importance. The simplest ideas are often valuable.

Suggestions lead to promotion and increased value. They show an interest in our work and organization, and a capacity for greater responsibilities. We invite suggestions upon methods or equipment, methods which will cause more speed, economy or better work, and other matters calculated to advance the interests of the business.

RULES COVERING SUGGESTIONS

All suggestions submitted will be under the supervision of Frank B. Gilbreth, personally.

Write your suggestion and mail it to F. B. G. marked "personal."

Suggestions will be considered promptly. For each suggestion that is accepted, the Company will award the suggester the sum of one dollar, which will be sent to the employee when he is notified that his suggestion has been accepted. We will then be at liberty to adopt the suggestion at any time at our option.

PRIZES

We will award monthly the sum of $20.00 for the most valuable suggestions received during the previous month. This amount will be divided as follows:

First Prize	$10.00
Second Prize	5.00
Third Prize	3.00
Fourth Prize	2.00
	$20.00

METHOD OF AWARDING PRIZES

On the first Monday of each month, employees who have made suggestions of the greatest value during the preceding month, will be awarded prizes in the order of the value of the suggestion.

As soon as the awards are made, the prizes will be paid in cash, and notices will be posted giving the names of the prize winners, together with a brief description of their suggestions.

Per Order
FRANK B. GILBRETH

Fig. 1. The Suggestion System

able suggestions. The use of suggestion systems is quite common today but the concept of seeking suggestions in Gilbreth's time was not generally practiced. While the cash awards were small, note the recognition of the value of publicizing the winners' names (see Fig. 1).]

Steady Pay Men

All steady pay men must arrive on the job before the first whistle is sounded, and must remain on the job until quitting time, regardless of weather, but men will not get time for hanging around the office and reporting for duty. They must actually be at work at such things as are mentioned below.

The intention of the above is to abolish the past customs regarding steady pay men, and applies to everybody, from the Superintendent down to the Apprentice Boy, inclusive.

Foremen and timekeepers must report to the Superintendent before starting or before leaving work.

Apprentices are subject to all the rules of Steady Pay Men.

When work is stopped by bad weather Steady Pay Men shall keep busy, if there is no other work for them, at the following:

A—Making trestles and patent horses.

B—Repairing wheelbarrows.

C—Repairing hods.

D—Mending hose.

E—Repairing engine houses and locker.

F—Putting handles in tampers.

G—Cleaning up tool house.

H—Cleaning transits.

I—Preparing staging and runs.

J—Sharpening saws.

K—Sawing off handles of worthless shovels.

L—Checking up lines and levels.

M—Checking up for dimensions—all steel, window and door frames, dimension stone, etc.

N—Cleaning and oiling steel tapes.

O—Cleaning roof, so that rain will not wash rubbish into conductor pipes.

P—Brushing off sills and projections, so that mortar will not make stains from rain.

Q—Cutting arches and other fancy brickwork.

R—Stamping and branding tools. Brands should not be heated too hot; if heated more than just enough to show red, the letters will burn off.

S—Examining lime to see that little or none is in powder.

T—Examining cement to see if *"condemned"* has been erased from barrel or brand.

U—Piling cement and lime at least 6″ above the ground.

V—Seeing if cement and lime are getting wet.

W—Packing cement bags.

X—Cleaning mortar from projections before it is set.

Y—Covering masonry projections to prevent chipping by falling brick.

Apprentice boys should be worked to their full capacity. Help them in every possible way to learn and get promoted. Answer all their questions about work and plans, that are asked in good faith.

Every superintendent, timekeeper and steady pay man must suppress subscriptions for presents, and all other forms of graft.

All steady pay employees, whether on the job or in the office, must keep the office notified of their *addresses* at all times. This rule also applies during vacations.

Foremen masons and foremen carpenters should each go out of his way to accommodate the other, and should grant the requests of each other promptly.

Foremen masons, foremen carpenters, foremen plasterers, and timekeepers, *must work in harmony,* because all steady pay men receive credit or blame according as the conduct of the job is good or bad. Teamwork and sacrifice hits are often more effective than "grand-stand plays."

We have in the past been awarded much work on the basis of *cost-plus-a-fixed-sum,* because we have the reputation of handling such work as if it were lump-sum contract work. *Maintaining this reputation* is the best service which can be rendered this firm, as we try to merit the award of contracts to us without *competition.*

Our steady pay men are the representatives of our firm: Therefore, their private character and their conduct outside of working hours will be counted in considering promotions.

Superintendents are expected to handle their work with such skill, promptness and efficiency that we shall continue to merit such unsolicited letters as [that shown in the accompanying illustration].

HOLLIS FRENCH & ALLEN HUBBARD
CONSULTING ENGINEERS
Albany Bldg., Boston.

November 8, 1902

Mr. F. B. Gilbreth,
Federal Street,
Boston, Mass.

DEAR SIR:—

We are very glad to be able to write you that the work which you have done for us on a basis of cost plus commission, notably in the work of altering the hotel at Bellows Falls and enlarging the power station canal at Garvins Falls has been most satisfactory.

The systematic way in which your accounts are rendered, and the prompt and efficient service which you have invariably given us has been a source of gratification to ourselves as well as to our clients.

Yours truly,
HOLLIS FRENCH & ALLEN HUBBARD

Photograph System

Gilbreth recognized the value of photographic records. They were used to keep office employees in touch with conditions on the jobs, for advertising purposes, for records in case of lawsuits, and for records of conditions of adjoining buildings to record any effects of settlement due to construction work on the Gilbreth project.

Photographs of conditions at the time of an accident were recognized as being particularly important.

Detailed instructions on time exposures, interiors, snap shots, and photographing moving objects were given, as well as instructions on camera and film care.

White List Cards

• •

We wish to keep track of those workmen who work in our interests, and to let them know when we need men. Get the addresses of those men who work faithfully. Make out a white list card for each good man when discharged or laid off.

As any business grows, the employees lose their individuality with their employer. This is discouraging to a workman who desires to have his efforts appreciated. We have devised a *"white list"* card so that we may know what each foreman thinks of an employee.

We shall send, to men of good records, postal card notifications which will put them on solid footing with any of our foremen, whether the men are known to them or not. We believe that the best class of workmen will appreciate our efforts and co-operate with us in making this system a success.

Workmen who spend the least time talking with one another during working hours, will, if other qualifications are equal, receive preference when the work slacks down.

Men who present *"white list"* notification cards must be given preference by our foremen at all times.

At the completion of the job, the Superintendent and Timekeeper must go over the time sheets and make sure that the proper White List Cards have been made out.

[EDITORS' NOTE: In devising the "white list" Gilbreth showed recognition of the importance of recording data on superior workers. Figure 2 is a rather simple merit-rating form, but evidence is presented that Gilbreth early realized that a record of performance was worth keeping. Further, he realized that as a company grew larger the employees lost their identity with their employer and that this was more discouraging to a workman desiring to have his efforts appreciated than to a poor workman. The purpose of the "white list" was twofold, then, to know what the foreman thought of an employee, and to give the employee the satisfaction of knowing that his efforts were appreciated sufficiently to give him preference in future employment. With the Gilbreth reputation it can be assumed that the "white card" carried prestige and value with other employers.]

Write Last NAME First	Trade
	Write Address on Back of This Card
(Cross Out the Answers You Do NOT Use)	
Number of Contract Where He Worked Last	
He Is a VERY PROFITABLE MAN and Should Be Sent for every Time We need Men of His Trade	
He Is a FAIRLY PROFITABLE MAN	
I Could Not Judge His Ability	
I Consider Him A	Class Man
Cause For His Leaving Us	
The Work He Is Most Profitable on Is	
This Card Was Made Out By	
Form 8–10/16/06 1000	

FIG. 2.   Rating Form Used in Preparing White List Card

2

CONCRETE
SYSTEM*

* *Concrete System,* by Frank B. Gilbreth, was published by The Engineering News Publishing Co., New York, in May, 1908.

Introduction—Publisher's Preface

••

The source or origin of the work is as purely practical as its purpose. The instructions are almost a stenographic report of what a successful concrete contractor said to his workmen; they contain his mandatory orders, his cautions, his reprimands, his suggestions for securing best quality and best speed of output. But—and here the work differs fundamentally from the typical book—there was nothing steady or consecutive in the process of writing it down; it was a gradual accumulation, the fruit of several years of slow growth. When an order was issued, or a caution given, or when a certain way of doing a thing was fixed as the standard, then a written memorandum was made, in the form in which the Rules appear here in the text. So, as the execution of successive concrete jobs brought them out, these Rules were gradually accumulated. Finally the time came when new accessions to the Rules were infrequent and entire large contracts were carried through without developing a new rule or changing a method. Then the collection of rules was grouped in a classified arrangement, as far as possible, for readier reference, and the result is the present "Concrete System."

Under these circumstances, of course, the reader need expect no thorough-going order of classification or arrangement, nor any exhaustive completeness. The one is impossible because of the very way in which the matter originated. Completeness, on the other hand, was not called for because the special tools and standardized appliances whose use is implied by the Rules are in the hands and before the eyes of the workmen, and thus do not require to be described in the text of the Rules; while at the same time the systematization of method, which permits only one way of doing a given thing on all Gilbreth contracts, forbids the description and discussion of the other possible methods for that operation.

21

General Outlines of the Concrete System

●●●

This Concrete System contains the written ideas of the most successful men in our organization. The illustrations are taken from our own works exclusively.

In printing it we have in view the following aims:

1. To HAVE THE BEST PRACTICE in all departments put in writing for the benefit of all employees.

2. To AVOID REPEATING ORALLY, by putting in writing, all those instructions from which there are no exceptions.

3. To MAINTAIN THE POLICY OF THIS FIRM, namely, that the best work will, in the long run, bring us the most profit, success, and satisfaction.

Maintaining this System has contributed to our success. It has enabled us to make a specialty of "speed work," because our superintendents, foremen, and timekeepers are trained in the "duplicate part" system.

As our organization is built thus, like a machine, we can supply additional foremen, who, being already trained to their duties, know what is expected of them and are able to take charge of the work immediately at any point.

Nothing in this System hinders progress. Improvements will be incorporated as approved. These rules in their present condition have been proved good by the great increase in our business during their use.

All employees must follow these rules to the letter, unless they receive written permission to suspend certain rules.

Employees who fail to abide by the spirit of these rules will not receive promotion.

We shall appreciate and will pay money for suggestions that will improve this system.

General Rules

●●

1   In the absence of any plans, specifications, or instructions to the contrary from our office, these rules must be carried out to the letter.

2   We have never had any concrete work fall down, and we never will have if the rules in this System are carried out. If we are obliged to do work in a different way from that which we believe to be the best way, we must protect ourselves by getting our views on record in writing.

3   If you receive orders from the owner, architect, or engineer that are contrary to any of these rules, you must notify our office of their wishes and request them to give their orders to you through our office. We are then able to put our protests on record, in writing, at the time we proceed in accordance with their orders.

4   Field work must be under the general supervision of the Main Office.

5   Field office, engine house, tool houses and all temporary buildings should wherever possible be built and equipped according to standard designs on file at the office.

6   The "Field System" shall govern any matters not covered by this System, such as accounting, receipt of materials, general orders, manifold books, and all other matters not pertaining to concrete.

7   Employees must not alter or change an architect's or engineer's plans or specifications under any conditions whatever.

8   Employees must not discuss an architect's or engineer's plans with any one except members of our organization.

9   No employee is permitted to have anything whatsoever to do with any job where there is not an architect or engineer employed by the owner.

(We have never deviated from this rule in the past, and shall not permit any violations of this rule in the future.)

10   The superintendent must be on the work during regular working hours, and at such other times as may be necessary.

11   When starting a new job, the superintendent shall have a line diagram made on tracing cloth, showing general layout of work, posts, girders, beams, panels, etc., and shall send a blueprint of same to Main Office daily with Daily Letter after having indicated thereon

---

Office of the
  President

                    MASSACHUSETTS INSTITUTE OF
                              TECHNOLOGY.
                          BOSTON, MASS.

        Frank Gilbreth, Esq.,
          176 Federal St.,
            Boston, Mass.

        DEAR SIR:—
            I have the honor to inform you that the Lowell Laboratory of Electrical Engineering, which you have built during the past summer, has been today inspected by the committee and accepted. I wish to express to you, at the same time, the thanks of the Executive Committee and of the Building Committee for the promptness, efficiency and skill with which the work has been carried through.
                                Yours very sincerely,
                                (HENRY S. PRITCHETT)
                                        President
        October 29, 1902

---

the amount of work accomplished, and what athletic contests have been carried out that day. Consult Main Office for instructions regarding method of marking up these blueprints.

12   Superintendents shall make up and send into the office a sketch of a plant and equipment layout, and also a system chart showing which men they recommend for assistants on their job. The office will return these to the job as soon as revised and approved.

13   A few sample charts showing layouts and routes of authority as submitted and approved are given on the following pages to show superintendents what is expected of them.

14   The superintendent must take enough photographs to keep the office in perfect touch with his job.

MASSACHUSETTS INSTITUTE OF TECHNOLOGY

BOSTON .... Nov. . 3, . 1902.........

Frank B. Gilbreth Esq
176 Federal St. Boston Mass

DEAR SIR,—
     In behalf of the Massachusetts Institute of Technology the building committee hereby accept the Lowell Laboratory of Electrical Engineering.
     The rapidity with which the work has been done is remarkable. The time stated in the contract seemed short, but you have completed the building much more quickly than the contract required. You have shown in all our dealings with you a most liberal spirit and we are glad to have this opportunity to express our thanks and hearty approval.

Faithfully yours,
Henry S. Pritchett,
Francis H. Williams,
George Wigglesworth,

Building Committee Mass. Inst. Technology
by (GEORGE WIGGLESWORTH,)
Treasurer

---

15   Superintendents must put all matters of importance on record in the Daily Letter. Records often prevent misunderstandings and lawsuits.

16   Superintendents must so conduct their work that they will receive letters from the owner similar to [that shown in the accompanying illustrations].

It is the feeling expressed in letters like these that will bring us repeat orders.

17   On jobs of sufficient magnitude the superintendent will, upon request, be assisted by an engineer who will give lines, levels, and grades, and look after such tests of cement, steel, and other materials as may be required.

18   All work is to be divided and assigned to foremen in charge of the following branches:

Carpenter work
Reinforcement
Concrete

19   These branches should be subdivided into subbranches, with a leader at the head of each subbranch.

20   There is too much talk to the effect that concrete men need not be skilled. Use only skilled men when they are obtainable. Break in unskilled men on work where they can do the least harm. It is always good practice to have the unskilled laborer put in charge of a skilled leader, as well as under a working foreman.

21   The number of men setting forms, setting steel, and concreting, should be regulated so that all three operations can be conducted continuously.

22   Too much stress cannot be laid on the importance of Athletic Contests to secure speed and economy.

24   Great care should be given to have the right number of men to each gang, or the contest will not be entered into with the same spirit that characterizes a contest where the men and the work are divided properly.

25   Work of this character should always be laid out so that the day's work in concrete will stop in a straight line in the middle of the span.

26   On jobs of comparatively small floor area, an entirely different method must be adopted. Use carpenters to get forms erected, and then transfer them to other work. Then put on the reinforcement gang for a few days, and then set them at other work. Next put on the concrete gang, and, when the floor is concreted, lay them off, and then it will be the carpenters' turn again.

27   While this method has many drawbacks, it is generally more economical than any other method.

28   This is much easier to carry out in cities than in small settlements, and is much easier when labor is plentiful than when it is scarce.

29   When laborers are secured through an employment agency, the following facts must be borne in mind:

30   Deal only with licensed agencies.

32   Do not hire men from an agent without the distinct understanding in writing that the men must actually go to work—we once had to pay fees for men who reported at the station but who never took the train.

33   When workmen are temporarily out of work, they should be kept busy with the following:

> Scraping out hoppers, wheelbarrows, and carts
> Cleaning off runs
> Cleaning up rubbish
> Greasing wire falls

Mixing

••

Superintendents must confer with the office regarding the design of the scheme of plant set-up. They should study the typical layouts used on other jobs and the catalogues of well-known manufacturers of mixer, hoist, and other apparatus. By giving this matter considerable attention and study, and by examining sketches of what has been done by other superintendents, much saving may be made in labor and generally much more speed can be obtained by eliminating unnecessary delay.

Set-ups should be designed so that gravity can be used for feeding, breakdowns will not stop the job, and materials will be handled the least number of times before they reach their final position.

In a very good layout for a medium sized job:

a. The stone teams drive up on a platform and dump their loads near the stone crusher, which is located in a hole dug in the ground.

b. The bucket conveyor takes the broken stone from the crusher and elevates it to a revolving screen, which deposits the various sizes of stone in three different bins. The left-hand bin is for dust, the middle bin is for stone $3/8''$ up to $1''$, and the right-hand bin is for stone over $1''$.

c. The bins open on the side and also on the end.

d. In case the crusher or conveyor breaks down, the storage bins will keep the mixer going until they are repaired. In case the mixer breaks down, the stone can be delivered on the platform and mixed by hand, or dropped into derrick boxes and deposited into measuring bins over another mixer. Breakdowns of any one part of carefully planned set-ups should not stop the job.

Temporary shut-downs are not only causes of delay, but they are often the cause of the workmen quitting the job if they lose a little time. If you want the best results from your laborers, you must look after their interests.

[EDITORS' NOTE: Once again Frank Gilbreth's emphasis on the search for "the best way" and his concern for the workers' interests are revealed.]

On jobs of considerable magnitude it will be found economical to dig a hole in the ground large enough for the concrete mixer. Build the platform over it heavy enough to support large piles of broken stone and sand. Build removable cover to measuring bins strong enough to support the wheel of a cart driving over it. This layout will often save one handling of the broken stone and sand, which can be shoveled into the measuring bins direct instead of into wheelbarrows.

Any kind of measuring hoppers, bins, etc., will flow freer and more evenly and will almost never choke if the interior angles where the sides come together are covered with a sheet-metal fillet, or even a wooden fillet. The curve should have at least $2''$ radius, and will work much better if it has $4''$ radius. If the machinery is located below ground, the platform should be grit and water-tight over the bearings of the engine and mixer. A tight fence of matched broads should be built around any opening in the platform. The gate-opening device for emptying the bins should be controlled from above and never from below, or the man below will surely empty the bins when they are not quite full, or before the proper amount of cement has been put in.

The remaining rules on mixing are quoted directly to show the

extent to which detail in planning was carried. The relatively unimportant items covered indicate the awareness of the men in the
organization in profiting from past experience.

177   When shipping engines, mixers, and other machinery, remove all oil cups, lubricators, and removable brass work, so that
they will not be stolen.

178   Brace everything thoroughly, so that the making up of trains,
etc., will not move the machinery about. This rule is not so important from the standpoint of the money loss of the value of the parts,
as from the delay in not being able to use the machines when they
arrive at the job.

180   Be sure that you put a tackle behind to prevent the mixer
getting away from the men and running down too quickly and injuring them.

181   When taking a mixer off a cart, do not forget to block up
under the rear part of the body of the cart, so that the front part of
the cart will not lift up and hurt someone, or perhaps break the
machine.

182   On jobs of this character the concrete mixer should be located as near as possible to the ground level, so that the feeders do
not have to wheel up-hill any more than necessary.

183   Dig a pit in the ground for the elevating bucket, so that the
mixer will discharge into it by gravitation.

184   It is seldom economical to put the elevating tower on the inside of the building, unless it can be done without leaving a hole
through the floors.

185   When a hoist is to be used for elevating the concrete, unless
the mixer is to be fed from overhead storage bins, it will almost invariably be found economical to place the mixer in a basement or
other excavation, so that the top of the charging hopper will be at,
or slightly below, ground level. The expense of operating steep runs
up to top of hopper will thus be avoided, and the work of the wheelbarrow men feeding the mixer will be made more economical, as
they will then be wheeling down-hill with loaded carts and up-hill
with empty carts.

186   One man cannot push a full-sized load in a two-wheeled cart
up-grade.

187   Other things being equal, use the sand, gravel, and stone that will best stand the roasting test. This is important, especially with the stone, as many hard stones, especially the lime rocks and granites, will crumble rapidly under a small amount of heat.

188   Experiment with screening and grading sands, gravel, and broken stone, and test the results to see if proper grading will not permit using less cement while obtaining the same strength of concrete. This is not only in the interests of economy, but also of constancy of volume.

190   Horses drawing scrapers go up over the top of the bridge and dump into the storage hopper. Carts are drawn underneath and the driver opens the gate and fills his own cart.

191   This arrangement will dig a cellar, or load gravel or sand for the concrete mixer.

192   The horses should have short outside reins to make them separate under a tight rein as they pass the hole on the center of the bridge.

193   The hole should be 6″ narrower than the scraper, and 4′0″ long.

194   A 4″×4″ cleat on the up-side will assist in dumping the scraper.

195   A 3″×4″ horizontal joist spiked all the way round the hole, 6″ down from the top of the platform, will give a horse a new footing in case he slips his foot over the edge of the hole.

196   On jobs of considerable size it is generally economical to build the railroad tracks up high enough to permit dumping the sand, gravel, and broken stone through the bottom of the cars instead of shoveling it out.

197   It is usually good practice to lay down plank to shovel on. The men will work much faster.

198   When men shovel against a plank, always use a square-pointed shovel. Use a round-pointed shovel at all other times.

199   During freezing weather the aggregates for concrete should be heated. This may be accomplished in various ways. If the weather is not too severe and the amount of aggregate to be used not too large, say fifty (50) yards per day, heating of the materials may be accomplished by building wood fires near the supply piles, that is, both sand and gravel or stone.

200   In extremely cold weather, when little thawing takes place during the day, it is better to build a supply hopper of sufficient capacity to store a day's run. At the discharge side, gates are provided in proper position so that they may feed directly into the feed hopper of the mixer. It is best to build the bottom of this supply hopper of sheet metal, containing a double bottom, so that an air space is provided directly under the sand and aggregates. The heat from a large salamander is led into this chamber and the necessary draft is supplied by having chimneys run directly through the stone pile.

201   Another effective and economical method of heating the aggregates is by using a steam coil. The aggregates and sand are simply thrown around the steam coil and left there a sufficient length of time to absorb the required amount of heat. This coil should preferably be placed near the cars that are being unloaded, so that the material can be thrown directly on the steam coil. It has been found from practice that this method of heating the aggregates gives better results and is more economical than the above-mentioned methods, but it limits the capacity of the material to the amount of room that may be used for the storage pile.

202   The use of chloride of calcium and chloride of sodium (common salt) in concrete during freezing weather should be avoided if possible, although tests show that adding small quantities to the mixture does not injure the concrete. In such cases, where pure water cannot be obtained, and sea water only is available, the latter may be used, but careful tests should be made at all times.

203   Bring the cars in as close to your mixing plant as possible.

204   Unload the cars and take the materials direct to the mixer.

205   Take stone and sand from storage piles only when there are no cars set.

207   Almost any type of batch concrete mixer will serve as a sand or gravel washer for small jobs. Simply fill with gravel, revolve the mixer, and let the hose play inside without stopping. When the mixer overflows, the water will carry all the foreign matter off.

208   For large jobs of sand and gravel washing, consult the office.

213   A working foreman shall be in charge of the mixer and shall be responsible for speed in feeding same, speed in removing concrete, for accuracy of measurements, amount of water used, cement used, etc.

214   The mixing gang shall start in sufficient time ahead of the regular force, so that when the second whistle blows the mixer will be in full operation with at least one batch of concrete in the hopper at the floor which is being concreted.

215   In feeding the mixer and in placing the concrete, arrange to have several good men as leaders whose pay will be somewhat higher than the regular pay and who will set the pace for the cheaper men.

216   Concrete mixers must be kept clean and no piles of waste concrete allowed to accumulate.

217   Before shutting down the mixer at noon, it must be thoroughly washed out, and at night it must be given a thorough cleaning so that all of the interior is bright.

218   Special attention should be given to the lubrication of bearings, etc., on concrete mixers. Where grease cups are used, they should be screwed down once every two hours. Where the bearings are of special design, the manufacturer's instructions regarding the oiling of same should be obtained and strictly followed.

219   A batch mixer is to be given the preference at all times.

220   Continuous mixers are to be used only under special conditions, and then only on mass work, like retaining walls, foundations, and dams.

221   When the Portable Gravity concrete mixer is used on our work, the manufacturer's instructions must be carried out to the letter.

222   If the Gravity, or any other form of continuous mixer, is used, it should, if possible, be fed with the Accurate Measurer and Feeder to insure even and continuous mixing of proper proportions.

223   The chief fault of continuous machines is the difficulty of feeding them properly. When the Accurate Measurer and Feeder is used, it is not enough to set the feed gates at the notches on the machine, but hand-measured quantities of the materials actually being used must be fed through the machine until it will feed from the cement, sand, and broken-stone bins the desired amounts simultaneously with an error of less than 3%.

224   The selection of the type of batch mixer to be used on a job should be governed by the kind of conveyors that will be used to take the concrete away.

225   If wheelbarrows are to be used, any standard type of hand discharge is all right, but if the concrete is to be handled in derrick buckets, the mixer should be one that will completely discharge its contents in less than four seconds.

226   Tests show that the average batch concrete mixer will require about forty seconds to mix the concrete, but that the strength is slightly increased if the mixing is continued a longer period.

227   We have therefore decided that the minimum times allowed for any batch mixer are as follows:

   a. Dry mixing 20 seconds.

   b. The water must be measured and the water pipe must be so arranged that it will take from fifteen to twenty seconds for the water from one batch to run into the mixer.

   c. Wet mixing 60 seconds.

228   Enough mixers shall be provided on the job to permit every batch to be mixed with the minimum time of each of the three processes as fixed above.

229   On large jobs where batch mixers are used, use a feeding device that will measure the ingredients by weighing.

230   This machine can be had in any size. Its advantages are speed of measuring and accuracy.

231   The feed gates in the storage bins are opened by hand. The gates close automatically when the desired weight is in the measuring bins. No leveling off of the top of pile to measure marks is required.

Transportation

RUNWAYS TO MIXERS and from mixers to forms where concrete is to be used should be built double width or in double sets, so that men wheeling in one direction will never obstruct the passage of those going in the opposite direction. Arrange runways so that men will travel in a continuous procession,—out by one route and return by another. In this way the great loss of time occasioned by the men stopping to turn carts or wheelbarrows around will be avoided. Spending a little extra money to make runways convenient and easily moved from place to place is good economy.

Detail one man to see that the runways are kept in good condition, so that the pushcarts and wheelbarrows can run at all times without interruption or obstruction. Keep runways free from dirt. A larger load can be wheeled on a clean runway with no obstructions on it than on a dirty one. When men are idle for a few minutes for any reason, have them clean off the runs.

With a two-wheeled pushcart, one man will wheel as much concrete, under favorable conditions, as three men can with ordinary wheelbarrows. A two-wheeled cart requires a fairly level runway 36 inches wide and should be capable of carrying a load of about 1000 lbs. In general it will be found economical to use two-wheeled carts in all cases where there is a comparatively large amount of concrete which can be placed from level runways, and where the extra expense of building wider runways is justified. When two-wheeled carts are used, it will be found advantageous to dump from the pointed end when dumping over the edge of the platform, and from the round end when dumping through a hole in the platform. In the latter case turn the cart completely over and let the handle strike with force against the platform. This will assist in shaking out the concrete and keep the cart clean. The handle of the two-wheeled cart is bolted on to the body of the cart, and by simply removing the bolts and reversing the handle, dumping can be done from either end.

3

....

BRICKLAYING
SYSTEM*

* *Bricklaying System*, by Frank B. Gilbreth, was published by The Myron C. Clark Publishing Co., New York and Chicago, in 1909.

Introduction

•••

The art of bricklaying is unique in that the fundamental principles of brick work today are not unlike those exemplified by the oldest ruins of thousands of years ago. The bricklayer also stands almost alone, as one who has not been obliged to compete in his trade with women, with machinery, or with foreign manufacturers.

Each old country has had its local methods of bricklaying; but not until the last score of years have bricklayers, coming to America from all countries, bringing their best local methods with them, learned from each other and adopted the best of each others' methods.

The purposes of this book are as follows:

(a) To put in writing that knowledge which has been handed down by word of mouth from journeyman to apprentice for generations.

(b) To record methods of handling labor, materials and plant on brick work that will reduce costs and at the same time enable the first-class workman to receive higher pay.

(c) To enable an apprentice to work intelligently from his first day, and to become proficient workman in the shortest possible time.

Training Apprentices

•••

[EDITORS' NOTE: The following paragraphs are quoted directly to show the extent of detail considered for proper apprentice training.]

1   There is no immediate profit from apprentices unless large numbers of them are employed on the same job at the same time. As

large numbers of apprentices invariably cause trouble between the employers and the bricklayers, it is necessary to limit our apprentices to those boys who, when they have become trained, will make valuable additions to our organization.

2   Hire only those apprentices who will apparently make good foremen, unless bricklayers are scarce.

3   Two or more apprentices on the same job work out better than one, as there is a spirit of rivalry between them, and they can be matched against each other in speed contests.

4   The term of apprenticeship shall be at least three years; additional time for lost time and vacations.

5   Apprentice shall not be permitted to work without overalls until he is out of his time.

6   The first day that an apprentice is put to work he is to be provided with a brick hammer and trowel at our expense. Procure an old trowel that has been broken in by some good bricklayer on the job. The foreman bricklayer should make it his special duty to see that the trowel is slightly undersized, also the best and the handiest trowel on the job. He should give the bricklayer a new trowel.

7   At the end of six weeks, if the apprentice has done well, he is to be given a new spirit plumb rule with two plumb glasses and one level glass. This plumb rule should be 3 ft. 6 ins. long.

8   As soon as he has progressed far enough to warrant it, he shall be given another large trowel, brick set and jointer. He shall furnish himself with everything else that he needs.

9   An apprentice should be taken in charge by an intelligent bricklayer, who should be responsible for his actions and work, for a period of one week. He should be put under a different bricklayer every week for at least a month. At the end of that time he should be put on that part of the work where he can earn his money and at the same time learn the most. In other words, we do not want our apprentices to be kept on heavy work, if they are constantly doing their best. At the same time, we do not want them promoted any faster than they can earn their money.

10   Apprentices must be worked to their full limit of endurance.

11   Apprentices must not be hazed nor misled after their first day at the trade. Foremen must answer every question that they ask in good faith, regardless of how simple it may seem.

12   An apprentice is supposed to do a man's amount of work on filling in the middle of the wall after the first month. He is supposed to do a man's amount of work on all common brick work after six months.

13   First of all, an apprentice should be taught that all brick, even common brick, have a top and a bottom, an inside and an outside.

14   The outside is generally determined by the way the bricks have been stacked in the kiln, but if the natural outside is chipped, oftentimes the natural inside is the better side.

15   All bricks made by hand in a mold are a little wider at the top or open side of the mold than at the bottom of the mold. This is sometimes caused by the molds being made slightly smaller at the bottom than at the open top, sometimes by the contact of the front and back side of the brick being slightly distorted by contact with the sides of the mold as the soft wet clay slides out of the mold.

16   In hand made brick, and in nearly all brick except wirecut brick, the natural top can be told from the natural bottom because it is much rougher. The top can generally be easily told from the bottom by feeling, if the brick is held in the usual position used just before laying. The bottom being narrower than the top, the brick can be held by less pressure of the fingers on the front and back of the brick when it is right side up than when it is upside down. A few minutes will enable a novice to detect a very small difference in the width of the top and bottom of a brick, by observing how much pressure of the fingers is needed to sustain the brick.

17   Brick must be laid with the wide surface uppermost. . . . All bricks must be laid with slightly overhanging faces, so that the appearance of the wall will be similar to beveled siding or clapboards upside down. The reason for this is that the bricks vary greatly in thickness, and one edge only is laid to line. This is the top edge. The lower edge is not laid to line. It is, therefore, not so straight, and is set slightly inside the line of the top edge of the course below it to hide its inaccuracies. While the amount of overhang and set-in of each course is slight, it is enough to show very plainly. If you sight down the face of the wall you will see nothing but mortar. If you sight up the wall you will see nothing but brick. If a course is laid with considerable overhang it is called "rolled." If a course is laid with a batter it is called "lipped."

18   *One of the worst mistakes that can be made in the training of an apprentice is to expect him to do perfect work first, and fast work later. A boy taught after this scheme is sure to get into bad habits of laying brick with too many unnecessary motions that will prevent him from ever laying brick fast. This is very important.*

19   *The right way is to put the apprentice at work where the appearance of the work is not of importance. Insist that he lay as many brick as a journeyman, even if they are not laid quite so well. Teach him to lay a brick with the least possible number of motions, and, intsead of correcting all of the little faults on one brick, to try to lay the next brick without the same faults as attended the laying of the preceding brick. This last method will teach speed, and skill will surely soon follow, with sufficient practice.*

20   Of course it is not intended by these directions that an apprentice be permitted to do any work that would affect the stability of the work. It is simply a matter of looks, and he must start where looks are not important.

21   "Motion study" is of the greatest importance in teaching a trade quickly. It is also the most profitable method of teaching a trade.

22   An apprentice must be made to lay brick with quick motions, even on his first day. Speed and the least number of motions must be uppermost in his mind at all times. The apprentice must be made to lay brick with the method outlined in this system even if it is necessary to have a bricklayer go over his work as fast as he lays the brick, to make his work right.

23   As soon as an apprentice has formed a fixed habit of laying brick with only a few, and with no unnecessary motions, he must be constantly reminded that the quality of the workmanship will be remembered long after all other considerations are forgotten.

24   The rules in this system must be construed as solely for the purpose of eliminating unnecessary delays, unnecessary labor, and unnecessary expense, and never for any short cuts that produce speed, economy or profit at the expense of the best workmanship.

25   Leave the so-called "tricks of the trade" to those persons who have not served a proper apprenticeship and who do not know how to do the best work.

26   Show the apprentice how to lay a brick without disturbing the line. Impress upon his mind that his fingers must not even touch

the line, or the line will be pushed out of place while the other men are trying to use it as a guide.

27   An apprentice should be taught to hold his trowel like a razor, with two fingers only, and with the thumb on the top of the handle. The thumb should never be put around the handle of the trowel. The handle of the trowel should be kept perfectly clean at all times.

28   Regardless of the locality in which an apprentice works, he should be taught to lay brick both "Eastern" and "Western" methods, not only so that he can have the experience for his own use, but also that he can boss both kinds of bricklayers to the best advantage.

29   The "Eastern" method is to "pick-and-dip" brick and mortar at the same time; the mortar being in a tub, or in a mortar box with beveled sides.

30   The "Western" or "stringing mortar" method is to use a much larger trowel than could possibly be used in a tub. This necessitates a mortar board or mortar box, and first spreading mortar enough for several brick ahead, and then picking up only brick.

31   Each method has its advantages and disadvantages. Some conditions make the "Eastern" method preferable, some the "Western" method.

32   If the apprentice is taught both methods, he will know, instinctively, which is the better to use under varying conditions. The kind of sand, the proportions of the cement, lime and sand, the dryness of the brick, the methods employed by the men on the leads—all these go to determine which method will give the most speed, economy and quality.

33   When an apprentice reaches to pick up bricks, see that he picks them up with both hands at precisely the same time.

34   When he reaches for mortar with one hand and brick with the other, teach him to pick up both at the same time. He should look at the mortar as he starts to reach for it, but he should pick it up by the feeling, and his eyes should be only on the brick that he is picking up with the other hand at the same time.

35   To appreciate fully the importance of this rule, watch several bricklayers a few moments. You will notice that the man who unconsciously is picking up with both hands at the same time, can do his work faster, and with much less effort to himself, than he who is pick-

ing up first with one hand and then with the other. This is largely a matter of habit. If an apprentice is allowed to pick up first with one hand and then with the other, it will be hard to break him of it.

36   The bricks nearest the wall should generally be picked up first, so as to maintain a clear place to stand and a clear place for the tenders to walk, in case they find it necessary to pass on the scaffold.

37   An apprentice should, at first, be taught to throw only enough mortar for one brick at a time on the line. After he is fairly proficient, he should be taught to throw his mortar for at least two brick, even when laying the pick and dip method. He can pick up mortar for two or three bricks just as quickly as he can pick up mortar for one brick. With practice, he can throw the mortar for three brick just as quickly, as he can for one brick, and he can certainly lay the extra one or extra two brick faster if he does not have to dip and throw the mortar more than once to two or three brick.

38   An apprentice should be taught that the bricklayer depends on sighting with his eye to get plumb corners nearly plumb, and that the plumb rule is used to correct the inaccuracies of his eye. The first three courses should be plumbed accurately to furnish a guide to the eye. A corner can be "sighted" quickest and most accurately, by sighting one side at a time, i.e., putting the eye exactly over the corner to be plumbed and moving the eye in the plane of one face of the corner, and in the direction away from the wall. Moving the eye back and forth to a point a slight distance from and exactly plumb with the corner, will make the corner apparently change from a point to a line. Any inaccuracy from a straight line is quickly detected. After one face of the corner has been corrected, sight the other face in the same manner. When the two faces are plumb, the corner will be plumb. Do not try to make the corner appear straight both ways at once. The method is slower, and it may appear straight when in reality it is not.

39   It is a simple matter to describe to the apprentice the best methods of laying brick for the greatest strength. It is a very difficult matter to explain to him how to lay pressed face brick in a manner that will make a large, plain, blank wall appear accurate and uniform under the most critical examination.

40   The following rules will help the apprentice to make the best appearing work on pressed brick face work:

(a) Use the thinnest line obtainable, that will stand a hard hauling without sagging or breaking.

(b) Build small leads, so that as much of the wall as possible is built to line, instead of built as a lead.

(c) Make the line fast around the end of the wall, and wound around a brick on the lead, so that a tight hauling will not pull down the lead. Another reason for doing this is that if the nail is used in the lead and the lead pulls down, some bricklayer may lose an eye by the nail flying through the air.

(d) See that the line is placed 1-32 in. outside the top edge of the brick and exactly level with it.

(e) See that no brick touches the line.

(f) See that the line is disturbed as little as possible when laying a brick.

(g) Do not lay a brick that is thinner, thicker, shorter or longer than the others, even if it is of the same cull. Use it for filling.

(h) Use the right amount of mortar. If you use more than the right amount it will squeeze out, and daub the brick underneath it.

(i) See that the lower edge of the brick is distinctly back of the line of the top edge of the course under it. The amount that it should be back varies with the brick and the conditions. It should never be less than 1-32 in. and seldom more than 1/8 in. Work looks decidedly better with too much set in (or roll) than not enough. This is one of the most important rules for good looking brick work.

41　　　The work of the apprentice differs from that of the journeyman in appearance largely because the latter is able to make the set in, or roll, or overhang, of all brick exactly alike.

42　　　An unskilled man can use a story pole to get brick courses the right height. He can use a plumb-bond pole, and mark exactly where the end joints should come. He can use a tight line, putting the top edge of each brick to it. He can cover up inaccuracies with good jointing and hide the differences of the thickness of the brick by skillful ruling. He can make every brick touch a plumb rule and straightedge, by tapping back the projecting brick with a hammer before the mortar has set. Yet the wall will have a bad appearance unless it looks uniform and each brick has the same amount of set-in. There is no way of correcting the amount of roll after the bricks are laid.

43   This is where skilled practice counts. It makes for uniformity. This is where the journeyman makes the good looking wall and where the apprentice finds difficulty and must lay the most stress; for when the sun moves from a position in the plane of the face of the wall and begins to throw long shadows on that wall, the inaccuracies are greatly exaggerated by the sunlight and the shading, due to lack of uniformity of set-in and roll.

44   Apprentices must study carefully the rules, photographs and charts in this system, especially those relating to methods. They must observe the work done by the various bricklayers, and must, after study of this system, the work they see, and their own work, make out charts of their own processes.

45   They must comply with all rules of the Field System, as well as of this Bricklaying System, and must be made to realize that they are a part of the organization, and that a knowledge of it and the systems by which it operated, are absolutely essential to any advancement.

46   Apprentices must be shown that the bricklayer's trade is one of the oldest, most respectable and most desirable of trades, and one worthy of the entire attention of any bright, educated and determined American boy; that the knowledge gained on the trade can never be taken away from the one who has once obtained it, regardless of what ill fortune has overtaken him; and that $25 to $100 per week will always stand ready for the man who can lay brick, or who has sufficient knowledge of the trade to supervise the work of other bricklayers.

Methods of Management

Foremen will be rated and paid according to the quality and not according to the quantity of work that they secure from their men. Not only an account of the greater pleasure that all derive from doing the best work, but also as a business proposition, the most permanent success will come from having earned and deserved the reputation of doing the best work. The foreman must see that all work is laid out in a systematic manner. The men should be so selected and grouped that, the job once started, speed and efficiency will be apparent and can be fittingly recognized. On small jobs a foreman may know exactly what each bricklayer is doing every minute during the day. On large jobs, if the foreman knows this, it is because he is neglecting to look after some points that are of much more importance.

A foreman should study to arrange his men so that the work of the slow men will show up automatically to their disadvantage. This can be arranged in many ways, one of which is to divide the gangs into units, the number of men in a unit to be determined by the character of the work.

Take, for example, a wall of nine piers, separated by eight windows. On this wall there should be nine bricklayers, if the piers are of about the same size. If the piers are not the same size, the number of bricklayers should be increased or reduced, so that their work will be equal, and the slow man will be shown up quickly. The foreman should watch the bricklayers to see which man is standing up idle. He is standing up for one of three reasons: (a) he is loafing; (b) he is out of stock; (c) he has finished his bit.

If it is for the first reason, he should be dealt with. If he is out of stock, the leader of tenders needs attention. If it is for the third reason, his speed should be recognized, and the mason who is behind and delaying the raising of the line to the next course should be investigated.

It is sometimes difficult to divide a wall that is not symmetrical into equal parts so that each bricklayer will have the same sized section; but with a little study almost any wall can be divided fairly. For example, if the wall is cut up by openings so that the piers are not the same size, it is often economical to put fewer men on the wall and apportion several piers to each man. In this way it can be divided evenly enough to make conditions favorable for a contest. Sometimes the trig can be put enough off center of the wall to compensate for some extra plumb work in a break or chimney flue. Again, a small pier in the wall may be assigned to an apprentice.

On a long wall, it is often economical to provide one or two special men to take care of a large irregularity in the wall, and to hold the contest on the remaining straight or symmetrical parts of the wall.

In any case, the foreman should watch the first few courses as laid, then shift the men enough to make the stints as nearly equal as possible.

The work of a bricklayer is generally indicative of his personal character. If he is dishonest he will do dishonest work and cover it up if possible before the flaw is seen. If he is honest he will leave his job before he will do scamp work, even at the suggestion of his foreman. If a bricklayer is ever caught doing a scamp piece of work he should never be absolutely trusted again.

Sometimes the athletic contest spirit and desire to outclass the others leads some of the bricklayers to do careless work, especially where it cannot be seen, as in the middle of the wall. One of the best methods of counteracting this is to write the name of each bricklayer on the plan, showing where each worked, and to let the bricklayers see that their names are being written on the plans. There is, of course, nothing new about this scheme, as stone masons for centuries have put their own marks on stones. The name or mark on the work undoubtedly makes the workman take more interest in his work.

On engine beds and similar work, where the pieces are isolated, assigning gangs of men of different nationalities to the different beds will create extra interest in the contests. If this is not feasible, put the tall men on one bed and the short men on the other, or the single men against the married men, or the eastern "pick and dip" men against the western "string mortar" men.

While one who is not experienced at making his men really enthusiastic on their work cannot appreciate how athletic contests will interest the men, it is the real secret of the success of our best superintendents. It not only reduces costs, but it makes for organization, and thus saves foremen's time.

There is no way that continued interest in athletic contests can be maintained so well as by having a fair and correct score kept of the results of the labors of the different men.

When it is not possible to divide the work so that each man's work shows up all by itself, the best arrangement is to divide the men up into two or more gangs of as few men as possible, generally with two, four, six or eight men to a gang.

If the character of the walls is similar, but if they are not the same dimensions, it is wise to provide some other form of measurement than the height of the wall, such, for instance, as a score on a large black board, so placed that it can be seen by all the men on all the gangs. This board should be ruled off, and the score should be carefully filled out.

The men can see the score and the contest can be carried out throughout the entire day. In the case of extra pay being given for particularly high records of brick laid, the bricklayers can see every half hour just how successful their efforts are.

In order that the bricklayers may always have a square deal, the method of estimating the number of brick that they lay per day shall be as follows: The story pole on the hauling end of the line shall be marked off in courses, as usual. At each mark, the number of brick in that course shall be plainly marked on the pole. In case of any dispute, any one can then check up the records, by actually counting the number of brick in each course.

As a general rule, the men should be separated so that the amount of their individual work will show up separately. This will bring about the best results, whether or not there is a well organized athletic contest in progress.

It is seldom good practice to have the tenders work individually instead of in small gangs, due to the difficulties of passing on narrow runs and foot stages.

Do not permit your hod carriers, wheelbarrow men or packet men to come up one at a time.

Have those carrying any one kind of material that are tending masons on any one wall fill their hods all at once, shank their hods all at once, and start all at once, but do not have them drop their hods at exactly the same instant, as it might endanger the stability of the scaffold.

Hold the leader responsible for the work of the entire gang. They must dump their material where the leader says they must dump it. They must never throw the brick from the hods in a manner that will scatter or break, or even chip the brick. They must empty the hod in a manner that will enable the bricklayer to pick up the brick the easiest, as bricklayer's time costs so much more than hod carrier's time that the hod carrier can afford to waste two minutes of his time any time that it will save one minute of the bricklayer's.

It may seem at first that making the men all fill at once and all start at once, and all go at once, is like holding the entire gang back to the speed of the slowest man. This is not so. On the contrary, it shows up the slowest man and he can be removed.

Have the men keep their place in the line. Have the last man who is set to work with the gang be the next to the last man in the line.

Pick out a good man for leader and pay him 10 per cent more than the rest, because he is expected to direct as well as work. He must see that he has more men when the bricklayers are backing up than when they are laying overhand.

In the event of the usual leader being absent, promote the rear leader to leader with leader's pay and the second man in the line to rear leader with 5 per cent more pay than the rest. This will make all the men in the line desirous of the leader's job with leader's pay. It will, if the rules are carried out, make the organization of the tenders automatic. The foremen will only have to watch the leaders in order to handle all the tenders.

Piling brick into a wheelbarrow is a matter that requires considerable attention. It is not enough to tell the tenders to fill the barrows with brick. The barrow gang must be shown how to do it in the quickest and least fatiguing manner.

The leader shall be paid at least 10 per cent more than each of the rest of the gang. He shall be carefully shown that the barrow must be placed as near the brick as possible. He must not be allowed to be leader unless he continually picks up brick with both hands at the same time and fills his barrow faster than the other men. He must convey the brick from the pile to the wheelbarrow in the shortest possible line, and both brick must be put in the barrow at the same instant.

It will be difficult to get every barrow man to abide by these rules, but the leader must be made to follow this method, and the extra money paid the leaders is an incentive to the others to work to be promoted to be leaders of gangs.

The men must be taught to pile the brick so that the load comes over the wheel, instead of on the legs of the wheelbarrow. This enables the man to wheel larger loads.

It should be decided by the brick foremen how many brick shall be put in the barrow by the leader, and he must count his load every time. The leader's load should be checked up occasionally, especially when his load appears to be small and if it is found short, he should be replaced by another leader. The number of brick, of course, depends on their dry weight, with due allowance when they are wet, and on whether the bricks are to be wheeled up an incline or on a level.

Rear end leaders are necessary on long trips where the last man leads the way back. Where the lap is continuous, a rear end leader is not necessary.

A rear end leader should receive 5 per cent more than regular tender's pay. He should be selected from the line of tenders, with the idea of promoting him to leader if he handles the gang promptly.

A properly organized and trained gang of tenders will do from 50 per cent to 200 per cent more work than an untrained gang.

When unloading cars of materials, try to have but one man to a car, and start several men at the same time. If this is not possible, start two men at the same time, but at opposite ends of the same car. This will enable the foremen to pick out the first-class men.

Reward the winner every time.

Too much stress cannot be laid on the necessity and value of having only first class men. Athletic contests have proved the surprising fact that first class men ordinarily do twice to three times the amount of work of other men whose methods of working disguise their slow pace until the athletic contest shows them up.

The difference in cost between the best work and the worst work is such a very small amount as compared with the entire cost of the undertaking that no firm or individual can afford to be identified with any but the best class. The features that increase the cost of work materially are, not working the men to advantage, and having them remain idle for any reason, such as for want of stock, lack of incentive for large output, lack of proper superintendence, etc.

Quality of the work must be given preference over quantity of output at all times.

The winners of the athletic contest should be paid higher wages than the rest of the men. They should furthermore be given first opportunity to make overtime wages and they should be kept till the last to finish the job.

Gilbreth Scaffold, Hod Type

• •

The Gilbreth scaffold accomplishes two things:
(A) Helps make better workmanship.
(B) Helps make more economical workmanship.
It helps make better workmanship for four reasons:

(a) It keeps the bricklayer at a constant height, where he can lay his brick with the most precision.

(b) It enables the bricklayer, even on overhand work, to keep the wall backed up solid, i.e., the entire width of the wall.

(c) The wall being always backed up solid, it can be properly protected from rain and sleet by simply putting the staging planks on it.

(d) The bricks can be best bedded because the work is always at a height that the bricklayer can best handle the brick and mortar.

(B) The Gilbreth scaffold makes more economical work because:

(a) It keeps the bricklayer at a constant height, and that height is such that no stooping over is required to pick up brick and mortar, and no stooping nor reaching is required to lay brick and mortar.

(b) It reduces the number and the length of motions.

(c) It does away with the bad practice of backing up 4 ins. or 8 ins. against the overhand or exterior face tier, and permits all filling of each course to be done the entire width of the wall at once.

(d) The bricklayers' platform is clear at all times, and there are no bricks underfoot.

(e) The bricklayer is out of the tender's way and the tender does not interrupt the bricklayer as he passes back and forth.

(f) When ordinary scaffolds are used, the wall is generally built 5 ft. above the floor. When the Gilbreth scaffold is used, the wall is not built more than 3 ft. 8 ins. above the floor. This 1 ft. 4 ins. when built from the floor is where the most reaching has to be done and consequently that extra time and labor is all saved by setting up the Gilbreth scaffold when the wall is 3 ft. 8 ins. above the floor.

(g) When the Gilbreth scaffold is once set up, and it takes no longer to set it up than it does to set up a trestle horse scaffold, there is no more worry, trouble or stage building for that wall in that story. No time is lost in shifting men from wall to wall. No athletic speed contests are broken up. This last feature alone is of great importance.

Watch carefully the circuit the tenders make when leaving the stock pile, dumping and returning to the stock pile. It is always economical to make return trips by special short cut runs.

When using wheelbarrows on tenders' run, be sure that the planks are laid so that the tenders will wheel down upon the next plank, not up onto the next plank.

Every time each hodcarrier passes a bricklayer on the same stage, he interferes with the speed of the bricklayer. Many different runs, will enable the hodcarrier to go and come the shortest way and pass the fewest bricklayers.

In many localities it is hard to procure skilled hodcarriers who can climb a ladder with a hodful of brick or mortar. Therefore, oftentimes a long cleated run will do away with the necessity of a ladder. For these runs use plank 3 or 4 ins. thick, so that they will not be springy and will not require props. If cleats are used, they should not be more than 1 in. thick, and they should be spaced at even distances.

It is not possible to make a rule covering all cases, that will state how far apart the cleats should be. The distance apart depends on the kind of men and the slant of the run, and is a matter of sufficient importance to warrant experimenting under the local conditions. All runs should be wide enough for men going up and down to pass one another.

A small amount of motion study will show the advantage of not being obliged to stoop to get the stock for that portion of the wall that is between the height of 3 ft. 2 ins. to 5 ft. above the floor; and, in time, analysis will show that no allowance will have to be made for the time that men are shifted from one wall to another while the staging is being raised.

Gilbreth Scaffold, Packet Type

The Gilbreth scaffold, packet type, is a modification of the Gilbreth scaffold especially adapted to the packet method and the fountain trowel. It is so designed that it may be set up and put in operation before the wall is built any higher than the floor on which the bricklayer stands.

There are several reasons for setting the scaffold up at once, as soon as the wall is level with the top of the floor.

First, it is easier, and quicker, consequently more economical, for the tender to unload the packs of brick from the wheelbarrow to the stock platform, than to lower them down to the floor.

Second, it is easier and quicker, consequently more economical, for the bricklayers to take their bricks from the stock platform than to stoop over to the floor for them. Furthermore, with this scaffold they can throw the mortar from the mortar boxes into the wall without stooping either at mortar box or at wall.

The average foreman underrates the necessity of having the scaffold at exactly the right height, because he sees that the bricklayer can stoop and bend and yet lay brick almost as fast as when he does not bend or stoop at all. Not being over-worried about the bricklayer's comfort, so long as he is laying brick fast, he forgets that men working at manual work, like bricklaying, cannot keep up the work every instant, and that, therefore, the percentage of rest absolutely required by such men must be greater than that of the men who are put to no exertion not absolutely necessary to laying a brick.

The bricklayer can then transfer the packs of brick from the stock platform to the wall without lifting the pack more than an inch or so, and if the stock platform is maintained at the relative heights here described, the bricklayer can do this transferring without stooping and with no bending of the back. Therefore, in reality, to transfer the pack of brick in a level plane from the stock platform to the wall requires no more work to be done than the stooping of the body and the straightening it up again.

The Gilbreth Packet System

The Gilbreth packet system consists of conveying bricks upon packets from the pile in the street to the top of the wall.

If the bricks are brought "packed," i.e., side by side, on edge, to the job, then they are to be unloaded and placed upon packets regardless of whether or not they are to be used at once, except in the case of brick that are to be culled before they are used.

If the brick are brought "loose," that is thrown in, they are to be dumped out, if the car or cart is provided with dumping means. But if they are not dumped out, they must be put upon packets, carried out or wheeled out, whichever is the cheaper, and stacked up on the packets until ready to be used.

The packets shall be made of two pieces laid lengthwise, and so spaced that the outside edges of the packet are spaced exactly the length of the average brick to be carried. The space between the two pieces shall be wide enough to permit room for the men's fingers to clear without jamming.

The lengthwise pieces shall be held in place by one crosswise piece at each end, that shall be so spaced that the distance in the clear between them shall be $1\frac{1}{2}$ ins. greater than the length of the lower layer of brick on the packet. Round off all corners of the end pieces where the hands rub.

The method of handling the packs from the stock pile to the hoisting apparatus, and from the hoisting apparatus to the mason, depends upon circumstances. Sometimes it is cheaper to have laborers carry them in their hands, sometimes skeleton wheelbarrows holding three or four boards are the cheapest, and on long runs it is sometimes most economical to pile the packs of brick into the carts.

In buildings divided by brick walls into small areas, it is often difficult to build long sloping runs up for wheelbarrows. When a run cannot be arranged down from the floor above, packs can be passed from tender to tender, from floor to stock platform, by having a few stagings 3 ft. high one above another.

When the packs reach the bricklayers' platform, they are shoved over on the tracks by the tenders toward the bricklayer. It is a very simple matter to pick up 90 lbs. when the lift is straight up, but it is a very difficult matter to pick up 90 lbs. when the lift is not straight up. Therefore the bricklayer must have his brick put as close to the inside edge of the stock platform as possible, so that he can lift his load in the easiest manner.

The number of brick that shall be piled upon a packet varies in different localities on account of two factors (a) the size and weight of the particular brick used, and (b) the quality of the laborers obtainable.

The weight of the brick that should be put on a packet should, with the weight of the packet, be as nearly 90 lbs. as is possible, with an even number of brick. This is the weight which a first-class, high-priced laborer can handle to the best advantage. With inferior, low-priced laborers, the number of brick must be reduced so that the weight will be lessened in proportion to their strength.

The strength of the laborers and not the strength of the bricklayers is to be the controlling factor to determine the weight of the load on each packet.

Many small men who have been rated as first-class bricklayers can work rapidly with a light load of, say a brick in each hand. They could not possibly stand the strain of transferring the packs of brick from the scaffold in a horizontal plane to the wall.

Other bricklayers, who are able to handle 90 lbs. with ease, would much prefer to lift a pack containing 20 brick from the scaffold in a horizontal plane to the wall than to make ten trips with a brick in each hand each trip.

Any bricklayer who is not able to transfer the packet with its regular full load from the stock platform to the wall will be obliged to take off a few brick from each pack in the old method until the remaining load on the packet has been reduced to a point where he can handle the weight comfortably and thrive under the continuous exercise of it. Of course he cannot earn as high wages as the man who can handle the larger load.

The bricklayer must place the pack on the wall in the location that will give the shortest possible distance through which to carry each brick from the packet to its final resting place on the mortar.

The bricklayers do not realize the importance of this, and must be constantly instructed to place the pack as near the place where the brick are to be laid as possible, even with the packet method. Careful packing of the pack so as to save all the motion possible will diminish the distance that a bricklayer's hand travels from a quarter to a half mile of distance per day.

The advantages of the packet method are to be seen all through the process of bricklaying. The brick themselves will be kept in better condition. Unloading brick from a hod or wheelbarrow is sure to make more or less bats, and many chipped brick. With the packet method it is possible to have the brick arrive at the scaffold without a chip out of them. This means the saving of the time needed to discard bats and to select unchipped brick fit to lay to the line. It also, of course, means a better looking wall.

Motion Study

•••

The motion study in this book is but the beginning of an era of motion study, that will eventually affect all of our methods of teaching trades. It will cut down production costs and increase the efficiency and wages of the workman.

There is a tremendous field, in all branches of all mechanical trades, for descriptions and illustrations in print of the best methods used by the best mechanics in working at their trade. We particularly request photographs showing such methods to the best advantage.

To be pre-eminently successful: (a) A mechanic must know his trade; (b) he must be quick motioned; and (c) he must use the fewest possible motions to accomplish the desired result.

It is a fact beyond dispute that the fastest bricklayers, and generally the best bricklayers, are those who use the fewest motions, and not those who are naturally the quickest motioned.

A bricklayer can do no better service for his craft than to devise methods for laying brick with fewer motions than are at present practiced by bricklayers.

It is a recognized fact among bricklayers, that they use one set of motions when they are trying to exceed the speed of a fellow workman, and another set when they are not especially rushed.

When a bricklayer shows an apprentice how to lay brick he invariably teaches the slow method. The result is, the apprentice learns to place the brick in the right place with the right amount of mortar under and against it, but the method used involves a great many more motions than are necessary.

The apprentice, after becoming an expert in this way, must then attempt to get out of the slow habits, due to unnecessary motions, and to learn to lay brick by a method that will enable him to complete his portion in the time that is allotted to journeymen.

The rules in charts *1, 2, 3,* and *4* will narrow down his first lessons

Opera-tion No.	The Wrong Way. Motions per Brick.	The Right Way. Motions per Brick.	Pick and Dip Method. The Exterior 4 Inches (Laying to the Line).
1	Step for Mortar.	Omit.	On the scaffold the inside edge of mortar box should be plumb with inside edge of stock platform. On floor the inside edge of mortar box should be 21 in. from wall. Mortar boxes never over 4 ft. apart.
2	Reaching for Mortar.	4/4	Do not bend any more than absolutely necessary to reach mortar with a straight arm.
3	Working up Mortar.	Omit.	Provide mortar of right consistency. Examine sand screen and keep in repair so that no pebbles can get through. Keep tender on scaffold to temper up and keep mortar worked up right.
4	Step for Brick.	Omit.	If tubs are kept 4 ft. apart no stepping for brick will be necessary on scaffold. On floor keep brick in a pile not nearer than 1 ft. nor more than 4 ft. 6 ins. from wall.
5	Reach for Brick.	Included in 2.	Brick must be reached for at the same time that the mortar is reached for, and picked up at exactly the same time the mortar is picked up. If it is not picked up at the same time, allowance must be made for operation.
6	Pick up Right Brick.	Omit.	Train the leader of the tenders to vary the kind of brick used as much as possible to suit the conditions; that is, to bring the best brick when the men are working on the line.
7	Mortar. Box to Wall.	4/4	Carry stock from the staging to the wall in the straightest possible line and with an even speed, without pause or hitch. It is important to move the stock with an even speed and not by quick jerks.
8	Brick, Pile to Wall.	Included in 7.	Brick must be carried from pile to wall at exactly same time as the mortar is carried to the wall, without pause or jerk.
9	Deposit Mortar on Wall.	Included in 7.	If a pause is made, this space must be filled out. If no pause is made it is included in No. 7.
10	Spreading Mortar.	Omit.	The mortar must be thrown so as to require no additional spreading and so that the mortar runs up on the end of the previous brick laid, or else the next two spaces must be filled out.
11	Cutting off Mortar.	Omit.	If the mortar is thrown from the trowel properly no spreading and no cutting is necessary.
12	Disposing of Mortar.	Omit.	If mortar is not cut off, this space is not filled out. If mortar is cut off keep it on trowel and carry back on trowel to box, or else butter on end of brick. Do not throw it on mortar box.

CHART 1. Pick and Dip Method, Laying to the Line.

Opera-tion No.	The Wrong Way.	The Right Way.	Pick and Dip Method. The Exterior 4 Inches (Laying to the Line).
	Motions per Brick. $\frac{1}{4}$ $\frac{1}{2}$ $\frac{3}{4}$ 1	Motions per Brick. $\frac{1}{4}$ $\frac{1}{2}$ $\frac{3}{4}$ 1	
13	Laying Brick on Mortar.	$\frac{4}{4}$	Fill out this space if brick is held still while mortar is thrown on wall. When brick is laid on mortar it presses mortar out of joints; cut this off only at every second brick. It takes no longer to cut mortar off two bricks than one.
14	Cutting off Mortar.	Every $\frac{1}{2}$ 2nd brk	
15	Disposing of Mortar.	Butter $\frac{4}{4}$ End Joint.	When this mortar is cut off it can be used to butter that end of the last previous brick laid or it can be carried on the trowel back to the box.
16	Tapping Down Brick.	Omit.	If the mortar is the right consistency, with no lumps in it, and the right amount is used, the bricks are wet as possible without having them run, no tapping with the trowel will be necessary.
17	Cutting off Mortar.	Omit.	If the brick must be tapped, hit it once hard enough to hammer it down where it belongs. Do not hit the brick several light taps when one hard tap will do.
18	Disposing of Mortar.	Omit.	Do not cut off the mortar oftener than every second brick, and when you do cut it off do not let fall to the ground; save it; keep it on the trowel, and do not make another motion by throwing it at the box. Carrying it to the box does not count another motion.
	18	$4\frac{1}{2}$	Total number of motions per brick.

Chart 1. Pick and Dip Method, Laying to the Line (*continued*).

to a few vital principles and motions. They show what he should learn first, as well as how he should learn it.

These rules and charts will enable the apprentice to earn large wages immediately, because he has here a series of instructions that show each and every motion in the proper sequence. They eliminate the "wrong way," all experimenting, and the incompetent teacher.

We do not want any bricklayer not well acquainted with the method and motions herein laid down to waste either his own time or the time of the apprentice teaching the latter.

Now as to the journeyman bricklayer, himself, we have a difficult problem to handle. We have found that some bricklayers with good

Opera-tion No.	The Wrong Way. Motions per Brick. $\frac{1}{4}\frac{1}{3}\frac{2}{4}\frac{3}{4}$	The Right Way. Motions per Brick. $\frac{1}{4}\frac{1}{3}\frac{2}{4}\frac{3}{4}$	Pick and Dip Method. Center of the Wall.
1	Step for Mortar.	Omit.	If a step is necessary the mortar boxes are too far apart.
2	Reaching for Mortar.	$\frac{4}{4}$	When reaching for brick and mortar always pick the stock first which is the nearest to the wall. Use those brick that are the farthest away from the wall as a reserve pile to be used only when pile gets small.
3	Working up Mortar.	Omit.	
4	Step for Brick.	Omit.	If mortar boxes are not more than 4 ft. apart and the bricks are all piled near the wall no step will be necessary.
5	Reach for Brick.	Included in 2.	
6	Pick up Right Brick.	Omit.	The only selection of brick for work in the middle of the wall is to pick up those brick that are the least fit for the exterior 4 ins., i.e., chipped, broken, misshapen and discolored brick.
7	Mortar, Box to Wall.	$\frac{4}{4}$	When conveying mortar from box to wall carry it in the shortest and straightest line possible. Do not pause in the path. Keep the mortar going at an even speed from box to wall.
8	Brick, Pile to Wall.	Included in 7.	Convey brick from pile to wall in shortest line, and use momentum of brick to help shove the brick into the mortar.
9	Deposit Mortar on Wall.	Included in 7.	Deposit the mortar to the right of the place where the brick is to be laid. The depositing of the mortar and brick can then be done simultaneously without delaying the depositing of the brick.
10	Spreading Mortar.	Omit.	The mortar must be thrown so as to require the least amount of effort to shove the joints full of mortar when the next brick is laid on it.
11	Cutting off Mortar.	Omit.	No spreading should ever be required of mortar in the middle of the wall pick and dip method.
12	Disposing of Mortar.	Omit.	
13	Laying Brick on Mortar.	Included in 7.	Do not lay the brick on the mortar conveyed to the wall at the same operation. Lay the brick in a place to the left of the place where the mortar is deposited and on top of the previous trowelful.

Chart 2. Pick and Dip Method, Laying in the Interior Tiers.

Opera-tion No.	The Wrong Way. Motions per Brick. $\frac{1}{4} \frac{1}{2} \frac{3}{4} \frac{4}{4}$	The Right Way. Motions per Brick. $\frac{1}{4} \frac{1}{2} \frac{3}{4} \frac{4}{4}$	Pick and Dip Method. Center of the Wall.
14	Cutting off Mortar.	Omit.	The brick should be shoved only far enough to just bring the mortar to the top of the brick, and no more, and then no cutting off mortar will be necessary.
15	Disposing of Mortar.	Omit.	
16	Tapping down Brick.	Omit.	
17	Cutting off Mortar.	Omit.	
18	Disposing of Mortar.	Omit.	
	18	2	Total Number of Motions.

CHART 2. Pick and Dip Method, Laying in the Interior Tiers (*continued*).

intentions cannot be made to leave off their old habits of making a dozen or more motions per brick, because they have been laying brick in that way for many years. Yet, by hard and continued work, with little time spent in resting, they are able to do a profitable amount of work per day.

It is not wise to interfere with this type of man.

Again, there is the bricklayer who can adopt any method, but who cannot get such good results from new methods.

We must have the best work in spite of all other considerations. Therefore, it is not wise to have him change from the method under which he is most skillful.

Another type, which is the commonest of all, is the man who, unconsciously, uses our method when he is rushed, but who, unconsciously, uses other methods when he is not rushed.

It is our intention to increase the wages of those men who lay brick in the manner described in this system, because we know that with the usual amount of effort and the same number of motions our method will increase the number of brick laid by two or three times the number laid under unsystematic methods.

We shall, therefore, continue to rate our bricklayers by classes, as follows [see p. 62].

Opera-tion No.	The Wrong Way. Motions per Brick. $\frac{1}{4}\ \frac{1}{2}\ \frac{3}{4}\ \frac{4}{4}$	The Right Way. Motions per Brick. $\frac{1}{4}\ \frac{1}{2}\ \frac{3}{4}\ \frac{4}{4}$	Stringing Mortar Method. The Exterior 4 Inches (Laying to the Line.)
1	Step for Mortar.	Omit.	
2	Reaching for Mortar.	$\frac{1}{4}$	As a large trowel holds mortar enough for four brick, $\frac{1}{4}$ of a motion is the right amount to allow for one brick.
3	Working up Mortar.	Omit.	Have a laborer keep the mortar at the right consistency by tempering.
4	Step for Brick.	Omit.	If the mortar boxes are not over 4 ft. apart no stepping is necessary.
5	Reach for Brick.	$\frac{4}{4}$	
6	Pick up Right Brick.	Omit.	
7	Mortar Box to Wall.	$\frac{1}{4}$	Conveying mortar for four brick, equals $\frac{1}{4}$ motion per brick.
8	Brick, Pile to Wall.	$\frac{1}{2}$	Brick in each hand $=\frac{1}{2}$ motion per brick.
9	Deposit Mortar on Wall.	$\frac{1}{4}$	Depositing mortar for four brick at once $=\frac{1}{4}$ motion per brick.
10	Spreading Mortar.	$\frac{1}{4}$	Spreading mortar for four brick per motion $=\frac{1}{4}$ motion per brick.
11	Cutting off Mortar.	Omit.	Do not cut off any mortar until brick is deposited on mortar.
12	Disposing of Mortar.	Omit.	
13	Laying Brick on Mortar.	Included in 5.	
14	Cutting off Mortar.	$\frac{4}{4}$	
15	Disposing of Mortar.	$\frac{4}{4}$	
16	Tapping Down Brick.	Omit.	
17	Cutting off Mortar.	Omit.	
18	Disposing of Mortar.	Omit.	
	18	$4\frac{1}{2}$	Total Number of Motions per Brick.

Chart 3. Stringing Mortar Method, Laying to the Line.

OPERA-TION No.	THE WRONG WAY. Motions per Brick. $\frac{1}{4}$ $\frac{1}{2}$ $\frac{3}{4}$ $\frac{4}{4}$	THE RIGHT WAY. Motions per Brick. $\frac{1}{4}$ $\frac{1}{2}$ $\frac{3}{4}$ $\frac{4}{4}$	STRINGING MORTAR METHOD. THE CENTER OF THE WALL.
1	Step for Mortar.	Omit.	
2	Reaching for Mortar.	$\frac{1}{4}$	Mortar enough for four brick at a time $= \frac{1}{4}$ motion per brick.
3	Working up Mortar.	Omit.	
4	Step for Brick.	Omit.	
5	Reach for Brick.	$\frac{1}{2}$	One brick in each hand $= \frac{1}{2}$ motion per brick.
6	Pick up Right Brick.	Omit.	
7	Mortar, Box to Wall.	$\frac{1}{4}$	Mortar for four bricks at once $= \frac{1}{4}$ motion per brick.
8	Brick Pile to Wall.	$\frac{1}{2}$	One brick in each hand $= \frac{1}{2}$ motion per brick.
9	Deposit Mortar on Wall.	Included in 7.	
10	Spreading Mortar.	$\frac{1}{4}$	Spreading mortar for four brick to the motion $= \frac{1}{4}$ motion per brick.
11	Cutting off Mortar.	Omit.	
12	Disposing of Mortar.	Omit.	
13	Laying Brick on Mortar.	Included in 8.	
14	Cutting off Mortar.	Omit.	If the brick is not shoved too far on the bed of mortar the mortar will be shoved just to the top edge of the brick, and no cutting of mortar above top of brick will be necessary.
15	Disposing of Mortar.	Omit.	
16	Tapping Down Brick.	Omit.	
17	Cutting off Mortar.	Omit.	
18	Disposing of Mortar.	Omit.	
	18	$1\frac{3}{4}$	

CHART 4. Stringing Mortar Method, Laying in the Interior Tiers.

(a) Those who adapt themselves to this system. Men of this class shall receive a substantial increase above the minimum rate of pay.

(b) Those who can adapt themselves in part to this system. They will receive more money than the minimum rate.

(c) Those who are not able to adapt themselves to this system, but who can, by great and constant effort, accomplish a fair day's work. They shall receive the minimum rate.

(d) Those who do not ever attempt to lay brick in accordance with this system. They shall be employed only when regular bricklayers are scarce.

To save all the time possible, and to do the work with the least manual effort, is the purpose of the charts.

Apprentices must be taught to make up charts representing their own motions.

They must be permitted to use a reasonable amount of time in charting the times of the operation of our best bricklayers, that they may fully compare the bricklayers' methods with the charts in this book, and that they may also see their own shortcomings, by comparison.

Foremen must be careful to insist that the rules here given are followed by our apprentices. They will not only lay more brick by following them, but they will also become more valuable additions to our organization. They will make better foremen bricklayers for us than men with a much wider experience who have not been carefully trained under our system.

The following rules are made on the supposition that the work is being done from the Gilbreth scaffolds. When it is done on the floor, or from other kinds of scaffolds, the work should be done as nearly as is possible in accordance with these rules.

Stepping for mortar (1) and reaching for mortar (2) must be done exactly at the same time.

The same is true of stepping for brick (4) and reaching for brick (5).

The apprentice must make it a point to stand where he can pick up his stock with both hands at the same instant with the least effort.

After he has found that spot on the bricklayers' platform where each foot should be, he must stand there without stepping, and lay as far as possible in each direction, without making a step or lifting either shoe completely off the platform.

We find, after many years of actual practice, that if the scaffold horses are set up anywhere from 10 ft. to 10 ft. 6 ins. apart, and if two mortar boxes, each 2 ft. 2 ins. wide, are placed in each bay, one of them being hard against the left hand upright and the other divided evenly between that box and the right hand upright, then the bricklayer can stand on any part of the bricklayers' platform and reach into a mortar box and also reach the brick pile.

If the horses and mortar boxes are spaced as stated above, operations numbers 1 and 4 can be omitted.

We have found that 1 ft. 5 ins. is the shortest distance that the bricklayer can work in comfortably. Consequently, we have designated the patent horse so that when the foot is butted against the wall, the edge of the stock platform is exactly 1 ft. 5 ins. away from the wall.

We have also found that the bricklayer picks up his stock with the least fatigue from a platform 2 ft. above the level on which he stands. The same is true of the height of the wall on which he lays the brick. We have consequently made the stock platform 2 ft. higher than the bricklayers' platform. We have arranged the lifting jacks to work on 8-in. notches, so that the stock platform and the top of the wall will be at the same level. This is the most convenient and comfortable arrangement for the bricklayer. It cuts down the distance for reaching for mortar (2), reaching for brick (5), conveying the brick from the staging to the wall (8), and conveying the mortar from the staging to the wall (7).

The bricklayer should always pick up those brick first that are on the side of the stock platform that is nearest the wall.

He should pick up the mortar from that part of the box that is nearest the wall, in order to reduce the conveying distance.

He should use the stock that is far away only when he has none near the wall.

Working up the mortar with the trowel (3) should be dispensed with by having a tender on the stock platform with a water bucket and hoe to keep the mortar at the right consistency for the speediest bricklaying.

Even with a small number of masons, it pays to put a tender on the stock platform. He can not only temper up the mortar, but he can devote any spare time to piling up the brick on the inside of the stock platform with their faces up, so that the time of picking out the right brick (6), can be reduced to almost nothing.

The time needed to convey the mortar from the staging to the wall (7), depends not only on the distance that the mortar box is from the wall, but also on the amount of mortar that is taken at each trowelful. This is one of the points where the stringing mortar method outclasses the pick and dip method for speed.

Spreading mortar (10) should never require over one motion per brick. In most cases of common brick work, the mortar should be thrown from the trowel so as to require no further spreading.

The apprentice who spreads his mortar with two or more motions, or strokes of the trowel, should be watched carefully. He should be made to count the motions that he makes in laying each brick, until he is able to lay brick in the manner and with the same number of motions laid down in this system.

Cutting off the mortar that projects over the edge of the wall before the brick is laid (11), is entirely unnecessary. This should never be done on common brick work.

Cutting off mortar after the brick is rubbed into the mortar (14) will furnish the mortar for the next end joint.

Buttering the end joint (12) should be omitted at process (11), and should be done only at process (14).

Rubbing the brick into the mortar (13) will require almost no time or effort, certainly not over one-half a second, provided the joints are the right thickness and the brick are properly wet.

Foremen must, therefore, see that the brick are constantly kept at the right degree of wetness, not only to insure good work but also for speed.

Foreman must personally lay out the story pole for those heights of laying that will make the most speed as well as the best work.

Mortar on the trowel that is cut off from under the brick should be put on the end of the brick previously laid, for filling the end joint. It should never be thrown from the trowel back into the mortar box.

Many masons have the habit of constantly throwing the mortar back into the box. A large portion of this daubs up the bricks instead of landing in the box; besides, it means an unnecessary motion every time.

Tapping brick down to grade with the trowel should not be necessary, if the mortar is of the right consistency, the brick is wet enough and the joints are the right size; but if a tapping is necessary, tap the brick one hard tap, instead of several light taps. This reduces the operation of tapping to one motion of not over one-half second.

Nearly all bricklayers tap the brick from habit, not because it is necessary.

These charts of each case should be used as examples by apprentices as to the methods they should first learn and which motions they should use also as the total of motions for each process.

After the apprentice has learned the twelve different processes exactly as shown, he should be permitted to practice any other method that will accomplish the same quality of work in the same amount of time, as there are many different ways of laying brick.

In filling in the middle of a wall it is always quicker to lay those brick nearest the overhand side first and those nearest the inside face last. This order will allow the carrying of the brick from the stock platform to the wall with the most uniform speed, without a hitch or a change of direction of the motion.

Close watching of bricklayers will disclose the remarkable fact that years of constantly training the left hand to tell by feeling the top side from the bottom side of a brick, forms the habit of turning a brick over in the hand so as to have it right side up, even if it is being laid in the filling tiers. Few bricklayers realize that they do this, as it has become automatic with them to do it for the face tiers.

When seen to do this while laying on the filling tiers, they should receive a few reminders that they are not to do so, as it requires just so many more unnecessary motions and fatigues them for no purpose, making them require just so much more rest.

Teach them to make absolutely no motions and to have their hands travel no distance that does not give results.

In the selection of these methods as adopted here for the training of our young men, we have followed the best of the working methods of the men in our organization—which consist of bricklayers from many different nations, who have adapted themselves to the different conditions existing in various parts of the United States.

4

●●

PRIMER OF
SCIENTIFIC
MANAGEMENT *

* *Primer of Scientific Management,* by Frank B. Gilbreth, was published by D. Van Nostrand Co., New York, in 1914.

Foreword

●●●

In preparing this Primer of Scientific Management Mr. Gilbreth has performed a public service. His clear and simple instruction in the rudiments of the science will aid managers, superintendents, and foremen in their efforts to introduce it into their business. But the Primer will prove of greatest value in helping to remove from the minds of workingmen misapprehensions which have led some well-meaning labor leaders to oppose a movement from which labor has most to gain. That these labor leaders should, at the outset, have viewed the new management with suspicion was natural and proper. The "Beginning of Wisdom is Fear." But the second step in the path of wisdom is understanding; and courage should not lag far behind.

Scientific Management undertakes to secure greater production for the same or less effort. It secures to the workingman that development and rise in self-respect, that satisfaction with his work which in other lines of human activity accompanies achievement.

Eagerness and interest take the place of indifference, both because the workman is called upon to do the highest work of which he is capable, and also because in doing this better work he secures appropriate and substantial recognition and reward. Under Scientific Management men are led, not driven. Instead of working unwillingly for their employer, they work in coöperation with the management for themselves and their employer on what is a "square deal." If the fruits of Scientific Management are directed into the proper channels, the workingman will get not only a fair share, but a very large share, of the industrial profits arising from improved industry.

In order that the workingman may get this large share of the benefits through higher wages, shorter hours, regular employment, and better working conditions, the labor unions must welcome, not oppose, the introduction of Scientific Management to the end that the workingman through the unions may participate in fixing those wages, hours, and conditions.

Unless the workingman is so represented, there must be danger that his interests will not be properly cared for; and he cannot be properly represented except through organized labor. The introduction of Scientific Management therefore offers to Organized Labor its greatest opportunity.

LOUIS D. BRANDEIS.

MAY, 1912.

Definitions of Terms

••

SCIENTIFIC MANAGEMENT

What is scientific management?

Dr. Frederick W. Taylor says:—

"The art of management has been defined 'as knowing exactly what you want men to do and then seeing that they do it in the best and cheapest way' (Shop Management); also, 'The principal object of management should be to secure the maximum prosperity for the employer coupled with the maximum prosperity for each employee.'

"Scientific Management has for its very foundation the firm conviction that the true interests of the two are one and the same; that prosperity for the employer cannot exist through a long term of years unless it is accompanied by prosperity for the employee, and *vice versa;* and that it is possible to give the worker what he most wants—high wages—and the employer what he wants—a low labor cost—for his manufactures."

"Principles of Scientific Management." Harper and Brothers.

Mr. H. K. Hathaway says:—

"For its objects Scientific Management has the saving of energy, materials, and time, or in other words, the elimination of waste, and the increase of the world's wealth resulting from greater productivity of men and machinery. These it aims to achieve, in each industry to which it is applied, through bringing to bear upon each problem the analytical methods of investigation employed in the sciences; developing an art or science with well defined and codified laws, in place of uncertain tradition and rule-of-thumb opinion. This is a broad statement of the first principle of Scientific Management."

Mr. James Mapes Dodge says in Paper 1115, Transactions of A. S. M. E., entitled "A History of the Introduction of a System of Shop Management":—

"The Taylor System is not a method of pay, a specific ruling of account books, nor the use of high-speed steel. It is simply an honest, intelligent effort to arrive at the absolute control in every department, to let tabulated and unimpeachable fact take the place of individual opinion; to develop 'team-play' to its highest possibility."

Col. Theodore Roosevelt says:—

"Scientific Management is the application of the conservation principle to production. It does not concern itself with the ownership of our natural resources. But in the factories where it is in force it guards these stores of raw materials from loss and misuse. First, by finding the right material—the special wood or steel or fiber—which is cheapest and best for the purpose. Second, by getting the utmost of finished product out of every pound or bale worked up. We couldn't ask more from a patriotic motive, than Scientific Management gives from a selfish one.

"Now, the time, health, and vitality of our people are as well worth conserving, at least, as our forests, minerals, and lands. And Scientific Management seems to do even more for the workman than for raw materials. It studies him at his task. Of the motions he makes and the efforts he puts forth, it determines by patient observation, which are the ones that get the result. It experiments to see whether these cannot be further shortened, or made easier for him.

"When the right way has been worked out in every detail, Scientific Management sets it up as a standard for that job; then instructs and trains the workman until he can accomplish this standard. And so on with all other workmen and all other jobs. The individual is first made efficient; his productive capacity is raised twenty-five or fifty per cent, sometimes doubled. From these efficient units is built up an efficiency organization. And when we get efficiency in all our industries and commercial ventures, national efficiency will be a fact."

Mr. Brandeis says in "Scientific Management and the Railroads," published by *Engineering Magazine,* New York:—

"Scientific Management means universal preparedness, the same kind of preparedness that secured to Prussia a victory over France and to Japan a victory over Russia. In Scientific Management nothing is left to chance; all is carefully planned in advance.

"Every operation is to be performed according to a predetermined schedule under definite instructions; and the execution under the plan is inspected and supervised at every point. Errors are prevented instead of being corrected. The terrible waste of delays and accidents is avoided. Calculation is substituted for guess; demonstration for opinion. The high efficiency of the limited passenger train is sought to be obtained in the ordinary operations of the business."

Professor Roe of Yale says that "Scientific Management" consists of three things:—

1. Accurate determination of the method and time in which a piece of work should be done.
2. Detailed instructions for 1.
3. Rewards and penalties to secure 1 and 2.

Mr. Cleveland Moffat says:—

"The basis of Scientific Management, as it is of art, is the rigorous cutting away of superfluities—not one wasted motion, not one wasted minute."

Engineering and Contracting says, in an editorial in the April 5, 1911, issue:—

"As we conceive it, Scientific Management consists in the conscious application of the laws inherent in the practice of successful managers and the laws of science in general. It has been called management engineering, which seems more fully to cover its general scope of the science."

Mr. Arthur W. Page says on page 14049 of *World's Work:*—

"What is 'Scientific Management'?

"Many people get the impression that Scientific Management consists of slide rules, instruction cards, eight sets of shovels, and the like.

"In reality the appliances are the least important part of it. The main thing is, first, to get the accurate information and, second, to continuously apply it."

Mr. H. L. Gantt says:—

"A system of management, to deserve the term 'scientific,' should aim to meet the following four conditions:—

"1. It should provide means for utilizing all of the available knowledge concerning the work in hand.

"2. It should provide means for seeing that the knowledge furnished is properly utilized.

"3. It should award liberal compensation for those who do use it properly.

"4. It should provide liberal means for acquiring new knowledge by scientific investigation, with adequate rewards for success.

"In introducing such a system, my advice is to begin at the bottom and go slowly."

W. B. Laine says:—

"Scientific Management is that form of Management which—

"(1) Separates an operation into its elements and determines—by study, observation, and experiment of unit times and motions—standards of equipment and method with definite instructions for operation; and

"(2) Determines a definite task difficult of attainment, but possible of daily and continuous performance with conservation of the physical and mental health of the worker; and

"(3) Routes material and effort in accordance with determined standards, providing instruction by functionally operating and trained teachers for the worker; and

"(4) Determines methods of payment, assuring a wage considerably above the ordinary and giving a large reward for attainment of the task and a definite loss for failure; and

"(5) By the elimination of waste material and effort, lost time, idle machinery, and capital, assures the maximum of prosperity for the employer and the employee."

TAYLOR SYSTEM

What is the difference between Scientific Management and the Taylor Plan?

Dr. Taylor's functional foreman plan of management founded upon time study is the *basis* for all scientific management, *i.e.* for types of management where scientific laboratory methods of analysis are substituted for the rule of "thumb methods" that have been handed down by word of mouth.

The Taylor plan of management is generally known as "Scientific Management," although there are many plans of management formulated by scientists that do not conform to the laws of management as discovered by Dr. Taylor.

Why is not Scientific Management called "the Taylor System"?

That type of management founded upon the best recognized scientific principles of to-day *should* be known as Taylor's plan of management, and *would* be, but for the personal objections of Dr. Taylor.

Where is Scientific Management best explained?

Dr. Taylor's writings describe his work in full. See:—

Transactions of the American Society of Mechanical Engineers, Papers numbered—

647.—"A Piece Rate System." June, 1895.
1003.—"Shop Management." June, 1903.
1119.—"On the Art of Cutting Metals." December, 1906.

Also

American Magazine—March, April, May, 1911.
"The Principles of Scientific Management." Harper's, 1911.
"Shop Management." Harper's, 1911.

The value of Dr. Taylor's work was appreciated very early.

Mr. Harrington Emerson, industrial engineer, recognized the epoch-making value of A. S. M. E. Paper 1003 at the time of its presentation before the American Society of Mechanical Engineers, in 1903, when he said:—

"I regard the paper presented at this meeting by Mr. Taylor as the most important contribution ever presented to the Society, and one of the most important papers ever published in the United States."

TIME STUDY

What is "Time Study"?

Time study is the art of recording, analyzing, and synthesizing the time of the elements of any operation, usually a manual operation, but it has also been extended to mental and machinery operations.

It is one of the many remarkable inventions of Dr. Taylor while he was working at the Midvale Steel Works. It differs from the well-known process of timing the complete operation, as, for instance, the usual method for timing the athlete, in that the timing of time study is done on the elements of the process. Much ridiculous criticism has been put forward by well-meaning but uninformed persons, who claim that timing a worker down to a three hundredth of a minute is unkind, inhuman, and conducive to the worst form of slavery ever known. On the contrary, obtaining precise information regarding the smallest elements into which an art or a trade can be subdivided, and examining them separately, is the method adopted in all branches of scientific research.

For description of time study data by Mr. Sanford E. Thompson, C. E., see "Shop Management," Harper and Brothers.

For time study by Mr. R. T. Dana, see "Handbook of Steam Shovel Work," The Bucyrus Co.

MOTION STUDY

What is Motion Study?

Motion study is the science of eliminating wastefulness resulting from using unnecessary, ill-directed, and inefficient motions.

The aim of motion study is to find and prepetuate the scheme of least waste methods of labor.

By its use we have revolutionized several of the trades.[1] There is

[1] "Motion Study," published by D. Van Nostrand Company, 25 Park Place, New York.

probably no art or trade that cannot have its output doubled by the application of the principles of motion study. Among the variables affecting the motions most, are

VARIABLES OF THE WORKER

Anatomy	Experience	Nutrition
Brawn	Fatigue	Size
Contentment	Habits	Skill
Creed	Health	Temperament
Earning power	Mode of living	Training

VARIABLES OF THE SURROUNDINGS, EQUIPMENT, AND TOOLS

Appliances	Reward and punishment
Clothes	Size of unit moved
Colors	Special fatigue eliminating de-
Entertainment, music, reading, etc.	vices
Heating, cooling, ventilating	Surroundings
Lighting	Tools
Quality of material	Union rules
	Weight of unit moved

VARIABLES OF THE MOTION

Acceleration
Automaticity
Combination with other motions and sequence
Cost
Direction
Effectiveness
Foot pounds of work accomplished
Inertia and momentum overcome
Length
Necessity
Path
Play for position
Speed

Arthur Twining Hadley, President of Yale University, states in his book "Economics":—

"The ability of a community to pay high wages seems to depend more upon the avoidance of waste than upon increase of accumulations."

TASK

What is meant by the word "task"?

The quantity of work of prescribed quality to be done in a given time, or the time required to do a certain quantity of output in a certain way as prophesied by scientific time study, is called the "task." The task is determined by building up synthetically the easiest, least fatiguing, least wasteful method, and allowing a definite percentage of time for rest, and a definite percentage for unavoidable delays. This percentage seldom amounts to less than $12\frac{1}{2}$ per cent and often reaches to more than 30 per cent, and in some cases over 50 per cent.

The task is obviously, then, not a measure of how much a man can do under a short burst of speed, but instead is that maximum quantity that he can do day after day without speeding up and year after year with improvement to his health.

The task is the quantity that the man who is actually to do the work can do continuously and thrive.

FUNCTIONAL FOREMEN

What is the meaning of "Functional Foremen"?

Functional foremen differ from the usual type of foremen in that, while the latter have full charge of a certain number of men, the former have charge of a certain function in the handling of the men. For example, the principal functional foremen under the Taylor plan consist of

(a) Route clerk, and order of work clerk.
(b) Instruction card clerk.
(c) Time and cost clerk.
(d) Disciplinarian.
(e) Gang boss.
(f) Speed boss.
(g) Repair boss.
(h) Inspector.

All of these functional foremen must be specialists at their functions and must be prepared constantly to teach and help the individual workman with whom they work in direct contact.

The functional foreman under the scientific plan of management differs from the foreman under the traditional plan of management in that the latter has so many functions and duties to perform that he has to depend largely upon the individual workman to guess for himself as to which is the best way to do the work and to hold his job.

Regarding the savings and economic benefits accruing from the general principle of division of labor, Adam Smith said in 1776 ("An Inquiry into the Nature and Causes of the Wealth of Nations"):—

"This great increase in the quantity of work, which, in consequence of the division of labor, the same number of people are capable of performing, is owing to three different circumstances: first, to the increase of dexterity in every particular workman; secondly, to the saving of time which is commonly lost in passing from one species of work to another; and, lastly, to the invention of a great number of machines which facilitate and abridge labor, and enable one man to do the work of many."

Regarding division of mental labor, Charles Babbage said:—

"The effect of the *division of labor,* both mechanical and in mental operations, is, that it enables us to purchase and apply to each process precisely that quantity of skill and knowledge which is required for it; we avoid employing any part of the time of a man who can get eight or ten shillings a day by his skill in tempering needles, in turning a wheel, which can be done for sixpence a day; and we equally avoid the loss arising from an accomplished mathematician in performing the lowest processes of arithmetic."

Laws or Principles
of Scientific Management

••

TIME STUDY

What is the fundamental of Scientific Management?

The great fundamental of Scientific Management is time study.

On time study hangs the entire plan of the Taylor system of management. The apparently simple art of time study is in reality a great invention, for, previous to Taylor's discovery of it, there was no practical way of predetermining or prophesying accurately the amount of work that a man could do before he actually commenced to do it.

Any plan of management that does not include Taylor's plan of time study cannot be considered as highly efficient. We have never seen a case in our work where time study and analysis did not result in more than doubling the output of the worker. The greatest need to-day, as Dr. Taylor has already pointed out, is a handbook of time study data for assisting the workers to earn higher wages and the management to secure lower production costs. It is hoped that the day will soon arrive when the colleges will coöperate in undertaking this work in accordance with a definite plan, with a national bureau in charge of the entire work.

What are the purposes of Time Study?

The purposes of the scientific study of unit times are five, as follows:—

1. To obtain all the existing information about the art or trade being investigated that is possessed by the present masters, journey-men, and experts of that trade, who obtained the most of their information through the "journeyman to apprentice method" of teaching.

2. To get the most exact information regarding the time required to perform each smallest element of the operation, so that in building up the standard method synthetically the quickest elements and motions may be selected, in order that the workman can, other things being equal, use a method consisting of elements requiring the least time to perform.

3. To determine which motions and elements are the least fatiguing, that the worker may be caused no unnecessary fatigue in his work, nor any fatigue outside of his work of actually producing output.

4. To determine the amount of actual rest that each kind of work requires, that neither the management nor the man himself may injure the man by trying to make him do too much in order to obtain an increase over and above the unusually high wages offered by Scientific Management.

5. To determine the personal coefficient of each applicant for certain kinds of work, that he may be assisted in entering that vocation for which he is best fitted.

It will be seen by the above that it is necessary to obtain the most accurate and minute times if the greatest good to the worker and the management is to be obtained.

STANDARDS

Why is the establishment of standards of tools, methods, and devices of such vital importance as a preliminary?

This is best answered by Mr. Morris Llewellyn Cooke, in his valuable "Report to the Carnegie Foundation For the Advancement of Teaching." He says (p. 6):—

"A standard under modern Scientific Management is simply a carefully thought out method of performing a function, or carefully drawn specification covering an implement or some articles of stores or of product. The idea of perfection is not involved in standardization. The standard method of doing anything is simply the best method that can be devised at the time the standard is drawn. Improvements in standards are wanted and adopted whenever and wherever they are found. There is absolutely nothing in standardization to preclude innovation. But to protect standards from changes which are not in the nature of improvements, certain safeguards are erected. These safeguards protect standards from change for the sake of change. All that is demanded under modern scientific management is that a proposed change in a standard must be scrutinized as carefully as the standard was scrutinized prior to its adoption; and further that this work be done by experts as competent to do it as were those who originally framed the standard. Standards adopted and protected in this way produce the best that is known at any one time. Standardization practiced in this way is a constant invitation to experimentation and improvement."

In what way can the general adoption of standards save money?

Dr. Taylor in his Paper 1003 ("Shop Management"), American Society of Mechanical Engineers, says:—

"284. It would seem almost unnecessary to dwell upon the desirability of standardizing not only all of the tools, appliances, and implements throughout the works and office, but also the methods to be used in the multitude of small operations which are repeated day after day. There are many good managers of the old school, however, who feel that this standardization is not only unnecessary, but that it is undesirable, their principal reason being that it is better to allow each workman to develop his individuality by choosing the particular implements and methods which suit him best. And there is considerable weight in this contention when the scheme of management is to allow each workman to do the work as he pleases and hold him responsible for results. Unfortunately, in ninety-nine out of a hundred such cases only the first part of this plan is carried out. The workman chooses his own methods and implements, but

IS NOT HELD IN ANY STRICT SENSE ACCOUNTABLE unless the quality of the work is so poor or the quantity turned out is so small as to almost amount to a scandal. In the type of management advocated by the writer, this complete standardization of all details and methods is not only desirable, but absolutely indispensable as a preliminary to specifying the time in which each operation shall be done, and then insisting that it shall be done within the time allowed.

"285. Neglecting to take the time and trouble to thoroughly standardize all of such methods and details is one of the chief causes for setbacks and failure in introducing this system. Much better results can be attained, even if poor standards be adopted, than can be reached if some of a given class of implements are the best of their kind while others are poor. It is uniformity that is required. Better have them uniformly second class than mainly first with some second and some third class thrown in at random. In the latter case the workmen will almost always adopt the pace which conforms to the third class instead of the first or second. In fact, however, it is not a matter involving any great expense or time to select in each case standard implements which shall be nearly the best or the best of their kinds. The writer has never failed to make enormous gains in the economy of running by the adoption of standards.

"286. It was in the course of making a series of experiments with various air hardening tool steels with a view to adopting a standard for the Bethlehem works that Mr. White, together with the writer, discovered the Taylor-White process of treating tool steel, which marks a distinct improvement in the art; and the fact that this improvement was made, not by manufacturers of tool steel, but in the course of the adoption of standards, shows both the necessity and fruitfulness of methodical and careful investigation in the choice of much neglected details. The economy to be gained through the adoption of uniform standards is hardly realized at all by the managers of this country. No better illustration of this fact is needed than that of the present condition of the cutting tools used throughout the machine shops of the United States. Hardly a shop can be found in which tools made from a dozen different qualities of steel are not used side by side, in many cases with little or no means of telling one make from another; and, in addition, the shape of the cutting edge of the tool is in most cases left to the fancy of each individual workman. When one realizes that the cutting speed of the best treated air hardening steel is for a given depth of cut, feed, and quality of metal being cut, say sixty feet per minute, while with the same shaped tool made from the best carbon tool steel and with the same conditions, the cutting speed will be only twelve feet per minute, it becomes apparent how little the necessity for rigid standards is appreciated."

How can instruction cards be made out for laborers who cannot write or read any language, and who also cannot speak or understand the language of the management?

There are several ways of overcoming this difficulty. If the job is a long one of highly repetitive work, it is sometimes advisable to get an interpreter who can translate and teach the instruction card to the men. If the men read, it is possible to print the entire card in the two languages.

Where this has not been advisable, we have found that a full-sized exhibit of a complete unit to be constructed, maintained in all its various stages, and shown in detail as to method and result, has contained enough of the principles and features of the instruction card to serve the purpose.

We have found that stereoscopic (3-dimension) photographs and a stereoscope have been a great help, not only where the men do not understand the language of the management, but also in cases where they do.

Dr. Taylor says:—

"The instruction card can be put to wide and varied use. It is to the art of management what the drawing is to engineering, and, like the latter, should vary in size and form according to the amount and variety of the information which it is to convey. In some cases it should consist of a pencil memorandum on a small piece of paper which will be sent directly to the man requiring the instructions, while in others it will be in the form of several pages of typewritten matter, properly varnished and mounted, and issued under the check or other record system, so that it can be used time after time."

And any method or device that will enable the management to explain to the men exactly what is wanted, that they may do the performing exactly in accordance with the method required by the planning department, will perform the functions of the instruction card.

In whatever form or physical shape the instrument for conveying the information from the planning department is, one thing is certain, i.e. that the more explicit and definite this information, the better the results will be.

FUNCTIONAL FOREMEN

With so many functional foremen, who shall decide when they disagree?

Each functional foreman decides matters pertaining to his own work. In case of a disagreement, the disciplinarian decides as to questions of discipline and penalties.

On large works, where there are several foremen working at the same function, if they cannot agree immediately, the decision is left to their respective overforemen. If these, in turn, disagree, the question is referred to the assistant superintendent.

What is the advantage of a disciplinarian over a self-governing body?

The disciplinarian should be a trained specialist, who holds his job during good and efficient behavior. He should be free from the politics of election by a self-governing body. He should also be "of the management" in selecting employees, fixing base rates of wages, and determining promotion of deserving workers and foremen.

Don't the foremen have to spend too much of their time looking at papers instead of pushing the men?

The foremen in the planning department put their orders and teachings in writing on paper, defining clearly the standard method of doing the work.

The foremen of the performing department do not drive the men. Their duties are to explain the written orders of the planning department, and to see that they are carried out exactly as written.

Inasmuch as the papers show and describe the best-known method, it is essential that the foremen follow the instructions on the instruction card to the letter in order to obtain the best results.

How can a worker serve eight masters?

These eight so-called "masters" are functional foremen whose duties are to help the worker to do his work in the exact manner called for on the instruction card. Each man thus belongs to eight different gangs, or classes of instruction, and receives help from all eight teachers. "A man cannot serve two masters," but he can easily receive and accept help from eight teachers.

Mr. Wilfred Lewis, President of the Tabor Manufacturing Company, stated recently in an address on Scientific Management at the Congress of Technology, Boston, April 10, 1911, speaking of his own experience with the Taylor System:—

"Our wonderful increase in production is not due entirely to rapidity of performance, for in some instances very little gain in that direction has been made. A great deal is due to the functional foreman, whose duty it is to prepare and guide the way of every piece of work going through the shop.

"The old notion that a man cannot serve two masters or take orders from more than one superior is denied by the new philosophy, which makes it possible for a workman to have as many bosses as there are functions to be performed. There is no conflict of authority unless the functions overlap, and even there such conflict as may arise is salutary and to the interest of the company."

RATE OF COMPENSATION

How is it possible to pay high wages and at the same time have low costs of labor?

By finding the best way to do the work. This will enable the worker to produce much higher records of output at a lower unit cost, yet a higher total daily wage, than he received under the old form of management. For example, suppose that under the old plan of management a man turned out about 10 pieces per day and received a total daily wage of $4.00. That would equal forty cents apiece.

Now suppose that by analyzing the method of making, down to the minutest motions, and by discovering a new method that took less time with less effort and was subject to less delay, the worker was able to put out 25 pieces, for which he received twenty-five cents apiece. The man's pay is here raised more than 56 per cent, and the production costs have been lowered $37\frac{1}{2}$ per cent, out of which must be paid the cost of the investigation and of the planning department.

What are the essential differences between the different methods of payment and what are the good points and the failings of each?

(a) *Day Work.*—The most common method of payment of the worker, especially in establishments where but few men are employed, is the day work plan. Under this plan a man is paid for the time he works, and there is no agreement as to how much work he shall do in order to earn his day's pay.

Theoretically, this plan is very good, but in practice it is a great factor in decreasing efficiency, raising costs, reducing outputs, and, eventually, decreasing wages.

The day work system of payment would be an ideal method of payment of the workmen, from both the standpoint of the workers and the employers, if the employers could tell what rate per day would be the correct amount to pay each workman. But there is no way of determining that easily, consequently the men are paid by the position they hold and not for their individual merit, skill, or productivity. The workmen, seeing that their pay is determined by their class of trade, immediately recognize that it is useless to be particularly efficient because it will not affect their pay in the long run. Consequently all hands soon fall into that easy-going pace that is just fast enough to hold their job.

(*b*) *Old Bonus Scheme.*—The old scheme of paying a bonus has grown into disfavor generally because under it the amount of bonus was not determined scientifically; and, finally, it was used as a club over the heads of the workmen to drive them to greater efforts without adequate or just financial rewards. It also resulted in a poorer quality of finished output and oftentimes in accidents and injuries due to the generally careless methods resulting from the incentive to earn the extra financial reward.

(*c*) *Old-fashioned Piecework.*—Piecework would be an ideal method for paying the men if it were not for several facts not readily recognized as being of great injustice to the worker. First comes the difficulty of finding out the correct and just price that should be paid per piece. Then there is the injustice to the worker while he is learning to do the work, also the fear on the part of the worker that the employer will cut the rate if he earns what the employer thinks is too much. Finally comes systematic soldiering, which is the worst thing in any type of management.

(*d*) *Gain Sharing.*—This method of compensating the workman was invented by Mr. Henry R. Towne in 1886. This method is fully described in the Transactions of the American Society of Mechanical Engineers, 1889, Paper 341.

(*e*) *Premium Plan.*—This method of paying workmen was invented by Mr. F. A. Halsey and is fully described in the Transactions of the American Society of Mechanical Engineers, 1891, Paper 499.

Mr. Taylor discusses these two methods of management (see Transactions of the American Society of Mechanical Engineers, 1895, Paper 647, ¶¶27–30).

(*f*) *Task with Bonus.*—This system was invented by Mr. H. L. Gantt. It consists of paying a regular day's pay to the worker in every case, even while he is learning and is unable to produce much output. It also provides for a scientifically determined task of standard quality, for the accomplishment of which the worker receives from 30 to 100 per cent extra wages. For any excess of output over and above the quantity of the task, the worker is paid at the same piece rate as is the rate a piece for the task. This is, therefore, a simple yet remarkable invention, for it insures a minimum of a full day's pay for the unskilled and the learners, and piecework for the skilled. (See "Work, Wages, and Profits," published by *The Engineering Magazine*. See also Paper 928, Transactions of the American Society of Mechanical Engineers.)

(g) *Three-rate with Increased Rate.*—This system has many advantages in certain cases, and we have found it to be extremely valuable during the period of teaching the workmen how to achieve the task. It consists of—

(1) Paying a usual and customary day's pay to every worker, called the low rate.

(2) Paying a day's pay plus 10 per cent to a worker when he conforms to the exact method described upon the instruction card. This is called the middle rate and is used for the purpose of encouraging the worker and of inducing him to conform with great exactness to that method on which the unit times for work and percentage of time allowed for rest and unavoidable delays are based, and which has been determined by the planning department to be the best method that they have seen, heard of, or been able to devise by making a one best way from uniting best portions of many workers' methods. This middle rate is abandoned as soon as the worker has once achieved the task in the standard method. For the accomplishment of the task, which has been derived by scientific time study, an extra payment of from 30 to 100 per cent above the low rate. This is called the high rate, and for anything above the task a wage equal to the same piece rate for the increased quantity is paid. In some cases it is advisable to pay an increasing or differential rate for each piece when the number of pieces exceeds that of the task.

(h) *Differential Rate Piece.*—The Differential Rate Piece is an invention of Mr. Taylor, and, like everything he has done, is the most efficient of all methods of payment.

This method is undoubtedly the best method of compensating the worker. It gives unusually high pay for high outputs and unusually low pay for low outputs. It rewards the man who conforms to his instruction card so that he is most particular to coöperate with the management for the complete achievement of his task.

Paying an unusually low piece rate for failure to make obtainable output seems like a hardship on the worker; but it is absolutely necessary to penalize the lazy in this way because the "dependent sequences," as Mr. Harrington Emerson has described them, make it necessary to induce all men to work, by means of high pay for successful effort and low pay for lack of effort. In this way one worker, or class of workers, is not absolutely prevented from doing its work, which is dependent upon the preceding condition that the first workers achieve their tasks.

Example.—A bricklayer cannot achieve his task unless he is supplied with the brick, mortar, scaffold, and "line up" in the correct sequence at the right time, the right quantity, and of the right quality.

The mortar men cannot transport the mortar until it has been mixed. The mortar cannot be mixed until its ingredients have been received, etc.

While the Differential Rate Piece system is the most efficient, it should not be used until all the accompanying conditions for its success, including time study, the task, provision for proper inspection, methods and tools generally have been perfected and standardized.

While it is the most efficient, it requires a higher standard of management before it can be used to best advantage. It is particularly efficient on work that is repeated day after day and year after year.

It is hardly to be expected that any large establishment will ever have all employees working under one system of payment, therefore the system of payment must be selected according to the general condition of the management, whether or not work is sufficiently repetitive to warrant making entirely new time studies and instruction cards and many other factors controlling the situation.

Different methods of compensating workmen are explained particularly well in Chapter III of "Cost Keeping and Management Engineering," by Gillette and Dana.

It is necessary to say, further, that many ill-prepared antagonists to Scientific Management have stated frankly that they were "against any kind of a bonus scheme." It must be remembered, however, that "the method of payment is no more Scientific Management than a shingle is a roof," as Mr. Ernest Hamlin Abbott has so aptly stated.

Will not the use of different systems of payment make all kinds of confusion in an establishment?

No, on the contrary, the different conditions governing the work make it necessary to use several different forms of compensation to the workmen in order to secure the best results. In fact, the existence of a class of work on which the men are paid by the day provides one of the best forms of punishment for the use of the disciplinarian. After the men have gotten the high wages resulting from following the teachings provided for them, they dislike exceedingly to be put into the "day's pay" class. In the Link-Belt Co.'s works,—which are conceded to be of the most highly systematized,—there are at least four systems of payment, namely:—

(*a*) Day work,

(*b*) Piecework,

(*c*) Task with Bonus, and

(*d*) Differential Rate Piece.

The same is true with the Tabor Manufacturing Co., the Brighton Mills, Plimpton Press, Yale and Towne Manufacturing Co., and several works under the able management of Messrs. Dodge, Day and Zimmerman.

Why is not a coöperative plan better than Taylor's plan?

This question is best answered by quoting from Dr. Taylor's paper read before the A. S. M. E. in 1895, entitled a "Piece Rate System." We quote also pp. 73 to 77 inclusive of American Society of Mechanical Engineers, Paper 1003.

"73. Coöperation, or profit sharing, has entered the mind of every student of the subject as one of the possible and most attractive solutions of the problem; and there have been certain instances, both in England and France, of at least a partial success of coöperative experiments.

"74. So far as I know, however, these trials have been made either in small towns, remote from the manufacturing centers, or in industries which in many respects are not subject to ordinary manufacturing conditions.

"75. Coöperative experiments have failed, and, I think, are generally destined to fail, for several reasons, the first and most important of which is, that no form of coöperation has yet been devised in which each individual is allowed free scope for his personal ambition. Personal ambition always has been and will remain a more powerful incentive to exertion than a desire for the general welfare. The few misplaced drones, who do the loafing and share equally in the profits with the rest, under coöperation are sure to drag the better men down toward their level.

"76. The second and almost equally strong reason for failure lies in the remoteness of the reward. The average workman (I don't say all men) cannot look forward to a profit which is six months or a year away. The nice time which they are sure to have to-day, if they take things easily, proves more attractive than hard work, with a possible reward to be shared with others six months later.

"77. Other and formidable difficulties in the path of coöperation are the equitable division of the profits, and the fact that, while workmen are always ready to share the profits, they are neither able nor willing to share the losses. Further than this, in many cases, it is neither right nor just that they should share either in the profits or the losses, since these may be due in great part to causes entirely beyond their influence or control, and to which they do not contribute."

Isn't it really the old piecework scheme under a new name with a few frills added?

In its final analysis, all compensation is more or less piecework. Even "day work" is a kind of piecework, *i.e.* the employer in effect says "I'll give you so much per day." Then if he thinks that he is not getting enough pieces done for the money, perhaps he does not say anything more, but simply sends the blue envelope to the worker.

Another employer might say, "I'll pay you 25 cents apiece," he and the employee both thinking that the latter could make anywhere from 8 to 16 pieces per day. There is one great objection to this method that does not always show up immediately. When it does, it does more damage than enough to offset all its value; namely, when, by special effort on the part of the employee, he makes say 32 pieces per day, and the employer, knowing that there are plenty of men to be had who would be delighted to work for $2.00 to $4.00 per day, cuts the rate. As Dr. Taylor says, just two cuts of the rate for the same man, and he will then stop all planning except on the subject of how much output he can safely make without the fear of another cut. It is surely not for the employee's interest to make any extra effort unless he is to be compensated for it. This necessitates the setting of the piece rate scientifically and not by guess or arbitration or collective bargainings, and we say this emphatically, although we are thoroughly in favor of collective bargaining on many things, such, for example, as the minimum day's rate to be paid to the worker and the number of hours in the working day.

We will digress for a moment here and tell of an incident seen some years ago. We had occasion to visit a factory, and saw a girl putting four-ounce lots of the factory's product into pasteboard boxes. Her duties were simply to put exactly four ounces of merchandise into each pasteboard box and to put the cover on. She was doing her work in a most inefficient way—obviously so.

Knowing that all the employees in that factory were on piecework, we suggested to this girl that we could show her some economics of motions that would increase her output. She seemed much interested and watched our stop watch record an output several times greater our way than the way she had been working. She seemed delighted with the suggestion, and we were pleased to have shown her how she could do so many more dozen boxes per day. She followed the suggestion for about ten minutes, or until we walked away. When we came back, we saw that she was doing her work in the old way. We asked her why she did not do the work our way when it was so much more efficient. Her discouraged reply was, "What's the use; the boss here cuts the piece rate when any girl earns over $6.00 per week."

"Cannot the piece rate be cut under Scientific Management?"

Yes, and so can the throat of the goose that laid the golden eggs; but there are a great many incentives put upon the management not to cut the rate once it has been set. For example, for the best results the management must have established the reputation of never having cut a rate which has been set under Scientific Management. Then when a rate has been set and it has been found that no workman or gang boss teacher can teach the actual worker to do the work in the allotted time, the time allowed must be extended. On the other hand, if the time allowed is much longer than that required by the worker to accomplish his task, the management must stand by its mistake and take its medicine; but its medicine will not be bad for it at that. Such "candy work" can be used as a special prize for long service and special compensation for continuous merit.

The rate must not be set until the process and the method for executing the work have been completely changed. When the rate and the task and the method have been determined scientifically and not by rule of thumb, there will be no occasion or desire under Scientific Management to change the rate. We have seen cases where the earnings of the worker totaled to more than that of the gang bosses and, nevertheless, the unit costs were low.

What are the best remedies for soldiering?

There is but one remedy for soldiering, namely, an accurate knowledge on the part of the management of how much output constitutes a fair day's work, coupled with paying permanently unusually high wages, with no fear of a cut in rate.

Application of Laws
of Scientific Management

FIELD OF APPLICABILITY

If Scientific Management is so worthy, why are there so few places organized under it at the present time?

Because there are so few engineers and teachers capable of installing it, and they are all busy with more work than they can do. Until some definite method is adopted for increasing the number of teachers, the progress will be slow.

Can Scientific Management be applied to office work, i.e. work that is mostly mental work?

Yes, there are many cases where it has been as effective as in the shop or on the job.

On work of repetitive character we have, in several instances, doubled the amount of output per clerk, and shortened the working hours.

We have never seen the case where higher wages, greater output, and lower costs have not resulted when an office force operated under Scientific Management.

What happens when a business is too small or too large to operate under exactly eight functional bosses?

If too small to warrant eight different functional foremen, fewer foremen can be used and each be given a number of functions to perform. If the job is too large for exactly eight men, then there may be several foremen to each function, with an "over foreman" to each group of foremen of the same function. Under the traditional form of management one foreman performs all eight functions as well as the time will permit.

For a description of practical application of Scientific Management, see a series of articles entitled "Applied Methods of Scientific

Management," by Frederic A. Parkhurst, running in *Industrial Engineering* for 1911, and published in book form by Wiley & Co.

POSSIBILITY OF SUBSTITUTES FOR SCIENTIFIC MANAGEMENT

Why not get an extra good foreman and simply leave the question of management to him?

In the first place, "extra good foremen" are hard to find, and when found are more profitable to their employer and also themselves when acting in charge of that function for which they are specially fitted.

Furthermore, one man working alone cannot do such efficient work as can several specialists of less brilliancy, in team work, each at the function at which he is specially trained.

As Mr. Ernest Hamlin Abbott has said, in the *Outlook* for Jan. 7, 1911:—

"Scientific Management cannot be 'bought and delivered in a box,' but when it is once installed, it will bring results that cannot be achieved by a merely 'born manager.' If a man wants to practice medicine, it is well if he is a 'born doctor,' but nowadays it is not sufficient; it is not even necessary. So it will be with the manager."

Cannot the American workman devise efficient methods as well as the engineer?

As a proof that the workman cannot compete in devising efficient methods with the trained engineer, it is well to cite the paper 1010 of the Transactions of the American Society of Mechanical Engineers, by Mr. Carl G. Barth, entitled "Slide Rules for the Machine Shop as a part of the Taylor System of Management," in which he states:—

"Thus already during the first three weeks of the application of the slide rules to two lathes, the one a 27 inch, the other a 24 inch, in the larger of these shops, the output of these was increased to such an extent that they quite unexpectedly ran out of work on two different occasions, the consequence being that the superintendent, who had previously worried a good deal about how to get the great amount of work on hand for these lathes out of the way, suddenly found himself confronted with a real difficulty in keeping them supplied with work. But while the truth of this statement may appear quite incredible to a great many persons, to the writer himself, familiar and impressed as he has become with the great intricacy involved in the problem of determining the most economical way of running a machine tool, the application of a rigid mathematical solution to this problem as against the leaving it to the so-called practical judgment and experience of the operator, cannot otherwise result than in the exposure of the perfect folly of the latter method."

What is the reason that employees do not know how fast work should be done?

There are many reasons, such as—

(*a*) They have not investigated their problems by means of motion study and time study.

(*b*) They have not realized the importance of having each step in the dependent sequences carried out without delay.

(*c*) They have not been taught the saving in time caused by having all of the sequences obvious, and all of the planning and most of the brain work done by the planning department before the work is actually done.

(*d*) The workers have been taught, by the fear of running themselves out of a job or having their rate cut, that the safest plan for them is to soldier whenever possible.

(*e*) Lack of personal familiarity with stop watch records of elements of work of the best men, under standard conditions, is the cause of their lack of knowledge of how fast the work should be done.

Does not a good system of routing bring nearly all the benefits of Scientific Management?

A system of routing is but a small part of the entire plan of Scientific Management. It is a very necessary part, however, and the line determining just where routing leaves off and some of the other functions begin is arbitrary. One man has stated that even motion study is largely a matter of routing the various parts of the human body, particularly the hands, feet, eyes, and head.

For an illuminating discussion of routing and its relation to Scientific Management see "Industrial Plants," by Charles Day, published by *The Engineering Magazine,* 1911.

Is not loyalty and good will the thing that will make employees work most efficiently?

It is certainly a great factor in obtaining coöperation between the management and the workers. Scientific Management obtains good will by the square deal, by a division of the savings, by teaching, etc., while the old form of management sometimes endeavors to obtain it by jollying, "welfare work," picnics, self-governing committees, etc. The disadvantage of the last is that a self-governing committee does not get the best results, because it is not supplied with and does not know how best to use those data which have been obtained in a scientific manner.

PREPARATION FOR INTRODUCTION OF SCIENTIFIC MANAGEMENT

What preparation can be made for the advent of the Scientific Manager before he comes in?

There are many things that can be done. Among the most necessary and the easiest to do are four:—

(*a*) Establish standards of methods, and of tools everywhere.

(*b*) Install schedules and time tables.

(*c*) Place each man, as far as possible, so that his output and its unit cost shows up separately.

(*d*) Put present system in writing.

> (See "Cost Keeping and Management Engineering," Gillette and Dana.)

These improvements will pay for themselves from the start and will facilitate the work of the efficiency engineer very materially.

PLACE OF INTRODUCTION OF SCIENTIFIC MANAGEMENT

Where is the best place to begin to install Scientific Management?

It should be first installed where it will have the least effect upon the workmen. When changes are to be made that affect the workmen, it is most desirable that those cases should be undertaken first that show most plainly that workmen are benefited and that show up clearest as an object lesson to all the workmen and to all the employers, superintendents, and foremen as to how Scientific Management simultaneously increases wages for the workers and cuts down production costs for the owner. It is desirable to start the installation in many places at the same time. Therefore the establishment of standards everywhere, including standard instruction cards for standard methods, motion study, time study, time cards, records of individual outputs, selecting and training the functional foremen, particularly the foreman in charge of the function of inspection, are the features that should be undertaken at the very first. Collect the great special knowledge that the functional foremen should possess and see that they learn it. In choosing which of two things is to be done first, always give precedence to that which can be nailed down and held from slipping back into the old rut, once it has been made to operate under the new Scientific Management.

METHOD OF INTRODUCTION OF SCIENTIFIC MANAGEMENT

Is it not necessary, in introducing Scientific Management, to import a number of functional foremen, etc.?

That depends upon circumstances. In our business we have a Flying Squadron of "over foremen" for starting a new job properly. These men are trained to handle one or more functions each, and can therefore start the job under Scientific Management on the first day that they arrive. It is their duty to help the permanently assigned functional foremen to get their work into shape and planned ahead as far as possible. The Flying Squadron can then be spared for other work, yet be available in case of emergency. In starting any new undertaking, for best results a larger number of foremen are required than are needed after the job has progressed.

The Flying Squadron, therefore, is valuable at the start of the work for its actual services as well as for teaching the permanent foremen on the job.

How can you introduce Scientific Management into an organization without giving the business a jolt?

By beginning at those places where the savings will be immediate and where changes will affect the entire establishment least,—by installing it first where it affects the work of one man only at a time, and by progressing at that speed that will not cause a jolt to the business.

TIME NECESSARY TO INSTALL SCIENTIFIC MANAGEMENT

How long will it take to install it all?

It can never be "all" installed, because there is no end to it. The time required differs. For example, the Link-Belt Company spent several years putting Scientific Management into their works at

Philadelphia, while they were able afterwards to put the same system into their Western shops in less than the same number of months.

It takes much longer to put it in where the management itself must be taught than where there is a Flying Squadron ready to take up the installation of each function.

In construction work, is not the job nearly completed before Scientific Management can be installed?

As there is no end to Scientific Management, it can never be said to be completely installed. In construction work much benefit can be obtained immediately—greater speed, better quality, and lower costs of production. From the very nature of construction work, it is difficult to avoid waste under any plan of management, and particularly under the traditional plan of management. It, therefore, offers unusual opportunities for saving through Scientific Management installed from the first day by the Flying Squadron.

PRACTICABILITY OF SCIENTIFIC MANAGEMENT

Isn't it true that you cannot expect to get all of the men, in fact any man, to use all of the prescribed motions and only the prescribed motions in any one day, or day after day?

It is quite impossible to get perfection in anything. However, the savings in motions, due, for example, to putting the bricks on a packet the right way in the first place, and delivering the brick to the bricklayer exactly in that condition and position that will make it easiest for him to use the most economical motions, together with the gang boss who is specially trained to coach the bricklayer to use the fewest, most economical, and most efficient standard motions, will result in an extremely high efficiency which, even if it does not reach the 100 per cent mark, is nearer to it daily.

How can an engineer tell with a stop watch, by timing a worker for a few hours or days, how much he can do day after day at his work, and how can the engineer be sure that the worker being timed is not using up his reserve strength?

He cannot be sure without sufficiently painstaking investigation. That is why Dr. Taylor timed men for long periods before he found his laws relating to quantities of rest required for overcoming fatigue without calling upon the worker's reserve strength. No worker has

ever considered that he must actually rest two whole hours in a day,
yet Dr. Taylor found that some kinds of work required the worker to
rest over 50 per cent of his entire day.

PURPOSE OF SCIENTIFIC MANAGEMENT

**Is it not true that under the Taylor System the shop or the business
"exists first, last, and all the time for the purpose of paying dividends to its owners"?**

Yes, and that is also true about shops and businesses under any and
all other forms of management. Without dividends there is no doubt
that the best thing to do would be to sell off the machinery before it
was all worn out, and to do such other things as might be necessary to
get back the capital invested before it was lost.

EXPENSE

**Must one "go the whole game" with Scientific Management to get
real results?**

No. Especially is this true in the small concern where there are not
enough employees to warrant the installation of all of the features of
Scientific Management. A small concern can use many of the features,
however, very advantageously.

Can savings be made, and have savings been made, from the first day?

Savings by use of Scientific Management can undoubtedly be made
from the first day. Science investigations can undoubtedly be made
that will pay for themselves as they go along; but the relation of the
saving by Scientific Management to the expense of it varies at different periods, and depends upon how fast Scientific Management is installed and upon the nature of the business.

In our business, we can show hundreds of instances on the cost
records of substantial decrease in costs, in many cases of costs that
were halved as fast as the system was installed.

Is it not necessary to wait years after Scientific Management is introduced to get full reduction in costs?

Yes, in a business already highly systematized, it undoubtedly will
require from 2 to 4 years to get the full benefit of the complete introduction of Scientific Management. This time can usually be re-

duced when there is no interference from those who oppose through ignorance.

Does not Scientific Management occasion a large outlay for equipment and machinery?

The purpose of Scientific Management is not the installing of the best machinery, although the best machinery is of course desirable. It is using to best advantage the machinery available.

Scientific Management aims, primarily, so to handle labor with the existing machinery that the maximum prosperity will result for the employer and for all employees. But, as it deals largely with scientific investigation, it discovers laws, and points out the economic advantages of new devices and machines. While it makes the employee more efficient and the management of more assistance to the employees, it also predetermines and makes inventions in machinery as well as methods almost obvious. Whether or not additional machinery and equipment is acquired is not a vital part of Scientific Management.

Is not the expense burden of maintaining the planning department equal to all the savings that it can make?

Dr. Taylor answers this in a most concise manner in paragraph 155 in the Transactions of the American Society of Mechanical Engineers, Paper 1003 ("Shop Management," Harper and Brothers, pp. 55–56):—

"At first view the running of a planning department, together with the other innovations, would appear to involve a large amount of additional work and expense, and the most natural question would be whether the increased efficiency of the shop more than offsets this outlay.

"It must be borne in mind, however, that, with the exception of the study of unit times, there is hardly a single item of work done in the planning department which is not already being done in the shop. Establishing a planning department merely concentrates the planning and much other brain work in a few men especially fitted for their task and trained in their especial lines, instead of having it done, as heretofore, in most cases by high-priced mechanics, well fitted to work at their trades, but poorly trained for work more or less clerical in its nature."

Mr. H. L. Gantt says, page 18, in "Work, Wages, and Profits":—

"A scientific investigation into the details of a condition that has grown up unassisted by science has never yet failed to show that economics and improvements are feasible that benefit both parties to an extent unexpected by either."

Is not Scientific Time Study so expensive that the average job cannot afford it?

Scientific Time Study does not all have to be done on one job. There are certain features that will reduce costs from the first day that can be done on even small jobs. The average job, even the small job, can be helped by many of the features of Scientific Management; and the instruction cards of previous jobs can be used with great economy even on small jobs.

Why are so many more inspectors required if the work is done better under Scientific Management?

Because the instruction cards call for a definite quality. They do not call for having the "work done to the satisfaction" of anybody. The extra money paid to the workers under Scientific Management is contingent upon the prescribed kind of quality being achieved.

The inspector keeps a close watch of work under Scientific Management. It is his duty to detect mistakes or lack of quality before much damage is done. As an example, suppose a workman was ordered to make 100 duplicate pieces from the same drawing. The inspector would watch the first piece keenly during its making and would pass upon the first unit when it was finished, to make sure that the workman understood his duties, and what was expected of him, and also that the quality of the work was right in every particular.

To catch mistakes before they are made is the cheapest way to get the right results.

Furthermore, the inspector under Scientific Management not only inspects, but also assists and instructs the workmen directly instead of through the other functional foremen.

Isn't there a larger waste from spoiling materials under Scientific Management?

There is not, because, as stated elsewhere, the first functional foreman introduced is that of inspector. The work is inspected more systematically under Scientific Management. The bonus is not paid unless the quality is within the requirements of the written instruction card.

The method of inspection under traditional management is often wasteful, because the inspection is usually done after the material is fabricated. Under Scientific Management the inspection proceeds as does the work itself. Inasmuch as the gang boss gets no bonus if the quality is not in accordance with the prescribed quality, he has a constant incentive to play at team work with the workman, *i.e.* he sees that the workman is provided with tools and surroundings in the best condition to make the prescribed quality. It is a matter of history that the quality of output has invariably improved by the introduction of Scientific Management.

INDICATORS OF SUCCESSFUL MANAGEMENT

What indicates the quality of the Management?

The best indicator of the quality of the management is the difference between the *customary* wages given for a certain kind of work and also the usual costs of production for that kind of work in other establishments, compared with the wages given and the costs of production in the works under consideration; or, in other words, the amount that the wages are higher and the amount that the costs of production are lower than usual, indicate the quality of management —other qualities, such as sanitary conditions, being as good or better.

If Scientific Management is all that is claimed for it, why are not the dividends always larger than in any shop where there is no Scientific Management?

They would be, if the merit and quality of the management were the one determining factor in profits and dividends. On the contrary, business judgment as to what and when to buy and where to sell, good salesmanship, and ability to get business at high prices are often of such great importance that dividends can be paid in spite of bad management. On the other hand, there are some cases where the management is so good that dividends can be paid in spite of bad business handling.

Effect of Scientific Management on the Worker

••

ACCIDENTS

Does Scientific Management insure the workman against accidents?

It does not insure him, but it certainly does reduce the *number* of accidents, because the machines, scaffolds, works, and ways are made and maintained in the standard condition called for on the instruction card, and are regularly inspected and overhauled as directed, and as often as required, by the written orders that come regularly from the Tickler or Reminder File.

Does not intensive production cause rapid depreciation of machinery, causing bad work and accidents and injury to the men?

No, because the desired maintainable standard condition of the machinery is determined by the planning department, just the same as the speed at which it is to be operated. It is inspected, cleaned and oiled, and repaired at stated times, whether it needs it or not. It must be kept up to the standard condition, or the worker cannot get the big outputs called for in order to get his bonus.

Therefore, the machinery is maintained constantly in such a condition that it will not break down or cause accidents. In fact, this function of repairs and maintenance at prescribed condition is assigned to a functional foreman specially trained to look after this work in accordance with the written instructions furnished by the planning department.

Does not a bonus scheme cause the work to be slighted and result in accidents to those who work under such conditions?

Yes, it does, when the bonus scheme is applied under the old plans of management. One man has stated that "any bonus scheme for repairing locomotives should be prohibited by laws; because when so many lives are dependent upon the quality of repairs on a locomo-

100

tive, there should never be an incentive to hurry the mechanic doing the repairs."

Under all of the old forms of "bonus schemes" this is absolutely true. Dr. Taylor must have recognized this and all other perfectly obvious difficulties of management in his practice. Dr. Taylor also successfully provided for overcoming this difficulty in a most logical and efficient manner, as follows:—

First, he analyzed the problem.

Second, he broke it up into its several most elementary subdivisions.

Third, he applied science to solving the problem of handling each subdivision in the best way.

Fourth, he built up, by and with the advice and assistance of the best workmen and engineers obtainable, a complete new process synthetically.

Fifth, he caused to be put in writing the entire process, so that it could be used forevermore, with all the advantages that come from conserving the information of how to do a thing in the best known way.

Sixth, he created the function of inspector, with duties of constructive criticism and not destructive criticism. He made it the duty of the inspector to sign a separate paper, stating that each and every repair had been executed precisely in accordance with the demanded quality of workmanship—no better and no worse. He authorized the inspector to deal directly with the workman and to assist him to achieve the prescribed quality of workmanship.

Seventh, he required the foreman to sign a separate piece of paper stating the length of time required to complete the job in the prescribed manner according to the requirements of the instruction card, as certified to in writing by the inspector.

Eighth, he provided that if the workman did the job exactly as prescribed, and certified to by the inspector, and if he also did the job within a certain time, he got a bonus—otherwise he did not.

It is now obvious that on such important matters as repairs on locomotives the Taylor plan is the most efficient for prevention of accidents. In our own experience, we have found that Dr. Taylor's plan is of great assistance in preventing accidents; in fact, we know that it is the one simplest and most efficient method of protecting the workers from injury and loss of life.

Dr. Taylor's plan is usually discussed from the standpoint of reducing costs, raising wages, increasing speed of construction, etc.; but if it had no other merit than its great benefits in eliminating the horrors and wastes due to the injury and killing of human beings, both of the public and of the workers themselves, it would have warranted the life work of Dr. Taylor and his followers spent in the creation of the science.

BRAIN

How can you expect every laborer to understand Scientific Management when it takes an engineer so many years to learn it?

The laborer does not understand it, nor is he expected to understand it. He simply understands the assistance he receives from the functional foremen in learning how to do his work more efficiently. He recognizes that he gets fairer treatment from the disciplinarian, higher wages from the time and cost clerk, and much more help from all the functional foremen; but he does not always learn the theories of Scientific Management unless he is ambitious enough specially to study it and to follow the same road that is open to every one else.

A machinist who has worked under Scientific Management for about one half of the ten years of his experience was asked how he liked the system. His reply was that he didn't know much about the system, because he "personally did not come in contact with it." He further stated that about all he knew of it was that somehow it enabled him to earn about a third more money every week of his life and that he had never been treated as well in any other establishment.

How long will it take any man to learn it?

There will never be a time when the expert will not learn more about it. The more one studies Scientific Management the more one is able to see what there is to learn, and the more experience he has in it the faster he is able to acquire new facts about it.

At the present time it is considered that a liberal education, preferably in engineering, followed by the complete mastery of at least one and preferably several mechanical trades, followed by four to six years of the closest study of the practical applications of the laws of Scientific Management in several widely different kinds of work, should make one capable of installing nearly all portions of Scientific Management into any business. In other words, with the same quality of brains, application, study, and experience, about the same length of time is required as to become a skilled surgeon. The surgeon, however, has the advantage of having at his disposal a tremendous amount of literature on his subject and also educational institutions. These, though quite as desirable, are not in existence in the subject of management. It is to be hoped, however, that this condition will be altered in the future and the time necessary for preparation will be greatly reduced.

Does it not make machines out of men?

Now, this question is usually asked in just this form, but there seems to be a great difference of opinion as to exactly what the questioner means. Is a good boxer, or fencer, or golf player a machine? Is the highly trained soldier at bayonet or saber drill a machine? He certainly approaches closely the 100 per cent mark of perfection from the standpoint of the experts in motion study. It is not nearly so important to decide whether or not he is a machine as to decide whether or not it is desirable to have a man trained as near perfection as possible in accordance with that method that expert investigators, working in harmony with the best actual workers, have decided to be the best known method for executing a given piece of work.

"All-around experience" to-day often means undue familiarity with many wrong methods, and "judgment" too often means the sad memory of the details of having done the work in several inefficient ways with a memory good enough to prevent repeating the use of the worst methods.

It is the aim of Scientific Management to induce men to act as nearly like machines as possible, so far as doing the work in the one best way that has been discovered is concerned. After the worker has learned that best way, he will have a starting point from which to measure any new method that his ingenuity can suggest. But until he has studied and mastered the standard method, he is requested not to start a debating society on that subject. Experience has shown that, with the best men chosen for the special work of selecting the method and planning the various steps in the processes,—these men having facilities and data at their command that equip them for their jobs,— their way will, in most cases, be better than that of the worker who has not first qualified on their way.

Experience has also shown that, whether or not the men may be called machines, they fare better and profit more when the management takes the time to have a trained planning department coöperating with the best workmen, determining every step in the process, and every motion in the step, and the effect of every variable in the motion. Then, after the "machine" has done it that way,—in the time allowed for the way,—the "machine" will be paid unusually high wages in real money for any suggestions that will be more efficient. He will be promoted to teach the others his new accepted method. If he continues to make suggestions for better methods than those of the planning department, he will be promoted to it. The line of promotion continues still higher; in fact, this "machine" will find himself at the top, if the measuring methods and devices show him to be more efficient than his fellows, for Scientific Management boosts "machines" for efficiency, not for their bluffs, bulldozing, or snap judgment.

Doesn't Scientific Management keep the worker from being an all-around mechanic and instead make him a narrowly trained specialist?

Perhaps so. Is it not better so? When there is so much to learn about such a simple thing as transporting a brick from the street to its final resting place, it is not better for the worker to have 100 per cent of knowledge on one specialty than to have one half per cent of his total knowledge on each of 200 different ways of earning a living. In all the great professions, specialization is the order of the day.

The physician and surgeon is no longer also the dentist. The dentist no longer attempts to do everything in his profession, except in remote places. He specializes in one of the many subdivisions of dentistry. His mechanical laboratory work certainly requires a differently trained expert than does the specialty of orthodontia or prophylaxis.

There is so much to learn in any kind of work that the most highly specialized worker can never expect to learn it all. In the professions, specialization generally means increased standing, usefulness, and earning power. Experience has proved that this is also true in the arts and trades.

Dr. Taylor has spent years investigating the comparatively simple art of shoveling, and he has said that even yet he has not learned it all. In case any one feels cramped by narrow overspecialization, he has as further compensation the fact that, if he has learned it all, his brain will be in such rested condition at the close of the working day that he can attend some night manual training school, where motion study, time study, and standardization are *not* taught, and where the faculty prove nightly that the Taylor plan of management, as a practical proposition, is not worthy of his consideration, because if it were they would, of course, teach it.

Perhaps specialization does narrow the mechanic, from the viewpoint of some people, but it does make him a highly trained expert in his specialty.

In case he loses his job under Scientific Management, is he not too highly specialized and not enough of an all-around mechanic to hold a job anywhere else?

The answer is "No." For he has been taught a method of attack that will enable him to use to advantage all the brains he has. He will have been taught all economies from motion study. That, in itself, will enable him to excel quickly those workers who have not been so taught. He will have been taught the economies resulting from the use of the instruction card.

If he has been taught to a point where he has been "overspecialized," then he surely has been taught habits of work that will enable him to become quickly a profitable worker at any new work that he may undertake.

Does not the monotony of the highly specialized subdivision of work cause the men to become insane?

No. Until one has worked under Scientific Management, and consequently realizes what the subdivisions mean, one cannot realize the great amount of knowledge that it is possible to acquire on any one subdivision of any one trade. For example, it was not until after we devoted years to the study of the motions used by several mechanical trades that we discovered that with the aid of a few devices we could teach an apprentice to lay brick faster and make a better looking and stronger wall than could an experienced journeyman working in the old manner.

Further study shows that our more recent investigations cause the old methods of bricklaying to be obsolete, for we now can build brick walls by machinery, at a lower cost, with no question as to filling of the joints, stronger, quicker, and drier, and by the same methods can build any kind of arches, ornamental work, etc., as cheaply as straight and plain brickwork can be built under the old method. We now see possibilities of improvement under this new method that seem to have no end. Yet, generally speaking, is not the subdivision of the mason's trade, brickwork, considered as monotonous as any kind of work?

A few years ago it was a general custom all over America, and is still in remote places, for a "mason" to be a stone mason, stone cutter, bricklayer, plasterer, and cement worker. Modern conditions have reclassified these trades, so that even the subclasses of the bricklayers now are divided into several distinct classes. The best plasterers and stone masons can no longer compete with the best bricklayer on brickwork. The plasterer's trade is also subdivided, although not so much as it will be.

To the man who has no leaning toward brain work, there is an ideal place provided in the performing department. When he feels that his work there is monotonous, there are three opportunities open to him—

(*a*) He may join the planning department.

(*b*) He may become teacher of the other men who prefer the so-called monotonous work, relieved of all responsibility except to do their work as called for.

(*c*) He can plan the spending of the extra money that will be in his pay envelope on next pay day, and can consider the intellectual stimulus that the extra pay will purchase; for when work is so highly repetitive as to be monotonous, it will surely enable the man best fitted for that work to earn the highest wages that he can ever earn at any vocation, *because* he has had practice at that work so long that it has become monotonous.

No, he will not become insane, for if his brain is of such an order that his work does not stimulate it to its highest degree, then he will be promoted, for under Scientific Management each man is specially trained to occupy that place that is the highest that he is capable, mentally and physically, of filling, after having had long training by the best teachers procurable.

Does it not rest a man to use different motions and doesn't it refresh his brain to do the work in a different way each time?

As a general proposition, it does *not* refresh a worker to use different motions. When it does, the planning should and does take that into consideration when making out the instruction card. One of the most generally recognized instances of this is the bookkeeper's standing desk and high chair. He changes from sitting to standing and *vice versa,* to rest and refresh himself; yet the motions of work are identical whether standing or sitting. That doing work the same way requires less effort than doing it a new way is so well recognized that a condition finally results where it seems as if the fingers could do the work with no other assistance than the command from the brain to proceed. This condition is called being "fingerwise" at a piece of work. It is well illustrated by the simple process of "buttoning a button," an act most complicated to the beginner.

Different motions each time require additional effort, a new mental process and a complete decision with the accompanying extra fatigue. The same motions each time take advantage of automaticity of motions, which is often less fatiguing than less wasteful, though constantly differing, motions.

Does not the old-fashioned way of gaining experience or judgment give the worker a training that he would never get otherwise?

Yes. The methods of Scientific Management will deprive him of much of the unnecessary and unproductive part of his experience, in that it will teach him, in the quickest way, how to learn the most efficient method. If he gets such proper training first, it will provide him during his after life with a mental and manual equipment that will serve him in making quick decisions in selecting his future experience, and in judging the "old type of experience" wherever he encounters it later.

"Experience is the best teacher" is as meaningless a proverb as "You can't teach an old dog new tricks." When the best experience has been found, measured, and recognized, it should be made standard,—written down on an instruction card. In this form it can be depended upon to be the best teacher, for it will transmit the information and experience from one mechanic to another without any loss in transmission.

CHANCE FOR A SQUARE DEAL

How can any one think it fair to take stop watch records on the very best man obtainable and then expect the others of the rank and file to keep up with such records?

Scientific Management does not expect the inefficient man to keep up with the first-class man, neither does it expect a dollar watch to do the work of the $300 watch. But when standards are created they must be founded on the work of the best man procurable, *i.e.* they must be a "100 per cent standard man's" records. Then all due allowance must be made for the difference in quality between the record of the standard worker and the worker who is actually going to do the work.

The poorer quality of men are not able to equal the records of the best men, but the analysis of data will show at what speed each man should work for the best combined results of output and health. Obviously it would add too much to fixed charges to take time study on each man. The present method is, by comparison, cheaper and more just, fair, effective, and satisfactory.

What show of a square deal has a worker who has from "one to eight foremen standing over him at the same time, applying a sort of industrial Third Degree" to make him conform to the desired standard motions?

This question has nothing to do with Taylor's plan of management, for the reason that each foreman helps the worker to do his work in the prescribed manner; teaches him the standard method, and how to use the least fatiguing and non-wasteful motions. Regardless of the number that may be helping him at once, the gang bosses have nothing to do with any "third degree" nor with any other form of discipline. That is all taken care of by an unprejudiced specialist called the "disciplinarian," whose make-up is that of peacemaker and whose duty is the furthering of the square deal.

CHANCE FOR WORK

When Scientific Management is in full operation, can the management dispense with the good men?

On the contrary, under Scientific Management even the functional foremen are expected to acquire so much more knowledge about their one function than is customary under the traditional plan of management that it will always require particularly good men to fill their positions.

The men, in their turn, that will be required, on account of the large outputs and the close following of the instruction cards demanded, will have to be exceptionally good men of their class. Every man will be expected to be the best obtainable of his respective class. In fact, Scientific Management goes farthest into the subject of selecting men specially fitted for their work. It does, however, demand that a man shall have a great deal of knowledge about his specialty and life work, rather than a little knowledge about many kinds of work.

Not only does Scientific Management require good men after it is in full operation, but it also provides for definite promotion to retain a man after he has outgrown his job. As Mr. James F. Butterworth, a well-known English authority, summed it up in the *London Standard*—"Scientific Management not only quickly recognizes the first-class man, but attracts other first-class men to share in the bettered conditions."

Granted that Scientific Management is advantageous for the best worker, is it not a distinct hardship to the mediocre man?

It is not, because first of all, the best men are promoted out of competition with the mediocre man. Furthermore, every man, including the mediocre man, is taught and promoted to fill the highest place that he is by nature and special training able to occupy. In fact, every man is taught and coached and helped until he reaches an earning power that he never could expect under the traditional form of management. The average man, having been taught a systematic method of attack, is better prepared to handle any new work at which he is put than he ever could if he had not had the experience under the systematic working of Scientific Management.

Does not Scientific Management eliminate many men, i.e. actually reduce the number of men employed, according to Mr. Taylor's own words?

No, because the management is enabled to handle more men and thus get the work completed quicker. Furthermore, while it is true that on any one part of the work the men required might be fewer, it is also true that the method of selection itself often results in providing the men, who are eliminated because of natural unfitness, with work for which they in turn are much better fitted. Actual statistics show that there has never been a case where the total number of employees has remained less in any organization operating under Scientific Management.

What would happen if every concern suddenly were able to do its work with one third of its present number of men?

It will take two or three years to install the principal features of Scientific Management in any one concern. It would take a lifetime to install all of the refinements of Scientific Management now recognized and determined. There never has been a case yet where the business being systematized did not employ a total of more men the more highly it was systematized. As soon as the work in any one department can be done with fewer men, the business as a whole becomes so successful that it can underbid its competitors; in fact, it often creates a market for its goods and then requires more men in other departments.

What becomes of the men to-day under the traditional plan of management?

Under this old plan, often the efficient instead of the inefficient man is "weeded out." He is never sure of his job, because usually under the old plan there is no accurate measuring of his efficiency. Where there is, he very often has made a low record of output because of a fault of the management.

Perhaps in some "dependent sequence," his work has been held up by failure of the management to supply him something; for example, the carpenter cannot lay the floor if he is not supplied with nails. The shoveler's output might be low because he had not been furnished with shovels that would permit of 21½ pounds of material on the shovel regardless of the change in the kind of materials shoveled.

"By those who have grasped this fact it is universally held that increased production due to efficiency of labor accrues very largely to the laborers themselves." ("Economics," by Arthur Twining Hadley.)

What happens to unskilled labor under Scientific Management?

Under Scientific Management there is no unskilled labor; or, at least, labor does not remain unskilled. Unskilled labor is taught the best method obtainable, and is provided with a corps of teachers whose duty it is to assist the laborers to become highly skilled in that art or trade at which they work.

Furthermore, the men are promoted as fast as they are fitted to be promoted, and are specially taught to fill places commanding higher wages even while they are taught. No labor is unskilled after it is taught.

Will not Scientific Management result in putting unskilled laborers at mechanics' work?

Not while they are unskilled. It is a part of the system to train all men to perform the highest class of work which they are mentally and physically able to perform. It in no way, however, contemplates the superseding of mechanics; which, of course, would be bad for the mechanics. The mechanics need have no fear from that source; in fact, Scientific Management plans for and entails so high a degree of perfection that the one greatest difficulty it encounters is to secure mechanics of sufficient intelligence, training, and expertness to carry out its plan. It does not concur, however, with the once general belief and principle that a locomotive driver should also be an expert machinist who could build as well as run a locomotive.

Is it not specially hard on the "weaker brothers"?

Yes, if "weaker brothers" means unwilling incompetents. These, Scientific Management discards, as does every other form of management, as fast as they can be detected. Any body of workers who, by purposely hiding the "weaker brother" in the gang, thereby make it difficult and sometimes impossible for the old-fashioned management to detect the weaker brother, is paying for his support out of the pockets of the strong. If this is so, why not measure his ability, pay him accurately what he is worth, pay the strong ones accordingly, and let the strong pay him what extra amount they desire to contribute on account of his weakness? Meanwhile, perhaps, he could be taught, or put on work where he would be more efficient.

Oftentimes a worker is inefficient because he is naturally unfitted for his chosen work by reason of natural slowness of successive action or poor ability for retention in memory of spoken words. Those workers with high personal coefficient, where the inward end organ most used in the work is the eye, as in the work of proofreading, are often the fastest workers when changed to such work, for example, as short-hand, where the impressions on the brain are taken in at the ear.

Again, the measuring devices of Scientific Management often discover that the "weaker brother," or the inefficient sister, is really a square peg in a round hole. While all kinds of management endeavor to discard the inferior workers, Scientific Management is the one plan that makes definite and systematic effort to promote each worker to the highest notch he is capable of in his chosen life work. It tries to place each worker where scientific investigation and analysis of his individual peculiarities indicate that he will be most efficient.

Volumes could be written about the worker who is in the wrong life work, for which he is by nature totally unfitted. The recognition of this fact is the cause for the interest in vocational guidance throughout the country.

We believe that one great benefit derived from Scientific Management will be the utilization of its data for assisting young men and women in determining the life work for which their particular faculties will enable them to be most efficient. Scientific Management endeavors to discover for workers, before they go to work, that work to which they are best adapted. In fact, the selection of the worker is an act of great importance under Scientific Management, and is one on which great stress is laid.

Scientific Management also tries to discard no man who has been tried out and partially taught. It attempts to place him to better advantage to himself and also to the management.

What happens to the inefficient worker? Is he not thrown out upon the labor market?

There are several things that may happen to him.

(a) He may be taught so that he becomes extremely efficient.

(b) His efficiency will be increased, whatever it is.

(c) He may be placed at a kind of work for which he is better fitted.

(d) He may be placed on that portion of the work that has not been systematized. There has never been a case where the Taylor System caused a large number of unemployed.

Doesn't the Taylor System really plan to eliminate the hopelessly inefficient man?

Yes, and so does every other plan of management. The other plans are not fair in that they do not always determine which are the really inefficient, but leave it to an overworked, busy, uninformed, prejudiced foreman or employer; while under the Taylor System the man is taught, shifted, and taught again, until he is placed at that work at which he is most efficient, and tried and tried until he has demonstrated his entire unfitness. Meantime, while he may not have been able to earn the maximum wages, he will have earned much higher wages than he could earn anywhere else on similar work under the old form of management.

HEALTH

What regard has this System for the physical welfare of the men? Does not this System call upon the reserve force of the worker, and thus wear him out before his time?

This question is answered at length by Mr. C. A. E. Winslow, Associate Professor of Biology, College of the City of New York, and

Curator of Public Health, American Museum of Natural History, New York, in an intensely interesting paper read before the Congress of Technology on the fiftieth anniversary of the granting of the charter of the Massachusetts Institute of Technology. Professor Winslow states in the closing paragraph:—

"The cleanliness of the factory, the purity of the drinking water, the quality of lighting, the sanitary provisions, and a dozen other points will suggest themselves to the skilled investigator when on the ground. He may find in many of these directions economic methods by which efficiency may be promoted."

Have observations ever been made on any one man long enough to determine if Scientific Management benefits him?

Yes, and on hundreds of men. A visit to the Tabor Manufacturing Co., the Link-Belt Co., and the J. M. Dodge Co. will convince any one who looks the employees over. There one finds that the men are happier, healthier, better paid, and in better condition every way than the men found in similar work in that vicinity. These places above named are among the shops where Scientific Management in its highest form has been in operation the longest time.

Does not the "speed boss" speed up the men to a point that is injurious to their health?

"Speed boss," like "task," is an unfortunate name, but, as Mr. James M. Dodge has said, the word "task" will probably have to be used until a word that is more descriptive can be substituted for it.

The same thing is true of "speed boss." We have heard one orator state that "the speed boss is the man who drives the slaves." He is right if you call the *machines* the slaves, for the "speed boss" does not tell the men how fast they shall make their motions. He does, however, tell the men at what speeds their machines shall run. He does not drive the men at all. He is their servant. When they cannot make the machines work at the speed called for on the instruction card, it is up to him to do it, then to teach them, or else to report to the planning department that he cannot, and then its members must show and help him. Under the traditional plan of management, swearing at a man is supposed to make him work faster, for the time being at least. The speed boss's job is to swear at the machine if he wants to, but he must attain the speed called for, no faster and no slower, or he does not earn his bonus.

Under the old form of management it sometimes happens that the foreman gets so angry at the machine that he discharges the operator, but the speed boss can not do this under Scientific Management. All cases of discharge must be handled by a trained, quiet disciplinarian, who disciplines the operator, the speed boss, and any one else who needs it, even the superintendent himself. This, in itself, is so unusual that in many cases the average workman cannot understand how it is that he is being treated so fairly.

As a general practice, do the people want a standard of efficiency so high that it requires a stop watch to get "the last drop of blood"?

There is no "last drop of blood" about it! The stop watch is a measuring device that has no more to do with making men work than it has when used by a physician to determine at what rate the pulse is beating. The stop watch is used to determine the correct time necessary for doing a certain piece of work, and to determine how much the worker should rest in order to achieve and maintain his best physical and mental condition.

It must be admitted, even by those who do not understand Scientific Management, that there is some rate of speed which is the correct speed at which the individual worker should work, and that this speed varies according to the man—his birth, education, training, health, and condition.

This correct speed is not the speed at which he would like to work if he were just naturally lazy, but it is the best speed at which he can work day after day, month after month, and, if he has reached the zenith of his promotion, then also year after year, and thrive, and continually improve in health.

The stop watch must be used to insure that the instruction card, the output, the percentage of rest for overcoming fatigue, and the pay shall be based upon that exact speed.

Taylor has found, by use of the stop watch and by timing thousands of cases, that some work requires that a man shall actually rest over 50 per cent of the entire day, and that practically all work requires more than $12\frac{1}{2}$ per cent rest. Now, that is one hour in an eight-hour day, and it does not sound nearly as much like "taking the last drop of blood" as does the old method of management, under which, if the manager heard that the man rested one half hour every day, he saw to it that the man was discharged.

Wherein does it cost the employer anything to lose a worker by wearing him out?

It takes time and costs money to specially train him, and old workers are therefore usually the most desirable.

INITIATIVE

What has Scientific Management to take the place of the ingenious man?

It has nothing "to take the place of the ingenious man." It does not supplant him. On the contrary, it furnishes a specially equipped planning department to help him to further and conserve systematically his ingenuity. This department works out problems of improvement of methods and conditions.

Such a department puts the services of the ingenious man and the inventor on a business basis and provides measuring devices and methods for determining the numerical measure of the efficiency of the new methods as compared with the old.

Does not the management lose the initiative and the bright ideas of its ingenious employees when they are obliged to follow implicitly the detailed written orders of the instruction card?

No. On the contrary, there is a special department for the employment of those men whose make-up and training specially fit them to make the most numerous and most valuable suggestions for improvements.

The value of the ingenious suggestions of the workmen is specially recognized and provided for by Scientific Management. Not only is a department created and maintained for fostering, conserving, and specially inventing such forms of improvement, but also a cash prize system is in operation for further obtaining the suggestions of those workmen who are outside the regular planning department.

It is seldom appreciated by the layman that the only inventions and improvements that are not wanted are those that are offered by the employee *before* he has first qualified on the standard method of procedure in accordance with the much tried out instruction card.

The condition precedent to an audience for offering a suggestion for an improvement is to have proved that the suggestor knows the standard method, and can do the work in the standard way of standard quality in the standard time. Having thus qualified, he is in a position to know whether or not his new suggestion is a real improvement.

Scientific Management offers the first standard method of obtaining high efficiency from those best qualified to invent and to make new methods. The ingenious employee is specially protected, assisted, and encouraged.

Does not standardization dwarf, wither, and preclude innovation and improvement?

On the contrary, standardization offers a base line from which we can measure efficiency. Inasmuch as the value of the entire scheme of scientific management hangs on time study, much time study must, therefore, be taken and used. This consumes time and costs much money. The fewer the standards the less quantity of time study need be taken.

Therefore, for the best net results, a few well-chosen, first-class standards are much to be preferred to many ill-chosen imperfect standards.

Standardization enables, and offers a constant incentive to, employees to try for better standards, not only for the joy of achieving, but also for the money reward that comes from making a better standard. The history of Scientific Management shows greater improvement under it than under any other plan.

When a man is paid under the day work plan for his time instead of for the quantity of output of prescribed quality, there is little to cause him to devise new methods or ways to increase his efficiency or productivity.

On the other hand, under Scientific Management he being paid for his productivity, there is every incentive to do all that he can,—to invent new ways, less wasteful ways, and to keep himself in the best physical condition to work.

What is there in it for the workman who makes the suggestion?

There are various rewards for accepted suggestions: sometimes cash; sometimes promotion to teacher or gang boss; sometimes the saving that the suggestion makes for a definite period of time; or a combination of the above accompanied by the recognition of having the accepted new tool or method named after the suggestor.

INSTRUCTION

Do not men dislike to be taught by teachers from outside?

Sometimes they do dislike it at first, but they usually like obtaining additional information about their life work, regardless from what source it comes.

Furthermore, the teaching usually comes mostly from the men who have been selected from their own number. The extra money that the teachers get is an added incentive to them to learn, earn more while learning, and thus be better fitted for promotion to the position of teacher.

Don't the workers think they "know it all" to start with?

Many mechanics believe that the best workmen of their trade do know nearly all that is worth knowing about their trade, but the unit cost columns and other devices for measuring efficiency soon shows them that "the way we have always done it" can usually be improved upon.

Do the men really benefit much by the teaching, or does not the benefit all go to the employer?

In re teaching, Mr. William Dana Orcutt says:—

"The ambitious workman of the past has sought to advance himself by attending night school, and in other ways which are a strain upon the time which he requires for rest and recreation. Scientific Management gives him this opportunity, under the most skillful instructors, while actually employed in his day's labors, fitting him, at the expense of the concern which employs him, to become qualified to earn higher wages from the very source which gives him his education."

What incentive has the teacher to see that the workers are properly trained?

The teacher's promotion depends on his success in getting results from the workers under his instruction.

He also gets a bonus every time that a worker gets a bonus and a second or double bonus every time that every worker in his entire gang gets a bonus.

Does not Scientific Management do away with the old "journeyman" idea, and is not that of itself a distinct disadvantage to the men?

It does sometimes do away with the "old journeyman idea" in many ways, especially with several of its wasteful aspects. It does away with teaching the apprentice by word of mouth by the traditionally taught journeyman, who has no idea of pedagogy. It does away with taking advantage of an apprentice for a certain definite number of years, just because he is an apprentice. It pays the apprentice in accordance with the quality and quantity of his output, instead of paying him a boy's wages even when he does a man's quantity of work.

It does away with the infamous and common practice of limiting the age at which an apprentice may start to learn his trade. It recognizes no such rule as that a boy shall not begin to lay brick after he is eighteen and shall not be out of his time before he is twenty-one, regardless of how expert he may be. It accords no special favors to any boy because his father was of the trade at which the boy works.

It substitutes for all this a square deal and a more efficient method of teaching the trade to a boy. It enables him to learn faster, to learn the science of his trade, to learn the best method that science can devise. It furnishes specially taught teachers to give "post-journeyman instruction" to even its best men. It makes available for use as a wage-earning device all of the expert knowledge that constant investigation, analysis, and study can devise, collect, and conserve.

Does not the paying of the bonus to the foreman make him help the best workers and let the poorer workers shift for themselves?

He must also help the poor workers or he does not get his second bonus, as the task set is achievable by any persistent worker. As the records of the foremen's gangs are watched by the superintendent, any foreman who does not teach all of his men so that they all can attain their task would not last long at his job.

LEISURE OR REST

Granted that workers "soldier," what is the harm? Does not that rest them?

A certain percentage of rest is necessary for the workers. It is absolutely required for their health. Under Scientific Management the amount of rest is determined scientifically; it is not guessed. The men are required to rest. On our own work we have demonstrated that regular enforced rest periods have invariably resulted in reduced costs of production. Soldiering is a case of making believe that outputs are produced when they are not. It is the worst form of cheating that there is. It often makes men work as hard in pretending to work as they would in actually producing output. Soldiering results in lower wages to the workers and in a business decline to the community.

LIFE, LIBERTY, AND THE PURSUIT OF HAPPINESS

Does not Scientific Management interfere with the workman's personal liberty?

If by that is meant the privilege of doing the work any way he chooses, or by any method, or on a standard of quality other than that prescribed, the answer is certainly "yes." But in every other respect, "no." His freedom from petty graft and holdup, and the protection and square deal offered him, give him more net liberty than he receives under any other plan of management.

Does not the forcing of the workmen to use the specified motions of the System only, from the time they arrive in the morning until they leave at night, take away their liberty and enforce slavery conditions upon the workers?

It has never been contemplated to prescribe each and every motion from the time of arrival to the time of departure in a mill or on a job any more than on a golf course or a baseball field. It is, however, hoped and expected that those motions that are of no use will be eliminated as far as possible, and that the motions used will be limited as far as possible to those that produce output or cause restful exercise. Surely no thinking man wants the work so arranged that the worker makes useless motions,—useless either to himself or to his employer.

Go to any library or sporting goods store, and you can obtain many books with copious illustrations reproduced from photographs to illustrate how to make the exact motions for the greatest efficiency in many different kinds of sports. But in how many trades can similar books be found? The best example to date of applying the motion studies of the arts of war to the arts of peace can be seen in Dr. Taylor's book "On the Art of Cutting Metals." In this he shows photographs of the stages in forging and sharpening metal cutting tools.[1]

Is it slavery to insist that a column of the same figures shall always be added up to the same total?

[1] See also "Bricklaying System," M. C. Clark & Co., Chicago, and "Motion Study," D. Van Nostrand, New York.

It seems reasonable, for the greatest efficiency and earning power, that each workman should be taught the exact prescribed motions that have been found to be the most productive, the least fatiguing, and the least wasteful. There is more to the benefits of teaching the exact motions than is commonly appreciated by the layman.

The advantage in speed, productivity, and ease of performance that come from habits of exactly the same sequence of motions and the absence of the mental process of making a complete decision for each motion cannot be appreciated by any one who has not made this subject a life study. The saving from this feature is a large one. For the best results, the best sequence of the best motions should be taught first,—taught and insisted upon until that sequence of those motions has become a fixed habit. Necessary and advisable deviations from this sequence will take care of themselves thereafter.

A book could be written on the *advantages of teaching the right motions before insisting upon perfection in the product manufactured.* In other words, Scientific Management insists that the novice shall use certain motions in a certain sequence until he can execute the work in the standard way, for the gains made by this process more than pay later for any cost of the time of the skilled worker going over and fixing up the first work of the unskilled worker. The ancient belief that a worker should do his work of *right quality of output first,* and fast afterward is wholly wrong. He should do his work with the *right motions first,* and either he or some one else should afterwards correct his work, or else throw it away, until he has formed habits of the correct motions. This method not only teaches him much quicker, but it also makes him much more efficient his whole lifetime.

I have never known a mechanic who had been taught the right motions who did not pity those who had not. Those who have only an academic knowledge of perspiration as a means of earning a livelihood should be comforted by the knowledge that the "slave of motion supervision" will have a pay envelope of much greater purchasing power to compensate him for his "slavery."

Does not Scientific Management "trammel the workman in the durable satisfactions of life"?

Not unless it is dissatisfying or unsatisfying to receive the best instruction obtainable and to do work in that method which time and experience have shown to be the least wasteful, the most productive, and the least fatiguing.

Furthermore, the working hours represent but about one half of the total time that the worker is awake. Under Scientific Management he has to work more regularly, and more constantly, but usually at not much greater speed. If this goes against his grain, it is more than compensated for by the greater amount of "durable satisfactions of life," as Dr. Eliot phrases it, that can be purchased with the excess money in the pay envelope earned under Scientific Management.

Why insist that men work separately instead of in gangs when, if they are in gangs, the best men will cause the slow and lazy men to work harder?

Experience proves that the output—when all men have their outputs measured separately—is much greater than when their collective outputs are measured as a gang. Furthermore, the workers sooner or later argue to themselves in this wise, *i.e.* "What is the use of my working harder than any one else, since the results of my efforts are divided up among the gang?" Furthermore, a man realizes that, even if he rests considerably, it affects the average output of the entire gang very little proportionally,—and, as a matter of fact, the men do not make the lazy ones work. For an example of this see "Philosophy of Management," page 75.

In exactly what way can the men produce more output under Scientific Management?

In *Harper's,* February, 1911, page 433, Mr. William Dana Orcutt, after seeing the results of the installation of the Taylor System by Mr. Morris L. Cooke at the Plimpton Press, says:—

"Every task of the operative is preceded by preparatory coöperation on the part of his employer. When the order reaches him, every detail has been provided for: he has no questions to ask; the proper tools are placed beside him, and the materials themselves are near at hand. All his time is spent upon productive labor, and his output is proportionally increased."

PROMOTION

What opportunity for promotion or development has a young man in a plant operated under Scientific Management?

Every opportunity that there is, except pull. Pull might get the job for him; but he must have the merit, or the record of production and the unit cost records will show him up at his true value.

H. L. Gantt says, page 135 in "Work, Wages, and Profits":—

"The development of skilled workmen by this method is sure and rapid, and wherever the method has been properly established, the problem of securing satisfactory help has been solved.

"During the past few years, while there has been so much talk about the 'growing inefficiency of labor,' I have repeatedly proved the value of this method in increasing its efficiency, and the fact that the system works automatically, when once thoroughly established, puts the possibility of training their own workmen within the reach of all manufacturers."

How can every man be sure that his merit will be discovered and that he will be promoted to the highest notch he can fill?

Because under Scientific Management the output of each man is recorded separately and the relative scores show up constantly.

High scores of output are accompanied by correspondingly high wages.

High scores and wages attract the attention of the management, which needs the services of teachers selected from those men who can make high records of outputs.

From the position of teacher the upward progress for the capable man is rapid.

Admitted that Scientific Management is better for most employees, what have you to offer to the successful all-around foreman under the traditional plan?

The "all-around" foreman, as his very name indicates, has to do many kinds of work, and to perform many different subdivisions of the several functions.

Not only is he in all probability much more efficient in some of his "all-around" duties than in others, but he is also using his valuable time in handling work that could be done by a lower-priced man.

Scientific Management offers such a foreman an opportunity to work constantly at his high-priced specialty. Thus he is more efficient, and we all enjoy that work most that we can do best. His earning power is also increased by putting him on high-class work on which he is most productive, and relieving him of ALL PAY-REDUCING DUTIES that could and should be done by a lower-priced man.

Further, he is taught the best methods that science can discover, —which raises him as a producer and earner above the earning power of his best work at his specialty.

Is it not a system of promotion based upon the contest principle—i.e. that the man who has the least regard for his fellows, coupled with the most ability, wins?

The traditional plan of management is sometimes based upon the contest principle; and so in a way is the Taylor plan, but under the Taylor plan, the winner does not win the loss of the loser, as he does under the old plan. On the contrary, the man even with the lowest score is paid unusually high wages, if he achieves his task, regardless of how much more some other worker may do. In other words, all may be winners under Scientific Management. It is not a case of *who* will get the prize by beating the others. It is a case of *how many* will get the prizes. For there are prizes for each and all that can be obtained by paying attention to business constantly.

SPEED

At what speed does Taylor's plan expect any man to work?

At that speed which is the fastest at which he will be happy and at which he can thrive continuously.

Does Scientific Management permit speeding up in case two girls wish to race?

There is nothing in Scientific Management that would prevent two girls from racing if they chose to do so. While Scientific Management does not encourage racing, it could not step in and stop any one from producing as much as he wished without being accused of desiring to limit the amount that could be earned in a day.

The quantity of output prophesied by time study as being the correct amount of output a worker should do in a day can invariably be exceeded by a spurt or a race.

One honest investigator was much disappointed by discovering that Scientific Management did not place a maximum on output of some women workers,—not realizing that such an occasional race to determine which was the smartest between girls who did not have time to enter athletic sports, gave them much pleasure as well as considerable extra money. They had no fear of a subsequent cut in their rate. Their racing record also proved that the set task based upon a high percentage of absolute rest for overcoming fatigue was so far below the record of race output that it was in no way unreasonable for everyday performance.

"Shortened hours combined with increased speed make the conditions of employment more favorable for high-grade labor and less favorable for low-grade labor. The better laborer does not dislike the speed and enjoys the time saved."—Arthur Twining Hadley in "Economics."

Do athletic contests between workers of different nationalities cause race feeling?

We have used the principle of the athletic contest for raising the efficiency of management for a quarter of a century.

Before and since we began the study of Scientific Management we have never seen any reason for criticism of the athletic contest. A periodical recently said that by means of putting different races against one another in athletic contests, we created race hatred. On the contrary, we have never seen a case of race prejudice result from athletic contests, but we have often seen a keen interest and joy created by such contests. Furthermore, the workmen coming from the same country or district often have the same or similar methods of working, and much can be learned when two or more gangs with different methods are having a friendly contest against each other. The workers are given the pleasure of sport together with a day that passes quicker and brings higher earnings.

Does not the giving of a bonus to the foreman every time that a man earns a bonus result in the foreman driving the men unmercifully so that he can get the bonus offered to tempt his selfish interest?

No, because the task is set by carefully timing actual performance with the proper allowance of time for rest and unexpected delays. No driving is necessary after the workers have been taught the improved method devised by the best workers coöperating with the planning department. After the workers have learned the right improved method they will find it possible to do their task every day by simply working steadily without rushing. When this is not perfectly possible, the task has been set wrong and must be corrected without delay.

Does the practice of paying a bonus to the gang boss for each workman under him, and a double bonus to the gang boss for every day that every man in his gang earns his bonus, result in cruel driving of the worker, and abuse, discharge—in fact everything

possible to coerce the worker into earning his bonus even on days when he is sick?

The "gang boss" gets one bonus for each time that the man under him gets a bonus, and a double bonus when every man under him earns his bonus. This makes the interests of the workmen and the gang boss identical. It makes them pull together. It causes the gang boss to do what he can to surround himself with the men who are best fitted by nature to do their allotted work. After these men have been selected, it is for the gang boss to protect and help them in every possible way to earn their unusually high wages, for he cannot get his otherwise. He uses all the brains he owns to help them from morning till night, regardless of how unsympathetic he may be by nature. He will spend no time scheming to get the old employees out and his friends and relatives in, for he realizes that the management has accurate measuring devices of the efficiency of the men under him and of him as an executive. He cannot bluff them. The facts will show up in their true condition in the unit cost column and on the chart showing fluctuations of outputs and individual earnings. The gang boss cannot discharge the workmen, for that is not his function. He will not recommend discharge for slight infractions, personal grudges, etc., because he realizes that to discharge a workman means to train a new one,—with a period when it is probable that at least one workman will not be able to earn his bonus. This means that during all that period the gang boss loses his double bonus plus the single bonus for the one or more men who did not make their bonus. Thus the gang boss thinks more than twice before he disturbs the usual daily working conditions.

Thus it will be seen that the effect of the single and double bonus on the gang boss is, in many ways, to make the employment of the employee more stable and permanent, and an incentive to conserve and use the special ability and efficiency of the trained worker. The gang boss cannot discharge or fine; and it is of no use to abuse the worker, for to recommend punishment that is not approved by the disciplinarian makes the gang boss ridiculous and subject to discipline himself.

Therefore the one thing left is to help the worker,—to help him to do his work, to achieve his task; to see that he gets his tools and materials without delay; and to see that the indication of hindrance or delay by breakdown is reported immediately to the repair boss, whose functions are to make inspections at stated intervals and to keep all machinery in the prescribed condition of repair so that breakdowns do not occur. Under the old scheme the gang boss usually "feels his oats." He abuses or ridicules, and is too busy to help the worker who is discouraged or is falling behind in his record of output.

Under Scientific Management it is better for the gang boss to risk ruin to his suit of clothes by jumping in and helping a man who is delayed by the happening of the unexpected than to let that one incident prevent him from earning the double bonus. Every time he thus helps himself he is helping the worker. There is no parallel to this under the traditional plan of management, except in the very small business where the employer is his own and only gang boss. This condition of scientific management has also many by-products of benefit to the workman. It fosters good feeling between the men and their employers. The men have more contented minds. They dare to push their work, knowing that when they really want help they can always get it. They soon learn to know that the gang boss is working for them, instead of their working for him. Their instructions are in writing on the instruction card. The gang boss can't change those instructions. If they work in accordance with the directions on the instruction card, the disciplinarian will stand by them. If they do not understand their instructions or cannot obey, they send for the gang boss. He is their coach, their tutor, and as the worker is paid more money for being more efficient, so also is the gang boss tutor paid in the form of bonuses and double bonuses in proportion as he is efficient as a teacher—not as a driver. The extra bonus offered to the worker is sufficient to induce him to put forth his best maintainable effort without the additional driving method of the "good old-fashioned" method of management.

UNIONS

Is not the real plan of Scientific Management to disband the unions?

The plan of Scientific Management in no way contemplates the disbanding of the unions. In fact, all followers of Taylor recognize the general necessity for the existence of unions. No one can study the subject of management without appreciating the good that has come as a result of the unions insisting upon more sanitary conditions of the shops and safer conditions of the buildings. It is unfortunate that the unions have not always been right, but they have not. Neither have the employers associations always been right. The many times that each side has been wrong have been due to fear of injury in the future or revenge for real or fancied wrong in the past. But Scientific Management now provides accurate measuring methods and devices for determining the merit and efficiency of different methods of procedure, and the greater the accuracy of such measuring devices, the fewer the misunderstandings between the employer and employees.

The measuring devices find the facts and thus eliminate the largest part of the cause for labor disputes. Mr. George Iles, in his intensely interesting and valuable book, "Inventors at Work," calls attention to the absolute dependence of advance in all sciences on the use of measuring devices. It was the discovery and adaptation of the simple measuring methods and devices by Dr. Taylor that enabled him to make the greatest progress in the science of management and to eliminate war between the employer and labor unions.

These methods of measuring the relative efficiency of methods and men assist to eliminate industrial warfare. Instead of having war, the unions will recognize that under Scientific Management they obtain more money, shorter hours, fairer treatment, better teaching, and more sanitary conditions than their union asks from employers operating under the old-fashioned or traditional plan of management. There must always be unions; there must always be collective bargaining by the unions for some things; but the union that attempts to interfere by collective bargaining with the installation or progress of Scientific Management will, if unsuccessful, have its members left out in the cold, and, if successful in interfering with the management's installation, will so discourage the management that they will decide to postpone, for the time being or permanently, that one plan of management that will enable the workers to obtain unusually high wages. Neither the followers of Taylor, nor any one else, is able to install Scientific Management and simultaneously participate in a debating society or risk results of unfavorable decision of a well-meaning but uninformed board of arbitration.

I cannot emphasize too strongly to any and all labor unions that my advice is to offer no resistance whatever to any employer who is honestly trying to put in Dr. Taylor's plan of management.

After it has been put in and is in fairly smooth running order, the union men will find that their wages are much higher; that the hours are at least no longer—in fact are often shorter; that conditions are better from a health standpoint; and that, further, the square deal really does and must exist. Incompetents holding down positions due to graft, relationship, marriage, and "affinities," are measured up to their true value, and all can see this. The worker's job is sure, so long as he is efficient; the worker is reproved, disciplined, punished, laid off, or discharged by a trained disciplinarian and not by the whim of a suddenly exasperated gang boss, foreman, superintendent, or new manager. When the new manager handles this function of disciplining in any other way than with the square deal, then there is no longer Scientific Management.

This plan of Scientific Management extends and prolongs the years of productivity of the worker, not only because he is treated better, but also because it is entirely a teaching plan; and the old employee can teach for years after his usefulness would have ceased under the old plan of management.

There is no call for unions to cease or disband. If they do disband, it will be because they themselves decide that there is another way of obtaining a better result. The unions have nothing to fear from Scientific Management except that their own acts may unintentionally prevent its rapid installation.

If Scientific Management is a good thing for the workers, why do the labor leaders all oppose it?

They do not all oppose it. Some oppose it for the simple reason that they do not understand it; the others have visions that Scientific Management is something that will reduce the value of their jobs, —and all are afraid, because of the bad treatment that workmen as a whole have had in the past, that Scientific Management is simply a new "confidence game," presented in a more attractive manner than ever before. Because of the many cases of unfair treatment that the workmen have themselves experienced and have seen on every side, they simply cannot imagine Dr. Taylor or any other practical man working for their interests unless there is a "comeback" somewhere.

I have heard gentlemen considered well balanced in every other particular admit privately on one day that they knew nothing of the details of Scientific Management, and harangue a crowd on the following day telling of the evils of Scientific Management to the workingman.

As a matter of fact, there are but few men who, after having first become proficient mechanics in at least one trade, and after having been in direct responsible charge of engineering or mechanical construction, or manufacturing, for several years, can grasp in less than three to five years the fine points of Scientific Management that are necessary to make its operation successful.

Dr. Taylor and his followers, therefore, ask all those who do not understand this plan of management to suspend judgment not only until they understand it, but also until after they have had time and opportunity to talk to those mechanics and laborers who have worked and prospered under it for several years.

In this connection I would recommend for such interviews as typical examples of happy, loyal, intelligent, well-treated, and well-paid workers, employees of the Link-Belt Co., the James M. Dodge Co., and the Tabor Company at Philadelphia.

Is it absolutely necessary to have no collective bargaining in order to install the Taylor System of Management?

No. But it will take longer if such bargaining is introduced. It would be like collective bargaining of the doctors with all the patients in a hospital as to what medicine Patient No. 40 should take.

WAGES

If the worker produces three times more output under Scientific Management than he does under the traditional plan, why does he not get three times as much wages?

If all of the saving by use of Scientific Management were given to the worker, the management could not afford to maintain the corps of investigators and teachers who are necessary under Scientific Management. The saving by means of better processes, easier conditions, and more efficient teaching is so great, however, that increases in wages of 25 to 100 per cent to the workman are always paid. The balance of the saving goes to pay for the cost of maintaining the conditions of Scientific Management and also for reducing costs of production.

In other words, the corps of investigators and teachers is what enables the worker to achieve three or more times the size of the output customary under the "good old-fashioned" management. The savings caused thereby must first pay for this corps, then the balance is divided between the employer and the employees.

What guarantee has the workman that the rate will never be cut?

There may be no guarantee to the workman that the rate will never be cut; but there will be no Scientific Management left if the rates are once cut, because the entire framework of Scientific Management hangs on first having the rate set by Scientific Methods and then never cutting the rate. Scientific Management represents the highest form of coöperation between the employee and the management. No management can expect any coöperation if the workmen have experienced a cutting of the rate with its after effects, namely, systematic soldiering. When the workers are caused by the cutting of a rate to figure out the greatest amount of output they can safely produce without another cut in their rate, there cannot be any further coöperation. Any one who has studied the subject of management enough to install Scientific Management will realize that the rates must be set right the first time and *never* cut. This is the best guarantee the worker can have.

What does the workman get if he exceeds the task?

That depends upon the method of payment that is used. Sometimes a higher piece rate for the entire number of pieces, as under Taylor's differential rate piece system; sometimes the same piece rate for all the additional pieces as the rate per piece of the task. If he exceeds the task much, he will be given a chance at the job of teacher or of gang boss, at either of which positions he can earn high wages.

Does not the management sometimes take advantage of the disciplinarian's power to fine the workmen and increase fines in times of business depression?

No, for the reason that under Scientific Management the fines collected go back into the pockets of the workman in some form or other.

Bitter strikes have occurred in many of the textile trades under the old plans of management, because the fines which were established primarily to compensate the employers for the injury caused by the employee were afterwards used as a means of reducing production costs, by the simple process of fining the workers for everything for which an excuse could be found.

Under Scientific Management the fines collected by the management for carelessness, disobedience, injury to machines or product are contributed to by the workers, gang bosses, functional foremen, and even those still higher up, at any time that the disciplinarian, in the exercise of his fair judgment, so decides. The money which is so collected is the nucleus of a sick benefit, insurance or entertainment fund, and is spent wholly upon the workers.

Such an arrangement offers no inducement to the manager or his disciplinarian to be unfair. The worker does not so much begrudge the money he has to pay, and every time the others hear of a fine being imposed they laugh in their sympathy, because they know the offender must pay and the management does not profit thereby. There is, therefore, no incentive for increasing fines in times of business depression, or at any other time. Then there is another benefit from the worker's standpoint. It is to the interests of the management to help the workers to do their work with the smallest amount of fines, because the management does not get the income from the fines, and any kind of fines, even necessary fines, cause some hard feeling. It puts the incentive on the management to remove the cause for fines.

What do you do with the bonus if the union refuses to allow the workman to accept it?

When the men refuse to accept high pay that has been offered to them, it should be deposited in a local savings bank subject to their order at any time. If they have earned the bonus that the management has promised them, then the management certainly should not keep it. Depositing it in the local savings bank shows good faith on the part of the management. When the worker gets old and helpless, he may change his mind and draw out his money.

Relation to Other Lines of Activity

What can the colleges and schools do to help Scientific Management; or, what place have the colleges in Scientific Management?

This question is too large to attempt to answer in this book to the extent that it deserves. (See Bulletin #5, Carnegie Foundation, by Mr. Morris L. Cooke, M. A. S. M. E.)

There are five things, however, that would help tremendously:—

1. The colleges should arrange for the collection and interchange of time study data through a central bureau, preferably a national bureau at Washington.

2. They should establish laboratories for the study of methods for shortening the hours of the working day and for increasing the efficiency of the workman, foreman, and manager, that their earning powers may become greater.

3. They should study the reclassification of the trades, that they may be less wasteful and better suited to modern conditions. At the present time nearly all the trades are practiced to suit conditions now obsolete.

4. They should disseminate information and data regarding the economic benefits to the workers themselves, as well as the country at large, from having everybody as efficient as possible and constantly producing as large outputs as possible *per unit of time consumed,* so that honest men will not oppose labor-saving machinery because of ignorance of facts.

5. They should disseminate the new method of teaching the trades, realizing:—

(*a*) That the best and fastest workman and the one who can accomplish the greatest output with the least fatigue is he who has been taught the right motions first, speed second, and quality third;

(*b*) That the worker's accuracy at first should be judged by his accuracy in conforming to the standard method and not by the degree of accuracy of his resulting work;

(*c*) That this method is not a scheme for teaching slipshod results but, on the contrary, greater precision. Habits of correct method will result in habits of correct results.

How does Scientific Management affect the general welfare of the country?

Will Irwin says, page 949, *Century,* April, 1910:—

"To get the most out of a day's work and that without injury to the workman's permanent powers, this is the greater formula upon which the pioneers of the new régime are working. Carry the formula to its logical conclusion and it embraces all those movements, formerly in the hands of philanthropists and charitable organizations, which seek to ameliorate working conditions. As a matter of self-interest, it incorporates the golden rule into the theory of production."

What relation has Scientific Management to industrial education?

Scientific Management concurs with the new thought that ideal teaching in the school and college is but the putting of the student in condition to learn his real lessons, namely, those that he will learn out upon the work; and there is no end to these lessons.

Under the old plan the journeyman of each trade is supposed to teach the apprentice his trade. This method is an acknowledged failure, because there is more incentive to the journeyman to keep the apprentice from learning than there is to teach him. This is indirectly recognized by the unions in their laws governing more favored apprentices, such, for example, as the son of a member of the craft whom they know will have the best training that his father, at least, and perhaps his father's most intimate fellow-craftsmen, will give him.

The apprentice is taught so poorly and becomes efficient so slowly that he oftentimes becomes discouraged of ever learning his trade. These two conditions have in the past caused the term of apprenticeship to be five to seven years in England and America, and in the former country that is still the term in many trades. This length of apprenticeship is supposed to give the employer sufficient time to obtain enough profit from the boy's latter years to make up for his former years, when he was unskilled and wasted much material. In fact, the apprentice was so profitless that the master usually made him do other work, such as heavy labor outside his trade, chores about the master's house, errands, etc., in order to get some profit out of the apprentice during the first years of his apprenticeship. The apprentice, obtaining little or no money for wages, in some cases going into debt to pay the employer to teach him his trade—his life work—was usually in constant trouble because he was not being taught as fast as he thought he should be, and was put to other unpleasant work, on the one hand, and was not working as hard as he should, on the other. Under the best of the conditions, he was paid for his time and not for his output—was working on a "day work" basis with an agreed upon wage for a term of years without any definite agreed upon quantity of output that he should deliver in return. His teachers were of two kinds: those that did not care to teach him, and those that were not selected for their ability to teach, even if they were willing. Furthermore, if they happened to be those that were willing and could teach, they taught what *in their opinion* was the best and most efficient

method—without any help of modern methods of research and pedagogy. Consider the stupendous waste of this method as compared with
the method of teaching the trades under Scientific Management,
where the teacher holds his position because of his measured efficiency to teach the one best way that science and coöperation have
determined and selected.

It is here that the teachers in the trades schools will soon come into
their own. In the past they have suffered from a lack of the proper
method of attack that made them become content with graduating
boys who, with a little actual "experience" after graduation, could
earn journeyman's wages. These were, even then, looked upon as
"incubator chickens." Now, with the method of attack furnished by
motion study, time study, and exact methods and devices for measuring the ultimate subdivisions of mental and manual effort and fatigue, the teachers of our trades schools will soon be able to turn out
"teachers of mechanics," that is, foremen; and the journeyman who
does not learn his trade with the right motions first, and with all
other recognized methods for the elimination of unnecessary waste,
must take the place of him with the lesser skill.

The faithful old journeyman was a most inefficient worker at best
—a less efficient teacher for lack of knowledge and incentive.

The best teacher of the present in the trades schools suffers in salary for lack of appreciation. The teacher of the future will be the best
obtainable. He will be able to prove his efficiency by the measured
quality of his output. This incentive for the teaching of the apprentice by specially trained teachers or functional foremen continues
through the entire life of the worker. There is no end to the period
of learning. Under Scientific Management a worker is better prepared each day to learn the new lessons that the investigators of the
planning department have discovered or synthesized. The functional
foremen and teachers of the management are better prepared each
day to pass their information on. The appreciation of the merit of the
best teachers of the trades in the future will carry with it an adequate
financial compensation.

Is Scientific Management a factor in securing industrial peace?

Mr. William Dana Orcutt says, *Harper's,* February, 1911:—

"It has commonly been accepted that the interests of capital and labor
ought to be identical yet, as a matter of fact, they have rarely been so
considered.

"The new force, which is called 'Modern Scientific Management' says, 'If they are not identical, then make them so,' and having flung the banner bearing this slogan to the wind, it has thus separated itself from the systems and systematizing, from card indices, vertical filings, and cost tabulations. It recognizes all these as necessary details of system, which in turn is a necessary ingredient of Scientific Management—but as a science it concerns itself with cause and effect rather than with records or figures, which are usually obtained so late that they possess only historical value."

Is it not a scheme that will wedge apart the college man and the mechanic into opposed classes?

On the contrary, it is the one thing that will show the college-trained man and the young mechanic their interdependent relations. It furnishes an accurate measure of their relative importance. It shows them that for the best and most lasting efficient results they must work together and pull together; that each is absolutely necessary to the other in this plan of Scientific Management, not only during the period of transition from the traditional plan of management, but also after it has been installed and is on a permanent basis.

Does not Scientific Management remove the worker farther than ever from the management?

On the contrary, it brings him into closer touch with the management. He is treated as an individual and is not herded into a gang and treated always as one of a gang. He finds that by coöperating with the management in enforcing its system he raises his own wages, helps his fellow worker to earn more money, and helps the management to get lower production costs. This in turn helps his employer to compete successfully and therefore to secure more business, thus helping to prolong the employment of the workers.

NATIONAL INDUSTRIAL SUPREMACY

Would it not be better to nip the whole Scientific Management movement in the bud because of what will happen to us when the Chinese and Japanese, with their few requirements and low cost of living, discover and apply our methods of attack and laboratory methods as applied to the Science of Management?

Even if there were any force to this argument, it would be lost because it is now too late.

Native Asiatic engineers who have been educated in American

colleges have already started the movement of giving their countries the benefits of Scientific Management.

How does Scientific Management affect reclassifying the trades?

First, its records show what parts of the work cause a lowering of the pay of the highly skilled man.

Second, Scientific Management endeavors to have each man so placed that he may work continuously on that kind of highest paying work that his skill, experience, and knowledge will permit him to do.

What place has Scientific Management in vocational guidance?

The preparation of the workman for his life work should begin while he is at school.

See "The Vocational Guidance of Youth," by Meyer Bloomfield, Director of the Vocation Bureau of Boston, lecturer on Vocational Guidance, Harvard University.

What place has so-called welfare work in Scientific Management?

The word "welfare" is usually disagreeable to the ears of the workers. Their viewpoint is that if there is any money to spare for welfare work they would rather have it distributed *pro rata* in their pay envelopes every Saturday night. Any kind of welfare work is better than nothing, and will help some; but to be permanent in its effect such work must be of a kind that enables the worker to be more efficient, to earn more wages, and thus take care of himself without any outside help.

The most beneficial "welfare work" would be the creation of a government bureau for the collection, preservation, and dissemination of data referring to Scientific Management.

Scientific Management hangs upon the science of time study. Dr. Taylor first called attention to the need of a book of time study data on the arts and trades, in 1895. There is not such a book on the market to-day, seventeen years later. Yet the government has employed experts to study how to increase the productivity of sheep, hens, cows, bees, pigs, and Rocky Mountain goats.

Who will be the man to receive the everlasting fame of being the first to start the movement for the permanent creation of a bureau and museum at Washington for the study of Scientific Management and methods of increasing the efficiency, longevity, and productivity of human beings?

Politicians recognize the great value of such a government department, but they are "vote shy." They fear the votes of a great number of workers who honestly believe that the sum total of "working opportunity," as they call it, is fixed and constant, and that to make one man more efficient and thus cause him to be able to do two men's work is simply displacing one more man to be added to the great army of the unemployed. The fact that this may be so this week blinds them to the fact that Scientific Management will quickly bring lasting benefits to them in the immediate future.

The case of the man who made the knitting machine for silk stockings in the time of Queen Elizabeth; the struggles to introduce the sewing machine, and the fountain trowel, and all the wars against the installation of labor-saving machinery since, are too well known to warrant writing about here. These improvements have come and are coming. Nothing can resist them permanently.

It is, however, a national, yes, a world calamity, that there are so many against any plan for saving labor. I am not able to see why, for example, certain unions insist, as did the bricklayers of Glens Falls, that outputs shall be limited by such crude methods as insisting that the bricklayer shall not lay down his trowel when he is picking up brick. They insist that the bricklayer shall not pick up brick with both hands unless he also keeps the trowel in his hand.

I do not understand by what measuring device or method they have determined that that procedure is the exact one that is best for their craft. If small outputs and long hours are desired, why not go the limit and say that no bricklayer shall have a trowel larger than the pie knife used in that vicinity, or that the wristband of the left shirt sleeve of each bricklayer shall be pinned to the leg of his trousers between the hours of eight to twelve and one to five? This surely sounds ridiculous, but four hours of it daily would cut down outputs less than the other less noticeable rules of the Glens Falls bricklayers.

No friend of the working men can do his fellow man so much good as to teach the truth about the benefits to the workmen from increased outputs,—for increased outputs are the one thing, or condition, that will permit raising wages permanently and reducing production costs permanently.

The benefits to the workman from raising wages speaks for itself. The benefits to the worker from reduced cost of production are not so obvious, but just as real, for when production costs are lowered the condition is made that creates greater "working opportunity."

Furthermore, reduced costs of production mean greater purchasing power of the wages of the workman, and reduced costs of living.

Scientific Management eliminates human waste as does nothing else.

Let us not be wasteful in earning money, even though we may be wasteful in spending it for those things individually most desired.

"Give back the singing man!" and give him something to sing about and to sing with, and give him plenty of hours in which to sing, and furnish him with conditions during his work hours that will make him feel like singing after his day's work is done; and during the reduced number of working hours concentrate on how to eliminate human waste, unnecessary fatigue, and the workman's presence under working conditions any longer than is necessary to achieve the proper sized day's work.

5

....

MOTION
STUDY*

* Motion Study, by Frank B. Gilbreth, was published by D. Van Nostrand Co., New York, in 1911.

Introduction

··

When the editor of a live journal hears of some new development in the field to which his paper caters, he is neglecting his duty if he does not make every possible effort to secure a powerful article by the highest authority on that development for his readers. Some months before "Motion Study" first appeared in the columns of *Industrial Engineering*, we heard that Mr. Gilbreth had, by some method or other, made wonderful records in the construction of buildings and other engineering works. We were curious to know how this had been accomplished, and sought an interview. We then learned that for years Mr. Gilbreth had been studying the actions of his workmen, the conditions surrounding their work, and all the other variables which go to help or hinder them in the actual construction work. He had paid particular attention to the motions made by a given man, say a bricklayer, in getting a brick from the pile made by the tenders to its final resting place in the wall. He had discovered how the number of these motions could be cut down, by having the brick brought to the bricklayer in a different way than usual, by placing them in a somewhat more convenient position, by arranging the scaffolding in an improved manner, and by various other little changes, some of them slight in themselves, but all together totaling an immense saving of time and motions.

This appealed to us as forming the basis of a good "story," and we immediately made arrangements with Mr. Gilbreth to prepare for *Industrial Engineering* a serial article showing the importance of these studies in the improvement of working conditions in all trades, and how they benefited both employer and workman. When the manuscript of "Motion Study" was first placed in the writer's hands, as editor, he examined it with considerable interest, but without any idea of the immense importance of what he had done in securing this contribution. It was then merely another good story for the paper. It seemed to him a trifle unfortunate, however, that the author had

141

chosen practically all of his illustrations from the bricklaying trade. On rereading the article more carefully it was apparent that these illustrations were of secondary importance and had been drawn from a trade with which every one was familiar and which any one could observe, also from one so old that it hardly seemed possible that it could be improved. It therefore became evident that the *principles* laid down were applicable to every trade and industry. This idea was confirmed later, when "Motion Study" appeared in serial form.

We were a trifle disappointed, at first, that it attracted less attention than we anticipated. We thought that perhaps we were somewhat in advance of our time, and that the public was not yet prepared for so long a step forward. It now appears, however, that the apparent lack of interest was due to the fact that we had presented a subject so entirely new that it required some little time for people to comprehend its importance and to realize its value. By the time the third installment had appeared, requests for the earlier installments were flowing in steadily, and since its completion many firms have sent for all the issues of the paper containing it. To show the wide application possible of the principles laid down in "Motion Study," requests for the complete series have come to us from the iron and steel industry, from the shoe manufacturing industry, from book-printing and book-binding establishments, and many other industries. It was when we began to receive these requests that we realized that we had done something worth while, and had published an article which was of stupendous value, not to one trade or group of trades, but to the whole world.

The writer, in handling the successive installments of "Motion Study," became more and more impressed with the possibilities which were involved in it. He resolved to apply some of these principles in his own office. Naturally the first point of attack is the one where the greatest saving can be accomplished. In our case, it happened to be the outgoing mail. A publication has, particularly in its circulation department, an amount of outgoing mail entirely out of proportion to the volume of business transacted by it, when measured by the standard of other industries. A circulation campaign will involve the sending out of perhaps twenty thousand duplicate letters, each with one or more inclosures. Evidently the saving of but one motion on each letter would, in the aggregate, show an immense saving of time. Formerly the girls folding and sealing the letters were permitted to arrange the work to suit themselves. A short observation of their work showed that there was much room for improvement.

The writer studied the question for a short time and made several experiments to determine in just what order each movement should be made to fold the letter, pick up its inclosure, pick up the envelope, and insert the letter and inclosure in the envelope. The first attempt was crude, but immediately doubled the output of the girl. Further study resulted in improvements which not only eliminated motions, but shortened the distance which the hands had to move in those that remained. The final result was an arrangement of pieces and a sequence of motions by which each hand, at the completion of one motion, was in position immediately to begin the next. The final motion, that of throwing the filled envelope on the pile, was eliminated entirely by having a large basket on the floor, directly under the point where the letter was inserted in the envelope. The girl simply let go of the envelope, and it fell into the basket, gravity doing the work formerly done by the girl. The output under the new conditions was about four times that obtained when the girls were allowed to do the work their own way.

Several other routine jobs in the office were handled in the same way, with a marked improvement in each case. By this time the office force had become interested and were studying motions on their own account, and improving methods of doing work without any suggestion from the writer. One of the girls devised a method of stamping envelopes which enabled her to work at a speed of between one hundred and one hundred and twenty envelopes per minute. She piled the letters on edge in a long pile, the addressed side facing her. The stamps were torn in strips, crosswise of the sheet, so that the stamps were side by side instead of one above the other. She fastened to the forefinger of her right hand a small wet sponge, and taking a strip of stamps in that hand, fed them across the sponge, using her thumb to move the strip, and to guide the stamp into place on the corner of the envelope. The left hand drew the stamped envelope forward from the pile, the thumb of the left hand giving the necessary pressure to the stamp while it was being drawn forward, to assure its being firmly affixed to the envelope. The motion of drawing the envelope forward tore the stamp from the strip, and the operation was complete. The work was done with marvelous rapidity, yet the girl hardly seemed to make any motions, except to pull the envelopes forward, and to reach for strips of stamps. We do not know just what processes were followed in developing the method, as the girl studied it out and put it in operation while the writer was taking a vacation.

These incidents, and others, convinced us that there was much more to motion study than appeared from a hasty survey of the subject. We then began to look around in earnest, to discover what had been done in this line in other trades than those with which Mr. Gilbreth was familiar. We found that practically nothing had been done in a systematic, scientific manner, except in certain shops where scientific management had been installed.

We further found, that even in these shops motion study had not been made in the scientific manner outlined in Mr. Gilbreth's articles. It was a by-product, an incident in the installation of scientific management, rather than a science of itself. Nevertheless, even treated as an incidental branch of management it had conferred much benefit on those shops in which it had been made. We shall refer to this later.

The reduction of the number of motions can be accomplished in two radically different ways: (1) By analyzing every step of a process, as outlined by Mr. Gilbreth, studying the motions made, and improving or eliminating them as a result of the analysis, or by devising an entirely new way of accomplishing the same object. (2) By substituting a device which is an improvement over that formerly used, but which required a greater number of motions to operate it, or by the substitution of new motions or processes as they occur to the observer, rather than by any systematic study of the subject. This last method is the one most generally used. It might be termed the "accidental" method, as contrasted with the scientific one developed by Mr. Gilbreth.

An example of this latter kind of motion study is familiar to every man, woman, or child who lives in even a moderate-sized city. In the city fire departments much thought has been expended on the problem of enabling the firemen to start out to a fire in the shortest possible time after the alarm has been received. At first the horses stood in their stalls with their harness on them. The hitching of the horses required the fastening of several buckles. Some one then invented the drop harness, now universally used, and the number of motions in hitching a horse was reduced to three,—snapping the collar round his neck, and the fastening of the two reins to his bridle by bit snaps. Later the horses were moved from the rear of the house to a point alongside the engine, so that they had only to travel a matter of a few feet to be in position under the harness. Some one else then invented a device which released the horses from their stalls automatically with the sounding of the alarm on the fire-house gong, effecting a further saving in time and motion. Instead of having the firemen descend stairs from their sleeping quarters, the sliding pole was thought of, which eliminated a great number of individual motions and saved many seconds. And so on, as one device after another was perfected which saved motions, and thereby time, it was adopted, until now the "motion efficiency" in a fire house is one hundred per cent. It is useless to improve it further, because it has reached a point where the company is ready to start to a fire before it has received the number of the box. The men and horses do their part in less time than the electric telegraph transmits the complete signal. Yet to attain this efficiency has required a period of perhaps thirty years. The subject was not studied in a scientific manner.

Turning now to the machine shop, let us see what motion study means there. In an editorial in *Industrial Engineering,* in August 1910, we said:

Before a task can be set intelligently it is necessary to know just what can be accomplished by the best type of workman. This usually involves a time study of the job under consideration. The time study is more than putting a clerk with a stop watch alongside the workman, with instructions to see how long it takes him to do the job. A proper time study requires that a certain piece of work be divided into its component operations and that each operation be studied separately, and also in conjunction with other operations to which it is related. The time of performing these operations is recorded not once, but many times, until a fair average has been determined. The results are then analyzed to see if the time required can be cut down. Usually it will be found that it can. A single instance will suffice for illustration.

In a certain shop with which we are familiar a piece had to have several holes of different sizes drilled in it, a jig being provided to locate the holes. The drills and the sockets for them were given to the workman in a tote box. The time study of this job revealed several interesting facts. First, after the piece was drilled the machine was stopped, and time was lost while the workman removed the piece from the jig and substituted a new one. This was remedied by providing a second jig in which the piece was placed while another piece was being drilled in the first jig, the finished one being removed after the second jig had been placed in the machine and drilling started. It was also found that the workman lost considerable time hunting in the tote box for his drill, and for the socket to fit it. The result was the provision of a socket for each drill, which was fitted to it in the tool room, and the further provision of a tray alongside the machine on which the man could lay out his drills in the order in which they were to be used. He was thereby enabled to pick up the correct drill without losing any time hunting for it. It was also found that it took considerable time to verify the size of the drill and socket, due to the figures stamped on the drill by the manufacturer being so small as to require the workman to go to the light to hunt for the figures. Consequently, numbers one-half inch high were placed on the drills, so that they could be seen in almost any light. To do this it was necessary to grind a flat spot on the drill to accommodate the large-sized figures. This had the desirable but unsought for result of enabling the workman to locate the figures by the sense of touch, and consequently no time was lost in turning the drill round and round to search for the size.

The above changes, simple in themselves, resulted in an increase in output on this particular job of about four times that usually obtained before the time study was made.

The incident related above is one that the writer discovered after he began to investigate motion study in other lines than those discussed by Mr. Gilbreth. It, too, is typical of the "accidental" method. It is sufficient to show, however, what scientific motion study could do if applied to an entire industry.

The following letter from Mr. H. L. Gantt to the writer illustrates how little people, even the most expert in their line, know about the most economical way of doing work:

Editor Industrial Engineering:

The series of articles on "Motion Study" by Frank B. Gilbreth are particularly valuable as illustrating what a man, having an analytical mind and a quick comprehension of details, can accomplish. They also illustrate the fact that in order to accomplish such results the subject must be given a great deal of study. The articles are unique in that they describe for the first time the detailed application to an art of principles which have often been described in more general terms.

On the other hand, the man who becomes interested in making this kind of a study will, if he has the right kind of mind, become so fascinated by it that it is on his mind almost all the time. The subject opens up so many possibilities that those men who can appreciate it are simply carried away. While in London with the American Society of Mechanical Engineers, Mr. Gilbreth cornered an old friend of his and explained to him the wonderful results that could be accomplished by motion study. He declared that he did not care what the work was, he would be able to shorten the time usually required, provided that nobody had previously applied the principles of motion study to the work.

A few days before, this friend had been at the Japanese-British Exposition and had seen there a girl putting papers on boxes of shoe polish at a wonderful speed. Without saying what he had in mind, Mr. Gilbreth's friend invited him to visit the exposition, and in a most casual way led him to the stand where the girl was doing this remarkable work, with the feeling that here at least was an operation which could not be improved upon.

No sooner had Mr. Gilbreth spied this phenomenal work than out came his stop watch, and he timed accurately how long it took the girl to do twenty-four boxes. The time was forty seconds. When he had obtained this information he told the girl that she was not doing the work right. She, of course, was greatly incensed that a man from the audience should presume to criticize what she was doing, when she was acknowledged to be the most skillful girl that had ever done that work. He had observed that while all her motions were made with great rapidity, about half of them would be unnecessary if she arranged her work a little differently. He has a very persuasive way, and although the girl was quite irritated by his remark, she consented to listen to his suggestion that he could show her how to do the work more rapidly. Inasmuch as she was on piece work the prospect of larger earnings induced her to try his suggestion. The first time she tried to do as he directed she did twenty-four boxes in twenty-six seconds; the second time she tried it she did it in twenty seconds. She was not working any harder, only making fewer motions.

This account the writer heard in Manchester, England, from the man himself who had put up the job on Mr. Gilbreth, and it is safe to say that this man is now about as firm a believer in motion study as Mr. Gilbreth is.

H. L. GANTT.

NEW YORK, Oct. 1, 1910.

Enough has been said, and sufficient instances drawn from widely diversified trades have been given, to show that motion study is a problem of the most vital importance to the world. Some day an intelligent nation will awake to the fact that by scientifically studying the motions in its trades it will obtain the industrial supremacy of the world. We hope that that nation will be the United States. Already rated as the most progressive nation the world has ever seen, it will take a position far in advance of all, once it begins to give its earnest attention to this subject. Certain it is, that if we do not some other people will, and our boasted progress and supremacy will then be but a memory.

When one looks about him and sees the wasted time and money in every walk of life from useless motions, the mind becomes weary in contemplating the magnitude of the task. The bricklayer, the carpenter, the machinist, the shoveller, the clerk, even the editor in writing with his pen, make twenty motions where one would suffice. The actual wealth of the nation is in what it takes from the ground in the shape of crops or minerals plus the value added to these products by processes of manufacture. If by reducing the number of motions in any of these processes we can increase many fold the output of the worker, we have increased by that amount the wealth of the world; we have taken a long step in bringing the cost of living to a point where it will no longer be a burden to all but the very wealthy; and we have benefited mankind in untold ways.

Words fail the writer when he tries to express his appreciation of what Mr. Gilbreth has done in blazing a trail for future investigators. The work he outlines of investigating and reclassifying the trades by means of motion study is worthy of the brains of the most scientific investigators; it is worthy of the endowments of a Rockefeller or a Carnegie; it is worthy of the best efforts of the national government. Properly carried to its logical conclusion it would form the mightiest tool for the conservation of resources that the country could have. Our scientists could engage in no more important work than this.

ROBERT THURSTON KENT,
Editor Industrial Engineering.

Description and General Out-line of Motion Study

••

NECESSITY FOR MOTION STUDY

Professor Nathaniel Southgate Shaler astounded the world when he called attention to the tremendous waste caused by the rain washing the fertile soil of the plowed ground to the brooks, to the rivers, and to the seas, there to be lost forever.

This waste is going on in the whole civilized world, and especially in our country. Professor Shaler's book, "Man and the Earth," was the real prime cause of the congress that met in Washington for the conservation of our natural resources. While Professor Shaler's book was right, and while the waste from the soil washing to the sea is a slow but sure national calamity, it is negligible compared with the loss each year due to wasteful motions made by the workers of our country. In fact, if the workers of this country were taught the possible economies of motion study, there would be a saving in labor beside which the cost of building and operating tremendous settling basins, and the transporting of this fertile soil back to the land from whence it came, would be insignificant. Besides, there would still be a surplus of labor more than large enough to develop every water power in the country, and build and maintain enough wind engines to supply the heat, light, and power wants of mankind.

There is no waste of any kind in the world that equals the waste from needless, ill-directed, and ineffective motions. When one realizes that in such a trade as bricklaying alone, the motions now adopted after careful study have already cut down the bricklayer's work more than two-thirds, it is possible to realize the amount of energy that is wasted by the workers of this country.

The census of 1900 showed 29,287,070 persons, ten years of age and over, as engaged in gainful occupations. There is no reason for not cutting down the waste motions in the vocations of the other almost half (49.7 per cent) of the population ten years of age and up-
149

ward who do *not* engage in gainful occupations. The housekeepers, students, etc., on this list have as much need for motion saving as any one else,—though possibly the direct saving to the country would not be so great. But taking the case of the nearly thirty million workers cited above, it would be a conservative estimate that would call half their motions utterly wasted.

As for the various ways in which this waste might be utilized, that is a question which would be answered differently by each group of people to whom it might be put.

By motion study the earning capacity of the workman can surely be more than doubled. Wherever motion study has been applied, the workman's output has been doubled. This will mean for every worker either more wages or more leisure.

But the most advisable way to utilize this gain is not a question which concerns us now. We have not yet reached the stage where the solving of that problem becomes a necessity—far from it! Our duty is to study the motions and to reduce them as rapidly as possible to standard sets of least in number, least in fatigue, yet most effective motions. This has not been done perfectly as yet for any branch of the industries. In fact, so far as we know, it has not, before this time, been scientifically attempted. It is this work, and the method of attack for undertaking it, which it is the aim of this book to explain.

PLACE OF MOTION STUDY IN SCIENTIFIC MANAGEMENT

Motion study as herein shown has a definite place in the evolution of scientific management not wholly appreciated by the casual reader.

Its value in cost reducing cannot be overestimated, and its usefulness in all three types of management—Military, or driver; Interim, or transitory; and Ultimate, or functional—is constant.

In increasing output by selecting and teaching each workman the best known method of performing his work, motion economy is all important. Through it, alone, when applied to unsystematized work, the output can be more than doubled, with no increase in cost.

When the Interim system takes up the work of standardizing the operations performed, motion study enables the time-study men to limit their work to the study of correct methods only. This is an immense saving in time, labor, and costs, as the methods studied comply, as nearly as is at that stage possible, with the standard methods that will be synthetically constructed after the time study has taken place.

Even when Ultimate system has finally been installed, and the scientifically timed elements are ready and at hand to be used by the instruction card man in determining the tasks, or schedules, the results of motion study serve as a collection of best methods of performing work that can be quickly and economically incorporated into instruction cards.

Motion study, as a means of increasing output under the military type of management, has consciously proved its usefulness on the work for the past twenty-five years. Its value as a permanent element for standardizing work and its important place in scientific management have been appreciated only since observing its standing among the laws of management given to the world by Mr. Frederick W. Taylor, that great conservator of scientific investigation, who has done more than all others toward reducing the problem of management to an exact science.

VAST FIELD FOR MOTION STUDY

Now tremendous savings are possible in the work of everybody,—they are not for one class, they are not for the trades only; they are for the offices, the schools, the colleges, the stores, the households, and the farms. But the possibilities of benefits from motion study in the trades are particularly striking, because all trades, even at their present best, are badly bungled.

At first glance the problem of motion study seems an easy one. After careful investigation it is apt to seem too difficult and too large to attack. There is this to be said to encourage the student, however:

1. Study of one trade will aid in finding the result for all trades.
2. Work once done need never be done again. The final results will be standards.

PRESENT STAGE OF MOTION STUDY

We stand at present in the first stage of motion study, *i.e.,* the stage of discovering and classifying the best practice. This is the stage of analysis.

The following are the steps to be taken in the analysis:

1. Reduce *present* practice to writing.
2. Enumerate motions used.
3. Enumerate variables which affect each motion.
4. Reduce *best* practice to writing.

5. Enumerate motions used.
6. Enumerate variables which affect each motion.

VARIABLES

Every element that makes up or affects the amount of work that the worker is able to turn out must be considered separately; but the variables which must be studied in analyzing any motion, group themselves naturally into some such divisions as the following:

I. *Variables of the Worker.*

1. Anatomy.
2. Brawn.
3. Contentment.
4. Creed.
5. Earning Power.
6. Experience.
7. Fatigue.
8. Habits.
9. Health.
10. Mode of living.
11. Nutrition.
12. Size.
13. Skill.
14. Temperament.
15. Training.

II. *Variables of the Surroundings, Equipment, and Tools.*

1. Appliances.
2. Clothes.
3. Colors.
4. Entertainment, music, reading, etc.
5. Heating, cooling, ventilating.
6. Lighting.
7. Quality of material.
8. Reward and punishment.
9. Size of unit moved.
10. Special fatigue-eliminating devices.
11. Surroundings.
12. Tools.
13. Union rules.
14. Weight of unit moved.

III. *Variables of the Motion.*

1. Acceleration.
2. Automaticity.
3. Combination with other motions and sequence.
4. Cost.
5. Direction.
6. Effectiveness.
7. Foot-pounds of work accomplished.
8. Inertia and momentum overcome.
9. Length.
10. Necessity.
11. Path.
12. "Play for position."
13. Speed.

In taking up the analysis of any problem of motion reduction we first consider each variable on the list separately, to see if it is an element of our problem.

Our discussion of these variables must of necessity be incomplete, as the subject is too large to be investigated thoroughly by any one student. Moreover, the nature of our work is such that only investigations can be made as show *immediate* results for increasing outputs or reducing unit costs.

The nature of any variable can be most clearly shown by citing a case where it appears and is of importance. But it is obviously impossible in a discussion such as this to attempt fully to illustrate each separate variable even of our incomplete list.

Most of our illustrations are drawn from bricklaying. We have applied motion study to our office and field forces, and to many of the trades, but our results on bricklaying are the most interesting, because it is the oldest mechanical trade there is. It has passed through all the eras of history, it has been practiced by nations barbarous and civilized, and was therefore in a condition supposed to be perfection before we applied motion study to it, and revolutionized it.

Since first writing these articles for *Industrial Engineering* it has been of great interest to the writer to learn of the conscious and successful application of the principles involved to the particular fields of work that have interested various readers. It was thought that unity might be lent to the argument by choosing the illustrations given from one field. The reader will probably find himself more successful in estimating the value of the underlying laws by translating the illustrations into his own vocabulary,—by *thinking* in his own chosen material.

The practical value of a study such as this aims to be will be increased many fold by coöperation in application and illustration. The variables, at best an incomplete framework, take on form and personality when so considered.

Variables of the Worker

•••

ANATOMY

A careful study of the anatomy of the worker will enable one to adapt his work, surroundings, equipment, and tools to him. This will decrease the number of motions he must make, and make the necessary motions shorter and less fatiguing.

Examples.—1. If the bricklayer is left-handed the relative position of the pile of packs to the mortar box is reversed.

2. The staging is erected so that the uprights will be out of the bricklayer's way whenever reaching for brick and mortar at the same time. [Fig. 1 omitted.]

3. Packs can be piled at a height with reference to the height of the mortar box that will enable stock to be picked up more easily by bending over sideways than by bending forwards. This latter case is, of course, on work where the non-stooping scaffold is not used.

4. The planks on the bricklayer's platform of the non-stooping scaffold, if made of two unconnected planks, will enable the bricklayer to lean either toward the stock platform or toward the wall without any other effort than that of throwing his weight on one foot or the other, taking advantage of the spring of the planks. (See Fig. 2.)

5. The inside plank of the bricklayer's platform must extend in under the stock platform, or the bricklayer's leg will strike the edge of the plank of the stock platform when he reaches for stock.

6. The stock platform must not be wider than the minimum width that will permit holding the packets, or the lower-priced packet man will not place the packs exactly in that position that will require the least amount of straining of the high-priced workman, the bricklayer.

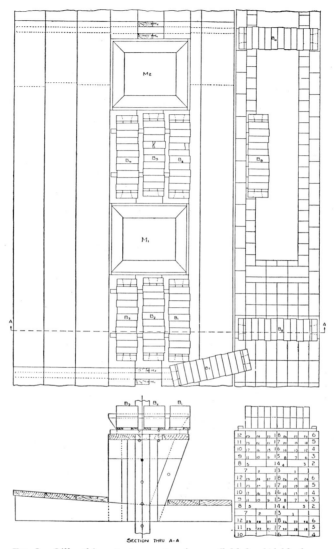

Fig. 2. Gilbreth's patent non-stooping scaffold for bricklaying.

The numbers show the correct sequence of courses and tiers as laid from the non-stooping scaffold for the fewest, shortest, and most economical motions under the "Pack-on-the-wall" method.

BRAWN

Workmen vary widely as to their brawn and strength.

When the actual work is being done, due consideration should be given to the percentage of efficiency that the men available possess. But all calculations should be made on the basis of using first-class men only. All data should be gathered from observations on first-class men only. In fact, so-called first-class men are not good enough. The best man obtainable anywhere is the best for observation purposes. The data gathered on that best man will then be considered as 100-per-cent quality. The men finally used can then be considered as of a certain percentage of perfect quality, and it should then be the aim of the management to attain 100-per-cent quality. This is one of the most important factors in the success of intensive management. The manager who wins is the one who has the men best suited for the purpose. Intensive management must not only recognize quickly the first-class man, but must also attact first-class men.

Everybody concedes that the size of the output depends, first of all, on the quality of the men.

Example.—We have found that a first-class laborer, if his work is so arranged that he does not have to stoop over, but can do his work with a straight back, can handle ninety pounds of brick on a packet day after day and keep in first-class physical condition, while laborers of a class that does not have the right food cannot handle continuously over sixty to seventy pounds of bricks on a packet. [Fig. 3 omitted.]

It is obviously better to have all one class of men, so that all instruction cards will be as nearly alike as possible. The size of the shovel, the weight of the hammer, the number of brick on the packet —these are variables that must also be considered when making out the instruction card—and these are all influenced by the brawn of the worker.

CONTENTMENT

Contentment affects the output of the worker. If he is contented, he will have his mind on his work, and he will be more willing to carry out the motions exactly as directed on the instruction card.

The contented worker does not require so large a percentage of rest for overcoming fatigue from his intensive efforts.

Contentment makes for loyalty to the management, for coöperating for maintenance of the best conditions, and for the protection and preservation of the property of the employer.

CREED

The term "creed" is used to cover religion, nationality, etc.,— everything that might act as a bond of sympathy between workers and the people with whom they come in contact. On work where the output of each man is recorded separately, the question as to whether the creed of the workman is the same as that of his foreman, or superintendent, or employer, is of little consequence.

In places where the output of each man is not recorded separately, it is a recognized fact that instructions of the foreman or employer will be more apt to be carried out where there is a bond of sympathy between the employees, the foreman, and the employers. A bond of sympathy between the workman and the people who are to occupy the edifice upon which they are working will also increase the output.

The motions of a bricklayer working upon the wall of a church differing from his own religion are often vastly different from those that he is careful to make when the congregation to occupy it coincides with his belief.

In planning athletic contests also, it is well to group men according to their affiliations.

Example.—On engine beds and similar work, where the pieces are isolated, assigning gangs of men of different nationalities to the different beds will create extra interest in the contests. If this is not feasible, put the tall men on one bed and the short men on the other, or the single men against the married men, or eastern "pick-and-dip" men against western "string-mortar" men.

EARNING POWER

The matter of classifying men by their relative earning power is as important as classifying them by their relative brawn. It is better, of course, to have men as nearly as possible of one class only, and that the best class. Classing men by their earning power simplifies the work of the planning department in many ways. It enables it to prescribe the same motions to the entire class of men, to place them all under nearly the same conditions, to prescribe the same tools and surroundings, to place them together, and, finally, to have an athletic contest between the men of the same class.

Furthermore, the motions to be made are often entirely different for workmen of different earning power.

Examples.—1. With masons and laborers of low earning power it is sometimes advisable to place the brick on the packets any way that will give the fewest motions for loading the packets, and to let the bricklayers lay them with their customary numerous motions, until men of higher earning power may be obtained to take their places.

2. With bricklayers and laborers of high earning power it is better

to have the laborers pile the brick upon the packets so that the brick will be in that position that requires the least amount of motions of the bricklayer to pick them up and to lay them.

It is obvious that all motions performed in handling or transporting material before the material is used, cut up, or fabricated, should, theoretically, be performed by low-priced men, and that the work done by the high-priced men should be limited as far as possible to the work of permanent character. As an example of this, the carrying of the brick and mortar to the scaffold is done by the mason's helper, while the carrying of the brick from the packet to its final resting place in the wall is done by the mason.

This same principle can be carried much further in all trades than is usually customary to-day. For example, we have found that piling the brick face up and with the top side nearest the palm of the bricklayer's hand when his arm hangs in a natural position will save an average of one motion of the high-priced bricklayer per brick. [Figs. 4, 5, 6, and 7 omitted.]

We have found a great increase in the number of brick it is possible to lay, and a decrease in the cost of laying them if the brick are placed by the low-priced man in the nearest practicable place in feet and inches from the place where they will finally rest in the wall. Not only this, but the receptacle must be left with the material on it, so that the higher-priced man can lift the receptacle and its contents simultaneously at the exact time the materials are wanted to a place still nearer to the place where the material will be finally used, to be transported from there to their final resting place by a still higher-priced man. (See Fig. 2.) [Fig. 8 omitted.]

This use of "low-priced men" does not mean the use of mediocre men. The men used, of whatever price, should be the best men of that class obtainable.

EXPERIENCE

That previous experience is an element to be considered is obvious. This fact is so well recognized that the expression "You can't teach an old dog new tricks" may be heard around the world. While this may be true with dogs, it is not true with workmen. On a short job it may not be advisable to attempt to change radically the lifetime customs of a local workman. But recording the output of each man separately will tell whether or not it is advisable to make out the instruction card in accordance with the previous experience of the workman, or in accordance with the way in which actual records have proved to be productive of the highest outputs. Experience varies widely, and the habits formed are often difficult to overcome.

Examples.—A bricklayer from certain sections of New England has been accustomed to pick up mortar with a trowel at the same time that he picks up brick with the other hand. This is called the "pick-and-dip method." The size and shape of his mortar receptacle, the arrangement of the brick and mortar on his scaffold, the shape of the scaffold itself, the sequence in which he builds the vertical tiers and the horizontal courses, and, finally, the labor-union rules themselves, are fashioned after the consequences of using a small trowel, just large enough to pick up sufficient mortar for one brick only.

A bricklayer so trained finds it difficult at first to adapt himself to the "string mortar" method of the West. The western-taught bricklayer experiences the same difficulties in adapting himself to the "pick-and-dip" method with the speed of the eastern bricklayer. But their difficulties are nothing compared with those that the employer experiences who puts the good points of both systems on any one job.

Not only do habitual motions become fixed, but also the previous experience of the bricklayer is often the cause of his making *too many motions, i.e.,* unnecessary motions. He seldom, if ever, has been rigidly trained to use a certain number of definite motions. It takes time and patience to induce him to adopt a standard method.

On a small job it is advisable to select those men for the leads and the trigs who are best fitted to be leaders, that is, who are best prepared by previous experience to carry out without delay the requirements of the instruction cards—but give due consideration to the previous experience and habits of work of the workmen.

On a large job, however, it is most economical to insist on standard methods and standard motions that will produce the highest outputs, without regard to the previous training of the workmen. Attract and retain those workmen who can follow out their instruction card and as a result produce the high records of outputs.

FATIGUE

Fatigue is an important variable to consider when selecting those motions that will give the most economy and that make the "standard motions." It goes without saying that the motions that cause the least fatigue are the most desirable, other things being equal.

Fatigue is due to a secretion in the blood.

To quote from an article signed "I. M. T." in the *American Magazine* for February, 1910:

"The toxin of fatigue is the phrase the physicians have given us with which to jar the attention of those who can only be stirred by harsh words. It has been demonstrated in the last few years that fatigue is due to an actual poison not unlike the poison or toxin of diphtheria. It is generated in the body by labor. But the system takes care of itself and generates enough anti-toxin to take care of a normal amount of toxin or poison. If it continues to be produced in abnormal quantities the system cannot grapple with it. There is a steady poisoning of the body, with all the baneful effects, mental and moral, as well as physical, that poison produces."

Continuous hard work, however, like proper training, puts the body into that condition that best overcomes fatigue.

Fatigue is due to three causes:

1. Fatigue due to coming to work improperly rested (fatigue brought to the job).

2. Unnecessary fatigue, due to unnecessary work, unnecessary motions, or uncomfortable positions, surroundings, and conditions of working.

3. Necessary fatigue, due to output.

Every motion causes fatigue. The same motions in the same trade cause about the same fatigue for all first-class men, and they all require about the same amount of rest to overcome fatigue, provided their habits and mode of living are the same outside of working hours.

The amount of fatigue caused and the percentage of rest required in many different kinds of work have been computed by Frederick W. Taylor with great exactness. He has assigned the various workers to classes and accurately computed the "task" from his records.

We have no such records as Mr. Taylor has gathered, but we have numerous records of outputs of different men on several kinds of work. We know that the amount of rest actually required by a workman increases with the discomfort of the position in which he works. We also know that the speed, hence the output of the worker, decreases rapidly if there is much fatigue to overcome.

Example.—A bricklayer can lay brick for a few minutes quite as quickly when he picks up the brick from the level of the platform on which he stands [Fig. 9 omitted], as he can when he picks up the brick from a bench twenty-four inches above the level of the platform on which he stands [Figs. 10, 11, and 12 omitted], but he cannot keep that speed up, because he requires more rest to overcome the greater fatigue.

It is not simply for the welfare alone, although that reason should be sufficient, but for economic reasons as well, that the men should be so placed and equipped that their work is done under the most comfortable conditions.

Examples.—1. It is a recognized fact that a cluttered-up floor under a workman's feet will tire him quite as much as the productive work that he is doing. A smooth-planked floor will enable a bricklayer to lay many more brick than will earth that has been leveled off.

2. A bricklayer can stoop over and pick up anything from the floor with one hand with much less fatigue if he has a place to rest his other hand while he is stooping, because he puts his weight on one foot and lifts his other foot out behind him, which does not tire the muscles of his back nearly so much.

Slow motions do not necessarily cause less fatigue than quick motions, and, per unit of work done, may cause much more fatigue than quick motions.

The amount of work done per motion may not be fatiguing proportionately to the size of the unit.

Example.—Lifting ninety pounds of brick on a packet to the wall will fatigue a bricklayer much less than handling the same number of brick one or two at a time. Consequently with the same amount of fatigue the workman will handle several times as many brick on packets as he can handle one or two at a time.

We have, then, under this variable two tasks to perform:

1. To eliminate unnecessary fatigue. This we do by studying and fixing the variables; that is, by standardizing the work.

2. To provide for rest from necessary fatigue, and to utilize rest time.

Under old forms of management workmen "should keep busy at something," even if prevented from doing their regular work. An idle workman was considered a disgrace. The consequence of this was that the workman took his rest while working, or made believe work while resting. The old-fashioned kind of rest is called "systematic soldiering." It is the curse of the military type of management. It is a form of cheating that has been made respectable by the conditions forced upon the workers by the employers.

Under scientific management the evils of soldiering are elimi-

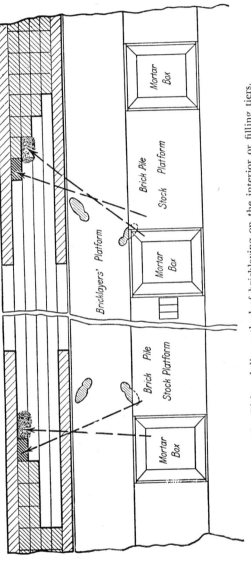

Fig. 13. Pick-and-dip method of bricklaying on the interior or filling tiers.

Working from left to right.—The mortar should be laid to the right of the brick and deposited on the wall at exactly the same instant that the brick is deposited on the previous trowelful. Otherwise the brick would wait until the mortar was deposited.

Working from right to left.—The mortar and brick are deposited in different tiers, so that they may be both deposited at the same time. The apprentice must be taught on his first day the right positions for his feet and the right motions for the greatest economy.

162

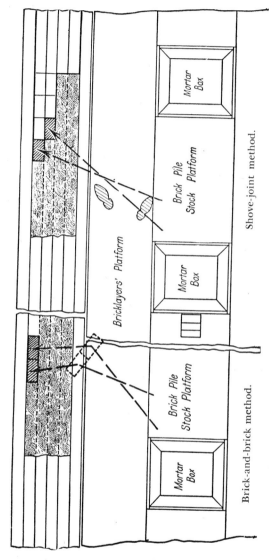

Brick-and-brick method.

Shove-joint method.

FIG. 14. Stringing-mortar method of bricklaying on the interior or filling tiers.

Brick-and-brick method of bricklaying, working from right to left.—In the brick-and-brick method the brick are picked up simultaneously, put together end to end in the air, and guided as one brick to place for the greatest speed. This method is not used when shove joints are desired.

Shove-joint method of bricklaying, working right to left.—The two brick are deposited in different tiers at the same time.

nated, and the correct definite percentage of rest required is recognized and provided for. When a man is prevented by causes beyond his control from doing his regularly assigned work, he is told to use the opportunity for rest,—not to take such rest as can be obtained by making slow and useless motions, that will give him an industrious appearance to the casual observer, but to rest, the 100-per-cent kind of rest.

There are cases where chairs and reading tables have been provided with beneficial effect for workers to occupy when delayed for a few minutes. They get the rest, and their presence at the table acts as a danger signal to the management.

When a man is fatigued to the point where it is impossible for him to do his best work he should be made to rest. He must not do anything but rest until he is in that condition that will enable him to fly at his work and perform it with the fastest standard motions possible.

Rest does not necessarily mean idleness. The worker can spend the rest period reading his instruction card, or filling out his record of output on the card, or in some other form of restful work. A change of work is often a rest. By performing the above two tasks well, we secure the greatest output per day and the fewest hours per day without injury to the health of the men.

HABITS

The habits of the workman have much to do with his success in eliminating unnecessary motions and in adopting quickly and permanently standard methods. The term "habits," as here used, includes not only personal "habits," so-called, but also habits of thinking, habits of working, etc.

Habits brought to the work may act as a deterrent or as an aid to its best performance. They embrace a group of sub-variables which are difficult to describe and analyze, and are of immense importance in influencing output.

That acquiring good habits of work makes the worker more versatile as well as more efficient is forcefully stated by Mr. Gantt in his book on "Work, Wages, and Profits." He says:

"The habits that a man has to acquire to become efficient in one class of work stand him in good stead in becoming efficient in other work. These habits of work are vastly more important than the work itself, for it is our experience that a man who has become efficient in one thing, readily learns to become efficient at doing other things."

HEALTH

The health of the worker may be affected by:

1. Other things than his work and the conditions under which it is done.

2. The work.

Consideration of other things than the work may properly be left to the welfare department. This department can most successfully define the scope of its work by attempting to improve the man himself and his surroundings in every way that will make him a better and more successful worker. This criterion will satisfy both employer and employee as to the appropriateness, justness, and utility of the work of the welfare department.

The life of the man when away from work is only in so far subject to the inspection and jurisdiction of the so-called "welfare" department as that department can show itself able to make of the man a more valuable economic unit to himself and to the community.

If the welfare department makes an efficient workman the product of its work, the philanthropic by-products will take care of themselves.

The work itself should be laid out in such a way that its performance will add to and not subtract from health. A proper study and determination of the variables that affect the surroundings and the motion will go far to insure this. Moreover, standardized work will transform the workman.

Henry L. Gantt, in a most stimulating paper on "Training the Workmen in Habits of Industry and Coöperation," read before the American Society of Mechanical Engineers, December, 1908, says of workmen:

"As they become more skilled, they form better habits of work, lose less time, and become more reliable. Their health improves, and the improvement in their general appearance is very marked. This improvement in health seems to be due to a more regular and active life, combined with a greater interest in their work, for it is a well-known fact that work in which we are interested and which holds our attention without any effort on our part, tires us much less than that we have to force ourselves to do."

This Mr. Gantt says in speaking of the benefits of the "task and bonus" system; but the same thing is undoubtedly true of men working under standards derived from motion study.

MODE OF LIVING

Mode of living has been more or less touched upon under "health" and "habits." It is a complex variable, difficult to analyze and difficult to control. Its effects on output are for this reason all the more far-reaching and demand scientific investigation.

NUTRITION

This is a subject that has been investigated much more scientifically with regard to horses and mules than with regard to workmen, but cases are seen on every hand where it is more profitable to furnish the most nutritious food to the men gratis than to permit them to have the usual poor food of the padrones' storehouse. In the building of a new town in Maine it was found to be economical to spend considerable sums of money for supplying food for the men at less than cost, rather than to have them eat the food provided by the local boarding houses. The nutritive value of various foods and the amount of energy which various diets enable one to put forth have been made a study in training soldiers. There must be many data available on the subject, and the government should collect them and issue a bulletin for the use of the welfare departments of large employing organizations. The army might also serve as an example in many other ways to the student of economics. The "Tactics" are admirable "instruction cards," conforming to many of the laws of motion study. It seems unfortunate that the governments of the world up to the present time have confined all of their attempts to standardize motions to the arts of war, and have done nothing in this line in the arts of peace.

SIZE

Size of men, with relation to their motions, has much more influence than is usually realized.

Short men are usually the best shovelers where the shovelful need not be raised much in doing the work, such as in mixing mortar and concrete. Few foremen realize that this is because a short man does fewer foot-pounds of work in doing the same amount of shoveling. On the other hand, when men are shoveling in a trench, the taller the men, usually, the more the output per man.

Oftentimes a staging is built at a height below a set of floor beams that enables the men to work to best advantage. On such a staging men should be selected of as nearly the same height as possible.

SKILL

The workman with the most skill is usually the one who can adapt himself quickest to new methods and conditions.

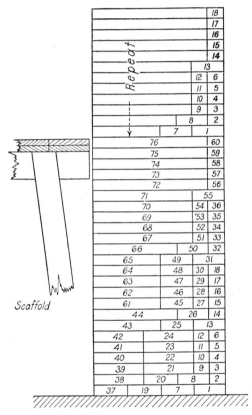

Fig. 15. The numbers show the correct sequence of courses and tiers as laid from the ordinary scaffold for the fewest, shortest, and most economical motions.

Example.—A bricklayer who has great skill in his trade can instantly lay a brick in the same manner that he is once shown. To get him to do so constantly when not supervised is difficult, but that can be quickest impressed upon his mind if he is shown the reason for every change demanded of him.

To make sure that the worker of the future acquires his skill prop-

erly, is the most important task here. This can be done only by insisting continuously on conformity to scientifically derived standards
from the beginning of his training.

Example.—The best results from a motion-study standpoint can
be attained only by teaching the apprentice from his first day to lay

Foot of
Patent Scaffold

```
                              79
                      78    | 72
                      77    | 71
                      76    | 70
                      75    | 69
                      74    | 68
                      73    |  67
                      66    | 60
                      65    | 59
                      64    | 58
                      63    | 57
                      62    | 56
                      61    |  55
                      54    | 51
                      53    | 50
                      52    | 49
                      48    | 33
                      47    | 32
                    46    |  31
                    45    | 30 | 18
                    44    | 29 | 17
                    43    | 28 | 16
                    42    | 27 | 15
                  41    |  26  |  14
                  40  |  25  | 13
                  39  | 24  | 12 | 6
                  38  | 23  | 11 | 5
                  37  | 22  | 10 | 4
                  36  | 21  |  9 | 3
                35  |  20  | 8  | 2
                34  | 19  |  7  | 1
```

Fig. 16.   The numbers show the correct sequence of courses
and tiers as laid from the non-stooping scaffold for the fewest,
shortest, and most economical motions. This scaffold permits
a much larger percentage of the brick to be laid as "filling in,"
instead of as "backing up," consequently requiring less skillful
motions.

the brick with the standard motions regardless of the looks of the
work. If the work is not good enough to permit the brick to remain
on the wall, a skilled bricklayer should fix it, until the apprentice
can lay the brick with the prescribed standard motions in a manner
good enough to permit the work to remain as a part of the structure.

The apprentice should not be permitted to depart from the standard motions in any case until he has first acquired them as a fixed
habit. The most pernicious practice is the generally accepted one of

first having an apprentice do perfect work and then attempting to make speed later. The right motions should be taught first, and the work taken down and rebuilt until it is up to standard quality. This is the *only* way to get the full benefits of the economics of motion study.

The workman who will make the highest outputs of the future will be he who has as a *habit* those standard motions that are the most productive when operated under standard conditions.

TEMPERAMENT

The temperament of the man has more to do with the motion he uses than one usually supposes.

Example.—Many expert face bricklayers would quit a job rather than lay common brick on interior walls, even though they might earn higher wages on the inside work. Other bricklayers prefer to lay common brickwork,—not that they doubt their ability to lay the face brick, but because they like the strenuous athletic contests for high scores of output and high pay. To them there is no monotony in laying common brick day after day, for to the skilled mason brick are not so nearly alike as are human beings.

A bricklayer interested in his work will often remember the characteristics of one certain brick years after he has forgotten the wall upon which it was laid.

Therefore the temperament of the man must be taken into consideration when placing the men. When they are best placed they follow their instructions on the subject of motion, and higher scores will be the result.

TRAINING

"Training" is so closely related to "skill" and "experience" that it is difficult to separate it from them. We use the word to mean both the worker's theoretical and practical equipment for his work, his entire preparation. The problem is to see that the worker has both kinds of equipment, acquired in the most useful, balanced method possible.

The training of the available worker must always be considered in estimating the time that it will take him to acquire standard methods and the output that can be expected of him. The training of the worker of the future should be planned to fit him for standard work. The training of the apprentice on the work to-day is usually defective because he has little or no training in theory at the same time that he is getting his practice. Furthermore, the journeyman who is his instructor not only has had no training in pedagogy, but often lacks the benefits of the elements of a common-school education. The usual time of apprenticeship in the building trades in this country is three years, or until the apprentice is twenty-one years old.

On the other hand, the boy taught in the trade school lacks training under actual working conditions. The question of dollars and cents to make for the employer, special fitting for high wages for himself, and the knowledge of the principles underlying the requirements necessary in order to obtain specially high outputs from intensive management, are wholly lacking.

The present apprenticeship system is pitiful and criminal from the apprentice's standpoint, ridiculous from a modern system standpoint, and there is no word that describes its wastefulness from an economic standpoint.

SUMMARY

Before turning to the variables of the surroundings, it may be well to summarize. The variables of the worker consist of the elements of the equipment that the worker brings to his work, both those that he was born with and those that he has acquired. These are mental and physical.

We have concluded:

1. That first-class men should always be secured if that be possible.

2. That everything possible should be done to preserve and to add to the natural powers and capacities that the worker brings to his work.

3. That standard practice derived from motion study does add to the natural powers of the worker, and both shortens his hours of work and adds to his output.

4. That training based on the laws underlying standard practice will enable the worker of the future to attain still higher efficiency and output.

Variables of the Surroundings

●●●

We turn now to the variables of the surroundings. These differ from the variables of the worker in that we can influence them more quickly and more directly. In discussing the variables of the worker, we deal more or less with the past and the future. The variables of the surroundings are each and all distinctly of the present.

APPLIANCES

The "standard conditions" maintained by the employer are a most important factor for high outputs. It is obvious that the appliances furnished the workman and the motions used are interdependent on each other.

Examples.—1. The bricklayer could not be expected to pick up the brick so that he would not have to spin or flop it in his hand unless it were delivered to him in the right position on a packet.

2. The bricklayer could not be expected to have so high an output if he had to stoop over in order to pick up his stock as he would have to do if the scaffold did not have a bench that obviated bending.

3. The bricklayer could not be expected to lay brick without turning around or bending over unless he was provided with packs of bricks that could be lifted bodily and placed upon the wall in units as large as could be economically handled.

4. The bricklayer could not be expected to do away with those motions that are necessary to remove the lumps from under a brick if there were holes in the sand screen and no pug mill to break up the lumps.

It is most important that the workman should be given "handy conditions" under which to work, that is, the "most comfortable," or those that require the "least percentage of rest" to overcome fatigue.

Examples.—1. The bricklayer must obviously have a scaffold to stand upon that permits adjusting the height of the platform on which he stands to a standard distance below the top of the ever-

171

growing wall on which he is laying the brick. We have found that the best height is from twenty-four to thirty-two inches below the top of the wall. If the wall is being laid overhanded, the height should not be over twenty-four inches, while if the wall is not being laid overhanded, thirty-two inches is the better height.

It is obvious that the bench from which the stock is picked up should be maintained at a standard distance above the platform on which the man stands. Also the platform on which the laborer walks should be located at the standard distance below the stock platform that will enable him to deposit the brick and mortar in a manner that will cause the least fatigue. Therefore, the three platforms for bricklayer, stock, and tender should be fixed with relation to one another, and movable in relation to the top of the wall, capable of being hoisted as the wall grows without stopping or disturbing the men.

2. The elevator for hoisting the brick and mortar should always be arranged so that it can, when desired, land above the top of a staged wall, and thus the brick and mortar can be wheeled down to the scaffold on the floor below. Then the tenders can wheel down with full loads and wheel the empty barrows up to the floor above.

3. Make a table, barrel, or box to put near the workman, no matter what his trade is, so that he will not have to stoop over and pick up his tools. Provide something to lean his shovel against or to hang his shovel on when he is alternately shoveling and wheeling to cut down time and to reduce the fatigue of stooping over and picking up the shovel.

The motions to be used and to be avoided are largely determined and affected by the appliances used; therefore for the highest outputs the right appliances must be devised, standardized, used, and maintained; otherwise the motions cannot be standardized. Furthermore, it is much easier to standardize motions with standard appliances than without them.

CLOTHES

The clothes that the workman wears may be a hindrance or a help to him in his work. Tight or ill-fitting clothing may restrict motions. Fear of ruining clothing may seriously cut down the speed of the worker.

On the other hand, clothing designed and specially adapted to the work that the worker has to do may increase output to a surprising extent.

Not till the advantages have been appreciated of having working clothes made the subject of study from the motion-economy standpoint will manufacturers provide the garments needed. But they are only too anxious to meet every demand as soon as they are conscious of it. Once let the specialized clothes for the worker be standardized and they will be placed immediately upon the market in inexpensive, durable, and attractive shape.

As for their reception by the worker, as soon as he realizes that they increase his efficiency, and are a badge of specialization and not of servitude, he will be ready and glad to welcome them.

COLOR

The stimulating effect of color upon workers is a subject to be investigated by psychologists. The results of their study should be of great benefit, especially to indoor workers. Motions could undoubtedly be made simpler by the proper selection of the color of painting and lighting in the workroom.

In our work we have to deal chiefly with color as a saver of motions. Color can be seen quicker than shape. Therefore, distinguishing things by their color is quicker than distinguishing them by the printing on them.

Examples.—1. The various pipes in a pipe gallery can best be recognized by painting them different colors.

2. The right-hand end of the packet is painted black, in order that when carried in the right hand of the laborer it can be placed so that the bricklayer can pick up each brick without spinning or flopping the brick in his hand.

3. Painting tools different colors, and also the place where they are to be placed in the drawer or the chest the same color, saves motions and time of motions when putting them away and finding them next time.

4. When low-priced men bring packages of any kind to higher-priced men to use or handle, the packages should always be painted, stenciled, or labeled with a distinguishing color on one end and on top. This will enable the low-priced workman to place the package in the manner called for on the instruction card with the least thought, delay, and motions. It will also enable the high-priced man to handle the package with no such lost motions as turning the package around or over.

5. Oftentimes the workmen who are best fitted physically for their

work cannot read, or at least cannot read English. Even if they could, it would take some time to read the stenciled directions on the non-stooping scaffold to the effect that "this side goes against the brick wall." It will greatly reduce the number of motions to paint the side that goes next to the wall a different color from the side that goes away from the wall.

ENTERTAINMENT

Music.—The inspiring and stimulating effect of music has been recognized from ancient times, as is shown by the military band, the fife and drum corps, the bagpipe of the Scotchman, down to the band that rushes the athlete around the track or across the field.

The singing of gangs at certain kinds of work, the rhythmic orders that a leader of a gang shouts to his men, and the grunting in unison of the hand drillers, show the unifying as well as the motion-stimulating effect of music and rhythm.

That some of the trades can have their motions affected in time and speed by music, to a point that will materially affect the size of their outputs, is a recognized fact.

Some of the silent trades have used phonography and musical instruments to entertain the men while they were working. It was found it paid the employer to furnish stimulating records at his own expense, so that the workmen would make more and quicker motions, rather than to permit the employees to furnish phonographic records at random at their own expense.

Reading.—Reading as a stimulus to output has been used with excellent results among the cigar makers.

It is also interesting to read in an article on "Three Months in Peonage" in the March, 1910, issue of the *American Magazine,* that story-telling may produce the same good results.

"The four packers under me," says the writer, a German white, who was working with peons at packing tobacco in Mexico, "knew no greater joy than to listen to a fairy tale with the regulation princess and dragon, and if I could but tell them one, or one of their number did so, the work went twice as fast, and they were happy."

The excellent and direct effects of entertainment upon health, fatigue, etc., are subjects for the scientist to study and the planning department and the welfare worker to apply. The effects of entertainment upon output should be studied by the student of motion economy. This variable alone furnishes a vast field for investigation.

HEATING, COOLING, VENTILATING

Heating, cooling, ventilating, and humidizing are closely allied, because all can be done with one and the same apparatus, and all greatly increase the workman's comfort, health, and possible number of motions.

Maintaining desired temperature in summer as well as winter by forcing into workrooms air that has been passed over heating or refrigerating coils has a great effect on the workman. Many factories, such as chocolate factories, have found that cooling the air for better results to the manufacturing process also enables the workers to produce more output—an output quite out of proportion to the cost of providing the air.

In many trades requiring great alertness and physical strength the proper heating and ventilating will allow the workman to dress in a costume specially adapted to his work, or to strip almost to the athlete's suit, with a consequent increased number and effectiveness of motions.

The degree of temperature and the percentage of humidity desired for each day of the year should be determined. The man in charge of the heating should receive no bonus for small consumption of fuel unless he also maintained the temperature and humidity called for on his instruction card.

The subjects of heating, ventilating, etc., are well covered by Mr. Hugo Diemer in his book on "Factory Organization and Administration." The proper time to consider these subjects is when the building is designed, but too often at that time the all-important question is,—How cheaply can the building be built? Ultimate saving will justify almost any conceivable first costs.

LIGHTING

The subject of lighting has, indirectly as well as directly, as great an influence upon output and motions, as upon the comfort of the eye. Upon it depends, to a large extent, the comfort of the whole body.

The arrangement of lighting in the average office, factory, or house is generally determined by putting in the least light necessary in order that the one who determined the location of the light may be able to see perfectly. This is wrong. The best light is the cheapest. By that is not meant that which gives the brightest light. In fact, the light itself is but a small part of the question. Go into any factory and examine every light, and you will notice that as a rule they are obviously wrong. A light to be right must pass five tests:

a. It must furnish the user sufficient light so that he can see.

b. It must be so placed that it does not cause the user's eyes to change the size of the diaphragm when ordinarily using the light.

c. It must be steady.

d. There shall not be any polished surfaces in its vicinity that will reflect an unnecessary bright spot anywhere that can be seen by the eyes of the worker.

e. It must be protected so that it does not shine in the eyes of some other worker.

The use of polished brass and nickel should be abandoned wherever it will shine in the worker's eye.

For work done on a flat surface, like the work of a bookkeeper or a reader, the light should be placed where the glare will reflect least in the worker's eyes; where the work is like the examining of single threads, the relative color and figured pattern of the background, as well as good light, is important. This is obvious. So is nearly everything else in good management. Go into the buildings among the workers, the students, and the scientists and see how rarely it is considered. All of this is not a question of getting the most out of the light. Light in a factory is the cheapest thing there is. It is wholly a question of fatigue of the worker. The best lighting conditions will reduce the percentage of time required for rest for overcoming fatigue. The difference between the cost of the best lighting and the poorest is nothing compared with the saving in money due to decreased time for rest period due to less fatigued eyes.

It is a similar case to the taxicab concerns—they charge their drivers with gasoline and tires and mileage, accidents, etc., but they furnish the lubricating oil free. The fallacy of the common practice of putting the lighting in the hands of the man whose merit is measured inversely as the coal bill is obvious.

The sub-variables involved make the problem as to exactly what lighting is most desirable difficult of solution. The proper solution will have such a beneficial effect, not only upon the man's work, but also upon his welfare, that no time or effort expended upon it can be too great.

QUALITY OF MATERIAL

It is essential to the use of standard motions and the resulting large output that all material used shall be in exactly that state in which it can be most easily handled by the worker.

Examples.—1. If there are lumps in the mortar, due to pieces of brick or shavings or lumps of lime, or cement or coarse pebbles in the sand, it is impossible for the bricklayer to do his best work.

2. If the sand is not selected with reference to the thickness of joints, if the sequence of tiers and courses (see Figs. 15 and 16 [pp. 167–68]) and the thickness of joints is determined by the whim of the bricklayer on the lead, instead of by the planning department, it is out of the question to expect high outputs. On the other hand, if the material is of exactly that consistency with which it can be best handled, and the other conditions are determined on the instruction card, much better speed can be obtained.

3. When using cement mortar made of cement and sand and no lime, the bricklayer will do more and better work if a tender is kept on the stock platform tempering the mortar to just the right consistency for the bricklayers.

4. If the brick are all handled in packs on packets from the time that they arrive upon the job until they reach the bricklayer's hand, they will each be of better quality, due to there being little or no chipping from handling and throwing about. The bricklayer will then be saved the useless motions of picking up brick that are chipped and discarding them again, to be used only when laying in the filling tiers.

REWARDS AND PENALTIES

The stimulus that rewards and penalties give motions is obvious. The discussion of reward and punishment would come under the head of compensation. It must be left to the cost reducing system to determine just what system of compensation will induce the men to do their swiftest, best work.

SIZE OF UNIT MOVED

The most advantageous size of unit to use is a difficult problem to solve, and is often controlled by some outside factor. For example, the most economical size of brick has been determined by the cost and other conditions relating to the making and baking, and not by the conditions of handling and laying. When the conditions of laying are studied scientifically, as they are to-day, one is forced to the conclusion that, for the greatest economy, the size of common brick should be changed materially from that of the present practice in America. The usual size of the brick used in England is much larger than the customary size used here.

It is obvious that there is some size of unit that is the most economical to make the standard package for handling brick in bulk. We have found it to be ninety-two pounds for a first-class laborer, either for piling or loading and unloading brick from carts. [Figs. 17 and 18 omitted.]

Careful examination of brickwork with the object in view of selecting the most profitable motions has entirely revolutionized the methods of bricklaying. For example, the size of unit that is picked up when loose brick are handled must be one brick for each hand. The packet enables us to pick up about eighteen brick at once.

The fountain trowel permits us to pick up and carry to the wall and spread mortar for twenty-one brick at one time without dropping the regular trowel which forms a temporary handle to it. [Fig. 19 omitted.]

The two-wheeled trucket permits carrying twelve packets, or 216 brick [Fig. 20 omitted], while the hod carries 18 brick, and the one-wheeled barrow carries 60 loose brick.

SPECIAL FATIGUE-ELIMINATING DEVICES

Only the careful student of management realizes how much the output of the worker can be increased by providing him with all possible aids toward doing his work.

Mr. Fred. W. Taylor, in his paper on "Shop Management," tells of a study he made of overhauling a set of boilers.

"He [the writer] did all of the work of chipping, cleaning, and overhauling a set of boilers, and at the same time made a careful time study of each of the elements of the work. This time study showed that a great part of the time was lost owing to the constrained position of the workman. Thick pads were made to fasten to the elbows, knees, and hips; special tools and appliances were made for the various details of the work. . . . The whole scheme was much laughed at when it first went into use, but the trouble taken was fully justified, for the work was better done than ever before, and it cost only eleven dollars to completely overhaul a set of 300 horse-power boilers by this method, while the average cost of doing the same work on day work without an instruction card was sixty-two dollars."

In reading this, it must be remembered that the fatigue-eliminating devices were only one element in increasing speed and reducing costs. But, on the other hand, it must be remembered also what a large element they were in adding to the comfort and ultimate well-being of the worker.

SURROUNDINGS

"Surroundings" have been previously discussed under "Fatigue," "Appliances," etc. It is only necessary to say here that the surroundings of the worker should be standardized, the standard being derived from a study of all the variables.

It is obvious that the highest possible records of output cannot be obtained unless the workers are furnished with a standard instruction card made out by the best man obtainable, one who knows more about their work than they do, and who can, and does, provide them with standard conditions that fulfill the most economical conditions of motions. Even then daily outputs and unit costs must be watched, so as to take advantage of the slightest change of conditions that affect costs. In practice, the unit costs must always also include the wages of the recorder, otherwise one cannot tell when the wages of the recorders are not deceiving as to actual unit costs under this intensive management.

TOOLS

The influence of the tools used upon the output is large. No workman can possibly comply with standard motions unless he has the standard tools. No worker should ever be obliged to furnish his own tools, if large output is expected. When workmen are obliged to furnish their own tools (due to their having too much thrift, lack of money, or fear of having them stolen), they usually use one size only of the same kind of tool. On many kinds of work greater output can be obtained by using two or more sizes of a tool.

Example.—The bricklayer should use a smaller trowel on pressed brick and a larger trowel on common brick.

Again, where workmen furnish their own tools, they use them after they are too much worn. A shovel with a worn blade will require several motions to push it into the material to fill it. It is cheaper in this case to cut off the handle of the shovel, so that the men cannot use it. Where no records are kept of their individual outputs the men always choose the shovel with the small blade.

It is especially important that apprentices should be supplied with proper tools. According to the usual practice the apprentice is taught with any tool procurable. He becomes adept and skilled, but often becomes so accustomed to the poor tool he has used that he finds it difficult to adapt himself to the use of a better new tool. This seriously hinders his complying with demands for standard quantities of output.

Tools should be of standard size and pattern. Workmen should invariably be made to use a tool that will enable them to make standard-sized outputs instead of using a tool that may seem "handier" to them. You cannot expect a man to comply with standard motions unless he has the standard tool for which his standard instruction card was made out.

The customary method in the past for determining the best weight of tool to use was to guess at it, and to use that size of tool which was thought to be the "handiest," or which it seemed could be used with the least fatigue.

Makers of hand tools cater to the whims of the local workmen, and, as a result, hand tools are made of many different designs in different parts of the country. Makers spend and waste great sums of money making experiments and conducting selling campaigns of odd or new designs of tools that have no merit from a motion-economy standpoint. There should be a bureau of testing, where the actual value of new shapes, designs, and sizes of tools could be tested and rated in percentages of efficiency from the standpoint of motion study.

Critics will say that such a scheme will crowd out new designs, and the benefit of the individual's inventions will be lost. But it would not; on the contrary, the testing would give great stimulus to inventors, designers, and tool makers, for they could then obtain the immediate attention of the buyers, because they would have the standard stamp of merit that comes from the record of a test that excelled previous standards.

We have testing stations for everything else. Think what the societies for testing materials have done for the progress of the world! Their records are usable forever, in any part of the world, once they are made.

When machines have to be tended, two separate sets of motions must be provided for:

1. The set that the worker uses when he is tending the machine.

2. The set that the worker uses to prepare tools and material for the machine while it does not require his attention.

All machines have to be tended more or less. Even automatic machinery has to have attention, and it is most important here to have motion study, because of the earning value of the machine being lost while it is shut down.

One sees occasionally a machine that can have any and every lever operated without the operator taking a single step, but comparatively few machines are constructed with this in mind.

Machines requiring constant starting and stopping and hand feeding or adjusting should have their various levers so positioned that the "laws of least effort of simultaneous motions" are complied with.

These laws will be discussed under "Variables of the Motion." It is only necessary to say here that motions should be similar on each side of a fore and aft vertical plane passing through the body. It is so necessary to have the motions similar that often counterbalances and springs can be installed to reverse the motion, thus also causing the hardest work to be done in the most convenient direction.

Anything that is used very often can be returned to place better, as well as with less motions, by gravity, or by the application of the gravity by some such means as a string and a weight. It requires some skill to use a wrench, but it requires no skilled motion or thought to return the wrench to its exact resting place with handle pointing in the most economical direction for picking up the next time it is used.

The average machine to-day is designed for a short demonstration of quick output, with less regard for the least percentage of rest required for overcoming fatigue due to continuous operation. With demand will come supply of machines that fulfill all economical motion requirements.

UNION RULES

The local rules of some unions are sometimes a hindrance to standardizing motions and thereby increasing output. The higher wages from higher outputs under intensive management soon convert the desirable members, however.

Many unions believe that extremely high outputs per man are against the interests of the union as a whole, on the theory that they may "work all of their members out of a job." Furthermore, they often think that the sacrifice that their one union may make in the world's endeavor to reduce the cost of living generally, is not properly offset by having any one trade or any one locality practicing intensive outputs. A few practical object lessons of the general increase in business resulting from higher wages and simultaneously created lower-production costs will, however, always convince the most prejudiced believer in artificially restricted maximum outputs.

The compensation of workers will not be discussed here, although the basis of compensation does affect motions.

WEIGHT OF UNIT MOVED

Generally speaking, the weight of the unit moved is of three kinds:

1. The weight of that part of the body that is moved.
2. The weight of a tool used, such as a hammer or a trowel.
3. The weight of material used, such as a brick, or the mortar on the trowel.

Other things being equal, the less of the body moved the less fatigue.

The weight that the tool should be is determined by the use of the tool. In the case of a sledge hammer, increased weight means increased efficiency. A twenty-five pound sledge might break a block of granite in halves in five blows, while a ten pound hammer might require one hundred blows. In the case of a trowel, increased weight means decreased efficiency. The heavier the trowel, the greater the fatigue—with no accompanying gain in output.

We have determined that a cutting-out hammer for brickwork should weigh, exclusive of the handle, 3.75 pounds, but that a hammer for drilling plug holes in granite, for making dog holes in heavy stone blocks, should weigh 4 pounds.

The weight of units moved should be standardized.

Example.—There is undoubtedly a certain sized load in a shovel that will enable a first-class man to accomplish the largest output with his maximum effort. Taylor has found his weight to be 21.5 pounds. The size of shovels that should be used should therefore be designated on the instruction card accordingly, and exactly 21.5 pounds should be the standard unit of weight of material shoveled.

SUMMARY

This discussion of the variables of the surroundings, etc., is not detailed—because general discussion is self-evident, and detailed discussion must be too specialized to interest the general reader.

It is only necessary to call attention to the general laws, logical and psychological, which underlie these variables, and their effect on standardizing motions. Each student naturally applies these laws to his own field, and sees for himself the opportunities for further study and application.

Variables of the Motion

A discussion of variables of the motion opens up a field so large that it is only possible here to attempt to show the method of investigation, and to show that each variable is a necessary factor in making motions standard, leaving to the universities and to properly created and equipped bureaus of the national government the task of reducing motion study to an exact science.

ACCELERATION

In considering acceleration of speed as an element of any motion, we must determine:

1. The amount of acceleration that it is possible or economical to obtain.
2. The means by which the acceleration can be obtained.
3. The effect of the acceleration on
   a. Economy in time required to make the motion.
   b. Economy in time required for rest to overcome the fatigue of having made the motion.

Examples.—1. Laying brick on a wall from a floor, from the height of the floor level up to three feet eight inches high above the floor, can be done with greatest speed when the brick to be picked up are each maintained at a height of one foot three inches, plus two-thirds the height that the wall is higher than the level of the floor on which the bricklayer stands. The brick to be picked up should never be higher than three feet eight inches under any circumstances.

By maintaining the height of the brick to be laid in this relative position to the height of the wall, the brick will always be in a position that permits the bricklayer to accelerate the speed of transportation of the brick by using the path of the quickest speed.

While bricklayers know nothing about this in theory, they very soon discover it in practice by means of their higher recorded output. Greater outputs will be noticeable as an immediate result of maintaining the brick as nearly as possible at the heights above stated.

2. In laying the filling tiers in any one course, it is most economical to lay the farthest filling tier first and the next farthest tier second, and so on. This enables the bricklayer to accelerate the speed of transportation of the brick up to the instant that it is deposited in the mortar.

The above practice is, of course, much more important on shove-joint work than on brick-and-brick construction.

3. The possible benefits from acceleration should be taken into consideration when determining the sequence in which the tiers shall be laid. The position of the feet of the bricklayer is an important factor in obtaining the acceleration desired. For the best results the feet should be on separate springy planks, so that the transportation of the brick can be speeded up, in addition to the speed of the arms by simply throwing the body by the aid of the spring of the plank. (See Fig. 13 [p. 162].)

AUTOMATICITY

Nearly all often-repeated motions become automatic. This is especially true of motions that require no careful supervision of mind or eye.

The automaticity of motions is of great assistance to the worker whose training and methods conform to standardized motions. This fact makes it necessary to have the apprentice taught the right motions first, last, and always.

The automaticity of motions is a hindrance to the worker who has been accustomed to old-fashioned surroundings, equipment, and tools, and who must adapt himself to standard surroundings.

Example.—A remarkable example of making unnecessary motions as a matter of habit is noticeable in places where the local bricklayers have been accustomed to laying brick that have a decided difference in the top and bottom. This difference makes it necessary to lay no brick upside down on the line. When these bricklayers first worked from packets with the brick in the right position to seize right-side up, they would invariably flop and spin each brick in their hands, first wrong-side up and then back again to the original right-side-up position.

The worker who has been trained wrong also finds it difficult to change his habits when he conforms to standard methods.

Example.—Occasionally we find the bricklayer who will spin or flop a brick that is to be laid in the middle of the wall, although it makes no difference which face of the brick is uppermost in these tiers.

The best way to cure motions that are not necessary but that are made from force of habit is to count the motions aloud, endeavoring to keep down to the standard number of standard motions.

When work is done by both hands simultaneously, it can be done quickest and with least mental effort if the work is done by both hands in a similar manner; that is to say, when one hand makes the same motions to the right as the other does to the left.

Most work is accomplished when both hands start work at the same time, and when the motions can be made at the same relative position on each side of a central fore and aft vertical plane dividing the worker's body symmetrically.

Even if motions cannot be planned to be similar for each hand and performed simultaneously, the plane in which the work is to be done should be carefully located.

If motions are so arranged as to be balanced, as suggested, it is possible not only to take advantage of automaticity, but also to cut down jar to the body. It is on this well-known principle that the shockless jarring machine is built. Balanced motions counteract each other. The result is, less bracing of the body is necessary, and less fatigue ensues.

COMBINATION WITH OTHER MOTIONS, AND SEQUENCE

A motion may be combined with motions that are (*a*) similar to it, and (*b*) dissimilar to it.

(*a*) If the motions combined are similar to it, advantage must be taken of the automaticity. Care must also be taken that all the motions made in a series of similar motions are necessary. Sometimes one effective motion is preferable to several not so effective.

Examples.—1. When tapping a brick down to grade with a trowel, one brisk tap will do the work as well as several light taps, and with much less time and effort.

2. If it is necessary to spread mortar on a face tier, one stroke of the trowel will do the work as well as several.

(*b*) If the motions combined are dissimilar, two motions may often be transformed into one.

Example.—The motion used to spread mortar may be combined with the motion used to butter the end of the brick laid just before the mortar was thrown. Thus, the two operations may be transformed into one, and a saving of time and motions will result. In fact, so doing may have other distinct advantages, such as leaving better keying for plastering direct upon the wall.

This subject of combinations of motions can barely be touched here. Its full treatment involves all other variables, and it can never be considered standardized till each separate motion is a standard.

COST

The cost of motions, absolute and relative, is a subject too large for any person, firm, or corporation to hope to cover. If complete data are ever to be gathered on it, the cost keeping, recording, and deducing will have to be done by the government.

But all work done by the individual investigator will result in real cost reducing, with increase of output, which is the ultimate purpose of all motion study.

The relative cost of labor and material must be considered.

Examples.—1. A bricklayer should never stop to pick up dropped mortar. The mortar dropped is not so valuable as the motions necessary to save it.

2. That quality of mortar that is easiest handled by the bricklayer is usually cheapest. The cost of grinding up the lumps in the sand, cement, and lime is less than the cost of the motions necessary to pick the lumps out with a trowel.

3. It is usually cheaper to fill a closer, say less than one-half a brick in size, on the interior tiers, with even the best of cement, than it is to cut a special piece of brick to fit or to walk a few steps to find one the right size. The extra cost of the mortar is negligible compared with the cost of the motions.

The relative cost of motions of higher and lower grades of labor must also be considered.

It is obvious that, other things being equal, it is cheaper to have a low-priced man instead of a high-priced man make the same motion; but only the most careful study can determine all of the motions that could be taken from the high-priced man and allotted to one or more grades of lower-priced men. This can never be wholly or properly accomplished until our present trades, with their inherited conditions and traditions, have been reclassified to meet modern conditions.

In some trades it is very difficult to effect such division of work, as unions are opposed to having anything relating to skilled work done by laborers.

Examples.—1. In the most highly unionized districts carpenters only are allowed to unload the rough lumber from the cars, and none but carpenters are allowed to transport, lift, and erect, as well as to fabricate it.

2. In bricklaying the case is slightly different. The work of transporting the brick to the place where they are to be laid has always been done by tenders and laborers. The bricklayer never wheels or carries brick. This is a tradition long handed down. Yet he is most jealous that no part of his own work shall be done by a tender or a laborer.

During the time that brick construction was practically without competitors in its field, the bricklayer could insist on his ancient privileges and prosper.

The inroads of concrete, both plain and reinforced, however, have changed conditions, and the bricklayer himself is, more than any other one factor, the cause of many cases of substitutions of concrete for brick.

The architecture of any country is determined by the relative cost of building materials in place, and the history of the world shows that the way to get the most of any one thing used is to make it the lowest in price.

The one thing that will reduce the price of brickwork more than any other is *to reduce the cost of the motions.*

After the laws underlying motion study have all been applied, the cost of motions can still be reduced from one-third to one-half by separating the motions of the bricklayer into at least two classes, such as, for example:

1. Those that require skill.

2. Those that require nothing but strength, endurance, and speed.

Those that require skill should be divided into several classes, according to the amount of skill required; those that chiefly require skill should be handled by mechanics, and those that chiefly require strength, endurance, and speed should be handled by specially trained laborers. This is the only way to enable brickwork to compete with concrete, when all of the architects, engineers, owners, and contractors shall have learned the full possibilities of concrete.

It will be urged that such division of the work of bricklaying will lower the general skill of the bricklayers as a class. Far from it! All operations requiring skill will remain in the hands of the bricklayer, who, escaping all work that unskilled hands could do, will have the more time and energy to devote to the "art" element of his work.

But we are not at this time discussing "brickwork as a lost art"— we cite bricklaying here as an example of the cost of motions, the result of the effects of cost of motions, and of the possibilities and importance of motion study as a method of attack in cost reducing and in standardizing the trades for the greatest possible economy.

What greater service can the bricklayer do both his trade and the people who own or occupy houses than to reduce the cost of the motions in brickwork without reducing his own wages or increasing his hours?

The elimination of wastes is the problem that has been forced to the attention of the entire world to-day, and of America particularly. The elimination of wastes in the trades offers the largest field for savings.

Every trade must be reclassified, and must have the brawn motions separated from the skill motions. Scientific division of the work to be done is as sure to result in higher wages and lower production costs as did F. W. Taylor's separating the planning from the performing.

The reason that our country is not astounded and confused at the appalling unnecessary loss to its inhabitants on account of unnecessary, wasteful, and improper motions of its workers is due to ignorance of the existence of this loss, and to ignorance of any method of eliminating it.

The loss due to the present classification of the trades alone is probably more than sufficient to pension, under full pay, one-half of the workers of the country; is certainly enough to enable all of the women and children in the trades to remain out of the trades and be paid at their regular wages.

While such action is not even recommended, the illustration is used to emphasize the enormous waste going on daily and yearly.

That we go on year after year submitting to this waste because our present trades are handled in accordance with ancient conditions entirely out of place in our present civilization, is no longer necessary and without excuse.

Let the government call its scientific managerial experts together and make a test of one trade, reclassify it, and publish the data. The object lesson thus presented will cause to be taken the necessary further steps to remedy the present system of handling the trades. The workers will each be able to earn higher wages when the unions see that they are benefited, and the labor interests will coöperate. The cost of living will be reduced as by no other means, and all this by scientifically reclassifying the trades!

DIRECTION

In most cases, the direction of a motion that is most economical is the one that utilizes gravitation the most.

Oftentimes delivering material to a high-priced workman by leaving the material in a high position also makes easy unloading for the low-priced workman.

Example.—Stacking up packs 2 feet high saves motions, and saves stooping when the laborer unloads his trucket. [Fig. 21 omitted.]

"Direction" admirably serves as an illustration of the close interrelation of the variables. It is closely connected with "path." It involves discussions of anatomy, acceleration, and speed. It demands consideration of all variables of surroundings, equipment, and tools.

The best "direction of motion" is not only important in itself for increase of output; it must also be kept constantly in mind in standardizing the placing of both materials and men.

EFFECTIVENESS

Effectiveness has been touched upon in discussing "combination with other motions."

An effective motion is one that produces the desired result. Oftentimes whole processes, methods, and operations can be so changed as to make the succeeding motions much more effective.

Example.—The introduction of the fountain trowel, used in connection with an ordinary trowel, made each motion in handling mortar much more effective. [Figs. 19 and 22 omitted.]

FOOT-POUNDS OF WORK ACCOMPLISHED

After all, a human being or a work animal is a power plant, and is subject to nearly all the laws that govern and limit the power plant.

It is a law of motion study that, other things being equal, the less number of foot-pounds of work done by the workman, the smaller percentage of working hours he must devote to rest to overcome fatigue.

It is therefore of great importance in obtaining the largest possible output that the work shall be so arranged and the workman so placed that he can do his work with the least possible amount of foot-pounds of work done per unit of output accomplished. This is where the philanthropic employer has often been rewarded without knowing it. In his desire to make conditions such that the workman was most comfortable while working, he reduced the number of foot-pounds of work to that which was absolutely necessary to do the work. He surrounded the workman with conditions that enabled him to have no fatigue, except that which was acquired from the motions of the work itself. He made conditions such that the workman was enabled to overcome the fatigue from his motions in the quickest possible time. [Fig. 23 omitted.]

INERTIA AND MOMENTUM OVERCOME

There are two ways by which the amount of inertia and momentum may be reduced.

1. By standardizing surroundings and equipment so that the inertia and the momentum are limited to practically that of the materials, and not the materials plus arms and body.

Example.—Picking up ninety pounds of brick at one lifting.

2. By so standardizing motions that as few starts and stops as possible occur from the time the material leaves the stock pile till the time it is in its final resting place in the work.

Example.—In laying brick by the "pick-and-dip" method on face tiers, a brick is lifted in one hand and a trowel full of mortar in the other. The brick must come to a full stop in the bricklayer's hand while the mortar is being laid and the bed prepared, and then move to its final resting place, unless brick and mortar are dropped in two different places.

In laying brick by the "stringing-mortar" method, the mortar is laid and the bed prepared before the bricks are lifted. The brick are conveyed from the pack to the wall without interruption or delay.

Standard methods of performing work may enable the worker to utilize the momentum.

Example.—If the bricks are conveyed from the stock platform or pack to the wall *with no stops,* the momentum can be made to do valuable work by assisting to shove the joints full of mortar. If, instead of being utilized, the momentum must be overcome by the muscles of the bricklayer fatigue, not full joints, will result.

The ideal case is to move the brick in a straight path and make the contact with the wall overcome the momentum.

LENGTH

A general rule of motion economy is to make the shortest motions possible.

Eliminating unnecessary distances that workers' hands and arms must travel, will eliminate miles of motions per man in a working day as compared with usual practice.

Example.—Put the wheelbarrow body as close as possible to the pile that is to be put into it, so that the distance the packets are carried from the pile to the barrow, or the sand from the pile to the barrow, will be the shortest distance possible.

Of the necessary distance to be walked or reached, have as much of it as possible done by the low-priced man, and have as little of it as possible done by the high-priced man.

Example.—With bricks, have the tender put the pack of brick as near the final resting place of the brick as conditions will permit, so that when the high-priced man picks up a pack of, say, eighteen bricks, he requires a short motion only.

Have the high-priced worker always use first the stock that is nearest, this rule requiring the shortest motions in conveying the stock to its final resting place.

Example.—In picking up brick from a packet or a scaffold the nearest brick should be picked up first. The brick that are farthest away serve as a reserve stock pile, to be picked up only in the emergency of not having any others nearer to pick up. It may be that the brick farthest away may not need to be used on that piece of work at all, or at least their place will not be occupied so many times by bricks to be transported with longer motions.

Standard tools, equipment, and surroundings are essential if length of motions is to be made standard.

As already said when discussing clothes, the workman of the present should have even his overalls, belt, and clothes so designed that they will hold the different kinds of tools that are oftenest used, so that they may be picked up in the shortest time—that is, with pockets for nails, clips, clamps, etc. The tools should be so placed that the least and shortest motions can be used after they are picked up, as cartridges are placed in a cartridge belt.

NECESSITY

The necessity of the motion is such an important variable that an investigator is tempted at first glance to divide all motions into necessary and unnecessary, and to eliminate with one stroke those that appear to him unnecessary. A more thorough investigation will be apt to prove that no such summary elimination is advisable.

A motion may be unnecessary motion in a necessary sequence, or it may be a necessary motion in a certain sequence, but the whole sequence may be unnecessary or inadvisable.

Example.—In opening a paper bag of cement the average untrained laborer usually cuts the bag in two and removes the paper in several pieces and with many motions. The correct way is to cut the bottom with a shovel and pull the bag upward in one piece by grasping the bag just above the string.

This example shows both how motions may be unnecessary in themselves and how they may belong to a sequence that is unnecessary.

The only final solution as to the necessity of a motion will come when the trades are completely standardized. It is impossible to determine whether or not a motion is absolutely necessary until the method of doing the work in which it is used is standard.

Examples.—1. Motions which were relatively proved necessary in laying brick by the "pick-and-dip" method or "stringing-mortar" method, the brick being lifted from the stock platform, became absolutely unnecessary when the "packet-on-the-wall" method of handling brick was adopted.

2. The same thing is true of motions eliminated by handling mortar in a fountain trowel.

The final solution of the problem of necessity of motions will be discussed later, though the subject is so large that no amount of discussion could do more than touch it.

PATH

The determination of the path which will result in the greatest economy of motion and the greatest increase of output is a subject for the closest investigation and the most scientific determination.

Not until data are accumulated by trained observers can standard paths be adopted. The laws underlying physics, physiology, and psychology must be considered and followed. In the meantime, merely applying the results of observation will reduce motions and costs and increase output to an amazing degree.

The path most desirable is usually that which permits gravitation to assist in carrying the material to place.

Example.—We have found that the most economical height for laying brick is twenty-four inches above where the bricklayer stands, while it is most economical to pick the brick from a height about three feet above where the bricklayer stands; that is, about one foot higher than the top of the wall where the brick is to be laid.

The path is affected by the direction that the material is to be shoved as it moves into its final resting place.

Examples.—When the packet is placed on the wall it should be placed so that the brick can be picked up and moved in a comparatively straight line with the direction that the brick will be shoved for filling a joint.

In theory the ideal path would be in a line of quickest speed from the stock platform to the wall.

In practice it is seldom that the most economical path for carrying a brick or mortar from the stock platform to the wall is exactly a straight line from one to the other. It will generally be most economical to move the brick in the path that will bend the arms the least and that will permit almost a swing from the shoulder.

PLAYING FOR POSITION

Each motion should be made so as to be most economically combined with the next motion, like the billiard player who plays for position.

The direction in which a motion is made may affect the time required for a subsequent motion.

Example.—In laying brick the motion of placing the mortar for the end joint can be done the quickest if it is done in the direction of the next motion, such, for example, as the next motion that puts the trowel in the position to cut off the hanging mortar.

The sequence of motions in bricklaying, that determines when the particular motion is to be made that puts the mortar in the end joint, depends upon whether the "pick-and-dip" or the "stringing-mortar" method is used.

When the motions are made in the correct sequence, many of them can be combined so that two, and in some cases three, motions can be made as one motion, in but little more time than is required for one motion.

Example.—Cutting off mortar, buttering the end of the laid brick, and reaching for more mortar all as one motion, in the "pick-and-dip" method.

SPEED

Usually, the faster the motions, the more output. There are other advantages to speed of motions besides the fact that they require less time. Speed increases momentum, and this momentum may be utilized to do work.

Example.—The momentum of the brick helps to shove the mortar better into the joint.

Again, high outputs are generally the result of the habit of speed in motions. Habits of speed are hard to form, and they are hard to break.

Next to fewest motions, speed of motions is the most important factor of high record of outputs.

The list of variables here given makes no claim to being complete. The field of study is so immense that it is impossible as yet to give a complete and detailed method of attack.

It will be noted in reading the discussion of the variables that it has been found extremely difficult to handle each one separately. It is needless to tell the student, the investigator, the cost-reducing manager, that, difficult as the task is, for the best results each variable must be studied alone. The effects of all variables but one must be eliminated, or, better perhaps, all variables but one must be maintained constant.

Quicker results may often be obtained by studying several variables simultaneously, and for short jobs this may be advisable. But for long jobs of repetitive work there is no way so accurate and satisfactory as studying one variable at a time.

Past, Present, and Future
of Motion Study

WORK ACCOMPLISHED

Considered in relation to the time during which it has been applied to the trades, scientific motion study can show most satisfactory results.

The workers in the field as well as in the office have been quick to appreciate and adopt the new methods suggested by motion economy.

This has been especially the case in the crafts. Nearly every proficient workman loves his trade. He loves the joy of achievement. He can achieve most when useless motions have been eliminated for him, and he welcomes improvements, as the bricklayers have welcomed the brick coming right side up on the packet.

MAGNITUDE OF WORK TO BE DONE

To the casual reader it may seem that the task of evolving standard practice from usual present practice, and from the best practice, is simply a case of observing, recording, and eliminating. The student will see that it requires the closest concentration to do even the necessary scientific observing and recording, while to deduce and systematize standard motions for any one trade would furnish a life work for several trained scientists.

It is a difficult task for an inexperienced or untrained observer to divide an operation correctly into its motions. Enumerating the variables that affect each motion is a task big enough to satisfy the most ambitious student of waste elimination.

VALUE OF CHARTS

We have found it helpful in recording our observations to use charts. Some such form as that shown [in the accompanying chart is used. EDITOR's NOTE: This chart is now reproduced as chart 1 on pages 56–57 of the present book].

195

This chart is one made during an observation of bricklaying before the invention of the packet, the packet scaffold, and the fountain trowel.

The operation of laying a brick was divided into the motions of which it consisted (column 1). The usual (present) practice of the time (given as "the wrong way," column 2) showed the units into which the operation was divided. The best practice of the time ("the right way," column 3, now obsolete) was charted in such a way that its relation *from a motion standpoint* to the usual practice was clearly shown.

Column 4 shows how the usual practice may be transformed into the best practice. It would serve as an instruction card to the workman, showing him not only where his method needed to be improved but also exactly how to improve it.

This chart, together with a plan showing the workman where he should put the stock and where he should place his feet (Fig. 14 [p. 163]), and with pictures showing how he should lay the brick, etc., proved most successful for instruction as well as for recording.

At first glance this chart, and the others like it, which we used at that time, seem very crude. In fact, compared to what has since been done to standardize operations, they *are* crude. But they mark a distinct phase of motion study. They show plainly, as careful reading will prove, that an earnest study of motions will automatically promote the growth of the study.

For example, study of column 4 in the sample chart given led to the invention of the packet scaffold, the packet, the fountain trowel, and several other of the best devices, and the "packet-on-the-wall" method now used in brickwork.

These inventions in their turn necessitated an entirely new set of motions to perform the operation of laying a brick.

So, likewise, the progression also went on before the days of conscious motion study: observation, explanation, invention, elimination, and again observation, in an upward helix of progress.

The great point to be observed is this: Once the variables of motions are determined, and the laws of underlying motions and their efficiency deduced, conformity to these laws will result in standard motions, standard tools, standard conditions, and standard methods of performing the operations of the trades.

Conformity to these laws allows standard practice to be attained and used. If the standard methods are deduced before the equipment, tools, surroundings, etc., are standardized, the invention of these standard means is as sure as the appearance of a celestial body at the time and place where mathematics predicts that it will appear.

It is as well to recognize first as last that real progress from the best present method to the standard method can never be made solely by elimination. The sooner this is recognized the better. Elimination is often an admirable makeshift. But the only real progress comes through a reconstruction of the operation, building it up of standardized units, or elements.

It is also well to recognize the absolute necessity of the trained scientific investigator. The worker cannot, by himself, arrange to do his work in the most economical manner in accordance with the laws of motion study. Oftentimes, in fact nearly always, the worker will believe that the new method takes longer than the old method. At least he will be positive that many parts, or elements, of the process when done under the new method take longer than under the old style, and will not be in sympathy with the scheme because he is sure that the new way is not so efficient as his old way. All of which shows that the worker himself cannot tell which are the most advantageous motions. He must judge by the fatigue that he feels, or else by the quantity of output accomplished in a given time. To judge by the quantity of output accomplished in a given time is more of a test of effort than a test of motion study, and oftentimes that element that will produce the most output is the one that will cause the least fatigue.

The difference in amount of merit between any two methods can perhaps be best determined by timing the elements of the motions used in each. This is the method of attack usually accepted as best, because it separates each motion into its variables and analyzes them one at a time. It is out of the question to expect a workman to do such timing and to do his work at the same time. Furthermore, it is an art in itself to take time-study observations, an art that probably takes longer to master than does shorthand, typewriting, telegraphy, or drafting.

Few workers have had an opportunity to learn the art of making and using time-study observations, because our school educators have not had any mental grasp of the subject themselves. Add to the difficulties to be overcome in acquiring the knowledge of observing, recording, and analyzing the time-study records, the knowledge necessary to build up synthetically the correct method with each element strictly in accordance with the laws of motion economy each by itself and when used together in the particular determined sequence, and you will see the reason why the worker by himself has not devised, cannot, and never will be expected to devise, the ultimate method of output. It does not then, after all, seem so queer that the workman's output can always be doubled and oftentimes more than tripled by scientific motion study. Again, scientifically attained methods only can become ultimate methods.

Any method which seems after careful study to have attained perfection, using absolutely the least number of most effective, shortest motions, may be thrown aside when a new way of transporting or placing material or men is introduced. It is pitiful to think of the time, money, strength, and brains that have been wasted on devising and using wonderfully clever but not fundamentally derived methods of doing work, which must inevitably be discarded for the latter.

The standardizing of the trades will utilize every atom of such heretofore wasted energy.

The standardizing of the trades affords a definite best method of doing each element.

Having but one standard method of doing each element divides the amount of time-study data necessary to take by a number equal to the number of different equally good methods that could be used.

The greatest step forward can be made only when time-study data can be made by one and used by all. A system of interchange and co-operation in the use of the data of scientific management can then be used by all persons interested.

This reduction and simplification of taking time study is the real reason for insistence upon making and maintaining standards for the largest down to the smallest insignificant tool or device used.

Much toward standardizing the trades has already been done. In this, as in almost countless other lines of activity, the investigator turns oftenest with admiration to the work of Frederick W. Taylor. It is the never-ceasing marvel concerning this man that age cannot wither nor custom stale his work. After many a weary day's study the investigator awakes from a dream of greatness to find that he has only worked out a new proof for a problem that Taylor has already solved.

Time study, the instruction card, functional foremanship, the differential rate piece method of compensation, and numerous other scientifically derived methods of decreasing costs and increasing output and wages—these are by no means his only contributions toward standardizing the trades whose value it would be difficult to overestimate; they are but a few of the means toward attaining standards which have been placed by Taylor, their discoverer, within the hands of any man willing to use them.

FUTURE WORK IN STANDARDIZING THE TRADES

The great need to-day in standardizing the trades is for coöperation. In other times all excellent methods or means were held as "trade secrets," sometimes lost to the world for generations until rediscovered. The day for this is past. Thinkers of to-day recognize that the work to be done is so great that, given all that every one has accomplished and is accomplishing, there is room and to spare for every worker who cares to enter the field. Coöperation and team work is the crying need.

Conservation and comparison of knowledge, experiments, data and conclusions are what we need. The various engineering journals are to be commended for recognizing the importance of this, and for furnishing an excellent means for recording and spreading much needed information.

The ideal conservator of knowledge in this, as in all other branches, would be the United States government. The government should maintain a permanent bureau, with experiment stations, as is done with the Department of Agriculture.

Individual investigators, corporations, and colleges, all would be willing to turn over the results of their work to such a government bureau. The colleges would coöperate with such a bureau, as do the agricultural colleges with the Department of Agriculture. The bulletins of such a bureau would be invaluable to the men in the trades, as are the agricultural bulletins to the farmers.

The Department of Agriculture is an excellent model. The form for a department or bureau of trades is all at hand. It is only necessary to translate the language of agriculture into the language of labor. It is only through such a bureau that the trades can formally be standardized.

Such a bureau would have two main tasks: (1) To subclassify the trades; (2) To standardize the trades.

The first task should be successfully completed before the second is undertaken.

We have spoken briefly, in considering cost of motions, of the necessity of separating those motions that require skill from those that require nothing but strength and endurance.

This sub-classifying of the trades according to the types or grades of motions that they use, or according to the brawn, brain, training, and skill required to make the motions, will cut down production costs. It will raise the standards of all classes. It will do away with differences between employers and employees. It will eliminate unnecessary waste. It will raise the wages of all workers. It will reduce the cost of living.

We might call such a sub-classification as desired a "functional" classification of the trades.

For example, for brickwork we recommend five classes:

Class A.—Ornamental and exterior face brick and molded terra cotta.

Class B.—Interior face tiers that do not show at completion, where strong, plumb, and straight work only is needed.

Class C.—Filling tiers where only strength is needed.

Class D.—Putting fountain trowels and brick packs on the wall near the place, and in the manner where the other three classes can reach them with greatest economy of motion.

Class E.—Pack loaders, brick cullers, and stage builders.

The pay of the A and B classes should be considerably higher than is customary for bricklayers. The pay of the C, D, and E classes should be lower than is customary for bricklayers, but much higher than the pay of laborers. This classification will raise the pay of all five classes higher than they could ever obtain in the classes that they would ordinarily work in under the present system, yet the resulting cost of the labor on brickwork would be much less, and each class would be raised in its standing and educated for better work and higher wages.

In the case of brickwork this new classification is a crying necessity, as the cost of brickwork must be reduced to a point where it can compete with concrete. Improvements in making, methods of mixing, transporting, and densifying concrete in the metal molds of to-day have put the entire brickwork proposition where it can be used for looks only, because for strength, imperviousness, quickness of construction, lack of union labor troubles, and low cost, brickwork cannot compete with concrete under present conditions.

Having sub-classified the trades, the second step is to standardize them.

And both classification and standardization demand motion study.

The United States government has already spent millions and used many of the best of minds on the subject of motion study as applied to war; the motions of the sword, gun, and bayonet drill are wonderfully perfect from the standpoint of the requirements of their use. This same study should be applied to the arts of peace.

It is obvious that this work must and will be done in time. But there is inestimable loss in every hour of delay. The waste of energy of the workers in the industries to-day is pitiful. But it is far more important that the coming generation of workers should be scientifically trained.

The science of management of the future will demand that the trades be taught in accordance with the motion standards of a United States Bureau of Standardization of Mechanical Trades. The present method of teaching an apprentice is the most unbusinesslike event that takes place in any of our industrial institutions.

We have never heard of a trades school, manual training school, or technical school that makes any attempt to solve questions of motion study. The usual process is to teach a student or apprentice to do his work well first, and after he has finally accomplished the art of making or doing the thing in question, then to expect him to learn to do it quickly. This process is a relic of the dark ages. A novice should be taught to do what he is trying to do with certain definite motions, and to repeat the operation until he is able automatically to use the standard motions and do good work.

If an apprentice bricklayer, blacksmith, or tool sharpener, for example, is not instructed to count his motions when doing a certain piece of work, he will surely get into the habit of making extra motions that cannot be omitted later without almost as much effort as that spent in learning the trade. There is little incentive for an old mechanic to teach a boy so that he will excel his teacher, and perhaps run him out of a job about the time that he, the apprentice, becomes expert.

One of the most common causes for neglecting the important subject of motion study is that the boss of the establishment is not himself really a master of the trade that is being taught, or, if he was master once, has forgotten it because there are no books or systems that have so described, charted, and illustrated his trade as to refresh his memory.

Again the teacher is often a mechanic who is not trained to impart what knowledge he has, has never studied pedagogy, and is expected to do a full day's work at the same time that he is teaching his apprentice.

The arts and trades of human beings should be studied, charted, photographed, and motion-pictured, and every employer, apprentice, and student should be able to receive bulletins of his trade for a sum equal to the cost to a farmer of a bulletin from the Department of Agriculture instructing how to increase the outputs of cows, hens, and bees.

One great aid toward cutting down the work of every one out of the trades as well as in, would be the standardizing of our written alphabet to conform to the laws of motion study. The most offhand analysis of our written alphabet shows that it is full of absolutely useless strokes, all of which require what are really wasted motions.

Consider the single example of the first stroke on the first letter of each word. Here is a motion that can be eliminated wholly. While its existence is necessary in type that represents handwriting or imitates engraved plate work, and in enameled separate letters of window signs, its adoption and use in handwriting is of no purpose and is wrong from the standpoint of motion economy.

Each letter of our written alphabet is a natural deviation from our printed alphabet that is the result of leaving the pencil on the paper.

Now the time has arrived for revising our written language by means of a new scientifically invented alphabet specially devised for the purpose of securing clearer writing, made of connected letters, each designed of itself and in connection with all the other letters, so that it conforms to the laws of motion economy. This is not a suggestion that we should adopt stenographic signs for words or sounds, although a general knowledge of one standard stenographic system would also be a great benefit to a nation.

The suggestion is, that in as much as it is the aim of our nation that all citizens should be able to read and write, a new written alphabet should be devised for us that shall conform to the laws of motion study,—that we all can increase either our outputs in writing or else that we all may be able to do such writing as we are obliged to do in less time.

It is to be hoped that an international society of highly trained educators, similar to those composing the Simplified Spelling Board, may be called together, as was the Simplified Spelling Board, to give this matter immediate attention. A written alphabet for all languages of the world should be determined and used not only by the users of each language, but also by the societies advocating and promulgating such world's second or international languages as Volapük and Esperanto.

One great drawback to the more rapid progress of any artificial or second language has been the difficulty of reading the correspondence between enthusiasts who were proficient in speaking their thoroughly agreed upon international language.

It would not be desirable to abandon our present written alphabet. There are now literally hundreds of different styles of lettering that all can read, yet how few of them can any of us make with pen or pencil.

To add one more style of lettering to the now existing hundreds could scarcely be considered as confusing by even those who are constitutionally opposed to changes in anything.

Therefore, there should be devised one more style of lettering, specially adapted to cutting down the time of writing and adding to the general legibility when written quickly.

Let this be our second written language. Let us use the present system and the new one. Let the generations to come have the benefit of the application of science to their future writing, and let the present style be also used, provided it does not die the natural death in the combat of the survival of the fittest.

We may have to wait for international coinage, international postage stamps, international courts, international arbitration, and international weights and measures; but there can be no reason for not having an international system of written alphabetical characters, and while having it let us decide in favor of that system that fulfills the requirements of motion study, both of the hand in making, and of the eye in reading.

THE FIRST STEPS

In the meantime, while we are waiting for the politicians and educators to realize the importance of this subject and to create the bureaus and societies to undertake and complete the work, we need not be idle. There is work in abundance to be done.

Motion study must be applied to all the industries. Our trade schools and colleges can:

1. Observe the best work of the best workers.
2. Photograph the methods used.

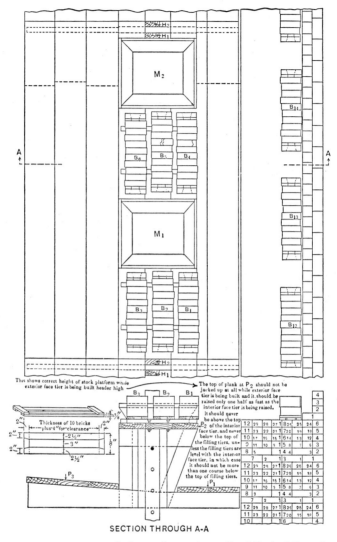

SECTION THROUGH A-A

Fig. 43. Location of the pack on the wall while building the exterior face tiers. Pack-on-the-wall method.

3. Record the methods used.

4. Record outputs.

5. Record costs.

6. Deduce laws.

7. Establish laboratories "for trying out laws."

8. Embody laws in instructions.

9. Publish bulletins.

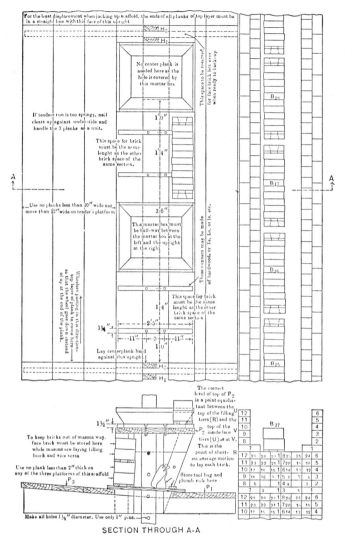

FIG. 44. Location of the packs while building the interior face and filling tiers. Pack-on-the-wall method.

10. Coöperate to spread results and to train the rising generation. This is the era—*now*. We have a scientific method of attack, and we have also scientific methods of teaching.

The stereoscopic camera and stereoscope, the motion picture machines, and the stereopticon enable us to observe, record, and teach as one never could in the past.

The following motion study pictures, [Figs. 24–42 omitted] charts, [see Chart 4, p. 61] and diagrams [Figs. 43 and 44, pp. 204–5] are typical and have been used for teaching journeymen and apprentice bricklayers our standard methods.

The economic value of motion study has been proved by the fact that by means of it workmen's outputs have been more than tripled, production costs lowered, and wages increased simultaneously.

This book is written for the express purpose of calling to the attention of the nation that what has been done in a few trades can be done in each and every trade.

The most important matter before the public to-day is the creation and operation of a department at Washington for discovering, collecting, conserving and disseminating data relating to Taylor's method of Intensive Management commonly called Scientific Management.

6

APPLIED

MOTION

STUDY*

* *Applied Motion Study*, by Frank B. and Lillian M. Gilbreth, was published by Sturgis and Walton Co., New York, in 1917. All of the seventeen illustrations of the original have been omitted.

Preface

●●

This book aims—

1. To describe Motion Study as applied to various fields of activity.
2. To outline the principles and practice of Motion Study in such a way as to make possible its application in any and all kinds of work.

Motion Study is a means to permanent and practical waste elimination,—hence a prerequisite to efficient preparedness that shall be adequate, constructive and cumulative.

Foreword

●●

This book aims to present in outline

1. The field where motion study has been and can be applied.
2. The methods by which it is applied.
3. The effects of the application.

It shows the results of actual practice in waste elimination. It enumerates past savings, and points out present and future possible savings.

It is offered as a contribution to the solution of the great national problem of "Preparedness."

Introduction

••

Blessed is the man who makes two blades of grass grow where only one grew before. More blessed is he who multiplies the harvests of toil not merely two-fold, but three-fold or more-fold, for he vitrually lengthens life when he adds to its fruitage. Such a man is Frank B. Gilbreth who tells in this book just how he wrought this wonder. For years he has closely watched workers at tasks of all kinds; he has discovered how much they lose by moving unprofitably hither and thither, by neglecting to take the shortest and easiest paths. In the ancient trade of bricklaying he has increased the output almost four-fold by doing only what must be done, and using a few simple devices of his own invention. In this volume Mr. Gilbreth describes and pictures the simple photographic process which enables one to record in detail the motions of a handicraft, or a manufacture, so as to bring them by criticism and experiment to their utmost economy of energy and time. When once the best practice is reached in any particular field of work Gilbreth motion-pictures make it easy to repeat that practice anywhere and at any time.

This most fertile means of record and of teaching enters the world of industry at an opportune moment. War to-day is destroying wealth at a rate beyond computation. National debts are mounting billion upon billion, entailing burdens of taxation such as mankind never faced before. Mr. Gilbreth meets this dire emergency with a readily applied method of increasing the results of toil, of reducing all waste of human exertion to its minimum. Not the least telling branch of his activity is in extending aid and comfort to maimed soldiers. He opens a door of hope, because a door of usefulness, to the thousands of brave men who have lost their limbs, their sight, or their hearing, on fields of battle.

His pages teem with suggestive facts: take, for example, his discovery that the best way to perform a task unites the methods of several dexterous and original operators. Again we are shown that wisdom

210

rests not even with the most gifted man, but appears only when men of the rarest ability join hands. Another point: our author has found that learners should strive first for Quickness; when speed is acquired they can best pass to good quality in their work. The levy paid for Dawdling is plainly beyond all estimate. A third point: Mr. Gilbreth argues that to repeat a task should not mean monotony. Let a task be fully studied, let all its possibilities be brought into view, and the operator will be too keenly interested to complain of "monotony."

This is a book written from the heart as well as from the brain. Its good will is as evident as its good sense. Frank B. Gilbreth is a versatile Engineer, an untiring observer, an ingenious inventor, an economist to the tips of his fingers: first and chiefly he is a man. To his wife, co-author with him, this book owes much. Every page has taken form with the aid and counsel of Mrs. Gilbreth, whose "Psychology of Management" is a golden gift to industrial philosophy. And thus, by viewing their facts from two distinct angles we learn how vital phases of industrial economy present themselves to a man and to a woman who are among the acutest investigators of our time.

GEORGE ILES.

New York, June 14, 1917.

What Scientific Management Means to America's Industrial Position[1]

●●●

There is some confusion to-day as to the meaning of scientific management. This concerns itself with the nature of such management itself, with the scope or field to which such management applies, and with the aims that it desires to attain. Scientific management is simply management that is based upon actual measurement. Its skilful ap-

[1] Reprinted from "The Annals" of the American Academy of Political and Social Science, Publication No. 935.

plication is an art that must be acquired, but its fundamental principles have the exactness of scientific laws which are open to study by every one. We have here nothing hidden or occult or secret, like the working practices of an old-time craft; we have here a science that is the result of accurately recorded, exact investigation. Its results are formulated, or are being formulated, into such shape that they may be utilised by all who have the desire to study them and the concentration to master them. The leaders in the field are, as rapidly as possible, publishing these results, that progress may take place from the stage of highest present achievement, and that no time or effort may be wasted in remaking investigations whose results are already known and accurately recorded. The scope of this management, which may truly be called scientific, is unlimited. It applies to all fields of activity, mental and physical. Its laws are universal, and, to be of use in any particular field, require only to be translated into the vocabulary of the trained and progressive workers in that field.

The greatest misunderstandings occur as to the aims of scientific management. Its fundamental aim is the elimination of waste, the attainment of worth-while desired results with the least necessary amount of time and effort. Scientific management may, and often does, result in expansion, but its primary aim is conservation and savings, making an adequate use of every ounce of energy of any type that is expended.

Scientific management, then, in attacking any problem has in mind the question—How may what is here available be best used? It considers the problem, in every case, according to the scientific method; that is, by dividing it into its elements and submitting each one of these to detailed study. Every problem presents two elements: the human element, and the materials element. By the materials element we mean the type of material used, the quality of material used, the quantity of material used, the manner in which the material is used, with conclusions as to why the material is chosen and handled as it is. In other words, we would apply to the material the familiar questions, what, how much, how, when, where, and why. These same questions are applied to the human element; that is to say, to all members of the organisation.

Having in mind now the principles and practice of scientific management, we can consider its relation to the industrial position of any country. Industrial growth, like all other growth, consists of progress and maintenance; that is, of advances over and beyond present achievement and of making adequate provision for holding any advantage that one may gain. It is generally realised that maintenance contains always the thought of conservation, that it is impossible to hold any advantage without making careful provision for using one's resources in the best possible manner. It is not so generally realised that progress also implies constantly this same conservation. The reason for this is the result of a confusion between saving, or conserving, and hoarding. True conservation contains no thought of miserliness or niggardliness. It is based upon a broad outlook on life and upon the needs of the situation, upon a willingness to pay the full, just price for what is wanted, but an unwillingness to pay any more than is necessary. Progress differs from lack of progress, fundamentally, not because the progressive man is willing to pay more than the unprogressive man will, but because the progressive man has a broader outlook and a keener insight, hence, a more adequate knowledge of where and when it is necessary to pay. The unprogressive man or nation suffers from a limited outlook that makes it practically impossible to make a just estimate as to what is worth while.

When we compare the various countries of the world, and try to estimate their relative industrial positions, we find a strong relationship between conservation in its highest sense and industrial supremacy. Again, as we turn to history, we find this same relationship constantly manifesting itself; that is, progress depending upon an ability to see what is worth-while, and a willingness to pay for that and that only, and stability or maintenance depending upon an efficient handling of available resources.

As we review history, and observe present conditions, we see that the differences between various countries are becoming less and less, as time goes on. Transportation, with its numerous by-products that affect both the material and the human element, is increasing the likeness between different countries at an astounding rate. This means that industrial supremacy will depend more and more upon the handling of available resources and less and less upon distinctive features in these resources themselves. The calamitous war, which is now apparently offering such a serious check to industrial progress, is contributing toward ultimately making working conditions more similar, in that many countries are being thrown upon their own resources for both materials and men, and are being forced to make discoveries that will more nearly equalise these resources.

Another outcome of this war, that should prove of advantage to the world, is the emphasis that is being laid upon the causes of industrial position and industrial supremacy and the resulting study that is being made as to the reasons for such supremacy. Such a study should be particularly profitable here in America. This country has always "conceded" her important industrial position. She has realised thoroughly her enormous natural resources and also her wonderful human resources in that she is "the melting pot of the nations." It is only within the lifetime of those still young among us that we have come to realise the necessity of conserving our natural resources. It has not yet reached the attention of many among us that our human resources are as worthy, in fact, infinitely more worthy, of being conserved.

It is self-evident, then, that to attain and maintain an industrial position of which she may be proud, America must conserve both her natural and her human resources. If she hopes for industrial supremacy, she must set about this conservation with energy, and must pursue it unremittently.

The writers have a thorough knowledge of European industrial conditions, through having done business simultaneously in this country and abroad for many years, through frequent trips abroad before the war, through having crossed the boundaries of many of the warring countries many times since the outbreak of the war, and through having observed carefully industrial conditions and methods. Their opinion, which is that of all who have made intensive studies of these conditions, is that America is far behind European countries in conservation of the materials element, both natural and manufactured resources. This statement needs no proof in this place. The fact it contains is universally accepted by serious thinkers and investigators. It is equally true that up to recent times European countries have done comparatively little toward conserving the human element.

The hope of this country lies, then, in equalling or surpassing foreign conservation of material and in maintaining or progressing beyond our present conservation of the human element. The material problem is being attacked along different lines in a more or less systematic manner. We all appreciate the benefits of scientific or intensive farming, until now our native farmers, working under the direction of and with the co-operation of the Department of Agriculture, get results that equal those of European farmers, in their native lands, or here in ours. The importance of laboratory analysis of materials and the help that applied science can render and is more and more rendering to the industries are also being recognised. Agricultural experience has taught the valuable lesson that it is possible to get great output, yet, at the same time, leave the producing force unimpaired, by a proper expenditure of money and brains. Experience with applied science has taught that by-products, as well as products, must be considered, and that the exact methods of science often bring results that are beyond those looked for or hoped for. It has been common practice to consider a transaction satisfactory, or better, if it fulfilled one's expectations, to lay emphasis upon the result rather than to standardise the means or method. Laboratory practice has taught that while the immediate results are important, the standardisation of the method is more important, since the unexpected ultimate results, sometimes called by-products, are often by far the most valuable outcome of the work. Certain industries in this country have gone far toward applying scientific methods to the material element, but no one of us need go outside his own experience to be able to mention other industries that as yet have no conception of what such work means.

Much has been done not only in the analysis of materials, but also with the handling of materials. America has cause to be proud of her machines and her tools. The chief criticism that we may make of present practice in this field is that of lack of standardisation. The reasons for this are many. One is business competition, though the feeling is gradually dying out that making one's product markedly different from that of all others is a strong selling advantage. Another is the strong feeling of independence and individuality that leads one to prefer a thing because it is different rather than because it is adequate to the purpose for which it is needed. A third is a lack of channels for direct and easy communication of ideas. This is being supplied both through organisations and publications. A fourth is the former lack of standardising bodies or bureaus, a lack which is also being supplied as the demand for such bodies increases.

Because of the highly specialised nature of much present-day work, few of us realise how widespread, almost universal, the lack of standardisation is. It is only necessary to turn, however, to such a field of activity as surgery, which engages the attention of some of the finest brains in the country, and which is apt to come, sooner or later in some way, into the field of experience of every one, to see a striking object lesson of lack of standardisation both of tools and of method.

It is the work of scientific management to insist on standardisation in all fields, and to base such standardisation upon accurate measurement. Scientific management is not remote, or different from other fields of activity. For example, in the handling of the materials element, it does not attempt to discard the methods of attack of intensive agriculture or of the laboratory of the applied scientists; on the contrary, it uses the results of workers in such fields as these to as great an extent as possible.

There is a widespread feeling that scientific management claims to be something new, with methods that are different from those used by other conserving activities. This is not at all the case. It is the boast of scientific management that it gathers together the results and methods of all conserving activities, formulates these into a working practice, and broadens their field of application. In handling the materials element, then, scientific management analyses all successful existing practices in every line, and synthesises such elements as accurate measurement proves to be valuable into standards. These standards are maintained until suggested improvements have passed the same rigid examination, and are in such form that they may be incorporated into new standards.

Turning now to the field of the human element—by far the more important field—we find that, while there is much talk of work in that field to-day, comparatively little has actually been accomplished. There have, in all places and times, been more or less spasmodic and unsystematic attempts to conserve human energy, or to use it for the greatest benefit of all concerned; but there has not been steady and conspicuous progress in this work for several reasons; 1. Because the methods used were not accurately measured and were not standardised. This made it impossible for the individual conserver to accomplish much of lasting benefit. 2. Because of lack of co-operation between such conservers.

It is the task of scientific management to supply both these wants. Success in handling the human element, like success in handling the materials element, depends upon knowledge of the element itself and knowledge as to how it can best be handled. One great work of scientific management has been to show the world how little actual knowledge it has possessed of the human element as engaged in the work in the industries. Through motion study and fatigue study and the accompanying time study, we have come to know the capabilities of the worker, the demands of the work, the fatigue that the worker suffers at the work, and the amount and nature of the rest required to overcome the fatigue.

Those not actively interested in the industries can scarcely realise that the process of keeping the soil at its full producing capacity and of providing depleted energy is infinitely more standardised and more widely used than the process of providing that the human organism overcome fatigue and return to its normal working capacity in the shortest amount of time possible. Scientific provision for such recovery in the industries, before the day of scientific management, was unknown.

It is even more surprising that only the pioneers in the work realise the application of any necessity for the laboratory method in the study of the human element as it appears in the industries. When making accurate measurements, the number of variables involved must be reduced to as great a degree as possible. Only in the laboratory can this be successfully done. It is fortunate for scientific management that its initial introduction in the industries has been made by engineers rather than by men who are primarily laboratory scientists, for this reason: the engineer has been forced by his training to consider constantly immediate as well as ultimate results, and present as well as future savings. Investigations of scientific management have, therefore, been made to pay from the start in money savings, as well as in savings of energy of all kinds. We note this in the results of motion study, fatigue study, and the accompanying time study.

As an example, take the laboratory investigations in motion study. These, where possible, are made by us in the laboratory, which is a room specially set apart in the plant for research purposes. Here the worker to be studied, with the necessary apparatus for doing the work and for measuring the motions, and the observer, investigate the operation under typical laboratory conditions. The product of this is data that are more nearly accurate than could be secured with the distractions and many variables of shop conditions. The by-product of this work, which is a typical by-product of engineer-scientists' work, is that the conditions of performing the operation in the laboratory become a practical working model of what the shop conditions must ultimately be. When the best method of doing the work with the existing apparatus has been determined in the laboratory, the working conditions, as well as the motions that make this result possible, are standardised, and the working conditions in the shop are changed, until they resemble the working conditions in the laboratory. In the same way, the length and periodicity of intervals to be allowed for overcoming fatigue, and the best devices for eliminating unnecessary fatigue and for overcoming necessary fatigue, are determined during the investigation, and are incorporated into shop practice.

The various measurements taken by scientific management and the guiding laws under which these are grouped determine not only the nature of the human element, but the methods by which it is to be handled. Motion study, fatigue study, the measures supplied by psychology,—these result in the working practice that fits the work to the worker, and produces more output with less effort, with its consequent greater pay for every ounce of effort expended.

Through scientific management, then, the individual conserver is enabled to progress constantly and to maintain each successful stage in the development. Scientific management can, also, and does, wherever permitted, provide for co-operation among conservers. It does this by:

1. Demonstrating the enormous waste resulting from needless repetition of the same investigation.
2. Providing standards which must be recognised as worthy of adoption, since they are the results of measurement.
3. Emphasising the importance of teaching and of the transference of skill, which depend upon co-operation.
4. Showing that maintenance depends, in the final analysis, upon co-operation.

We have formulated our programme for such co-operation into the following stages:

1. Each individual to apply scientific management to his own activities, individual and social.
2. Groups, such as industrial organisations, to apply scientific management to the group activity.
3. Trades to apply scientific management to the trade activity. This includes, ultimately, a reclassification and standardization of the trades, such as we have advocated in "Motion Study."[2] The trades must be classified according to the amount of skill involved in the motions used, and must then be standardized in order that the necessary training for succeeding in them can be given.
4. Industries to apply scientific management to the entire industry, with co-operation between the various trades involved.
5. A national bureau of standardization to collect and formulate the data from all the industries into national standards.

[2] D. Van Nostrand Company, New York, pages 94–103 (p. 139 of this book).

6. An international bureau of standardization to collect national standards and to work for international co-operation.

America's immediate industrial position depends upon America's realization of the need for conservation, as demonstrated by scientific management, and upon America's use of such means of conservation as scientific management offers.

America's ultimate industrial position depends upon America's realization that the highest type of conservation includes co-operation.

Individuals, groups, trades, and industries have realized and are realizing more and more, daily, that it is for the good of all that common practice be standardized and that improvements take place from the highest common standard. Nations have not yet come to any great realization that this same principle applies to international relationships.

If America desires to gain and maintain leadership in industrial progress, she must be the advocate of industrial conservation and co-operation, and must be the example of that readiness to derive and to share standards for which scientific management stands.

Motion Study as an Industrial Opportunity[1]

There is no waste of any kind in the world that equals the waste from needless, ill-directed, and ineffective motions, and their resulting unnecessary fatigue. Because this is true, there is no industrial opportunity that offers a richer return than the elimination of needless motions, and the transformation of ill-directed and ineffective motions into efficient activity.

This country has been so rich in human and material resources,

[1] Reprinted from "The Annals" of the American Academy of Political and Social Science.

that it is only recently that the importance of waste elimination has come to be realized. The material element received the first consideration, and in the comparatively few years during which the subject has received attention, an enormous amount has been done to conserve natural resources, to economise in the use of materials, and to utilize the by-products of industrial processes.

The human element is now receiving long-delayed attention. Vocational training, vocational guidance, better placement, and better working conditions have become subjects for serious consideration in all parts of this country and of the world. Savings in human energy are resulting from these investigations, but the greatest saving in time, in money, and in energy will result when the motions of every individual, no matter what his work may be, have been studied and standardized.

Such studies have already been made in many trades, and have resulted in actual savings that prove that the results of the practice confirm the theory. In laying brick, the motions used in laying a single brick were reduced from eighteen to five,—with an increase in output of from one hundred and twenty brick an hour to three hundred and fifty an hour and with a reduction in the resulting fatigue. In folding cotton cloth, twenty to thirty motions were reduced to ten or twelve, with the result that instead of one hundred and fifty dozen pieces of cloth, four hundred dozen were folded, with no added fatigue. The motions of a girl putting paper on boxes of shoe polish were studied. Her methods were changed only slightly, and where she had been doing twenty-four boxes in forty seconds, she did twenty-four in twenty seconds, with less effort. Similar studies have cut down the motions not only of men and women in other trades but also of surgeons, of nurses, of office workers; in fact, of workers in every type of work studied.

Motion study consists of dividing work into the most fundamental elements possible; studying these elements separately and in relation to one another; and from these studied elements, when timed, building methods of least waste.

To cite a specific example: The assembly of a machine is the piece of work under consideration. The existing method of assembling the machine is recorded in the minutest detail. Each element of the assembly is then tested,—the method used in handling the element being compared with other possible methods. In this way, the most efficient elements of an assembly are determined; and these elements are combined into a method of assembly that, because it is the result of actual measurement, is worthy to become a standard. Such an assembly is that of the braider, manufactured by the New England Butt Company. As a result of motion studies made upon this, where eighteen braiders had been assembled by one man in a day, it now becomes possible to assemble sixty-six braiders per man per day, with no increase in fatigue.

The accurate measurement involved in getting results like this includes three elements. We must determine, first, the units to be measured; second, the methods to be used; and, third, the devices to be used.

The unit of measurement must be one that of itself will reduce cost, and should be as small as the time and money that can be devoted to the investigation warrants. The smaller the unit, the more intensive the study required.

The methods and devices to be used are also determined largely by the question of cost. Naturally, those methods and devices are preferable which provide least possibility of errors of observation. Such errors have been classified as of two kinds: first, errors due to instruments; and, second, errors due to the personal bias of the observer. The newer methods of making motion studies and time studies by the use of the micro-motion method and the chronocyclegraph method exclude such errors. Fortunately, through an improvement and cheapening of the devices, it is now possible to make accurate records of motions, even when no great outlay for the study can be afforded.

The micro-motion method of making motion studies consists of recording motions by means of a motion picture camera, a clock that will record different times of day in each picture of a motion picture film, a cross-sectioned background, and other devices for assisting in measuring the relative efficiency and wastefulness of motions.

Suppose the process of assembly before cited is being micro-motion studied: The assembler is placed before the cross-sectioned background; the micro-motion clock is placed where it will record in the picture, yet not disturb the worker; near it is another clock which serves as a check on the accuracy of the special clock. The assembler, who has been rated a skilled worker under the old method, naturally does the best work possible, since a permanent record is being made of his performance. The observer operates the motion picture camera, which, however, allows him freedom to observe the assembly process continually, and to note possibilities for improvement.

From the data on the film and the observations of the observer, can be formulated an improved method. The standard method is seldom derived from the work of one observed worker only. It has been noted that *the ideal method seldom lies in the consecutive acts of any one individual;* therefore, many workers are observed before the final standard is deduced.

These micro-motion records give all the data required except the continuous path of a cycle of motions. This lack is supplied by the chronocyclegraph method. The chronocyclegraph method of making motion study consists of fastening tiny electric-light bulbs to the fingers of the operator, or to any part of the operator or of the material whose motion path it is desired to study. If it is merely the orbit of the motion that is to be observed, a photograph is made of the moving part to which the light is attached, during the time that this part is performing the operation. If the direction, relative time, and relative speed are to be noted, the path of light, through controlled interruption of the circuit, is made to consist of dots or dashes, or a combination of the two, with single pointed ends,—the point showing the direction. Through the micro-motion studies and the chronocyclegraph studies, then, the expert formulates the standard method. It is important to note the changes which the installation of a standard method implies. This method consists of improved motions, and implies, first, changes in surroundings, equipment, and tools; and, second, changes in the type of worker assigned to do the work.

During the motion study of the assembly, it was found that more efficient motions could be made if the machine assembled was placed on a special table, which could be turned on its side and transformed into a lower table, after the base group of the machine had been assembled. It was also found that speed was gained and fatigue eliminated, when the parts of the machine were arranged in an obvious sequence on a vertical packet.[2] These devices were immediately supplied at little cost and with great result in saving. Through these devices, and the other changes made by motion study, it became possible to accomplish nearly three and one-half times as much as-

---

[2] For description of the original motion study packet see "Bricklaying System" [pp. 52–54 of the present work].

sembly as had previously been done. Such changes are typical, and it is typical that the inventions *result from* the motion study.

As for the type of individual suited to the work,—the simplification of the process and the reduction of the motions to habits often made it possible to utilise workers with less initiative and skill, assigning the more skilled workers to a higher type of work. In the case cited of the assembly, the original assemblers were retained and enabled to do much more work with less fatigue. It has also been possible to train inexperienced men to assemble in much less time and with less effort than was formerly the case.

The result of the introduction of motion standards is an increase in output and wages, and an accompanying decrease in cost and fatigue. The decreased cost and the increased wages both depend, of course, on the increased output. The output is increased, because the motions used to make any one unit of the output are less in number and more efficient in results. The average cost of output increase is sufficient not only to provide for the higher wages necessary to induce the workers to do the work in the manner prescribed, and to enjoy doing it, but, also, to allow of at least enough profit to the management to cover the cost of the investigations that resulted in the standard.

The *quality* of the output is maintained through a new type of inspection, which considers not only the output itself, but the elements,—material and human,—which result in that output. Nothing is a higher guarantee of quality than insistence on a standard method.

Along with the laboratory investigations from which motion study standards are derived, goes a general campaign to arouse every individual in the organisation to think in terms of elements of motions. Such simple office equipment as pencil holders are motion studied, and every member of the organisation is encouraged to observe and record his own motions in performing the most elementary of operations. Motion study may be carried on with no devices, and every one is expected to know how to make at least the preliminary investigations. In this way, the spirit of motion economy grows throughout the entire plant, with a consequent elimination of waste motions and a growing interest in the more scientific methods of motion study.

What, now, are the results of this motion study upon the individual men doing the work, upon the factory group, upon the industrial world, and upon society at large? The men themselves become more efficient. They become specialists,—skilled workers. They learn the motion-study method of attack, and are thus more fit to undertake any type of work. They learn to think in elementary motions, and to eliminate waste in every activity of their lives.

The increased output of each individual worker does not result in the employment of less men in the plant. The transference of skill that maintenance of standards implies, means that many teachers are needed. These come, naturally, from the ranks of the skilled workers. The planning that is necessary is also usually done by workers promoted to the planning department. At present, at least, the demand for men trained under motion study is far larger than the supply; it will be for years to come,—certainly until the increased output results in the increased demand which is its inevitable consequence.

The industrial situation is bettered through the general spread of the ideas of waste elimination, and through the practical application if its principles in whatever relations those trained under it may enter. How far this influence upon the industries will extend will depend entirely upon the amount of work done by individuals, and upon their co-operation. At present, many individuals are engaged in, or are at least interested in, motion study and waste elimination. But there is not the proper degree of co-operation. Such co-operation can only come as motion study becomes a matter of interest to society at large. The whole social group is already being affected by the results of motion study. One typical result is the gradual filling in of the gap between the school and the plant. An intensive study of motions is proving that there are far greater likenesses in trades, and even professions, on the mechanical side, than we have ever believed possible. The demand of the industrial world will be more and more for young workers trained to be finger-wise, with a knowledge of the fundamentals of motion economy, and with an understanding of the relationship between efficient motions and success in the industries.

The industrial world is becoming more and more definite in its requirements for industrial training. This is making it possible for all types of schools to give their pupils a training which enables them to fit into working conditions without the customary, preliminary jolt, and months and years of adjustment. The training required is so general, yet so definite, that it may well prove an important part of the training of every young man or woman, whether or not he goes ultimately into the industries. This training is being given not only in the technical schools and in the trade schools but also to some extent, at least, in the ordinary public schools. It consists of making every pupil, to as great an extent as possible, "finger-wise"; that is, of training his muscles so that they respond easily and quickly to demands for skilled work. With this training goes an appreciation of the importance of such "finger training," and of its relation to motion economy. The pupils are also given an appreciation of the problems of industry, and of the relation of these problems to social development.

An effect of motion study in the industries upon society it its influence toward spreading the belief that real efficiency considers and conserves the human element;[3] that it makes fatigue study imperative; and that its fundamental idea is conservation, not exploitation.

The great need to-day, as in all fields where progress is to be made, is education. The community as a whole must be educated as to the importance of motion study, and as to the possibility of every man and woman making such motion study to some extent for himself. The technical press and the press generally are doing much to spread these ideas. Much is also being done by the colleges that are studying and teaching the subject. Such wide-spread education is absolutely necessary before we can hope for the reclassification and standardisation of the existing trades, which is a necessary future step. The trades must be reclassified, according to the amount of skill involved in the motions used; and must then be standardised in order that the necessary training for entering them and succeeding in them can be given. As an example of reclassifying a trade, we would recommend, for example, for brick work, five classes.[4]

The other great need, besides education, is, then, a national bureau of standards, where work done in motion study can be collected, classified, and put into such form that it will be available to every one. There is an enormous waste, at present, from repeating investigations along the same lines of work. There is not only the waste from the actual repetition involved, but also the fact that the time utilised in doing work already done could, instead, be devoted to original work, that is sadly needed.

It is the work of the United States Government to establish such a Bureau of Standardisation of Mechanical Trades. The standards there derived and collected would be public property, and original

---

[3] See "Fatigue Study," p. 10, Sturgis & Walton, New York.
[4] See page 199 of this book for these five classes.

investigators could invent from these standards upwards. Most important of all, perhaps, these standards would furnish the ideal means for teachings or transferring skill to the young workers who desire to enter a trade.

The reclassification of the trades and the Bureau of Standardisation are, then, the two great needs for motion study development. But these will come only when the individuals interested apply motion study to their own work, and show willingness to co-operate with others.

The industrial opportunity afforded by motion study is not, then, some great future opportunity of which we dream, or some remote and inaccessible opportunity for which we must collectively strive. It is an opportunity ready, here and now, to be grasped by each one of us individually,—and it is the greatest industrial opportunity that this century affords.

Motion Study and Time Study Instruments of Precision[1]

The greatest waste in the world comes from needless, ill-directed, and ineffective motions. These motions are unnecessary and preventable. Their existence in the past was excusable, because there was no knowledge of how to dispense with them. That excuse no longer obtains. The methods and devices of waste elimination are known and are being constantly used. But the knowledge of how to make these great world-wide economies is being disseminated at an astonishingly slow pace.

This paper is for the purpose of disseminating such knowledge, particularly as to the devices that are used for making the measurements that enable us to eliminate waste.

In the science of management, as in all other sciences, progress that is to be definite and lasting depends upon the accuracy of the meas-

[1] Presented at the International Engineering Congress.

urements that are made. There are three elements to every measurement:

1. The unit measured.
2. The method of measurement.
3. The device by which the measurement is made.

It is here our aim to show the development of the devices of measurement, that is, of instruments of precision that apply to one branch of the new type of management, namely, to motion study and its related time study.

The fundamental idea of the new type of management that has been variously called "Scientific Management," or "Measured Functional Management," is that it is based upon the results of accurate measurement. This fundamental idea has been derived as follows: Each operation to be studied is analysed into the most elementary units possible. These units are accurately measured, and, as the results of the measurement, the efficient units only are combined into a new method of performing the work that is worthy to become a standard.

Dr. Taylor, the great pioneer in time study, and his co-worker, Mr. S. E. Thompson, have clearly defined their conception of time study as "the process of analysing an operation into its elementary operations, and observing the time required to perform them." Time study has to do, then, fundamentally, with the measurement of units of time.

Now motion study has to do with the selection, invention, and substitution of the motions and their variables that are to be measured. Both accurate time study and motion study require instruments of precision that will record mechanically, with the least possible interference from the human element, in permanent form, exactly what motions and results occur. For permanent use the records must be so definite, distinct, and simple that they may be easily and immediately used, and lose none of their value or helpfulness when old, forgotten, or not personally experienced by their user.

There have undoubtedly been some vague motion studies and guess-work times studies made as far back as historical records are available, particularly in the arts of warfare. The importance of rhythm, for example, which is one of the fundamentals in motion study, was recognised in the Assyrian and Babylonian pictorial records which perpetuate the methods of their best managers, as examination of photographs of such records in our possession will plainly show. Babbage, Coulomb, Adam Smith,—all recognised the importance of the time element in industrial operations, for the purpose of obtaining methods of greatest output, but not methods of least waste. It was not, however, until Dr. Taylor suggested timing the work periods separately from the rest periods that the managers tried to find accurate time-measuring devices.

It is not always recognized that some preliminary motion study and time study can be done without the aid of any accurate devices. It is even less often recognised that such work, when most successful, is usually done by one thoroughly conversant with, and skilled in, the use of the most accurate devices. In other words, it is usually advisable in studying an operation to make all possible improvements in the motions used and to comply broadly with the laws of motion study before recording the operation, except for the preliminary record that serves to show the state of the art from which the investigation started. However, in order to make a great and lasting success of this work, one must have studied motions and measured them until his eye can follow paths of motions and judge lengths of motions, and his timing sense, aided by silent rhythmic counting, can estimate times of motion with surprising accuracy. Sight, hearing, touch, and kinesthetic sensations must all be keenly developed. With this training and equipment, a motion- and time-study expert can obtain preliminary results without devices, that, to the untrained or the uniformed, seem little short of astounding. When the operation has received its preliminary revision and is ready for the accurate measurements that lead to actual standardisation and the teaching that follows, devices of precise measurement become imperative for methods of least waste that will stand the test of time.

Early workers in time study made use of such well-known devices as the clock, the watch, the stop-watch, and various types of stop-watches attached to a specially constructed board or imitation book. Through the use of these it became possible to record short intervals of time, subject, of course, always to the personal error. The objection to the use of these methods and devices is their variation from accuracy, due to the human element. This is especially true of the use of the stop-watch, where the reaction time of the observer is an element constantly affecting the accuracy of the records. But the greatest loss and defect of personally observed and recorded times is that they do not show the attending conditions of the varying surroundings, equipment and tools that cause the differences in the time records, and give no clue to causes of shortest or quickest times.

As for motion study, Marey, with no thought of motion study in our present use of the term in his mind, developed, as one line of his multitudinous activities, a method of recording paths of motions, but never succeeded in his effort to record direction of motions photographically.

Being unable to find any devices anywhere such as the work of our motion study required, the problem that presented itself, then, to us who needed and desired instruments of precision, applicable to our motion study and to our time study, was to invent, design and construct devices that would overcome lacks in the early and existing methods. It was necessary to dispense with the human element and its attending errors and limitations. We needed devices to record the direction as well as the path or orbits of motions, and to reduce the cost of obtaining all time study and motion study data. These were needed not only from the scientific standpoint, but also from the standpoint of obtaining full co-operation of the mechanics and other workers. Many of these had, as a class, become suspicious of time study taken secretly by those who, they thought, did not know enough about the practical features of the trade to take the time study properly, and could not prove that the times were right after putting them on paper. Here was absolute pioneer work to be done in inventing devices that would record times, paths, and directions of motions simultaneously. With the older time study devices there was no way of recording accurately either the unit timed or the controlling surrounding conditions. The "elementary units" were groups of motions. They were elementary only with relation to the stop-watch, with which it is impossible to record accurately the time of an element of a motion, since it takes two decisions and two motions to press the stop-watch. These "groups of motions" were sometimes described at greater or less length, the accuracy of the description depending upon the power of observation of the recorder and the detail with which the time at his disposal, his willingness and his ability to observe, permitted him to set down his observations.

Through our earliest work in making progress records we recognised the necessity of recording time and conditions accurately and simultaneously, the records being made by dated photographs. This method was particularly applicable in construction work,[2] where progress pictures taken at frequent intervals present accurate records

[2] See "Concrete System," Engineering News Publishing Co., New York.

of the surroundings, equipment and tools that affect records of output of various stages of development.

In making more intensive studies of certain trades, such as shovelling concrete work, and bricklaying, we found it advantageous to photograph the various positions in which the hands, arms, feet, and other parts of the body involved in the operations were placed, and to record the time taken in moving from one position to another by one method, as related to the time taken in moving from the same first to the same second position by another method.[3] Our intensive study of bricklaying, which grew out of an appreciation of the unique history, present practice and doubtful future of this trade, led us to a more intensive study of the problems of motion and time study in general.[4] Bricklaying will always be the most interesting of all examples to us, for one reason, among others, that it was the first trade to use the principle of duplicate, interchangeable parts system of construction; had had six thousand known years of practice in all countries; and was, therefore, a comparatively finished art, but not a science, when we undertook to change it by means of motion study.

Fortunately, we are now able to use the motion picture camera with our speed clock, and other accessories, as a device for recording elements of motion and their corresponding times, simultaneously. Our latest microchronometer records intervals of time down to any degree of accuracy required. We have made, and used, in our work of motion study investigations of hospital practice and surgery, one that records times to the millionth of an hour. This is designed for extremely accurate work, but can be adjusted to intervals of any length desired, as proves most economical or desirable for the type of work to be investigated.

Having completed our microchronometer, we proceeded as follows: The microchronometer was placed in the photographic field near the operator and his working equipment, and against a cross-sectioned background or in a cross-sectioned field, and at a cross-sectioned work bench or table. The operator then performed the operation according to the prescribed method, while the motion-picture camera recorded the various stages of the operation and the position of the hand on the microchronometer simultaneously. Thus, on the motion picture film we obtain intermittent records of the paths, the lengths, the directions, and the speeds of the motions, or the times accompany-

[3] See "Motion Study," D. Van Nostrand Co., New York City.
[4] See "Bricklaying System," Myron C. Clark Publishing Co., Chicago.

ing the motions, these records all being simultaneous; and the details of the conditions of the surroundings that are visible to the eye are recorded without the failings of memory. This was a distinct step in advance, but we realised that there was a lack in the records. It was difficult, even for one especially trained and experienced to visualise the exact path of a motion, and it was not possible to measure the length with precision from the observations of the motion picture film alone, as there is no summary or recapitulation of all the motions of a cycle or operation in any one picture. To overcome this lack we invented the cyclegraph method of recording motions. This consists of attaching a small electric light to the hand or other moving part of the person or machine under observation. The motion is recorded on an ordinary photographic film or plate. Upon observing our very first cyclegraph records, we found that we had attained our desire, and that the accurate path taken by the motion stood before us in two dimensions. By taking the photographic record stereoscopically, we were able to see this path in three dimensions, and to obtain what we have called the stereocyclegraph. This showed us the path of the motion in all three dimensions; that is, length, breadth, and depth. It did not, however, contain the time element. This time element is of great importance not only for comparative or "relative" time, but also for exact times. This time element is obtained by putting an interrupter in the light circuit, that causes the light to flash at an even rate at a known number of times per second. This gives a line of time spots in the picture instead of a continuous cyclegraph light line. Counting the light spots tells the time consumed.

The next step was to show the direction of the motions. To do this it was necessary to find the right combination of volts and amperes for the light circuit and the thickness of filament for the lamp, to cause quick lighting and slow extinguishing of the lamp. This right combination makes the light spots pointed on their latest, or forward, ends. The points, thus, like the usual symbol of arrow heads, show the direction. The result was, then, of course, finally, stereochrono-cyclegraphs showing direction. These act not only as accurate records of the motions and times, but also serve as admirable teaching devices. Wire models of cyclegraphs and chronocyclegraphs of the paths and the times of motions are now constructed that have a practical educational value besides their importance as scientific records. These models are particularly useful as a step in teaching visualisation of paths by photographs alone, later.

Our latest apparatus in the field of recording devices apparently fulfils all present requirements of the time- and motion-study experts and their assistants and the teachers who are now devoting their lives to the transference of skill and experience from those who have it to those who have not.[5]

We have also devised and used many special kinds of apparatus; for example, devices for recording absolute continuity of motion paths and times, doing away with the slight gaps in the record that occur between one picture and the next on the cinematograph film, due to the interval of time when the film is moving, to get in place for the next exposure. To overcome this objection we have a double cinematograph, that one part may record while the other moves from one exposure to the next. In this way we get a continuous record of the operation. There have been occasional objections to all methods of making time and motion studies that involve the presence of an observer. Some of these have come from those working on what they consider their own secret processes, who object to having any observer record what they are doing, believing that the time study man is obtaining knowledge of their skill and giving them no information in return. Others have come from those who have seen or heard "secret time study" and "watchbook time study," and who regard all observers as spies because of general lack of understanding and co-operation; and there are some instances where they are right. For such cases we have designed an automicromotion study, which consists of an instantaneous modification of the standard micromotion apparatus, and also the autostereochronocyclegraph apparatus. This enables the operator to take accurate time study of himself. He can start the apparatus going and stop it from where he works, with one motion of his finger or foot. This invention supplies every possible requirement and feature for time and motion study processes, except the help and advice of a properly qualified observer, or the annoyance of having one not fitted by training, experience, or natural qualities to co-operate.

There is not space in this paper for a discussion of the educational features of observations made with these devices, or of their influence upon the new and much needed science of fatigue study, or of their general psychological significance.[6] It is only necessary to emphasise their adaptability, flexibility, and relation to economy. We have here

[5] See "Primer of Scientific Management," D. Van Nostrand Co., New York.
[6] See "Fatigue Study," Sturgis & Walton, New York.

a complete set of inexpensive, light, durable apparatus, adaptable to any type of work and to any type of observer or self-observation. It consists of systematically assembled units that may be so combined as to meet any possible working condition. Through a specially devised method of using the same motion picture film over and over again, up to sixteen times, and through a careful study of electrical equipment and of various types of time spot interrupters, we have been enabled to cut down the cost of making time and motion study, until now the most accurate type of studies, involving no human equation in the record, can be made at less cost than the far less accurate stop-watch study. This time study and motion study data can be used when it is "cold." No specially gifted observer, combined with the most willing and efficient recorder, can compete with it for observing and recording facts. It does not depend upon a human memory to "give up" its facts. It is usable at any time and forever, after it is once taken. Naturally, the requirements for refinement and the special set-ups to be used in any case must be determined after some study of the case in hand.

There are now available, therefore, instruments of precision fitted to make measurements as fine as the most exact science demands,—economical enough to make both immediate and ultimate savings, and that meet the demands of the most exacting industrial progressive. When the time and motion study is taken with such instruments of precision, there are still other by-products that are of more value than the entire cost of the time and motion studies.[7]

[7] See "Time Study; a Factor in the Science of Obtaining Methods of Least Waste." See "Psychology of Management," Sturgis & Walton, New York.

Chronocyclegraph Motion Devices for Measuring Achievement[1]

The great need of this age is the conservation of the human element.

It will be the aim of this paper to show:

1. That the human element can be more efficiently utilized, and conserved to a greater degree, by the elimination of useless, ineffective and ill-directed motions.

2. That permanent elimination of such motions necessitates standardizing the motions used in any activity.

3. That standardization demands accurate devices for measuring achievement.

4. That chronocyclegraph motion devices measure achievement accurately, and thus provide for standardization and, ultimately, for motion economy.

Stupendous as the financial loss to the entire world is, on account of the great war that is now being waged in many countries, and affecting all countries, it is as nothing compared to the world's loss of the human element. This is not only a loss that is being felt by this generation, but it is a loss that will be felt for many generations to come. It is, therefore, a great world problem, demanding the attention of all of us, to conserve and utilise humanity in every way possible. This problem has two aspects. The first is the utilisation of those directly affected by the war, either by being crippled or maimed through some injury received in the war, or by being forced to become productive members of the community through loss or crippling of the earning members of the family caused by the war. The

[1] A paper presented at the Second Pan-American-Congress at Washington, D.C., January 3, 1916.

234

second is the more efficient utilisation of all other members of the community, in order to make up, as far as possible, for the loss in productive power of individuals either killed or rendered in some way less efficient by the war.

The need for economy in the expenditure of human effort is not new. Even in the days of the Pharaohs there was the realisation that every ounce of strength of the worker was of value, as is plainly shown by photographs of the ancient carvings and other records of their industrial practice. There was, unfortunately, in those times little or no appreciation of the humanitarian side, of the need for conserving the worker for his own happiness and for the ultimate good of the race or the country. The practice was to extract every ounce of effort from the worker in the shortest amount of time possible, taking little account of the amount that the worker's life was shortened by the process. With the ages has come an appreciation of the greater benefit, not only to the individuals in society, but to society as a whole, to be derived by prolonging the life of the worker and increasing the number of happiness minutes that he enjoys. With the spread and growth of the movement for conserving material things, such as forests, mines and other natural resources, and the utilization of the sources of energy, such as water power, has come an appreciation of the field for conservation of the human element. With the growth of the science of management, and the emphasis laid on motion study and fatigue study, has come an appreciation of the methods that may best be used to effect this conservation. Now, with the enormous need, has come the realisation that practice of this conservation should be started immediately, and maintained permanently, or, at least, for generations to come, if the world ever expects to recover from its stupendous and almost incalculable war loss.

"Economy" has become the watchword of the day, and it is an excellent watchword, but the practice of *unstudied* economy is apt to lead to serious economic disturbances. The first step in rational economy consists of investigating the relation between economy and waste elimination. It is necessary to realise the need to eliminate the useless and the need to utilize to the fullest capacity everything that is of use. This requires

1. The determination as to what is useless and as to what is useful.
2. The determination as to the most efficient method of utilizing the useful.

That is to say, it requires accurate measurement applicable to activity. The problem is not simple, for along with the activity and its resulting achievement and output comes the fatigue accumulated by the worker while doing the work, and fatigue is a subject concerning which, as yet, little is known.[2] Permanent results in human economy demand accurate records of fatigue co-ordinated with records of achievement, and with records of the methods by which the achievement has been secured.

To find and apply the necessary measures for achievement and fatigue is primarily a task for the engineer. His training impresses him with the importance of measurement. His work makes him skilled in the use of measuring devices. Success in his profession depends chiefly upon the continued application of the most accurate measurement available, and this provides the incentive necessary for the maintenance of the scientific method. The engineer must secure the co-operation of the educator, the psychologist, the physiologist and the economist before he can hope to secure complete data, and to understand the full interpretation of what he finds,—but this is his duty

1. To make the investigation in the most scientific manner of which he is capable.
2. To submit his finds for comparative study by others and for the use of the world.

This paper describes and attempts to make useful the history of such an investigation, a search for and the devising of satisfactory devices for measuring achievement.

It is a fortunate thing to be born in an age like the present, when the scientific spirit prevails in all fields, and where everything can be legitimately submitted to measurement. The world-wide desire to ascertain causes made it a simple matter to realise that large output or achievement was not in itself so important as the reasons for this achievement, with the consequent placing of the emphasis upon the methods *and* their results rather than upon the results alone. The writers thus became impressed early with the importance of obtaining as accurate and detailed records of methods as possible, if achievements were ever to be accurately measured.

This methods study was formulated into motion study, and divided into three parts:

1. Study of the variables of the worker.
2. Study of the variables of the surroundings, equipment and tools.

[2] See "Fatigue Study," Sturgis & Walton, 31 East 27th Street, New York.

3. Study of the variables of the motion itself.[3]

It was possible to make fairly satisfactory records of workers and of surroundings, equipment and tools with an ordinary camera. These were supplemented by descriptions in great detail of the best methods observed, even to the making of diagrams showing the relative location of the worker's feet and the position of the working equipment. Through such records conspicuous wastes in human energy became at once apparent, and various inventions of devices that cut down the amount of effort necessary, or eliminated needless fatigue, were made.[4] With these inventions, and the comparison of the motions resulting from them with the motions used before the inventions, there was instantly an added appreciation of the importance of a study of the elements of the motions themselves.

With the writer's acquaintance with Dr. Taylor and his epoch-making discovery of the necessity for recording unit times, came an added appreciation of the need for including time study with motion study. The great problem was to record the motions used. The cinematograph was finally resorted to as an accurate recording device. The invention of a special microchronometer that recorded times down to the millionth of an hour, made possible simultaneous records of this microchronometer and the positions of the worker whose activity was being studied. Even the first records, though unsatisfactory in many respects, demonstrated the practicability and usefulness of these methods of recording motions. Little by little the method was improved. An ordinary, reliable clock was placed alongside the microchronometer, in order to serve as a check upon its inaccuracy, if any occurred, and also to provide a record of the time of day that the study was made, in the resulting picture. Temperature and humidity records were included upon the picture. Signs, describing the place where the investigation was being made, the name of the investigator and the date, were placed for an instant in the field, and thus became a part of the permanent record. The original white dial with black marks was subsequently changed, at the suggestion of a film reader, to a black dial with white divisions and white hands that left a clear, sharp record upon the picture, and recorded the elapsed time of each exposure. The worker and the timepiece were placed in front of a cross-sectioned background, in order that the motions might be more accurately located. The ultimate value of these rec-

[3] See "Motion Study," D. Van Nostrand, 25 Park Place, New York.
[4] See "Bricklaying System," Myron C. Clark, Chicago, Ill.

ords, called "micromotion records," far exceeded what had originally been expected. These records were useful, not only in deriving improved methods of performing work that were worthy of being standardised, but also in serving as most admirable teaching devices.[5] The negative films were used originally for the study that resulted in the standards, and either these negative films, or positives that appeal more readily to those not trained in film observation, were thrown upon the screen, and served as topics for discussion in the foremen's, managers' and executives' meetings, or as demonstrations of the best methods of those learning the industry. Through the application of the results of data gathered from these films, large savings in industrial practices were immediately gained. As a typical example, where eighteen to twenty textile machines had been assembled in a certain shop before the application of micromotion study, sixty-six were assembled after the results of the study had been incorporated in the shop practice. The savings were the direct result of the micromotion study, combined with the improved placement or assignment of the workers to the work, and the improved surroundings, equipment and tools with which the work was done, that occurred in connection with it. We have here accurate devices for recording achievement and for measuring the amount of time consumed by the achievement. The motions that made up the method by which the achievement was secured are also here accurately recorded.

If the aim of making motion standards had been simply to provide instruction or time study data for those already skilled in the art of doing the work, the micromotion records would probably have answered every requirement, but, important as it is that those who know how to do the work in any fashion shall be taught the best way, it is even more important, for the savings, that the *learner shall be taught the best way immediately, that is, from the beginning of his practice.* When it came to the transference of skill, the micromotion records were not completely satisfactory in enabling the workers to visualise the path of the motion easily. The average engineer, who becomes, through his training and the necessities of his work, a good visualiser, even though he is not one by nature, often fails to realise the small capacity for visualization possessed by the average person. A long experience in teaching in the industries made this fact impressive and led to the invention of the cyclegraph, and, later, the

[5] See "The Psychology of Management," Sturgis & Walton, 31 East 27th Street, New York.

chronocyclegraph method of recording, in order to aid the non-visualising worker to grasp motion economy easily. The device for recording the path of the motion consisted of a small electric light attached to the forefinger or other moving part of the body of the worker. The worker performed the operation to be studied, and the path traversed by his hand was marked by a line of light. An ordinary photographic plate or film was exposed during the time that he performed the work, and recorded the motion path described by the light as a white line, something like a white wire. A stereoscopic camera enabled one to see this line in three dimensions. This line was called a "cyclegraph," since it had been determined a cycle was the most satisfactory unit of motions to be thus recorded, and the method was called the "cyclegraph method of motion study." A study of cyclegraphs shows a need for an indication of time, and, while the path of the motions is apparent, the *time* of the motions is not shown by the plain cyclegraph. This time element is of great importance, not only for securing records of comparative or *relative time,* but also for securing records of *exact time.* The time element was eventually obtained by placing an interrupter in the current, that transformed the white line of the cyclegraph into a series or line of dots and dashes. This made of the cyclegraph a chronocyclegraph. The exact time is secured by using a tuning fork vibrating a known number of times per second as an interrupter. The record now becomes a series of timed spots, and the method becomes the "chronocyclegraph method." Through intensive study of the apparatus, it has become possible to devise differentiated time and speed spots, and thus to distinguish various motion paths in the same stereograph [Fig. 12 omitted]. This means that we can now attach any desired number of lights to different working members of the worker's body, and obtain synchronous chronocyclegraph records that are accurate, yet that differ in shape from one another to such an amount that it is possible to distinguish each, and to trace the continuous path of each light with ease.

The latest development in this study has been in the line of cheapening the cost of the apparatus. As in making micromotion studies it was found that the original method could be much cut down in cost by using the same film as many as sixteen times, so here it was found that cheaper types of interrupters can be used in place of the more adjustable tuning fork, made originally for the extremely accurate tests of the psychological laboratory. It must be understood that for the investigation of surgery and like types of activity, and for use in investigations in psychological laboratories, and in other scientific fields, the most expensive and elaborate of apparatus is none too fine; but it is possible, where first cost must be considered, and in much work in the industries, to make records accurate enough with apparatus that is within the reach of any one desiring to own it, and willing to devote time to learning to operate it.

With the study of the chronocyclegraph data has come the invention of the *penetrating screen,* which makes it easier to visualise and to measure the elements of the cycle being studied. It was desired to visualise simultaneously the time and space occupied by the motion. As is so often the case, invention was here held back by a belief. In this case it was, "Two objects cannot occupy the same space at the same time." It took years to realise that, while this is usually true, a photograph can show them as occupying the space at the same time. This multiple exposure method made it possible to place a cross-sectioned screen in any place, or number of places, in the picture. A screen may be placed in the plane in which the worker is performing his chief activity, before the worker, or back of him. The worker may be enclosed in a three, four, five, or six-sided box. The screen may be set at any angle. In short, a cross-sectioned screen of known dimensions can be introduced at any place where it will enable one to secure a more accurate record of the motion. This is done by the simplest and most inexpensive means. Take a sheet of black paper of the size of the space to be photographed, and cross-section it with white lines at any distance that may be desired. Then photograph this screen at any place, or places, desired, by exposing the film each time that the screen is at a different pre-determined place. It is important that the time of the exposure of the screen be right, otherwise it may either be difficult to see the screen, or, on the other hand, the screen may be so prominent that it interferes with seeing the records of the motions themselves easily. The cross-sectioning being properly made, expose the now cross-sectioned film, and photograph upon it the work being studied. The resulting photograph gives the path of the motion laid along the cross-sectioned plane divided into any space elements desired. The penetrating screen, therefore, now furnishes the last desired feature for measuring and recording, namely, exact distance of motions. This, in combination with the foregoing list, now gives us records of exact speeds.

For some types of activity, such as handling a drill press, a record taken from one direction was satisfactory, and its close study enabled one to double the output of the machine with no added fatigue to the operator. With other operations, such as the folding of cloth, it was desirable to take chronocyclegraphs from several points simultaneously, in some cases placing the camera in front of the operator, at the right side, at the left side, and also above. A study of these records led to the realisation that it would be a great advantage, if it were possible to study the motion from all angles. An advantage to the motion study man in eliminating all useless, inefficient and ill-directed motions and in his general education in motion study. An advantage, also, to the worker, who could thus see his motions as he never could while doing the work. A special advantage to the learner desiring to acquire the skill in the shortest amount of time, and with the least amount of effort possible.

This need was even greater in the case of surgery, where it was found impossible, because of the necessity for operating conditions, to take the photographs required in the usual manner. While the telephoto lens was a great help in making it possible to take necessary records from the amphitheatre of the operating room, thus neither disturbing the operating conditions nor adding a new variable, through the presence of an observer, that might affect the methods used, here also the need for viewing the motion at other angles remained. An intensive study of this need and possible means for overcoming it resulted in the invention of the motion model. This consists of a wire model that exactly represents the path, speeds and directions of the motion studied. As many cyclegraph records of the operation taken from different angles as are needed are made, the cross-sectioned screen being introduced at those places where the direction of the motion makes a decided change. These cyclegraphs, which are in every case stereochronocyclegraphs, are studied through a stereoscope. Motion models are made by looking at the path as shown through the stereoscope, and bending the wire to conform to this path. The wire model, when completed, is placed in a black box cross-sectioned in white, the cross-sectioning being placed at the same relative places as are the cross-sectioned screens in the original picture. If the photograph taken from the same angle that the original photograph was taken is exactly similar to the original photograph, the model is considered a success. Each and every subdivision of a chronocyclegraph has its significance, and, therefore, the model must be brought to this state of perfection before it is considered complete.

Where a chronocyclegraph motion model is desired, the spots on the chronocyclegraph are represented by spots painted upon the model. Black and grey paint being used upon the wire model that has been painted white, the result is spots of white fading through grey to black, that resemble closely in shape the white spots seen in the chronocyclegraph. It is possible also to use the ear in teaching. Through a new device consisting of a pendulum, a bell and a flashing lamp, time records, simultaneous with the other motion and time records, can be made. The same devices can be then set in operation while the work is being learned, and the learner can count by listening to the bell at the same time that he is learning through his eyes or his fingers by means of the motion model. The significance of all these devices to psychology and education can only be appreciated by a close examination of the models and cyclegraphs themselves, and an observation of their methods of recording *habit* or *lack of habit, decision* or *indecision, grace* or *awkwardness,* etc. Habit is best recorded by the stretched cyclegraph, which allows of the various lines recording habit being recorded accurately, yet in such a manner that they are easily distinguished from one another. These aspects of the motion models are important to the engineer in so far as he is a teacher and interested in the learning process.

Of perhaps greater importance, however, here, is the motion model as a means of devising, maintaining and improving standards. Through the study of the motion path, either as shown in the chronocyclegraph or in the chronocyclegraph motion model, and through a comparison of such graphs or models showing the paths of different operators doing the same kind of work, it is possible to deduce the most efficient method and to make this a standard. Moreover, each standard motion path is a help towards deducing other standard motion paths. Through an intensive study of motion paths followed in doing different kinds of work efficiently, there has come a recognition of the indications of an efficient motion, its smoothness, its lack of hesitation, its regular normal acceleration and retardation and its use of habit. The efficient method having been standardized, the motion model or cyclegraph then acts as a definite and tangible embodiment of this standard motion, thus enabling one to maintain the standard with comparative ease. It in no wise precludes improvement, nor suggests lack of progress toward the ideal. In fact, it suggests improvements because of its continued availability for observation and study. It furnishes a very definite starting point from which such improvements are to be made, as well as a measure by which they are to be rated and judged. Through a comparison of the motions used in different lines of work, in the industries, in surgery and in other kinds of activity, it can be shown that the same identical motions are used in doing what are usually considered widely different types of work. This allows of an instantaneous location of the place where skill is lacking, of a tremendous amount of transference of efficient methods from one trade, craft or profession to another; and of a consequent saving in time and energy. This is also the basis of our new classification of all activities in accordance with their motions and decisions. These models and graphs form also an important element in proper placement, since it is often possible to determine through them directly a worker's capability of learning and performing the work.

The data ascertained by these motion devices are placed upon the Simultaneous Motion Cycle chart. This analyses a motion cycle into its component parts, and indicates graphically by which member of the body, and in what method, each portion of the cycle is performed. The Simultaneous Motion Cycle chart is made on cross-sectioned paper with the various working members of the body used as column headings, and with the sixteen elements of the motion cycle placed vertically on the chart. By the comparison of the analysed motion model with the data on the chart, the possibility of the transference of work from one working member of the body to another is indicated, and the field for invention of devices or for more efficient placement is indicated. The Simultaneous Motion Cycle chart that is the outcome of the chronocyclegraph motion devices has been used by the writers for years in the industries, and has been presented by the writers for the benefit of the crippled soldiers, in whose interests they are at present engaged, with the collaboration of educators in Canada, England, France, Germany and Russia, in collecting data. The engineers of this country have been asked, through the American Society of Mechanical Engineers, to collect and send in all data available, that they may, by the use of this Simultaneous Motion Cycle chart and the models, be made available for teaching the most profitable motions to the crippled soldiers of all the warring countries abroad.

Important as the work for the crippled soldiers is, it is, as has been indicated, only a part of the conservation work that must be done. The other part, the conservation of all humanity to make good the great present loss, should be undertaken by a body like this Congress.

No matter what work is done by the individual, or by individual plants, or trade groups, or industries, or even by a whole country, to cut down waste by standardizing motions, there will be an enormous loss unless all nations co-operate in making and maintaining standards. There is no excuse here for holding secrets from one another, for reinventing, or for allowing any nation to fall behind the others. There is no excuse because the need is so overwhelming that all countries should hasten to start international standards. Let us use, therefore, chronocyclegraph motion devices as an aid towards making the much-needed international standards. This Pan-American Congress here assembled would serve as the most admirable headquarters for a Bureau of Pan-American Motion Standards. Undoubtedly, in every country here represented men have thought of the advisability of solving this great problem of human conservation, and have done what they could, each in his own restricted field, and largely without encouragement. It would be a wonderful help to these investigators, and to the world at large, if the work that has been gradually spreading from the individual to the group could now spread also from this representative group to the millions of individuals that it represents. The first step in this process is to enlist the interest of every member of this Congress in the necessity for human conservation, in the practicability of motion economy and in the belief that measured standards stimulate rather than stunt invention. The world must come to think of efficiency in terms of measured elements of motions and to concern itself with providing for efficient motions and sufficient rest for overcoming fatigue therefrom. This is not only a world problem and a pressing problem, but it is also a unifying problem. At war or at peace, every nation must realise the importance of the conservation of the human element. If we emphasise this, we not only make for efficiency in that more work may be accomplished with less effort, but we work also for permanent peace, in that we emphasise a common problem and suggest a common solution.

Motion Models: Their Use in the Transference of Experience and the Presentation of Comparative Results in Educational Methods[1]

This is the age of measurement. The motion model is a new device of measurement. It is for this reason that we are presenting the motion model to-day to this section of this Association, which stands for accurate measurement, and which believes that advancement must come through such measurement.

Your general subject for this meeting is listed as "The Scientific Study of Educational Problems." You are to be congratulated upon having chosen such a subject, and thus having shown your belief that advances in education, as in other fields of activity, depend upon the application of the scientific method to the solution of the various problems involved. The *art* of teaching need never lose its ancient respect and standing, but the *science* of teaching, which in no wise supplants or interferes with the art, enlists a new co-operation from all those engaged in like types of activity, and should arouse a new interest in educators themselves. Only where the scientific method is applied can one expect to find invention that is improvement, and progress that is continuous and permanent.

Now the continuous application of the scientific method demands three things:

[1] Presented at a meeting of the American Association for the Advancement of Science.

1. Units of measurement.
2. Methods of measurement.
3. Devices by which measurement can be made, and can be made at a decreasing cost.

Many such units, methods and devices of measurement, as applied to education, already exist. There has been in all fields where education is going on a lack of means by which behaviour could be accurately recorded, and the records used as data for predicting behaviour, and for outlining methods for attaining future desired results. *Motion models* supply this lack. They were derived in industrial experience, and were first applied in teaching in the industries, but their use is not limited to the industrial field, nor to teaching of manual operations.

The fact that this paper is presented here is indicative of the new feeling that is growing up in all fields of activity, of the necessity of correlation. This realization of the importance of correlation is the outcome of many things. One is the tendency of this age to think in parts rather than in wholes, in elements rather than in grouped elements. In the olden times, both material things and human beings were invariably thought of as entities, wholes; but with closer thinking, and the awakening of the scientific spirit of analysis, measurement, standardization and synthesis, has come the realization that the fact that the thing or persons as a whole is often far less important than the fact that the thing or person is a group, or community, or combination of parts. The material thing is analysed into its elements. The human being is thought of as a group of working members. The old-time operation is thought of as a combination of acts. Now, finally, the motion itself is thought of as a cycle or combination of elements and motions.

With this intensive study of elements has come also a realization of the importance of likenesses between things. This emphasis on likenesses may be given as the second reason for the realization of the necessity of correlation. The old-time wise man wondered at the differences between things, and the scientist for years and decades followed the old-time wise man, and placed the emphasis in his classifications upon differences. Our ordinary classifications of to-day are thus based: for example, classifications of the trades are based more or less indefinitely upon

a. Difference between the types of men who do the work.

    b. Differences in the ability and general education of the worker.

    c. Differences in the kinds of, or the value of, materials handled.

    d. Differences in the surrounding conditions.

Similar emphasis on difference marks the division of the trades from the professions, a difference so insisted upon that any attempt to correlate the work of, say, a surgeon, typist and bricklayer, meets with instant and almost universal disapproval. Yet the trend in science to-day makes it more and more apparent that all have neglected emphasizing the likenesses to an astounding degree, and that a heavy price has been paid for this neglect. The very idea of difference implies division. This has set up for years boundaries between experiences, professional experiences and teaching experiences, that it will require yeoman work to destroy.

    Yet splendid work is to-day being done in correlation. In the field of education the work done has not only a scientifically derived theory to support it, but can also show practical and successful results. This work is acting as a stimulus and a guide to workers in other fields of activity. Much undoubtedly remains to be done in correlating various types of teaching and learning in the schools, but what has been done is an indication of what can and will be done, and there need be no fear of the ultimate results. Educators are also to be congratulated on the beginnings made in correlating teaching in the schools and colleges and in the industries, such, for example, as in the half-time work now being increasingly introduced throughout the country. However, this correlation has usually been imperfect in that, while the teacher of such "half-time" pupils consciously adapts the school work to fit the shop needs of the pupils, the shop teacher and school teacher have not generally, as yet, compared methods and attempted to make the pupils' learning experience a unified one. Shop teaching, or to put it in a general phrase, "transference of skill and experience in the industries," is at present such an indefinite thing that one can scarcely blame either side for this lack of correlation. In this country, and in the same locality, are existing side by side to-day methods of teaching as old as the time of the guilds and the most modern methods of teaching, with an indefinite and surprisingly large number of steps, or grades of teaching, in between. It would undoubtedly interest, and it might profit, educators to trace the history of teaching in the industries; but this is not the place to present such a history. This, because the need for immediate correlation of teaching in the school and in the industry is so pressing and so great.

Never in the history of the world has there been such a need as there is to-day for economy in all lines, to compensate as far as possible for the enormous loss in human and material things caused by the great war. We have endeavoured to bring out in various recent papers the immensity of this loss, and to outline various methods by which it may be partially met. No body of thinkers realises more clearly than do the educators just what this loss means, and none has proved more ready to do their part toward meeting it, as is testified by the noble work done by educators in all the warring countries in standing ready and glad to do their part in the "making-good process."

We are presenting, therefore, what we believe to be the most advanced type of teaching in the industries, as a contribution towards that correlation for which we all long. This method is the result of years of experience as learners and teachers in many lines of activity. It has the increasing support of psychologists and teachers as well as of managers. We offer it not only hoping that it may prove of service in your various lines of activity, but with the assurance that you will immediately test it in every way possible by your own data and experience, and allow us to benefit by the results of the tests. We come with an equally hearty desire for co-operation, for this, in the final analysis, is the most satisfying incentive of all.

In order to make clear what this device, *the motion model*, is, and what the methods are in which it may be used, and by which it is used, it is necessary to trace, though only in outline, the history of its evolution.

The motion model is a wire representation of the path of a motion. It is the result of years of endeavour on our part to put a motion in such visible and tangible form that it may be visualised and measured with accuracy, and that the laws underlying

1. The behaviour that caused and affected the motion,
2. The behaviour that resulted from the motion,

may be scientifically determined. This desire to understand motions thoroughly has been a driving force with the writers ever since the start of motion study itself. The study of motions, of course, is not new. It must have existed, whether used consciously or not, ever since there was any activity at all; but what is now generally understood by the phrase "motion study" had its beginning in the year 1885. We quote here an earlier account, by one of the writers, of his first day at construction work. This will be of interest to this particular audience as not only outlining what occurred, but indicating to some extent the mental process that lay back of it. We quote:

"I started learning the work of the construction engineer on July 12, 1885, as I had been promised that a thorough mastering of at least one trade, and a general practical experience with many trades, would be followed by rapid promotion in my particular line of engineering. I was, accordingly, put to work between two specially selected, expert bricklayers, who were instructed that they were to teach me the trade as rapidly as possible. They gladly agreed to this. First one taught me, then the other, and, much to my surprise, they taught me entirely different methods. To make matters still more puzzling to me, I found that the methods that they taught me were not the methods that they themselves used. Now, I had the idea that, if I could learn one way thoroughly, I could be promoted in the shortest time possible to the higher position promised me. It seemed perfectly obvious that to learn two ways would take much longer than to learn one way, perhaps twice as long. Yet each man was an expert, whose methods were considered perfectly satisfactory, and each was turning out a large quantity of work excellent in quality. Hoping to discover which method taught me was the better, after a short time I quietly placed myself between two other bricklayers of my own selection. These were as willing to teach me as the first two had been, but I became more puzzled than ever when I found that their methods were different and that neither one taught me either of the methods shown me by my first two teachers. Naturally, the foreman soon sent me back from my own wanderings to my first location. All my friends, however, had one common rule for me, 'Keep at it on each brick until it is in true position.' I struggled on, trying to follow first one method and then another that was being taught me, and being constantly admonished by my first teacher, 'not to make so many motions.' Disgusted at my unsatisfactory results, I began watching this first teacher more closely, when he was working, and found that he used two entirely different sets of motions when doing his own work, both of these differing radically from the demonstration set that he used to teach me. That is, all three sets of motions were used to do identically the same type of work, the only difference being that Set One was used to teach the beginner, Set Two was used when working slowly, and Set Three was used when working rapidly. I looked at my second teacher. He also had three sets of motions. From that day I continued to observe as far and as fast as I could, and have found in practically every case that every worker has at least three distinct sets of motions for doing the same work.

"Naturally, as time went on, I came to ask my various teachers, 'What is the quickest way?' Each one had his own special 'kinks,' or short cuts, such as putting two bricks together in the air and then placing them together in the middle of the wall. Of course, I had to try out each of them, but soon found the great difficulty of achieving the first quality and, at the same time, using high speed motions while working.

"My observations involved certain fundamental questions:

"1. Why did the teacher use different motions when teaching than when himself working?

"2. Why did the teacher use different motions when working slowly than when working rapidly?

"3. Which of the three methods used was the right method?

"4. Why did each teacher observed have his own special set of short cuts, or 'kinks'?

"5. What was really the best method of doing the work?

"6. Was the insistence on quality first and right methods second advisable?

"7. At what speed should the beginner be taught to do his work?"

Through all these years we have been trying to find the reasons why the conditions that were so puzzling existed, and the answers to the questions here enumerated. Both reasons and answers depend upon a few simple and easily stated facts. We say "facts" advisedly, for the motion models have proved them to be such. We use the word with exultation, for, while we believed them to be facts for years, because the results justified the theories, we have often been ridiculed by students and investigators in all lines for so believing. Only since the motion models demonstrated the facts are they coming to be acknowledged as such, and are we receiving assistance in making them more generally useful.

The facts are as follows:

1. The motions are the elements to be considered in learning to perform an activity.

2. Right motions must be insisted upon from the beginner's first day at work.

3. Right motions do not lie in the conservative acts of any one person performing the activity, unless he has been specially taught the standard method.

4. Fast motions are different from slow motions.

5. Standard speed of motions must be insisted upon from the learner's beginning on his first day, if least waste of learning is the first consideration.

6. Right motions at standard speed produce right quality.

7. The best learning process consists of producing right motions at the standard speed in accordance with the laws of habit formation.

We might here turn immediately to the motion model and show how it demonstrates these facts, but the demonstration will be clearer if the steps in the process of the derivation are carefully stated. We shall, therefore, return to the seven questions listed above, and state in each case our conclusions as to the answer.

1. The teacher used different motions when teaching than when working himself because he did not recognise his activity as consisting of motion elements. He attempted to demonstrate to the pupil that method that would obtain the desired quality of work product. He placed the emphasis on quality of output rather than on speed of learning.

2. The teacher used different motions when working slowly than when working rapidly because of the different muscle tension involved. When placing the emphasis upon speed, he was favourably affected by the variables of centrifugal force, inertia, momentum, combination of motions and play for position.[2] When there was no such emphasis on speed he was differently affected by these variables.

3. While none of the three methods of any individual worker was at all likely to be the standard method, the method used when working rapidly was most likely to approximate the standard.

4. Each teacher had his own short cuts in so far as he had consciously or unconsciously thought in motion economy. These differed because it was not customary to compare methods, because working conditions sometimes imply trade secrets, and because there was no adequate correlation between existing methods;—the eye being able to recognise the slow motions only.

[2] See "Motion Study," D. Van Nostrand Co., New York.

5. The best method of doing the work did not at that time exist, because, due to lack of measuring methods and devices, it was not possible to record the elements, or motions, of all the different methods; to measure these, and to synthesize a standard method from the data.

6. The insistence on quality first and right methods second was entirely wrong, since it allowed of the formation of wrong habits of motions, the result of which is a lifelong detriment to the user. The proper insistence is upon right methods at standard speed first, and quality of work product second. It must always be understood that absolute accuracy of method and speed occur simultaneously only with the desired quality. That is to say, take care of the method and the speed, and the quality will quickly take care of itself.

7. The beginner should be taught to do his work immediately with motions of standard speed. Quality should be attended to, however, in every instance.

a. By having the learner stop constructive work long enough to correct what he has done, or do it over again until it is of proper quality, care being taken not to confuse the doing with the correcting.

b. By having some one else correct the work as many times as is necessary, until it becomes of proper quality.

c. By having the learner work where the finest quality is not essential.

The determination as to which of these three methods for providing that the resulting product be of desired quality be used depends upon the type of work done and the type of learner.

It is probably needless to tell a gathering like this assembled here what a storm of adverse criticism the answers to these questions, embodying our beliefs, has caused in the engineering, and also in the educational world. In fact, this storm of criticism still rages to-day, and we expect many objections to the teaching process here involved from you at the close of this paper. We ask, however, at this point that you suspend judgment in this matter. Set aside all of your prejudices and even, perhaps, your experience, to put yourself into our attitude in working out what we have stated are the most efficient processes, and then at the conclusion strike the balance and assist us with your criticism.

You can see that all of our conclusions rest upon the possibility of examining and comparing motions and their results. The first necessity, then, was to obtain an accurate record of the motion. We used the fewest motions, shortest motions and least fatiguing motions possible. We wrote, and collected, descriptions of motions. We made diagrams of the surrounding conditions, even to the location of the worker's feet, at the time when efficient work was being done. We recorded the best we found by photography, at first with an ordinary camera,[3] later with stereoscopic cameras. These gave us detailed records in three dimensions. We used the cinematograph to record the motions being made against a cross-sectioned background, floor and workbench. This enabled us to record and follow the motions more accurately. We then invented a special microchronometer for placing in the picture, when we could find none in the market that could give us fine enough intervals to record the relative times of different motions. This micromotion process, with its combination of the cinematograph, the special timing devices and the cross-sectioned screen, enabled us to obtain accurate and satisfactory records of methods used, except that it did not enable us to visualise clearly the path taken by the motions and the elements of the motions.[4] Our next step was to attach a miniature electric light to the hand of the worker; to photograph the worker, while performing the operation being studied, and thus to obtain the motion path under actual working conditions. Through the use of an interrupter in the light circuit we obtained the photography of time in a single exposure. Later, through a time controlled interrupter, we obtained photographs of exact even periods of elapsed time of any desired duration. Through the use of a special arrangement we obtained time spots that were arrow-shaped that gave us the invention of the photography of direction. Through the use of the penetrating screen we obtained exact distance, and thus exact speed, of motions. Finally through the use of the chronocyclegraph method, which is a combination of these various devices, we obtained a satisfactory record of a motion path, showing relative time, exact time, relative speed, exact speed, and direction of all motions in three dimensions. This chronocyclegraph now answers every requirement as a recording device, and also as a demonstrator of the correctness of our recommended practice, but it is not always a completely satisfactory device with which to demonstrate, simply because of the fact that the sterechronocyclegraph is not tangible. While it is possible to throw the stereoscopic records

[3] See "Bricklaying System," Myron C. Clark Company, Chicago, Ill.
[4] See works of Muybridge, Marey, Amar. See "Concrete System," Engineering News, New York.

upon the screen, it is not satisfactory to enable an entire audience to visualise a motion path simultaneously. We were forced to use individual, single or magazine stereoscopes. As a result, any group of learners, although provided with stereoscopes and with the same picture, or cyclegraph record, find it difficult to use or visualise the cyclegraph simultaneously. It is difficult to concentrate the group mind upon the individual subdivisions of the motion. The motion models overcome this difficulty, making the motion path actually tangible. They enable us to demonstrate to the group mind.

The chronocyclegraph is a perfect record. It is free from the errors of prejudice, carelessness, and all other personal elements. The motion model is the precise record made tangible, and transformed into a satisfactory teaching device. We must, however, establish the validity of our records before enumerating the advantages of our teaching devices. What does the chronocyclegraph show? We group the following in accordance with the seven facts stated before:

1. The chronocyclegraph shows that the subdivision of the motion cycle is the important element. The motion cycle can be accurately recorded, hence analysed into elements that may be standardised and synthesized into a recorded method. The time taken to do the work cannot be used as a preliminary standard, the worker being allowed to use any set of motions that he desires. The elements of such a set not being scientifically determined, the user of the motions will either take longer than necessary to do the work, or become unnecessarily fatigued. In order to come within the time, he must finally arrive at what would at least be a habitual cycle of motions, many of which are inefficient. If any wrong habit of motions occurs there will be a serious loss by reason of habit interference, with consequent unnecessary fatigue, and the likelihood of the time ever becoming standard will be greatly reduced. The quality of the output cannot be made the preliminary standard, since this would allow of unstandardised motions, with an ensuing decrease of speed, and would result in unstandardised times.

2. The chronocyclegraph shows plainly the effects of habit. We have convincing illustrations of loss in efficiency due to the intrusion of old habits. They show that a discarded habit will return and obtrude itself when a new method is for some reason insisted upon, and the existing habit cycle is broken down in order that the new one may be formed. Say, the worker used originally habit A, and has come to use habit B. If he be taught cycle C, which differs from A and B,

where he fails in C, he will be apt to introduce an element from A, not from B. The complication is evident. To profit by habit the laws of habit formation must be rigidly utilised.[5] These laws support the dictum, "Right motions first."

3. A comparison of the chronocyclegraphs of the various workers, studied in connection with the quantity and quality of the output achieved and with the standard method finally derived, shows that the best method does not lie in the motion cycle, or in the consecutive motion cycles, of any one individual. The micromotion records are of enormous benefit here, in that they enable us, at any time and place, to review the methods used by each worker, and to compare them.

4. The chronocyclegraph of the same worker performing the same work at different rates of speed demonstrated absolutely that fast motions are different from slow motions. They do not follow the same path or orbit. Micromotion records are here again of enormous assistance. Through them we were enabled to observe the worker performing the work at practically any speed that we may desire to see him use, as determined by the number of pictures projected per second on the screen. Those of you who have made a study of motion picture films, their making and projecting, and who have analysed trick films, where the people move far above, or below, the normal speed of real life, will at once realise the possibilities in motion analysis that lie here.

5. It having been shown that fast motions are different from slow motions, it becomes self-evident that, in accordance with the laws of habit formation, the learner must be taught the standard speed of motions from the first day. If he is not, he will not form properly the habit of using the forces that lie in his own body under his own control, of which he is usually at present unaware. It must not be understood that standard speed means always high speed. It does not. It means that rate of speed that will produce the desired results most efficiently. It must be remembered that there are a few motions that cannot be made at the standard speed at first by the beginner. In such cases the speed should be as near as possible that used by the expert.

6. The records of quantity and quality of output that are made simultaneously with the chronocyclegraph records demonstrate that right motions at the right speed produce the desired quality. This is,

[5] See "The Psychology of Management," page 234, Sturgis & Walton Co., New York City.

also, demonstrable through logic. The first thing to be standardised is the quality of the resulting product desired. The standard method is then made to be that method of performing the work that will produce this quality most efficiently. Through performing the standard method at the correct speed the standard quality does and must invariably result. During the learning process, of course, quality will seem to go by the board, but this is only during the period that the learner cannot succeed in performing the method described. The correlation between the methods and the quality is perfect. Therefore, the expected and desired result must come to pass.

7. The teaching must, therefore, consist of two things:

a. The right method must be presented at the standard speed. The right method, taken with the cinematograph at standard speed of motions, may be presented slowly by projecting fewer pictures per second on the screen, but in any case the motions must be made at the standard speeds when being photographed.

b. The right method must be followed during the determining length of time, with the proper rest intervals for overcoming fatigue, and always with sufficient incentive.

The learning process is the proper repetition of the desired method at the standard speed.

It remains but to show the relation of the motion model to the chronocyclegraph, the use of the motion model for teaching, and for comparing the results of various methods of teaching. The motion models are made by observing the chronocyclegraph through the stereoscope, and bending a wire until it coincides with the path of the motion observed. The chronocyclegraph is best made in combination with the penetrating screen, that enables the motion model maker to measure, and thus to transfer to his wire very small elements of the motion path. The motion model maker is provided with a cross-sectioned background against which he can hold his model during the construction period, to compare his results with the cyclegraph from which he is working. He is also provided with a cross-sectioned box in which he may place the model, for observation and analysis. As the original cyclegraph, by means of the penetrating screen method, may be inclosed in a box of as many sides as are desired, it is often possible to facilitate the making of the model by the use of a properly cross-sectioned box. This box is of wood painted black, with the cross-sectioning done in white. The motion model, upon its completion, is painted black. The spots upon the chronocyclegraph are represented by spots painted upon the model. These spots are made of white paint, shading gradually through grey to black, and when finished resemble very closely in shape the pointed spots seen upon the chronocyclegraph. The motion model, which has now become a chronocyclegraph motion model, may be fastened against a cross-sectioned background and photographed from exactly the same viewpoint from which the chronocyclegraph was taken. The photograph of the model and the chronocyclegraph record may then be compared. Unless they are exactly similar the motion model is not considered a complete success. In cases where the motion cycle recorded is complicated, it is of great assistance to take chronocyclegraph records from several different viewpoints, as such records assist in making the motion model more perfect. In some cases two or more viewpoints can be obtained by mirrors.

The motion model has all the uses of the chronocyclegraph as a recorder of standards. In addition it has its teaching uses. The first of these is an assistance in visualising the motion path. The motion model makes it possible actually to see the path that the motion traverses. It makes it possible to see this path from all angles. This was not possible with the chronocyclegraph, for, even where many chronocyclegraphs were made, the sum total of them only represented viewing the motion from the specific number of angles. The motion model can be viewed from all directions, from above, from below, and from all sides. A further importance of this in the industries is seen in the effect of the motion model upon the invention and redesigning of machinery to conform to least wasteful motions. The necessary limitations of shop conditions, machine operations, etc., make it often impossible to obtain a chronocyclegraph from more than one direction. Here we have all such limitations for viewing the motion removed. The motion model thus immediately educates its user by enabling him to see something that he has never before seen.

The motion model also teaches its user to make more intelligent use of chronocyclegraphs and cyclegraphs. These take on a new meaning when one has actually seen and used their corresponding models. In point of fact, a constant use of the motion model is a great help in visualising a motion path without a chronocyclegraph. Of course, such visualising cannot compare with the chronocyclegraph record, though it is often sufficient as a stimulus to motion economy and to invention. The motion model is also of use in that it enables one to teach the path of the motion. It makes it tangible. It makes the learner realise the problem of transportation involved. This has the byproduct of impressing the user with the value of motions. It is extremely difficult to demonstrate to the average person the reality and value, and especially the money value, of an intangible thing. The motion model makes this value apparent and impressive. It *makes tangible the fact that time is money, and that an unnecessary motion is money lost forever.*

The motion model is of peculiar value to its maker. The process of observing chronocyclegraphs and then bending the wire accordingly is not only excellent training in accurate observation, but impresses the maker, as probably nothing else could, with the importance of motions. He comes to be extremely interested in the significance of every curve and bend and twist and change of direction. He comes to realise the importance of the slightest change from a straight line, or a smooth curve. The elements in the motion cycle become apparent. He learns to think in elementary motions.

There are at least two methods, then, by which the models may be used to transfer experience.

1. By having the learner make such models.
2. By having the learner use such models.

The sequence with which these two methods should be used would be determined by the thing being taught, by the learner, by the teacher, and by many other variables. If the object of the teaching is to transfer some definite experience, or skill, in the shortest possible amount of time, it is better to give the completed model to the learner at the outset, and allow him to make a model later when he has learned the standard method, and may be stimulated to invention. If the object is to teach the learner the importance of motions and their elements, it is better to allow him to make a motion model first and to use the model later.

There is also a great difference between the method by which the motion model is used to teach the expert and to teach the beginner. The expert uses the motion model for learning the existing motion path and the possible lines for improvement. He notes the indications of an efficient motion, its smoothness, its grace, its strong marks of habit, its indication of decision and lack of fatigue. Nothing but a close study of an efficient motion, as compared with the various stages of inefficiency through which it passed, can make clear these various indications. The changes from awkwardness to grace, from indecision or hesitation to decision, from imperfect habit to perfect habit, have a fascination to those interested which seems to increase constantly. The expert, then, takes the model in whatever stage it may be, and through its use charts the lines along which the progress towards a more efficient path can be obtained. The motion model is to the expert a "thought detonator," or a stimulus to invention. On the other hand, to the beginner who is a learner, the motion model is a completed thing, a standard, and it should be in the most perfect state possible before being given to him. Through its use he can see what he is to do, learn about it through his eye, follow the wire with his fingers, and thus accustom his muscles to the activity that they are expected to perform. Moreover, he can, through the speed indications, follow the path at the desired speed, by counting, or by the use of specially designed timing devices that appeal to his eye, to his ear, or to both simultaneously. All of the sense teaching is thus closely correlated. A further correlation through books or through oral instructions concerning the significance of what he sees and touches, makes the instruction highly efficient.

This method of instruction may seem at first applicable to manual work only, but, as with its use the importance of decisions and their relation to the motions becomes more apparent, it will be seen that the complete field of use has by no means as yet been completely charted. So much for the motion model as a means of transferring experience, or of teaching.

We next turn to the motion model as a means for recording results. We have already discussed at some length the motion model as a record of a method of performing an activity. It can also serve as a record of the individual's, that is, the learner's response to the teaching. If at various stages of the individual's learning process his behaviour be chronocyclegraphed and then motion modeled, and the results compared with the motion model, we have a very definite and visible standard of progress. If various individuals at the same stage of learning be thus handled, we have not only a record of their progress, but also a record of the value of the method being used. If proper test conditions be maintained, and other individuals be trained along a different method, and the various sets of motion models be then compared, we have a comparative record of results. It will be seen that this method of comparing results may be used even where the motion model has not in any way been used as a teacher. The results of any number of educational methods that manifest themselves in any form of behaviour may be compared.

We have also a method that will record fatigue, and that, therefore, will make possible the determination of rest periods, their length compared to working periods, and also their distribution throughout the hours of the day.[6]

We have said many times that there is no waste in the world to-day that equals the waste in needless, ineffective and ill-directed motions and their resulting unnecessary fatigue. This means that there are no savings that can be made to-day that can compare with those made by eliminating useless motions, and transforming ineffective and ill-directed motions into properly directed and efficient motions. "Motion Economy," "Savings" and "Waste Elimination" must be the watchwords of the day; savings not only in money, but in the mental and physical elements that produce the money and the durable satisfactions of life. It is for you to conserve, to utilise and to increase this intelligence by training all people, and especially the coming generation, to become *thinkers in elements of motions*. The greatest wealth of the nation consists of the intelligence and skill of its people.

The Three Position Plan of Promotion[1]

●●

An adequate system of promotion is the solution not only of holding employés in an organisation, but also of the employment problem.

There is much emphasis to-day upon the proper *selection* of employés, and many and elaborate systems have been undertaken for a scientific, or near-scientific, *placement*. These are not in any wise to be criticised, for the selection of the individuals comprising any organisation is important, and any plan that will cause the employment manager to plan his duties carefully and to give each decision on the

---

[6] See "Fatigue Study," page 127, Sturgis & Walton Co., New York City.
[1] Reprinted from "The Annals" of the American Academy of Political and Social Science, Philadelphia, May, 1916. Publication No. 1001.

fortunes of others careful consideration is to be commended. It must be realised, however, that even more important is holding and helping these employés after they have been selected, and providing an adequate systematized plan of advancement for them. In the Three Position Plan of Promotion we have not only the true and proved answer to the problem of promotion, but also the means by which efficient placement becomes almost automatic, and a supply of desirable applicants for any vacant position is constantly available. No system of placement can hope to succeed unless such a supply of applicants is available.

We wish to emphasise then three points:

1. The necessity of attracting desirable applicants.
2. The necessity of holding, fitting, and promoting those already employed.
3. The interdependence of these two.

We have never known a better friend of the worker than Mr. James Mapes Dodge, and he was wont to emphasise and demonstrate the benefit not only to the employé, but also to the organisation of holding the co-operating employé, and the great and needless loss to the organisation, to the worker, and to society in a constant change of the personnel of the organisation. Now, no organisation can hope to hold its members that does not consider not only the welfare of the organisation as a whole, but also the welfare of the individuals composing that organisation.

The Three Position Plan of Promotion considers each man as occupying three positions in the organisation, and considers these three positions as constantly changing in an upward spiral, as the man is promoted from the lowest position that he occupies and into the position next higher than the highest position that he occupies. The three positions are as follows: first, and lowest, the position that the man has last occupied in the organisation; second, the position that the man is occupying at present in the organisation; third, and highest, the position that the man will next occupy. In the third position the worker occupies the place of the teacher, this position being at the same time occupied by two other men, that is, by the worker doing the work, who receives little or no instruction in the duties of that position except in an emergency, and by the worker below who is learning the work. In the second position the worker is actually in charge of the work, and is constantly also the teacher of the man next below him, who will next occupy the position. He is also, in emergencies, a learner of the duties of his present position from the man above him. In the first position the worker occupies the place of learner, and is being constantly instructed by the man in the duties of the position immediately above.

Naturally a plan like this demands a close co-ordination of all positions. This is provided for through the master promotion chart. This chart is in the hands of the man in charge of promotion. It is slightly different for each organisation. It consists of a schematic arrangement of all positions in the organisation, so arranged as to provide for lines of most rapid advancement, along the various functions and subfunctions, under which the measured functional management by which we operate, works. The great advantage of such a chart is that it makes possible visualising the complete problem of the organisation's needs in teaching and preparing its members. The direct product of this is that the man in charge of promotion sees clearly the needs and the means of filling them, the demand and the supply. The important by-product is the gradual evolution of permanent, rapid, direct paths of promotion. This means the abolishment of the "blind alley" job, that is, a position into which some member of the organisation drifts with no chance for advancement. Another by-product of this chart is the fact that the promotion head, the promotion manager, or chief of promotion, as he has been variously called, can arrange for shifting or transferring the worker easily, if he sees that he has been improperly placed, or, if he develops abilities along some unexpected line. This is often the case under this type of management where there is great opportunity for the development of latent, as well as apparent, abilities. This master promotion chart is the great educative force to the management as to the importance of proper promotion.

The interests of the individual worker and his education as to the importance of promotion are carried on through the individual promotion charts. Upon these the records of each and every member of the organisation are separately kept. These sheets are often called "fortune sheets," and it is this aspect of them that is of peculiar interest to the psychologist. When a worker becomes an interested, or particularly co-operative or efficient member of the organisation he is called into the department in charge of advancement or promotion, and given one of these fortune sheets. Upon it is shown his present position, and he and the man in charge outline together his possible and probable line of advancement. The sheet then becomes his fortune map, or fortune schedule. The projected line of promotion is outlined in green, and upon it are placed the dates at which it is hoped he may reach the various stages of advancement. At set times the worker and the promotion chief, or one of his helpers, meet, and the line of actual progress of advancement of the worker is traced upon the map in red, with the dates of achieving the various positions. The two then consult as to existing conditions, the special reading and studying necessary for fitting for the new positions, possible changes, or betterments. The direct product of this is that the worker understands what he is doing, gets expert advice for greater progress, and realises that there is, and must be, co-operation between him and the promotion department for the good of all concerned. The by-products are equally, or more, important. One is that the worker is glad to impart all information that would be of help to the organisation as to his history and antecedents, his home and other social conditions outside the plant, that help or hinder his plans of preparing, ambitions, etc. It is common practice in these days to present the applicant with blanks to be filled in with all this information. We use such blanks in selecting applicants, always with the proviso that, if the applicant shows any disinclination to fill out such parts of the blank as tell of his ambitions or other details, which he may consider confidential, he be not required to do so. This information has been invariably volunteered, when the fortune map, or schedule, is understood. Naturally the applicant must furnish such information as will show his ability and reliability; but, as we will see later, these are so supplemented by data obtained through other sources that it is not necessary to ask for information usually considered confidential before it is volunteered. The second by-product of these fortune sheets is directly connected with the solution of the problem of getting constantly a group of desirable applicants from which to select more wisely. Thus, when the worker looks at his fortune sheet, and understands the three position plan of employment, he recognises that he must train some one to take his position before he can hope to be most rapidly advanced. Naturally he first looks around in the organisation to see who is available, for it is always desired that those within the organisation be advanced first. However, if no such person is available, he reviews his entire acquaintance, and all possible sources for new workers, in order that he may obtain the most desirable person easy to train into that position. It is not necessary to dwell long upon the advantages of this system for holding members already in the organisation. No worker who is constitutionally able to become a permanent member of an organisation will wish to change, if he is receiving adequate pay and has ample opportunity for advancement, especially, if, as here, he is a member of a group where it is to the advantage—more than that—actually to the selfish interest, of every member to push all higher members up, and to teach and fit others to advance from below. Inseparably associated with this is the fact that any worker will be ready and glad to enter an organisation where such conditions exist, and a desirable applicant will automatically present himself, when needed, at the direct request of some one who knows his particular fitness for the job, and desires him to have it. This selecting of the worker by the worker is real democracy. An organisation built thus has proved to be the most satisfying to both management and workers.

Now there are various questions that may arise concerning this subject, that it is well to answer here.

What becomes of the workers who find exactly the positions that suit them, and have no desire to advance?

The answer to this is that, if a worker finds such a position, he is retained in it, and that others who go beyond it are trained by him in the work of that position until they know enough about it to advance to the next higher grade. This often happens, especially in the case of the workers who prefer positions entailing comparatively little responsibility, and who, arriving at some work that satisfies them, and that involves but slight responsibility, choose to make that particular work a life vocation. If, as is seldom the case, a second worker is found who desires to remain in the same position, it is sometimes advisable to place such a contented specialist in another organisation, as trained and satisfied expert workers and teachers are all too rare.

If promotion is constant, are not men constantly promoted or graduated out of the organisation?

The answer to this is "Yes, and always to waiting and far better positions."

What becomes of such well known "blind alley" jobs as that of elevator or errand boy?

These positions are transformed into training stations or schools. Through them the young worker is put in touch with various lines of activity in the organisation and his possibilities, capabilities and tastes are noted. Tending jobs under this type of management are also so used as training stations. The new work for crippled soldiers, which is now occupying so much of our attention, is also furnishing a means of filling such "blind alley" jobs. A position that might be deadening for a young, ambitious boy, or for a progressive worker, might prove the salvation of a maimed, or crippled, worker who might otherwise become an idle, unproductive, and worst of all, a discouraged and unhappy member of the community.

How can the close "human touch" that is essential to this system of promotion be maintained in a large organisation?

We maintain this spirit through what we call the "Godfather Movement." This is especially successful where there are many young workers. Some older man in the organisation, preferably in the same department, or interested in the same line of work, is made the godfather of several young, or inexperienced, workers, and keeps in touch constantly with their progress. We call this man "the Godfather" in all foreign countries, where the relation between godparent and godchild is an unusually close one, and is very similar to the sort of relation supposed to exist here between members of the same family. It resembles, perhaps, in this country more the "Big Brother" or "Big Sister" Movement now so popular.

What are the actual results of the workers already employed using this system of promotion?

They are most satisfactory in every case. In organisations where we have installed this system as a part of our plan of management we have seen

    a. Office and messenger boys pass through five positions in one year.
    b. A messenger boy become head storekeeper in three years.
    c. A mechanic become night superintendent in four years.
    d. A foreman become superintendent in two years.
    e. A receiving clerk become head production clerk in three years.
    f. A stenographer pass through five positions to motion study assistant in one year.
    g. A stenographer pass through five positions to assistant chief of the three position plan in one and one-half years.
    h. An office boy become assistant purchasing agent in three years.
    i. A half-time apprentice become foreman in three and one-half years.

j. A stenographer become head of the department of graphical presentation of statistics.

k. A labourer become superintendent in nine years.

and other cases too numerous to mention, many advancing in spite of predicted dire failure of the plan of selection, placement and promotion. The greatest good is, perhaps, not the individual advancement, but the increased interest and zeal of all the workers under this plan.

What are the practical results on supply of applicants and on better placement?

In our experience we have never failed when using this plan of promotion to supply all needs of the organisation almost immediately with most desirable and efficient workers. Every member of the organisation working under this plan has become an active and successful "employment bureau man."

What are the advantages of this whole plan to the man in charge of the function of employment?

He benefits by this plan, perhaps, more than any one else. He comes in close touch with every member of the organisation. It is to the advantage of every member to tell him exactly which individuals he thinks had better follow him, whether these are inside or outside the organisation. Imagine for a moment that you are such a chief. *A* comes in and says, "Mr. Blank, I should like *O* to follow me in my position." *B* comes in and says, "I should like *O* to follow me in my position." *C* comes in and says, "Mr. Blank, I should like *O* to follow me in my position." Naturally you would recognise the wisdom of getting better acquained with *O*. Or, perhaps, you suggest to *A,* "I think that *M* would be a good man to follow you," and *A* says, "No, I think I had better have some one else." You suggest *M* also to *B* and *C*, who reply somewhat along similar lines. There may be nothing fundamentally wrong with *M*, but the line you have planned will probably not receive so much co-operation as it should, and, in any case, there is something there worth investigating. Again, a worker comes to you says, "Mr. Blank, I know a man who is not in this organisation who would be just the person to follow me. You know there is no one available just now, as the man below me is satisfied with his job." Here follow particulars as to the desired man's education, training, etc., which act as the supplementary data before mentioned. The recommender is given a blank form of "recommendation" to fill out for filing, whether or not the proposed man is hired. This naturally leads to the question

Can any part of this plan of promotion be used without the other parts?

The answer is "Yes" and "No." "No," if the desired results are to be obtained in full, since the entire system is interrelated and correlated with the complete plan of Measured Functional Management. "Yes," in that the fundamental ideas underlying this plan can undoubtedly be worked out in many ways. The immediate success of this plan is fostered by a carefully devised set of forms and charts and other devices for visualizing the possibilities of individual success that have stood the test of time and use. The ultimate success of this plan depends upon the principles[2] that underlsy it, giving every man a square deal, a maximum chance for co-operation, advancement and prosperity, in other words, the opportunity for simultaneous individual and social development.

The Effect of Motion Study Upon the Workers[1]

• •

Motion study makes all activity interesting. While, at first thought, this fact may not seem of great importance, in reality it is the cause of many of the far-reaching results obtained through motion study. Motion study consists of analyzing an activity into its smallest possible elements, and from the results synthesising a method of performing the activity that shall be more efficient,—the word "efficient" being used in its highest sense.

[2] See "The Psychology of Management," Sturgis & Walton, New York City.
[1] Reprinted from "The Annals" of the American Academy of Political and Social Science, Philadelphia, May, 1916. Publication No. 1000.

The process of motion study is such as to interest the worker. While undoubtedly some success could be made of motion study through a trained observer merely watching the worker, we find it of utmost importance and mutually advantageous from every standpoint, to gain the full and hearty co-operation of the worker at once, and to enlist him as a co-worker in the motion study from the moment the first investigation is made. Our methods of making motion study are by the use of the micromotion, simultaneous motion cycle chart, and chronocyclegraph methods. All make it imperative that the worker shall understand what is being done and why, and make it most profitable to every one that the worker shall be able, as well as willing, to help in the work of obtaining methods of least waste by means of motion study. While the process of making motion and time studies through the use of the cinematograph, the microchronometer and the cross-sectioned screen have been so reduced in cost as to make them indispensable even from the cost standpoint, the process is made even more economical when the worker, or the observed man, does his best work, and endeavours to take a part of active initiative in deriving the motion standards. We find in our practice that the worker is only too glad to do this. In fact, it is usually he, oftener than the observer, who cries out, "Wait a moment till this is done in the best way possible," or "Wait a moment, please, I know a way that I believe is easier." Similarly, when using the chronocyclegraph device; the worker is not only interested in the electric lights and their various paths and orbits of dots and dashes, but is most anxious that these paths shall be those of the greatest skill and the fewest number of motions possible.

The various methods used with these various types of apparatus, which are usually new to the worker, present problems in psychology which are interesting to the worker as well as to the observer. The worker is quick to note that, with the new conditions attending the measuring work, his own process varies for a short time at the beginning from his unusual habits, because of the entering of the variables of the apparatus and the strange conditions that it involves. He is quick to notice, also, that this effect of strangeness soon disappears, and that he then works exactly in accordance with his normal method. This period of strangeness, far from being a disadvantage, is, on the contrary, often a great advantage. The worker is almost *sure to revert to the former habit,* and an investigator or observer often gains valuable clues not only to excellent standards, but to necessary methods of teaching those standards, particularly with emphasis on eliminating interference of many wrong habits acquired in trade learning prior to conscious effort for motion economy. It is, therefore, clear that during the period of making motion studies the effect of them upon the worker is educative to the highest degree, for not only does he become interested in what he does, but he learns to think of all activity in terms of motions and elements of motions. The by-products of this are also important, as he is always able afterwards to learn new work much faster and with comparatively little coaching, and as he has that success that usually attends the work of one who knows the least wasteful method of attack of learning the new problems of performing the new task.

The effects of motion study are particularly striking upon the observer or the man actually making the studies. This is true not only during the time of making the observation, but also during the time spent in embodying the data derived in simultaneous cycle motion charts and in motion models. These motion models, which are wire representations of the paths of the motion, made from the stereoscopic records derived from the chronocyclegraph process have a peculiar educative value that is well embodied in the following statement of a young engineer who spent some time making motion models as a part of that thorough training for motion and time study man which we believe so necessary:

"After making a number of models of motions I have changed from a scoffer to a firm believer. I believe not only in their value as an aid to the study of the psychology of motions, but also as to their educational value in the teaching of the motion study man.

"I consider them of the same value to the motion study man as is the model of an engine or a mechanical device to an engineer. If the engineer was to study, for instance, a railroad engine, and the only chance he had to study was to watch an engine going by him at express train speed, his impression as to the mechanical working of the engine would be, to say the least, vague.

"A motion, in itself, is intangible, but a model of a motion gives one an altogether different viewpoint, as it seems to make one see more clearly that each motion leaves a definite path, which path may be subjected to analysis.

"I have made motion studies since making models, and what I learned from making the models has convinced me of their value. In former motion studies which I have made, my attention was always divided, more or less equally, between the direct distance between the starting and finishing points of the motion, the equipment, and the surroundings. I have found that, since seeing a motion, as represented by a model, I am better able to concentrate first on the motion itself, and then upon the variables which affect the motion. This seems to me a more logical method, and I know that I have had better results.

"I believe a good method of illustrating how a motion model helps one to visualise is to compare it with the wake left by an ocean liner. When one stands at the stern of a liner, which changes its course often, and watches the wake he can visualize the change more readily than when unable to see the wake."

It is interesting to note here not only the interest aroused intensively in the subject of motion study itself, but also extensively in the correlation of processes in the industries with general processes outside. The motion study man is a specialist who, because of his work, spends a large amount of time in the close study of motions, but to some extent this intensive and extensive interest is aroused in all those engaged in motion study, whether as observers or observed.

After the results of motion study are actually installed the effects are as great or greater upon those who work under the derived standards. It must be understood that *motion study* always implies *fatigue study*,[2] for the best and least wasteful results cannot be obtained otherwise, and that the worker who operates under these standards, therefore, not only has time to do the work in the best way, but ample time for adequate recovery from the fatigue of his work. This procedure provides directly for his physical and mental well-being. Motion study lays particular emphasis upon this. The great bogey of all who argue against standardisation is "the awful resulting monotony." Now psychology,[3] as well as the results in actual practice, proves that monotony comes not from performing the activity the same way every time, but from a *lack of interest involved in, or associated with, the activity*. This interest is supplied not only directly by motion study, but indirectly by the other parts of measured functional management, such as devices for eliminating unnecessary fatigue and for overcoming necessary fatigue.

Besides all this there is the interest aroused and the education resulting from the graphic representation of the results of motion study data to the worker as well as the observer. The pictures of the micromotion films are projected at the normal speed of the moving picture. They are also examined one at a time. The chronocycle-

[2] See "Fatigue Study," Sturgis & Walton, New York City.
[3] See "The Psychology of Management," Sturgis & Walton, New York City.

graphs in three dimensions are shown through the stereoscope, on the screen, by means of the wire motion models to the workers at the foremen's and workers' meetings and are there discussed. All the traditional knowledge is literally collected, measured, sorted, tagged and labelled. These data, together with indisputable measuring methods is presented before those possessing the greatest craft skill of the old methods, and who can quickest actually learn the new knowledge and put it to use. The new knowledge is of no use to the employer without the co-operation of the worker. This fact puts the relations between the worker and his employer on a new basis. They *must* co-operate, or both pay an awful price. These new methods have demonstrated that there is so much to learn that the employer cannot afford to put on and lay off his employés in proportion to the receipt of orders. He must solve the problem of steady employment. He cannot afford to let his specially trained men "get away." This is of vital importance in its effect upon the mental condition and activity of the worker.

By these means the workers, who are the actual producers of the nation, become familiar in every day experience with motion study and time study instruments of precision and with the results of their use. Such knowledge in the hands of our workers is the means of their being able to take the initiative in acquiring greater skill in all trades and in all life works. This is one of the best forms of industrial preparedness. It must be emphasised that the facts concerning motion study here stated embody not only a program but a record. The actual every day practice of motion study shows these effects upon the worker not only in the intangible results of added interest and a different attitude towards the work, but also in such tangible results as a larger number and a more profitable set of suggestions in the suggestion boxes, better attended and more profitable foremen's and workers' meetings, a greater number of promotions, more co-operation, more reading and study of the science of management, and higher wages earned with greater ease.

Motion study has no right to claim all the benefits that accrue from measured functional management, but, as a part of this management, it shares in these benefits, and thus those who work under it are assured of unusually high pay, during and after the motion study, a chance for promotion, physical and mental well-being, and a co-operative atmosphere in which to work. Motion study has the right to claim as its own benefits an added interest not only in the activity involved in the particular work done in the office or plant or wherever the work place may be, but in all activity away from as well as at work. Motion study benefits employés and employers, as well as everybody else who adopts its methods, because *it makes "to do,"* *mean "to be interested," and to be interested means to be more efficient, more prosperous, and more happy.*

A Final Note

• •

In writing this volume with the aim of eliminating waste, we realise that progress in general waste elimination is always retarded by the feeling that it is for others rather than ourselves. In order that we might practise what we preach, we requested that this book be printed in accordance with the forms of spelling recommended by the Simplified Spelling Board, New York City. The publishers ruled otherwise, and to change the spelling now would cause delay.

New conditions confront the world to-day. These new conditions demand as never before that savings be made whenever possible. Simpler Spelling requires less time to learn, saves motions of writing, typing, setting type and eye swing in reading. It saves ink, pencils, paper, and consequently helps save forests. The saving of forests in turn eliminates floods. The elimination of floods saves the priceless fertile soil from being eroded and washed to the seas, there to be lost forever.

Some of the greatest scholars in the English speaking world gathered together as the Simplified Spelling Board have made certain standards for simplification without any confusion or loss of any advantages of the present forms of spelling.

Simpler spelling has been adopted by over 300 schools, colleges and publishers during the last year. Its adoption is progressing faster than is generally realised. There is no logical argument against the forms recommended.

Ignorance and custom are the great hindrances to progress. Every possible saving in time, materials and fatigue that enables us to get more out of life should be adopted.

LILLIAN M. GILBRETH,
FRANK B. GILBRETH,
Member Advisory Council Simplified
Spelling Board.

7

MOTION STUDY
FOR THE
HANDICAPPED*

* Presented at the Tenth Sagamore Sociological Conference, June 27–29, 1917.

The Re-education of the Crippled Soldier[1]

• •

There is no question more important, more interesting and more timely to-day than the question of education. It seems ridiculous to say that we are only now beginning to realize the importance of education, yet such is undoubtedly the fact.

Lack of education lies at the root of many of our troubles to-day, and wrong methods of education will account for most of the others. The great problems of waste and its elimination, that range all the way from the saving of the least bit of food or fuel material to the elimination of the needless losses of war, are all based upon lack of, or wrong methods of, education.

It is time that the world faced this situation squarely, and realized that not only for present prosperity, but also for future safety and happiness, we must acknowledge the importance of education and discover and standardize the most efficient methods, also that the time to begin the reconstructive work is NOW.

It is with this broadest aspect of the situation from an economic, educational and waste-eliminating standpoint in mind that we desire to emphasize the importance of re-education for the Crippled Soldier. Here we have a small branch of educational activity overwhelmingly prominent just now, that gives us an opportunity to demonstrate what can be done with efficient education and the effects of such education upon eliminating waste.

The need for re-educating the crippled soldier is self-evident. We have, in many countries of the globe to-day, the economic balance destroyed or threatened by the sudden withdrawal of the fighting men of the country. These, if they return at all, come back, many

[1] [EDITORS' NOTE: The thinking behind the work for the handicapped is as good to-day as it was after World War I. If allowance is made for the improvement in prosthetic devices, medicine, psychiatry, and the change in our colloquial vocabulary, the material is as appropriate in 1953 as it was in 1917.]

277

of them, changed, to a greater or less extent, in capabilities and demands. We have men of all types of education, or without education, crippled and wounded, and placed suddenly and without preparation in situations where their previous training, in its specific aspects, seems to stand them in little stead. This is especially true of those who have only a manual education, since when they are physically disabled they find themselves unable to adapt themselves to new occupations without considerable assistance.

The world needs the work of every person existing and able to be a producer, but most important of all is the cripple's own need for constructive activity, and for feeling that he is still able to do "a man's job" in the world.

It is most necessary to emphasize that while the re-education of the crippled soldier affords a most excellent place for demonstration as to efficient educational methods, it is no field for experimenting. Fortunately such experimentation is not necessary. Efficient methods of education have been worked out, and all that is needed now is the energy and skill to apply them. Having studied the problem of the crippled soldier abroad, both thru actual observation and thru correspondence with the foremost scientists engaged in the re-education there, and knowing the needs, we have worked out in the laboratory the methods by which suitable occupations for cripples of any type may be determined and also methods by which training in these occupations may be transferred to the crippled learner.

This has been done thru Simultaneous Cycle Motion Charts and Motion Models, which embody data gathered thru the application of the micromotion method, and the cyclegraph method of recording data.

With these methods it is not necessary that experiments be made on the cripples themselves. The experiments, many of which have already been made, can be made upon unmaimed learners or workers, and, thru the devices, the data from these experiments can be incorporated into data to be used for the cripples.

We have been fortunate in having secured quite splendid cooperation in making these investigations—the Hon. John Barrett, Director of the Pan-American Union, having been one of the first to demonstrate to his own satisfaction and that of others the possibility of performing activity usually considered "two armed" with but one arm.

The advantage of experimenting with the unmaimed subjects is that they possess to an exaggerated degree the awkwardness that characterizes the recent cripple. Hence methods that succeed with them succeed with even greater ease and speed when applied to the maimed worker who has become accustomed to lacking various working members.

The methods, therefore, are ready. It is trained teachers that we lack.

There are various methods by which we may prepare these. One is by cooperating with those who are re-educating cripples abroad. This might be done by sending those who are to do the teaching here into the foreign field to see what is being done. This method has the disadvantage of necessitating sending people to some distance to acquire their information, and a further disadvantage, in that much of the work in foreign countries, because done without adequate preparation, is really not fit to be used as a model for our work here. Therefore it seems best that the training be done here in this country, under laboratory conditions. The industries furnish ample supply of cripples of all types who may be used as sample learners if such are desired, with the added benefit to these individuals and to the industries to which they will return.

We have been fortunate here also in obtaining cooperation from industrial workers who have eagerly embraced the opportunity to make their experience of use to others.

It is perhaps but natural that there should be a feeling in this country that, with so many pressing problems, the problem of the cripple can be left until such time as the cripples do return. Such an argument is, however, very misleading. The chief errors into which the countries abroad have fallen have arisen from the fact that this very thing was done, that the solution of the problem was postponed until the return of large numbers of cripples made some sort of solution necessary. The result was "hit-or-miss" attempts to better conditions that have left much to be desired.

These all demonstrate the necessity for beginning the work *now*. It must be begun from various standpoints; first, those who are to teach the cripples must be thoroly trained, both in the schools and in the industries. Second, a thoro survey of industrial opportunities must be made both by trained survey makers who have received special instructions as to what is needed, and by those in the industries themselves, who must furnish the largest amount of the data, if this is to be accumulated with the greatest amount of speed. Again, we must make arrangements to have those trained in teaching sent to the base hospitals, that preliminary work in re-education may be undertaken as soon as possible. The moment a man is able to take his mind from the pain of his wounds, and perhaps even before this, the possibilities of re-education must be presented to him. Again, provisions must be made for seeing that this re-education is done under military regulations, that is to say, it must not only be *offered* to cripples but it must be *insisted upon,* exactly as it is in the highest type of work now being done, that in France. Again, every mind of the country must be focused upon discovering opportunities for the cripples. We must realize that these are of three kinds. They consist

1. Of so adapting cripples to jobs already existing, or so adapting such jobs to cripples, that cripples may become competitors with the whole worker.
2. Of finding occupations that do not exist, but which should exist for public prosperity, and assigning these to crippled workers.
3. Of reserving certain jobs for cripples, and putting them in these jobs on a non-competitive basis so far as uncrippled workers are concerned.

This is one part of the educational work that must be done for the general public. Another is arousing interest in the discovery, invention or adaptation of devices that will make it possible for the cripple not only to have a productive and paying occupation but also to "fit back" into all the ordinary activities of life. These may or may not be attached to the maimed limb of the cripple. They may be such simple devices as a tilting box and magnetized hammer to make possible nailing with but one arm. The more activities the cripples can master easily the more capable he will feel, and be.

If the most efficient methods are transferred with the least amount of waste—and if as many things are taught as can be adapted to, and useful to, the cripple—the resulting "re-education" will not only "make good" in itself, but will offer a model for all education to follow.

Motion Study for Crippled
Soldiers[2]

●●●

Motion study causes invention automatically. In such motion study invention lies a solution of the problem of enabling the crippled soldiers to earn high wages in the industries after peace has come. The lines along which the inventions are to be made are determined by accurate measurement. Hence, the resulting invention is a permanent improvement upon the best practice known.

The problem of the crippled soldier is no new one, tho it is seen in its most impressive and exaggerated form to-day. Furthermore, the problem of the mutilated soldier is really the same problem as that of the worker injured by an accident in the industries, so far as the engineer's particular field is concerned. While the soldier is still wounded or ill, his treatment lies in the province of the doctors, nurses, convalescents' homes, and other agencies for immediate relief. When the soldier is discharged from these as having been healed or repaired—to as great an extent as is possible—securing his usefulness, efficiency and happiness becomes a problem for the engineer, the motion study expert, and for the industries. There are some who think that it is the duty of their respective countries to support these crippled and maimed defenders for the remainder of their lives, and to require no work or activity on their part. Those who have been in close touch with actual conditions know that the last thing in the world the sufferer wants is such enforced or continuous idleness. The great horror of the majority of injured soldiers is that of becoming non-productive members of the community, as men who have done their work and are allowed to exist on sufferance. It is to be hoped that they will get pensions, but the enormous debts of their respective countries will make such procedure extremely difficult. In any case,

---

[2] A paper presented at a meeting of the American Association for the Advancement of Science, in Columbus, Ohio, December 27, 1915, to January 1, 1916.

281

it is the duty of the engineer, for he is best fitted to accomplish results, to provide as rapidly as possible the means and ways by which these men who wish again to become workers may accomplish their day's work satisfactorily to themselves and to their families and friends, without undue strain and fatigue, and with the greatest possible amount of personal satisfaction. The crippled soldier is like any other crippled worker who returns to his occupation. He may have suffered, however, from a greater shock and have more horrible recollections. If so there is all the more need for providing him with proper and suitable work quickly, so that his mind may be taken from his own misfortunes and occupied with other interests; and all the more reason for making the work attractive, inspiring and stimulating.

The maimed soldier, if he has been an industrial worker, will, in many cases, the same as his mates in the industries who have been maimed during their work there, prefer to return to his previous line of work. With the remarkable mechanical artificial limbs that now exist this may be quite possible; if it is impossible, to as nearly that type of work as he can. This being the case, many workers can be best provided for by some change that will adapt the work to the man. This may consist principally of rearranging the surroundings, equipment and tools. It may consist of slight modifications of machinery. It may consist of changing the method by which the work is done, that is, of allowing some other work member of the worker's body to perform the motions that formerly were made by a member that is now maimed or missing. In any case the need is for invention. In similar situations the need has always been for invention, and the need has been met in the best manner available. Perhaps it was found that the work could be done sitting as well as standing, in which case the worker was given a chair specially designed to fit his individual requirements. Perhaps it was found, as in a case of typewriting, that a motion for moving the shift key, formerly done with the hand, could be transferred to the foot, or that the injured operator could use another make of typewriter having a double keyboard, thus requiring no shift key, and enabling a one-armed man to become a successful operator. Such a change as this meant both the redesign of the machine and training a new member to do the work. However, the limitations of such "hit-or-miss" casual inventions are evident. Unless an improvement in equipment were obvious, there was formerly no precise method for knowing exactly along which line the change in design should lie. In the second place, it was difficult to visualize which members of the body were engaged simultaneously in the activity, and thus transfer of activity from one member of the body to another was, consequently, also difficult. In the third place, there being no headquarters, no definite channel, for the exchange of information, the benefit of the invention was apt to cease with the particular individual for whom it was made.

The problem, then, becomes one of visualizing

1. The existing surroundings, equipment and tools.
2. The best method for performing the work under existing conditions.
3. The standard or most appropriate type of worker to perform the work.

The visualization of the method (that is 2) enables us to see

a. The various members of the body engaged in performing the operation.
b. The motions and elements of motions used by these various members.
c. The relative and actual time consumed by each element of a motion.

We must be able not only to see these facts, but to see them all at the same time.

We have realized the importance of such visualization, and for years endeavored to obtain the device that would make it possible. This device we herewith now present in the form of the Simultaneous Cycle Motion Chart. This chart has been used by us in our work of installing Scientific Management and Motion Study in the industries and in surgery, and has been found applicable to all lines of activity where applied. In order to explain what this chart does, it is necessary to trace, tho only in outline, its history. Believing for years that the fundamental element in all activity is the motion, we started early to record the motions thru descriptions, thru ordinary and, later, stereoscopic photographs, and with the cinematograph. Thru this last, as we have before explained, in combination with the specially devised clock and the cross-sectioned background, we obtained satisfactory records of motions and elements of motions. We have in the micromotion films all the data necessary for complete visualization of worker, working conditions, and methods. There were but two things needed that were lacking in this record. One was a complete visualization of the entire path of the motion. The other was a visualization of the simultaneity of the different motions made by the different members of the body. It is difficult and practically impossible for the micromotion film, no matter how slowly it be run nor how often it be viewed, to note and hold clearly in mind what each member of the body is doing. We secured a satisfactory record of the path, direction and speed of the motion thru the chronocyclegraph records, and have, by transforming this chronocyclegraph into a motion model, made this path not only visible but tangible.

The Simultaneous Cycle Motion Chart overcame the second difficulty. This chart is made by recording the times vertically, and the various working members of the body horizontally. The ordinary decimal cross-sectioned chart paper is used. The data for the chart is all contained on the micromotion film. Because of the specially devised clock, recording intervals to the millionth of an hour and of any length desired, and the cross-sectioned background, we can read as small an element of the motion as the particular kind of work requires, and can immediately record it upon the chart. This chart is a motion cycle chart, because we have found the cycle the most satisfactory group of motion elements to handle.

A motion cycle consists of the following elements, arranged in varying sequence:

1. Search.
2. Find.
3. Select.
4. Grasp.
5. Position.
6. Assemble.
7. Use.
8. Dissemble, or take apart.
9. Inspect.
10. Transport, loaded.
11. Position for next operation.
12. Release load.
13. Transport, empty.
14. Wait (unavoidable delay).
15. Wait (avoidable delay).
16. Rest (for overcoming fatigue).

When the elements have all been listed, the chart, as is obvious, presents in chronological sequence, when read down any one column, the various activities performed by any member of the body, the posture during a complete cycle, and the time consumed by each element. When read across, the chart presents a record of all the working members of the body at any one time. Each of the seventeen elements of motion activity is represented by its individual color. This enables us to visualize certain desired groupings, and to see at a glance not only which members are working, and which are being delayed, are unoccupied, or resting; but at what they were working, and also to compare the records with records of similar motions in different kinds of work. The immediate use of these Simultaneous Cycle Motion Charts in the industries has been the discovery of the method of least waste, that is, the method of doing the work best fitted to become the standard method. This, of course, is always that method by which the most may be accomplished with no unnecessary fatigue and the least necessary fatigue to the worker. In other words, it enables us to find that method that will allow of the greatest saving of the worker and the greatest prosperity to both worker and employer.

Now, given a maimed worker, a simultaneous motion cycle chart is used

1. To adapt the method to the worker.
2. To assign the worker to an appropriate type of work, if he has no strong preference or aptitude for any particular kind of work.
3. To suggest inventions or changes that will make work and worker a better fit.

It is this "suggestion of automatic invention" that we desire to emphasize. Suppose, for example, that a worker who has lost his left arm desires to return to his former work, which is work apparently requiring both arms and both legs. We may find by looking at the chart that, say, two-thirds of his work is done by the right arm, the left arm doing comparatively little. We find that where both arms are occupied simultaneously, for a large proportion of the time either one or the other of the arms is engaged in "transporting empty." Only for two short intervals are both arms occupied simultaneously. We see at once that it is extremely likely that the left arm's operations can be transferred, with a slight change in the conditions, either to the right arm or the feet, which, while listed as working, since they were standing, are really performing no activity resulting in product. This same chart, which, as illustrated here, shows the bringing back the turret head of a chucking lathe and positioning a new tool ready to cut, shows that the work could be done perfectly under the existing conditions by a man seated, thus not requiring legs for the work. On the other hand, should a man who had done this job lose both arms, it is at once apparent that he should immediately be transferred to some other type of work that can be successfully done without hands. An adequate knowledge of exactly how these charts suggest invention can only be gained by a close study of many of the charts themselves.

It must be apparent, however, immediately, that each element of the body and what it is doing appear before one on the chart something as the chess men stand on the chess board. One can study the board and plan the moves and note the possible opportunities. Those of you who are economists as well as engineers will immediately become impressed with the frightful waste in industrial conditions and will ask at once:

1. Why do we assign whole men to-day to occupations that crippled or maimed workers could handle satisfactorily?
2. Why do we allow a man to occupy so much time in performing work, when assignment of idle members to activity would economize the working time enormously?
3. Why do we allow the accumulation of unnecessary fatigue by work being done standing continuously that could be done sitting a part of the time, and by work being done with fatiguing motions that could be done as well with far less fatiguing motions?

The answer to all these questions is because it has not been common practice to think of these things, and because the economic and social pressure has not been so great, in the past, that the industries were obliged to think of these things. It is selfevident that with the astounding number, literally millions, of crippled and maimed soldiers who must come into the industries, we *must* think of these things and *must* act upon the results of our thinking. The ideal method of attacking the great problem of waste would be, of course, to start at the very foundation and reclassify all the trades themselves, according to the results of Motion Study. Each type of work should be analyzed into its motions and elements of motions. The motions should then be classified according to the amount of strength, skill and numerous other variables of motion study that they require. By this method of division of labor we are able to build up trades with definite manual and mental requirements. This enables us to assign each man to learn and to do that type of work which he could best perform with most profit to himself, to his employer and the community; but this is a change, of course, that cannot be made all at once. However, it is now being made more slowly than is necessary. All this only means more specialization. We can see plainly that the crippled soldier is going to bring absolute demand for highly specialized work before the attention of the world. If a man has but one arm, if he has no legs, if he is blind, he must be assigned to some special type of work. The more work is specialized, the more quickly he can be so assigned, and the more thoroly he can get satisfactory results. There is still some fear, in many minds, as to the dangers of monotony due to specialization. This is not the place to argue that question. It need only be said that nothing is monotonous that is highly interesting, that monotony and fatigue are not synonymous, and that the remedy for so-called "monotony" lies not in supplying a different occupation, but in providing proper rest intervals, together with a sufficient interest and incentive. Remember, there is least monotony where the greatest skill is used. Reclassification of the trades, greater division of labor, and more specialization, these are coming and should come for the benefit of all.

The question now remains: What can we do now, to-day, towards hastening the day of their coming, and towards providing for the immediate need? The answer is: "Stimulate invention, and provide that this invention shall be from the best practice known at the present day." This means collecting:

1. All information as to how individual cripples have succeeded in becoming useful, efficient and happy.
2. All data on changes of machinery to make its use by maimed or crippled workers possible and profitable.
3. All data on the elimination of unnecessary fatigue, and the provision of rest for quickest recovery from necessary fatigue.

Start collecting such data immediately. Send it direct to any one you know who needs it. Send copies of it to us, that we may make it immediately available to the educators in all the warring countries, who are cooperating with us in this work of making their crippled soldiers happy, and also their enemies' crippled soldiers happy, in the least amount of time possible. We will immediately take these data, and, thru the help of the Simultaneous Motion Cycle charts, put it into such shape that it can be used not only to help particular cases like those from whom it was derived, but also to suggest adaptations and inventions that may help other different types of cases. The work of collecting these data may be ultimately that of an International Bureau of Standards. In the meantime, those of us who have actually seen the need firsthand, and heard the calls to help, must do what we can to see that available information is placed where it can do the most good. We can do more than this, in that we can arouse interest everywhere in the subject of Crippled Soldiers and Motion Study as a source of national wealth. No one who has not tried it can realize how extremely interesting all activity becomes when viewed and treated as a definite, measurable combination of motions and decisions. We have been astounded again and again to discover that someone who had lost a working member of his body is able, thru the loss, to find life more interesting, in that he has come to think for the first time in terms of motions, and how he can make his own motions more efficient. We are rejoiced to find again and again that some apparently hopeless cripple becomes actually more interested in life when he realizes the possibilities of motion economy and utilization of motion possibilities.

We have here not only a mechanical problem, but also a psychological problem of cheering the maimed worker during his learning period, and of making the man feel the worthwhileness of what he can do. It is not necessary to go abroad to the battlefields or the hospitals in order to begin this work. Start with the first case you see, and make him feel not only the possibilities of what he can do, but the possibilities of what he has done. Let him feel that his experience makes it possible for him not only to add to the world's useful knowledge, but to send encouragement and assistance to someone similarly handicapped, that no unmaimed individual could possibly give. This has been done time and time again. This can be done in more cases than any of us realize. Take up, then, at once these two aspects of the subject of furnishing to the crippled soldier a means by which he can live and work, and you will have made, perhaps, the greatest contribution towards happiness minutes that may ever be your good fortune to achieve.

How to Put the Crippled Soldier on the Pay Roll[3]

There are few problems before the world to-day more important than that of putting the Crippled Soldier back on the pay roll. If we broaden the term to include industrial cripples, we have a problem that affects all countries and all times. Because the war cripple appeals to popular sympathy, we are all vitally interested to-day in studying and solving this acute aspect of the problem, but our results are useable in the field of re-education of the injured of all types.

The problem of the crippled soldier is assuming greater proportions every day. The first stage of the solution of the problem is past; that is to say, in all countries has come a realization of the seriousness of the condition that exists, and of the necessity of doing something to better the condition immediately. With the knowledge of the seriousness of the condition has come a growing interest in the whole subject, and a desire to cooperate in putting these cripples on a self-supporting, happy and efficient basis as rapidly as possible.

There are those who object to putting the cripple on the pay roll, feeling that he has done his part, and that it is the duty of society to support him the rest of his life. There are many answers to this objection. It is a question whether society can afford to support such an enormous number of non-producers, no matter how just their claim to support. Partial support may be possible—time alone can determine this.

The real answer to the objection is that the health and happiness of the cripple himself demand that he be kept busy from the earliest stage in his recovery period that he is really able to work, and that he be re-educated at the earliest possible moment. Reports of convalescents of all the warring countries show that the greatest problem is

[3] Presented to the Economic Psychology Association, New York, January 26–27, 1917.

289

to persuade the man that life is worth living even in his maimed condition, and that he is still needed to do his part in the world's work. The injured man must be made to feel that he is not an object of charity, nor even a pensioner, but that he is a handicapped contestant in the world of active people, and that it is a sporting event what and how much he can do.

All who have taken part in or investigated work with cripples agree that it is essential that activity be attempted as soon as possible; the only question is, shall the activity be really productive or not. Surely in these times this is no question at all, and it is our duty to furnish real work to the cripple, work that he can do efficiently, and that will bring him returns in money, in satisfaction, in self-respect, and in the happiness that results from attaining these.

In order to do this we must:

1. Find types of work that a cripple can do.
2. Demonstrate to the cripple the advantages of working.
3. Find the type of work that the cripple can do and desires to do.
4. Adjust the cripple to the work.
5. Teach the cripple to do the work.
6. Persuade the uninjured man that it is hardly respectable to do work that can be done by a cripple.

These are all parts of the crippled soldier work, but it is not necessary to complete one part in order to start on another. In fact, all six of these are being done now.

We find work that cripples can do in two ways: first, by collecting records of cases where cripples have done various things; second, by studying the work of the injured workers, in order to find what members are used, and how the work may be reassigned to other members. This we do through the micromotion film and the Simultaneous Motion Cycle Chart, since they have been described already in available papers.

We demonstrate to the cripple the possibilities and the advantages of working by showing him these records of both types. It should be noted here that the cripples are only too happy to be helped to be useful, if the re-education is begun soon enough, before they have to contend with the bad advice of the ignorant, though well-meaning, friends, and the difficulties of overcoming habits of idleness. This is really understating the facts. We receive constantly pitful news of the desperate desire of the injured to be helped back to activity, and of the danger of the depression that inevitably results if hopes of re-education are not supplied immediately.

Finding the type of work that the particular cripple desires to do, and can be fitted to do, is largely a matter of tests that are at present being formulated and tried.

Adjusting the cripple to the work is done by two methods. These will be discussed in detail later.

The teaching is done through all the ordinary teaching devices, supplemented not only by micromotion films that show how the work is done and how long it takes to do it by elements and as a whole, but also by cyclegraphs, motion models, steroscopic photographs, and charts.

The uninjured man need not be made the subject of a harangue on leaving such work as he can do to the cripple. The average worker teaches the world the meaning of true brotherliness, and will be more than ready to do his part in adjusting the industrial world to accommodate the new type of worker, when he realizes the need.

We shall now discuss the problem of adapting the cripple to the work in some detail, as it is one toward whose solution we can all contribute. There are two distinct methods of attacking the problem, both valuable, each being supplementary to the other.

The European method is well exemplified by the work of the famous French scientist, Dr. Jules Amar, who, in typical papers, considers the device or contrivance that the cripple is to use as the fixed element, and adapts and equips each cripple so that he can use the devices of his trade, or of the new work that he has chosen to do.

The typical American attitude is, perhaps, exemplified by our work in considering the cripple as the fixed element, and adapting the device and method to the individual cripple who is to use it. It is but natural that the first method, that of the genius, Amar, should be used abroad, where many of the labor-saving devices in use come from America, or some other foreign country, and cannot be easily adapted. It is as natural that our methods should be in use here, where the devices are more easily changed, to suit individual workers, by the original maker of the machines.

As an example of the two methods, let us take the case of the cripple to be trained to be a typist. The Amar method is demonstrated plainly by the illustration herein included, furnished us through the courtesy of Professor Amar himself, whose cooperation on work for the Crippled Soldiers we are pleased to acknowledge. The other method we will describe in detail, hoping to arouse still further co-operation in this work in this country. Professor Amar's illustration shows a one-armed man operating the typewriter. We will illustrate the same subject and device as attacked by the other method by con-sidering the cripple as the fixed element. In considering any type of activity to which it is proposed to introduce the cripple, we first analyze this activity from the motion study standpoint, in order to find exactly what motions are required to perform the activity, and in what way these motions may be adapted to the available, or re-maining, capable members of the cripple's working anatomy, or eliminated by altering the device or machine itself.

Through a careful examination of the motions of many of the world's most expert typists, we found many interesting facts not generally known; for example, that the time required by the usual commercial typist to take out a finished sheet of paper and insert another in a position exactly level in the typewriter was about ten seconds. The time required to do this same work by Miss Hortense Stollnitz, the recent winner of the International Amateur Champion-ship, is less than three seconds, while Miss Anna Gold, who won the National Amateur Championship, requires still less time. Our first thought, then, naturally, was to find and transfer the activity requisite for that shortest, most efficient, method to the work method of the crippled to operate the machine. We found that Mr. Casey, the one-armed secretary to the Mayor of Boston, could, with a simple device of his own invention, insert the paper with much skill, and that he operated the shift keys of his Oliver typewriter by means of foot pedals of his own design.

At this point we found, however, a device that handled the paper in such a manner that all motions of inserting and taking out were eliminated from the ordinary work of the typist. With the coopera-tion of the leading makers of typewriters, such as the Remington, the Monarch, and the Smith-Premier typewriters, and particularly of Mr. George W. Dickerman, the devices were sent to our Motion Study Laboratory, where the motions of the machine and its operator were analyzed, measured and charted. How successful the results were is shown by the illustrations herein included. [Illustrations are omitted.] By means of this device, the one-armed soldier or industrial cripple can remove his paper and be ready with a new sheet inserted in place in two seconds.

When one original and several duplicates are made by the old method, the time required is, of course, longer for the commercial typist, because of the time and care required to handle the carbon paper and to keep the sheets of paper even and smooth. With the typewriting machine arranged for the cripple it takes no longer to handle two, three or four copies than it does to handle the single copy, because the duplicating is done by a permanent ribbon attached to the machine, and the trouble of handling the carbon paper is entirely done away with. If the rolls are kept free from the machine and hang on the wall, or other high support, they can be of any desired diameter, permitting a month's supply of paper if desired. The paper when attached to the machine is in rolls four inches in diameter. The process of tearing the paper into sheets of desired lengths is very simple, and can be done with one motion. The top and bottom edges of these torn sheets show an edge not quite as straight as if cut with the shears, but as straight as any paper torn against the sharp edge of a straight ruler.

Another example of the use of an existing device to facilitate the work of typing for a cripple is that of the double bank of keys such as exist in the Smith-Premier typewriter, and the use of a machine having all capitals and a single bank of keys as with the Remington or Monarch. By this means the motions of the shift keys are entirely dispensed with, and a legless, one-handed typist is enabled to equal the output of many of the commercial typists who are using but two of their ten fingers today; and a cripple with but a single finger can earn a living. We have also found dictating machines of use in decreasing the number of variables against which the typist works. When provided with a dictating machine, a typewriter requiring no shift key action and with the rolls of paper properly attached, a willing one-handed worker can compete successfully with the average stenographer-typist with the old equipment, and perhaps in some cases be able to earn more money than before being crippled. He can, in a small office, handle successfully dictating machine, typewriter adding machine and telephone.

This use of, or adaptation of, existing devices by no means does away with the necessity of the most careful motion study and fatigue study of the operation. It is only thru these that one is enabled to classify completely the motions involved, and to discover which ones of these can be handed over to available, securable or inventable devices.

We have so far found all manufacturers of devices approached more than willing to adapt their work to the requirements of those who are maimed and crippled. We hope by offering this paper to arouse still further cooperation in the makers and users of devices, that they may think in terms of cripples during the inventing, manufacturing and using periods.

This branch of the work, like all the other branches, demands the most careful investigation of the mental as well as of the physical side. There are certain types that will respond quickest to attempts to use the regulation equipment, and will be willing to adapt themselves, even to their own discomfort, in order to use it. There are others who feel that it is their right to have all mechanical aids at their service. There are some who find artificial limbs, and especially mechanical limbs, helpful and interesting. There are others who have no use for any such devices, and who prefer to show their adroitness by doing, with their limited equipment, all or nearly all that the ordinary uninjured man can do. Each individual must be studied, and the proper method of treatment applied.

But it is the work of all of us to supply the data with which the experts will work. The individual histories of cases where cripples have been enabled to cope successfully with their handicaps must be collected. The data must then be compiled, properly classified and cross-indexed, and incorporated into a series of books, copies of which should be put into every large library in the world. This work would eventually pay for its cost of compiling and distributing, and no one can estimate the good that would be done by having every cripple feel that he had actually books of cases of men injured like himself to refer to for help and encouragement. The histories should be not only of those who have been recently crippled, but also of old cases of the handicapped who became skilled. They should also include those born handicapped, as well as those injured later.

The great need is that everyone shall realize that there is a part in the work for him. It is the work of the psychologist, of the economist, of the industrial expert. True! It is just as much the work of every man, woman and child in the community. It is active, practical, interested cooperation that is needed—and it is needed now!

First Steps on the Solution of the Problem of Crippled Soldiers[4]

•••

The problem of the Crippled Soldiers stands before us demanding not only an immediate solution, but one that shall be of permanent value to the cripples and to the community of which they form a part. No delay is excusable, no half-way methods can be accepted, and a satisfactory solution demands not only a unified community willing to apply scientific methods but a change in attitude toward many existing activities.

There must be a great change in the general attitude of mind toward at least ten subjects of universal interest, and a refusal to accept any conclusions that are not the result of measurement. *First,* toward so-called "efficiency." At the beginning of the efficiency movement there was great admiration expressed not only for the ideals therein involved but for the practice into which these ideals formulated. Lately there has come a fashion of confusing efficiency with ruthlessness, with lack of art, or with "dry as dust" methods. Now it must not be forgotten that real efficiency consists simply of attaining the desired end with the least expenditure of effort possible. What that end may be is determined by ethics. It must be said, however, that the aim of efficiency both in the industries and out is usually understood to be durable satisfaction and happiness both to the individual and to the social community involved. With this thought in mind any effort to decry efficiency and to confuse it with other terms and to think of it as anything but a synonym for waste elimination, for utilization and for valuable achievements, must be condemned

[4] Presented at the Joint National Conference of the Western Efficiency Society and the Society of Industrial Engineers, Chicago, Ill., March 27–29, 1918.

if we are to get anywhere in solving such problems as that of the Crippled Soldier.

Second, an attitude of mind toward applied science must be changed, *i.e.,* the attitude that exists in the mind of many recent college graduates, unfortunately a preponderant number of them being women, that any science that has a practical end or is applied in a practical field thereby ceases to be "pure" and is not of the highest value. We must come to realize that thru applied science has come not only advances in the sciences working with material, but also in the human sciences, such as psychology. It has been applied science that has brought people in the industries to realize what actual measurement will do for them, and it is absolutely necessary that the thinkers of the world evaluate applied science properly if it is to accomplish its great work.

Third, the attitude toward "dignity of labor" must be changed. In theory the American people believe that any labor that is performed efficiently is dignified. In practice the same type that belittles applied science, belittles also anything but mental labor. The curriculum of the average college, and lack of training for the industries, the scorn of vocational guidance by those who are interested in so-called "cultural subjects" only, not only cuts off a large element of the community from such training as will result in ability to think and act in efficient motions, but also cuts off those who have been forced to content themselves with manual activity from a chance for that education that would insure all parts of the brain developing concurrently with those parts that develop accompanying the manual labor.

Fourth, there must be a change in attitude toward the necessity for reclassifying the trades. It has too long been thought that because in ancient times certain activities were considered as constituting a trade group there was something of Divine Right in this grouping which must be maintained. We are coming to realize, thru careful scientific investigations, and thru accumulating data that show the likenesses between various trades, that the division marks between them are poorly placed.[5] As women and cripples come into the trades it will become necessary to reclassify them from the standpoint of the type of thinking, of the manual skill demanded, etc. We must, therefore, if we wish to aid progress, come to accept the necessity for a reclassification of the trades and come to demand that this shall be

[5] See "Motion Study," D. Van Nostrand, 25 Park Place, New York City.

based on the results of actual laboratory measurements, and upon these only.

Fifth, there must be a general change of attitude of mind toward cripples. It is absolutely undeniable that the average man and woman alike has felt that the cripple, thru his maiming, became a different sort of member of the community, to be shielded and pitied perhaps, but scarcely to be welcomed back into the activities of life. Again, women have been largely to blame here, and this feeling must entirely change if the cripple is to be made, as he must be made, a productive member of the community, with a share in social as well as in industrial life.[6] The shameful neglect of industrial cripples in this country goes to prove what has been said. It is not the Labor Unions, with their well-known sympathy for the "weaker brother" who have been the prime movers, as Unions, in keeping the industrial cripples from coming back into the trades. It is the general feeling of individuals, as employers and employees alike, that the thought of a cripple re-entering competitive industrial life is repellent, that these people should be provided for by pensions in their homes. Through the new Crippled Soldier Work, where all cripples have been invited to give their histories and to contribute their experiences for the encouragement of the crippled soldiers, *for the first time* the cripples have been made to feel that they are an essential part of the community and that there is a call for what they can do.

In the *sixth* place there must be a different feeling toward industrial accidents. These have been in the past thought of as sad and calamitous but scarcely as criminal, which in many cases they are. The crippled-soldier problem, with the great number of men who inevitably are returning in a maimed condition, brings out clearly the shame and the crime of allowing men to be maimed in the peaceful pursuits of the industries. A strong emphasis on the seriousness of industrial accidents will be a great aid toward World Peace ultimately.

Seventh, there must be a general change in attitude of mind toward the Consumers League[7] and other allied activities that are aiming to supplement the work of the National Safety Council and other accident-preventing agencies by assuring to workers proper working conditions and hours. Those who wish to go into such work as the

[6] See "Measurement of the Human Factor in Industry." Presented before the Western Efficiency Society, National Conference, May, 1917.

[7] See "Industrial Liberty in Wartime," by Secretary of War Newton D. Baker. Delivered before the Consumers League, Baltimore, November, 1917.

Crippled Soldier Work must first be sure that they are utilizing all existing activities which can contribute toward the cause. Otherwise we shall have a reduplication of effort, which in the present critical condition of our National affairs is little short of scandalous.

Eight, there must be a general change of attitude of mind toward fatigue. Serious as accidents of all kinds are, the loss to the country is by no means so large as is the loss thru preventable, unnecessary fatigue. The whole subject of fatigue must come before the public mind and each and every one of us must determine that we will be instrumental in eliminating unnecessary fatigue and in providing rest for necessary fatigue before we can have done our share toward solving the new problem.[8]

Ninth, there must be a general change in the attitude of mind toward the position of women in industry, and particularly of those women who are coming into industries usually performed by men, many of them women who have never been in the industries before. The Canadian women have taught the world a splendid lesson by their attitude, which doubtless was also shared by the English women. In every case they signified a desire to *supplement* the work of the men rather than to supplant them, as is splendidly brought out by Mrs. Harry Heustis, first woman superintendent of the munition workers in the Ross Rifle Factory at Quebec.[9]

Coming in with this attitude, they slipped into their assigned positions with the least amount of friction possible, and the adjustment became easy of accomplishment. This same attitude must be held by women, and must be held by the men of the country toward the women, *i.e.,* that the women are coming in to do what is best for every one that they shall do, and in a cooperative spirit, or we can get nowhere.

Tenth and finally there must be a general change of attitude toward motion economy. It must be realized that all activities, consisting as they do of motions and of decisions, consume a certain amount of physical and concurrent mental activities; therefore, motion economy, performing an activity according to the best method and with the greatest amount of speed that it is possible to attain and at the same time not accumulate unnecessary or over-fatigue, is a National Duty.

---

[8] See "Fatigue Study," Macmillan Co., 5th Avenue, New York; George Routledge and Sons, Ltd., London.

[9] See Article by Mrs. Heustis in *Scientific American* of January 12, 1918.

With these ten changes of attitude in mind, and the fundamental character that they must have, understood, we may turn, second to the divisions of the Crippled Soldier Problem. We come at once to the problem of "first aid." The physical first aid is well understood and the need for immediate and constant, careful nursing. It it perhaps not so well understood that there is a concurrent psychological need, that the Crippled Soldiers demand from the first moment encouragement and accounts of those who have had similar experience and what they have been able to accomplish through the training and through the placement that is to become available. Along with this, or following shortly after, comes the necessity for early teaching. It is too late to wait till the crippled soldier returns to his home, it is too late to wait till he comes to this country, it is often too late to wait till he is in the camp. On his sick bed he must have the first mental and muscular training, if the re-education is to be as profitable as possible, and if he is to have the greatest use of the maimed member. Next on the list comes the need for psychotherapy, the more scientific re-education outlined so well by Mr. George Edward Barton of Consolation House, Cliften Springs, New York, in his little book on "Re-Education." The whole process must be conducted with the least amount of waste possible, considering the man's physical and psychological condition, his past experience, the training that is available and the ultimate opportunity that he is to have.

These first aids having been considered, we turn now to the training of the Crippled Soldier, and consider first the teaching. The teachers of the Crippled Soldiers in the past have too often been simply such teachers as were available, who taught not what the cripple needed but what they themselves knew best. As the result many a strong, hardy man became a weaver of baskets, a maker of toys, or a worker at some other feminine occupation. Now not only does the cripple himself crave to be back in the world of men and of actual production but also economic conditions demand that he be there. It is, therefore, our duty to provide immediately that fittingly trained teachers be available.

For this, of course, the next thing is money, and anyone who doubts his or her power to be of use in this problem can immediately be of great service, and learn more about the activities in the mean time, while collecting money for the cause. This the Red Cross Institute is already doing, supplementing thereby their work of collecting bibliographies, making studies of appliances, etc. The Association of

Collegiate Alumni have undertaken to do a part of this work and the Red Cross Institute will welcome all other workers as individuals or in groups. Besides the teachers and the money there comes the need for utilization of existing activities. Here again much is being done. The staff of Teachers' College of Columbia University connected with the nursing have cooperated with the New York Infirmaries, in order that teachers may be trained in the re-education of its cripples and at the same time that the present industrial cripples may profit by the care and attention. In this way not only are existing opportunities utilized but the training furnished benefits all concerned.

The next point to be considered is the need for preparing opportunities for these cripples when they have been properly trained. These may be of three sorts; *first,* new opportunities, that is discovery of work that needs to be done but has never been properly covered. As an example of this we may consider the occupation of the Dental Nurse, which is coming into existence in certain states and is being strenuously opposed in others. This work consists of taking from the already overcrowded work of the dentist, the work simply of keeping the teeth cleaned, and assigning this to a properly trained, certificated and inspected nurse. Through laboratory study we have discovered that this work may be satisfactorily done by a one-eyed, one-armed, legless cripple. The *second* type of opportunity is that of the "set-aside" occupation, which will be satisfactory for a cripple and which does not demand the capabilities of the whole man or woman. Such would be the running of a small store, the tending of a telephone, the running of cash register, etc. Again, thru laboratory experiments, we have demonstrated the possibilities of these occupations proving profitable. The *third* type of opportunity is that where the cripple is placed on a competitive basis with whole workers. This may be brought about in two ways, first, through artificial limbs or attachments. This we have called the Amar Method because of the wonderful work along this line done by Prof. Jules Amar of Paris. Second, through appliances fastened to the cripple or through changes in existing apparatus or machinery. Such has been the work in this country. For example, work with typists where, through attachments of multiple rolls and the use of ribbons instead of carbons, it is possible for a one-armed man to compete satisfactorily on short letters with a two-armed typist working according to present-day methods, and the second example that of magnetized hammer and rocking box which enables a one-armed man to accomplish nailing with as much speed and exactitude as can a two-armed man with the ordinary apparatus. This method is peculiarly fitted to the American type of mind, which delights in invention.

Perhaps the most important thing in the whole problem, the most significant, is the necessity for combining heart and brain in whatever work is done, the heart for the sympathy to provide the incentive. If we lose this attitude of pity, which has been the attitude toward the cripple of the past, we certainly lose our chief incentive to enter into the Crippled Soldier Work. No desire for a better economic condition, no passion for a new type of education, *nothing* can take the place of the warm human sympathy that sends one into the Crippled Soldier Work, and makes him ready and glad to welcome the returned cripple and to help him to the best of his ability. But this "heart" work by itself can accomplish little, and what is accomplished often has to be undone or done over. Along with this must come the brain work. Here arises the necessity of first discovering the *one best way*. Too long have we been satisfied, as educators and as people, to teach the *available* way and to allow the learner to come to some decision, by himself, as to what is the best way. A study of habit and of habit interference shows that we have here a most wasteful process. The learner vacillates from one method to another, and, if he is of a decisive type, often comes to a method which is not highly efficient. If he does come to an efficient method, he seldom really knows why it is efficient, and whether he is right in keeping it or not. Under the new education the *one best way* will be discovered according to laboratory methods. That and that only will be taught, and the learner will be forced to perform activity in that way until he understands it thoroughly. Then a suggestion will be in order, and will be carefully tested and incorporated, that the learner of the next generation may progress from the highest point that we have succeeded in reaching.

Accompanying the *one best way* will be the effective transference of skill: the knowledge that what one man has must be passed on to the others who need it, in the most efficient method possible. The learning process must be simplified by the fact that both teacher and pupil are trained for their functions, and that both know that what they are doing is for the ultimate and immediate good of themselves and the world. And with these two comes the attitude of mind that is fixed constantly on making measurements and on abiding by the results of measurement. There is a feeling, and has always been, that measurement is inartistic, that "hit-or-miss" is more beautiful, more stimulating, more satisfying. Yet all the great works of art conform absolutely to measurement, the great pictures, the great statues, the great symphonies, all make their appeals because they fulfill a fundamental human desire for accuracy. Expertness, skill is satisfying wherever it is found—in the sports, in the industries, in the professions. No matter what the work may be, where *skill*, where *accuracy* exists, where measurement is recognized, there we have smoothness, grace, beauty and satisfaction.

To solve the Crippled Soldier Problem, then, we must have a general change in the attitude of mind, a recognition of the fundamental necessities of the Crippled Soldier Problem, and the desire to enter into the solution not only with our hearts, but with our minds also. It is a big problem. Perhaps there is none more pressing facing the world to-day. Upon its solution will depend not only the possibilities of winning the war, but those far greater possibilities involved in Winning the Peace.

8

•••

FATIGUE
*STUDY**

* *Fatigue Study,* by Frank B. and Lillian M. Gilbreth, was published by Sturgis & Walton Co., New York, in 1916.

A Description and General Outline of Fatigue Study

●●

[EDITORS' NOTE: As in the work for the handicapped, allowance has to be made for recent developments. Note the logical approach to the problem of what fatigue is and the aims of the fatigue study.]

WHAT FATIGUE STUDY IS

Our fatigue study is an attack upon this unnecessary waste of human energy. It is a careful consideration of the problem of activity from the side of its results upon the human organism. It aims:

1. To determine accurately what fatigue results from doing various types of work.
2. To eliminate all unnecessary fatigue.
3. To reduce the necessary fatigue to the lowest amount possible.
4. To provide all possible means for overcoming fatigue.
5. To put the facts obtained from the study into such form that every worker can use them for himself to get more out of life.

RELATION OF FATIGUE STUDY TO MOTION STUDY

Motion study has been described as the dividing of the elements of the work into the most elementary subdivisions possible, studying and measuring the variables of these fundamental units separately and in relation to one another, and from these studied, chosen units, after they have been derived, building up methods of least waste. It is through the measuring of motions that one comes to realize most strongly the necessity of fatigue study.

There has come, in the past twenty-five years, a strong general realization that the important factor in doing work is the human factor, or the human element. Improvement in working apparatus of any type is important in its effect upon the human being who is to use the apparatus. The moment one begins to make man, the worker,

305

the centre of activity, he appreciates that he has two elements to
measure. One is the activity itself. This includes the motions, seen or
unseen, made by the worker,—*what* is done and *how* it is done. The
other is the fatigue. This includes the length and nature of the interval or rest period required for the worker to recover his original
condition of working power.

Any one who makes a real motion study, or analyzes motion study
data, cannot fail to realize constantly the relationship of motion study
to fatigue study. The fatigue is the more interesting element, in that
it is the more difficult to determine exactly. When we recognize this
close relationship between motion study and fatigue study, we see
that we have a body of data already collected and at our disposal.
What is even more desirable, we have a method of measurement
ready at our hand. Every observation of a motion may be used to give
information about fatigue. Is this information of immediate use to
the man who is attacking his fatigue problem for the first time to-day?
Yes, and no. Yes, in that it is at his disposal. No, in that he must determine his own particular problem before he can start to solve it.
The first step in this direction lies in classifying fatigue.

THE CLASSES OF FATIGUE

There are two classes of fatigue:

1. Unnecessary fatigue, which results from unnecessary effort, or
   work which does not need to be done at all. A typical example
   of such work is that of the bricklayer, who furnished one of the
   first subjects for motion study. Any one who has watched a
   bricklayer lift all of his body above the waist, together with the
   bricks and mortar from the level of his feet to the top of a wall,
   cannot fail to realize that bricklaying requires a great amount
   of energy as well as skill. Yet by far the most of the energy expended in the method of laying bricks, that had existed for
   centuries, was entirely unnecessary.[1]

2. Necessary fatigue, which results from work that must be done.
   The new method, which enabled this same bricklayer to lay
   three hundred and fifty bricks per hour, where he had laid one
   hundred and twenty bricks per hour before, did not eliminate,
   and did not expect to eliminate all of the fatigue accumulated
   in the working day. The bricklayer at the end of the day, by
   reason of motion study devices, laid more brick, but was never-

[1] See "Bricklaying System" [pp. 140–60]. Myron C. Clark Co., Chicago [1909.]

theless much less tired. Experimental work in his case was carried to a high degree of perfection, because he was recognized as a splendid type of efficient brawn.

THE METHODS OF FATIGUE STUDY

The methods used must rest on a scientific basis. These methods are the same for the expert and for the man making his first attack on the problem. They are as follows:

1. Record present practice, make an accurate and complete account in writing of what is actually being done.
2. Decide in what sequence things are to be measured, and put them in such shape that they can be measured.
3. Apply accurate measurement.
4. Determine standards synthetically from the measurement, and make such changes in practice as will make it conform to the standard.
5. Compare the new standard practice with the old practice. Determine exactly what improvements have been made, in order to be able to predict the line along which new improvements must lie.

This is the standard method of attack of measured functional management. It can be the more successfully applied to fatigue study in that the results can be checked at every point by the results of motion study, which bear a constant relation to them.

The Fatigue Survey:
What Is to Be Done

••

THE GENERAL SURVEY AND THE FATIGUE SURVEY

The fatigue survey should be a department of the general survey. A description of the apparent causes of fatigue, or of the devices present that eliminate fatigue, can mean little without the accompanying description of the worker, the conditions of the work and the work itself. The fatigue survey might be made without a general survey.

From the results, fatigue might be eliminated, or better means for overcoming fatigue provided, but there would be no assurance that the records applied would be efficient, or do lasting good, if the causes of fatigue were not understood. The causes could not be understood without the general survey. The fatigue element receives more emphasis than any other element of the general survey. We look for fatigue first, last, and all the time, but we record with it all the attending circumstances that we can observe or discover.

Preliminary Provisions for Rest for Overcoming Fatigue

PROVISION FOR REST

The first necessity in the fight against fatigue is to eliminate the causes of unnecessary fatigue. The second is to provide for proper rest to overcome fatigue, whether necessary or unnecessary.

If the worker goes home too tired each night, the first method of remedying this condition is to provide rest periods during the working day—to set aside time in which he may recover his proper and normal working strength. One method by which this may be sometimes done is by shortening the working day. This permits the worker to get into better condition either before work, after work, during a lengthened noon hour, or during the "second breakfast" and "tea recess" of many European organizations. The supposed advantage of this plan is that it gives little or no jolt to the working process. To this we might answer, as circumstances vary, that it does give a jolt, because speed must be increased in order that output should be maintained; or we might say that the jolt is really needed. The disadvantage, in some cases, of shortening the working hours is the effect upon the entire industry in the vicinity. This is a feature to be considered, for in the long run maximum prosperity is dependent upon largest outputs. There can be no doubt that in most cases it is advisable and profitable to shorten working hours, but how and when this is to be done is a serious problem. In our own office, our stenographers work every other Saturday till 1:00 P.M. only, and the alternating Saturday they do not work at all; that is to say, we give them a holiday of Saturday afternoon and Sunday every other week, and all Saturday and Sunday the other weeks, besides their regular two-weeks vacation in summer. We find that we get more and better work as a result. No plant, operating under the measured type of management, that we know of, has ever regretted shortening its working hours. It may be that the working hours formerly existing were so long that shortening the hours was the only immediate adequate remedy. The danger in shortening hours is that, if the whole problem is not thoroughly studied, the worker may not be sure of the same or a larger wage for work which he is able to do in the shorter time. Fatigue elimination is fundamentally the duty of the management. The worker cannot afford to pay for the fatigue elimination, directly or indirectly. Let the short hours be planned for and assured, but make sure before introducing them that everything is in such condition that wages can be maintained or raised. This is a matter requiring study of actual records and not "guess," "personal opinion," or "judgment."

There are other methods of providing for fatigue elimination or recovery, that do not involve so many elements. Such a method is providing rest periods during the working day. This is a method that may be used immediately. To whom are these rest periods to be given, then? Ultimately, of course, to every member of the organization whose work is of a nature that requires a fixed rest period. The work should, preferably, be so arranged that every worker, be he in plant or in management, would achieve larger outputs by having definite and properly located rest periods. It has been proved in most work that more output can be achieved by applying one's self steadily for short periods, and then resting, than by applying one's self less steadily and having no rest periods. This, of course, applies only to work which in itself provides no rest periods. At the beginning of the fatigue eliminating campaign, provide rest periods for those who seem to need them most. There are two, off-hand, quick methods of determining which workers these are. One is the appearance of the workers at various times of the day, and at the end of the day. The other is the amount of output and the rate that output is turned out by the worker during the day and during the various parts of the day. In some organizations, it has been the standard practice to take no chances when the worker looks or feels tired. They provide rest periods immediately, long enough to allow him to recover and go back to the work with zest. This is, of course, the immediate remedy. "Provide the rest period first. Discuss its efficiency later." This first-aid plan has worked splendidly for a long time among women workers in such industries as the drygoods trades. The typical welfare work may be unscientific from the standpoint of those familiar with highly organized methods, but it has sensed the trouble keenly and quickly, and provided at least a temporary remedy without delay. "Time to rest when one needs it." This is the first slogan of the campaign for eliminating the evils of overfatigue.

CHAIRS TO MAKE THE REST MOST EFFECTIVE

The merchants have again been the pioneers here, in realizing that reclining chairs or couches furnish the most effective rest. It is not necessary here to discuss the physiological effects resulting from a change of blood pressure. It should be noted that even a few minutes in a reclining position provides such rest as could not be gained in a much longer time if seated upright in the most comfortable of chairs. If attending conditions allow of reclining chairs or couches, for at least the exceptional and emergency cases, these should immediately be provided. It surely does take real courage for the management of an organization of strong and strenuous men to install reclining chairs, couches, and high foot-rests for rest periods; but fame awaits the one in this field, who can make the practice general. The brain worker of all types has long realized the benefits of the occasional use of the reclining chair. Flat couches without even the smallest of pillows are a part of the regular working equipment of some of our greatest brain workers. It is considered no disgrace, nor is it worthy of note, if a tired soldier flings himself flat upon the ground to rest. It attracts no attention for an exhausted worker to go to sleep on a hard wooden bench at noontime. But to put a couch in some quiet spot, or even a chair with extrahigh, large, flat, arm rests, where the same type of rest might be enjoyed most effectively, *this* seems radical, and "might make the men think we had gone crazy." It might be objected that the worker should not allow himself to become so fatigued that this type of rest is necessary. The answer is,—if rest in this position will overcome what is almost complete exhaustion, what increases in national efficiency and prosperity may it not cause in overcoming quickly less violent stages of fatigue?

Next to the couch or reclining chair, in efficiency, is the arm-chair.

There are "arm-chairs," and chairs with real arms specially fitted to the individual worker. These will be even more efficient if provided with a foot-rest. We have actually installed such arm-chairs out in the works with very good results. We have had many a case where even the workers laughed loudly when the special, unusual chairs were brought in. They began to use them more out of friendliness towards us than out of any belief in the special usefulness of these peculiar chairs. However, at the end of a few days of actual use, they were able to handle their work in greater quantities and with less fatigue. "It's a joke to work like that," one said. Some of the workers claimed that they did not need such a chair, but, after it became the fashion to use it, each one seemed glad enough for the better rest provided.

From this type of chair down to the smallest possible seat, the gradation is gradual and constant. In certain types of work, like selling in a drygoods store, the space is sometimes so narrow that the only type of chair practicable, under present conditions, is the small folding seat that can slip under the shelves or fold up against them when the girl is serving a customer. Such also is the type of chair that folds up under or next to a machine, which the operator is tending, and which can be pulled out during the periods when the machines need no tending, and the operator is simply inspecting or waiting for the next tending period. Every one realizes the advantage, as a resting device, of anything upon which one can occasionally sit. The two-inch, iron arm of a seat on a railroad train, the tiny seat that folds into a walking stick or umbrella, that the enthusiast at the races takes with him,—these are typical examples of seats that seem almost ridiculous, yet that have an enormous effect upon the amount of fatigue accumulated in a few hours, or in a day. "A chair to rest in"; this is the second slogan. If a chair is not procurable, then some sort of a seat, even a packing box with no back, even a post to lean against, or a rail to lean upon,—anything to shift the pressure is better than nothing. Far better a seat with no back, immediately, than the best type of chair in the indefinite future. Get some sort of seat for the worker to-day, and begin planning for the efficient chair at the first day possible.

The final word on chairs in this preliminary work is that some sort of a chair should be provided for every member of the organization. There is a wide-spread belief that one chair for every two or three or more workers is sufficient; that "they can change off using it." The argument was something like this: "No one needs to sit more than one-third of the time, therefore one chair to each three workers is enough," etc. The chief fallacy is the implied idea that the rest periods of the workers can be so arranged that the chairs can be in constant use, and that each worker will have a chair at his or her disposal at the proper time. Now in theory, of course, this is not an impossible arrangement. It might have to be made if chairs and seats cost many dollars apiece, and it probably would be done then, if there was a proper realization of the importance of overcoming fatigue. But when chairs are as cheap and plentiful as they are now, there is no excuse for thinking of such a condition. In practice, where there are not enough chairs for every one, at certain times of the day the chairs are empty, as every one is busy. At other times, when work is duller, the chairs are all used, and many workers are trying to rest as best they can, standing. These conditions can be noted in any dry-goods store, in any shop or factory where there is an inadequate supply of chairs. "A seat for each and every worker whether he needs it or not"; this is the third slogan.

BETTERMENT WORK

The third division of provision for rest falls under the general heading of betterment work, or what is popularly called "welfare work." The term "betterment work" is used by those who are interested in measured management instead of "welfare work," to emphasize a distinction in thought. Some welfare work implies that it is the gift of the manager to the workers. Betterment work is the same type of work, done with the distinct understanding that what is done is for the good and profit of the organization. It is the due of every member of the organization to have the best resting condition possible. Making these conditions better is betterment work. There is no intention to criticize welfare work. Most welfare work is betterment work. Some workers, however, object to welfare work as implying "charity," therefore, we say betterment work. It is the worker's due that he gets. Such work comprises establishing rest rooms, lunch rooms, entertainments—anything that can make the resting time more attractive and profitable. It may also imply the service of a betterment worker or a staff of such workers; or it may be that the organization itself takes up the work co-operatively, with no outsider to direct it. Doubtless some such activity already exists. If so, it would be the duty of the fatigue eliminators to recognize it and encourage it.

The fourth provision for rest is really a part of betterment work. It must be described at some length. This is the Home Reading Box Movement, which furnishes a definite means for making rest periods, both at work and at home, attractive and profitable. Before turning to a description of this, we may estimate the effect upon the worker of the preliminary work so far done.

RESULTS

The results of the preliminary work we have done are as follows:

1. The interest in fatigue becomes more vital. We have aroused more interest in fatigue elimination, and have made it general. With the establishment of properly distributed rest periods, chairs, seats, etc., the recovery process becomes interesting. As he knows how resting improves his working conditions, the worker becomes more warmly interested in the fatigue itself. It is a very different thing to talk about the evils of fatigue, or even to see the advantages of proper rest exhibited in object lessons, than it is to get proper rest in a specially designed chair for the first time in one's working life. Fatigue, which was *an* enemy, becomes now not only *my* enemy, but *our* enemy— mine, because I recognize it has affected me; *ours,* because we are fighting it together for our best interests, severally and collectively.

2. The interest in fatigue becomes more intelligent. Many workers, especially women, feel that it is to be expected that they will get exceedingly tired by night; that one cannot expect to do so much late in the day as early in the day; that stopping to rest is cutting down one's output, thus cheating one's self, if one is a piece rate worker, or cheating the management, if one is a day rate worker. The worker now comes to realize that he hurts the management *and* himself, when he gets too tired. "It is your duty to rest when you need it;" that is the fourth slogan. It must be remembered also that the rest periods provide time for clearer and more intelligent thinking. It is impossible to come to any valid conclusion when one is working at top speed part of the day, and in a state of exhaustion the rest of the time. We have now an opportunity to think, and brains rested enough with which to think.

3. The output increases. Usually, in practice, the output increases as a result of the fatigue-recovery periods. Increased outputs

encourage both management and worker. They must, however, be inspected and controlled. Some one with the proper training must be in charge, that excessive fatigue may not be accumulated, and the rest periods lose their purpose. With the increase in output must come added compensation in wages. If this is provided, the fatigue eliminating campaign will not be regarded as a new scheme for driving the worker. Better for the good of the management and the men to limit the output to its usual amount during this period, until the workers see that too much fatigue today interferes with the standard quantity of output to-morrow, than to attempt to allow increased output without increased pay. The world can better afford to lose the extra product, than the management to appear even for a moment to be trying to overwork the men.

4. The spirit of co-operation grows. The worker realizes instinctively, if the survey has been properly made, and if this preliminary work has been properly done, that the aim of fatigue study is the good of all concerned. There is a psychological element to this. It might be possible to question the motive of installing fatigue eliminating devices. There is no question as to the motive in installing the resting devices and rest periods. The rest periods allow time for development of the social spirit. "To know all is to understand all," a wise Frenchman has said. "I like every one whom I know," is the thought of another wise man. "Let's go at the fatigue survey all together," is the fifth slogan. The Home Reading Box Movement is, perhaps, the channel where this spirit of co-operation expresses itself most freely.

SUMMARY

Preliminary provision for rest for overcoming fatigue consists of establishing rest periods, providing chairs or other devices in which one may rest, and establishing or encouraging betterment work. These result in a more vital and intelligent interest in fatigue, and a spirit of co-operation. This work is embodied in five slogans. These are as follows: "Time to rest when one needs it"; "A seat to rest in"; "A seat for each and every worker whether or not he needs it"; "It is your duty to rest when you need it," and "Let's go at the fatigue survey all together."

Preliminary Fatigue Elimination: What Can Be Done Immediately, at the Very Beginning

••

THE LIGHTING PROBLEM

It is not necessary to have a scientific knowledge of motion study, physiology, and psychology, or even of hygiene, in order to make preliminary, anti-fatigue improvements in working conditions of any industrial organization that has not already had a regular fatigue survey made. We might profitably begin with lighting, since no fatigue is more wearing than eye fatigue. We attempt here only to ask a few general questions about the light. "Is there enough light, so that every one can see his own work perfectly?" "Is the light properly distributed?" "Is glare prevented?" etc. Nearly all factory managers of to-day are careful to provide enough light for the worker. In their desire to furnish light enough, many workers often have more light than is really comfortable, and are forced to adjust their eyes constantly in order to see distinctly. The lighting to be found in most factories is not properly distributed, and seldom strikes the work at the least fatiguing angle.

The greatest fatigue from lighting, however, lies in the question of glare and reflection. One sees examples of this everywhere. It is caused largely by a misplaced pride in equipment or machinery, and by keeping everything in a high state of polish. One is often disturbed and inconvenienced in even the best equipped public libraries by the glare of the electric lights upon the shiny, varnished, or otherwise highly polished surfaces of the desks. Oftentimes we see lights carefully placed so that the individual gets light enough with his light in the right location, while lights in the distance shine in his eyes. Even when the lights are provided with adjustable shades, it is almost impossible to place one's book in such a position that reflected light will not shine from the page to the eyes. The glare from nickel-plated machinery, be it a large factory machine or a typewriter, or any other kind of shop or office equipment, will cause fatigue, if the eye is required to work constantly in the vicinity; but the source of fatigue is not recognized. A dull black finished machine may not be so beautiful either to manufacturer or purchaser as would be a shiny, nickel-plated machine of the same design, but the main question is, "How much comfort will the operator take while using the machine?" The kind of finish of such machinery is usually affected greatly, if not determined wholly, by the question of salesmanship. Good appearances have always been a large element in making sales, and it is natural and right that the manufacturer should like his product to be attractive in appearance, and that the manager should take pride in the looks of his factory or office. But our entire standard of what is desirable in "good looks" in a work place has changed. We look now for efficiency and fatigue elimination rather than for ornament and glaring polish. We reduced fatigue, annoyance, and distraction on several pieces of work by having our clients paint nickel and other bright parts with a coat of dull black paint. For the best results to the eye, the same finish as that on the inside of a camera is to be recommended.

We are coming to realize more and more that the great test of everything is suitability, and that the mysterious and tangible thing called "suitability" simply consists of the measure of predetermined units of desired qualities. The operating room in the hospital is bare, with plain walls and rounded corners, with the least opportunity for dust lodgment, because that is most suitable to the type of work done there. The modern business desk is flat topped, with no tiny drawers or cubby-holes to collect papers and miscellaneous odds and ends, because this type of desk conforms best with present day systems of office management. In the same way all machinery and office equipment should be without socalled ornament or polish, because in this way the most work can be done with the least amount of fatigue. Our whole idea of ornament is changing. Suitability here also is the standard, and the artists have done noble work in setting an example to the trades. "Suitability" must become a slogan for every department in the organization.

The new doctrine will interest the selling department, who act as intermediaries between the manufacturing department and the public who is to buy the product. It will be a real part of the preliminary work in adjusting such conditions as lighting to take the sales department and purchasing department into conference on the subject. Let all interested see that nothing comes into or goes out of the plant until the question, "What is its relation to fatigue?" has been considered. We forget sometimes that a thing may have value not only because it has certain qualities that eliminate fatigue, but also because it lacks certain qualities that would cause fatigue.

Go, then, through your own plant with the question of glare in your mind. Examine and inspect every work place, and see what can be done. Not only for reasons of glare, but for other reasons we recommend that every work place should be inspected for unnecessary fatigue by having a man, competent in fatigue study, actually sit and stand in the working position in each and every work place in the establishment once every three months during the installation period, and not seldomer than once per year thereafter. Sometimes it will be found that moving the nearest light or shading a distant light will be all that is necessary. Sometimes a coating of dull black paint on some of the working equipment is required; sometimes the substitution of a dull-finished for a glossy paper. Sometimes dull-coloured blotting paper can be laid upon the place where the reflected glare comes. Perhaps a dull finish upon that would not only save the time of your workers, but also those who are to use the product after it leaves your hands. The world worked a great many years under the motto, "Give the public what it wants." We are beginning to realize to-day that the public will want just exactly what it is educated to want; also that the public is easily educated if the arguments that are used are based upon measurement, and are presented in attractive form. The lighting problem is but a small element of the problem of eye fatigue. This will, however, be left for later consideration.

THE HEATING, COOLING, AND VENTILATING PROBLEM

This problem has to do with different aspects of seeing that the worker is provided with proper air. We are beginning to realize that the air problem is much more complicated than was formerly thought. Recent investigations have gone to prove that the temperature of the air is fully as important as the supply of air, and that humidity is another important element. In this day no one can feel satisfied with his solution of the air problem who has not submitted it to an expert, and installed the results of his measured investigation.

In the meantime, safety lies on the side of providing more fresh air than is necessary. If there is plenty of fresh air, unless the work itself demands peculiar temperature or humidity conditions, the worker is fairly safe. The rest periods that are being installed will do much to solve the air problem, as they furnish an admirable opportunity for giving the work places a thorough ventilation, if not a complete "airing out." This is not in the least to underestimate the importance of proper temperature and of proper humidity, as will be noted later. All measured records of outputs should include records of the temperature and the humidity. The accumulation of this data is daily bringing nearer the time when standards covering these will be available. In the meantime, give the worker plenty of fresh air *all the time.*

FIRE PROTECTION

The average manager to-day realizes fully the necessity for fire protection. It is not, perhaps, so fully realized that the mere knowledge that there is adequate fire protection has a considerable effect upon the mental comfort of many of the workers. Nothing is more fatiguing than worry. When each worker in the establishment knows that in case of a fire he can leave the building with speed and perfect safety, he has absolutely no worry or distraction from the fire standpoint.

Fire protection should include not only seeing that the building and all it contains are made as fire-proof as possible, and installing all possible devices for putting out a fire should one start, but also the fire drill. Here the motto of the Boy Scouts is useful, "Be prepared." There is nothing so satisfactory as preparedness. The fire drill is not only a means of handling the organization during a fire, but it is also a splendid preparation for meeting an emergency. The great problem that arises in any unexpected situation is the problem of making a decision. If one can acquire the habit of making a decision quickly, and can also make habitual certain decisions in certain situations, the resulting speed and fatigue elimination is remarkable. Make the response to the fire situation, then, standard. You will be benefiting your workers not only by teaching them how to act in any fire anywhere, but also by teaching them how to respond to a signal in a standard way. These various sets of habits in response to various stimuli should be formed in the first years of the school life, if not before. They are being formed at this time to-day to a greater extent than ever before, but unfortunately the majority of adult workers in the industries have never had such training as children. It, therefore, becomes the duty of the management to form such habits as rapidly as possible.

SAFETY PROTECTION

Safety protection in its broadest sense covers not only protection from grave dangers, but from anything that might have a harmful effect upon the worker's body or mind. The standard to be set is that everything should be safe not only when the work is done by experienced adult workers, but even should it be done by inexperienced, immature or tired workers. We know how many accidents happen to the inexperienced worker, that would never happen to the experienced worker. We all know how many children are hurt, where an older person would see and avoid danger; and we note every day, more and more clearly, that the exhausted worker is to an enormous extent more susceptible to accidents than is the rested worker. It is usually the tired motorman who has the collision. The tired locomotive engineer passes the stop signal. The exhausted motorist is in the accident. The tired operator gets his fingers caught in the machine. The overtired sickroom attendant gives the wrong medicine.

One side of the fatigue elimination question is that fatigue elimination cuts down accidents. The other side is that cutting out the chance of accidents eliminates fatigue. Here again the question of worry is an important element. If one knows that the working conditions are absolutely safe, he can concentrate his attention upon the work in hand.

It is coming to be understood not only that it is mandatory that working conditions be made healthful, but also that it is perfectly possible, and, in most cases, easy to make such conditions healthful.

Look over your conditions, then. Put the proper safety devices on the machine, the tools, etc. Install the vacuum cleaners that will collect the dust and lint. Put the goggles or nostril-guard, or other device, on the worker, that will insure to him clean air and decent working conditions. Make a scientific attack upon the problem later, but put in a safety device now, even if you have to change some of it next week. You will gain the immediate return that will make the investigation pay from every standpoint in the changed attitude of your workers, if in nothing else. The Museum of Safety Devices, with its energetic and enthusiastic secretary, will show you what has been done and what can be done in the line of safety. "Safety First" has become the slogan of the day. If we make it "Safety First, beginning now," we shall have full working directions.

THE WORK PLACE

The working conditions that we have so far discussed have more or less effect upon all of the workers in a group. We come next to the inspection of the work place of each individual worker. The first consideration here is that he have room enough in which to work. There is an enormous amount of fatigue involved in doing work in an overcrowded work place, yet few workers or managers realize this. Again, habit is involved here, and the habit of order demands that the work place be kept in an orderly condition. Any one who has walked through factories, shops, or any places where work is going on must have noted the tired appearance of the workers among what is called "clutter." The girl selling ribbon, who walks up and down behind the counter through an accumulation of paper, cardboard cores, and other odds and ends, has not only the bodily fatigue of pushing the clutter ahead, or kicking it aside, but also the mental fatigue that comes from adjusting herself constantly to such conditions. The folder of cloth, who has barely enough room to move her hands because of the supply of finished and unfinished materials, is fatigued from the clumsy position, even though she and no one else realizes this. The office worker, whose finished and unfinished papers are heaped in confusion before him, expends not only useless motions in getting at and disposing of what he wishes to handle, but also mental energy, in constantly adjusting and readjusting himself to the work. There has been a popular idea that it "looked busy" to have plenty of work around, that to see work to be done would impress both managers and workers with the need for applying themselves to the work more constantly and with considerably more speed. This may be true if the work is arranged in an orderly fashion, but disorderly work is far more likely to discourage than to stimulate the worker. As for completed work, there is no excuse for leaving large quantities of it at the work place one moment longer than is absolutely necessary. Any encouragement that it might give the worker could better be given by a record of what he has done.

THE WORK-BENCH OR TABLE

Few work-benches or tables should be considered as absolutely satisfactory that do not permit the worker to do his work standing or sitting. Our ideas as to proper work-benches or tables, and as to the proper placing, height, etc., of machinery and tools have too often been prescribed to us by the manufacturers of the articles, who have thought more of what was convenient to manufacture than of what was least fatiguing to use. Such manufacturers are not to be blamed in the least for their attitude. They, naturally, have been guided by what would sell best. They have, as a rule, shown themselves more than willing to supply any legitimate demand. The user must demand what will be best for his work. It is no slight, short-time job to determine the proper height, positioning, and layout of a work-bench, using this term in a general sense to cover the place of any kind of work upon which the worker is engaged. As preliminary work, we may, usually, then, boost everything that can be so lifted to such a height that the worker, at his option, may stand or sit. If it becomes a case of single choice, that is, his either standing or sitting, arrange the work so that he does it sitting, and does the necessary standing or moving about during his rest periods.

The change in industrial conditions has made this problem important. The question once was, "*Can* we make it of a quality that will pass?" Since the day of intensive outputs, the question has become, "*How many* can we make of a given quality?" In the first case, any kind of workbench was good enough,—the worry being limited to the question of "*Can* we make it?" Now it is no trouble to make almost anything; but the worry is "Can we make enough so that the cost will enable us to pay the required wages and still compete, or must we give up manufacturing in this location?" This makes us think of the least fatiguing conditions and of making work-benches of two levels, etc.

THE CHAIR OR OTHER FATIGUE-ELIMINATING DEVICE

Closely related with the work place is the work chair. It is distinct from the rest chair in that it is specially devised to be used during work periods. The ideal work chair is of such a height that the worker's elbows will bear the same relation to the work place when he is sitting as they would if the work place were properly adjusted for him to do standing work. Types of chairs that have been designed and that are proving effective in eliminating fatigue while at work will be described more at length in the next chapter. The important point to be considered here is to adjust the work to the worker if possible. Where this is not possible, immediately, adjust the worker as best you can to the work. Make the relation of his elbows to the work the deciding point. If at present the work must be done standing, and the worker is too small, and it is easier to raise the worker than lower the work-bench or table, provide some sort of a stand or platform that will put him at the proper level. If he is large, raise the work-bench by lengthening the legs, or adding a false top, or, in some rare cases, by lowering the standing place. If the work is seated work, adjusting the chair will probably be the simplest change to make. Arm rests often afford an immediate and immense relief, but must fit the particular arm and be adjustable for best results. A head-rest may also be a valuable first aid, though often a later improvement in working methods will eliminate so much eye and head fatigue that the head-rest will not be needed. In other types of work, the foot-rest will often do the most immediate good. If every manager were made to sit for a certain number of hours to-day with his feet hanging, there would be an enormous increase in the number of foot rests in our industrial plants to-morrow morning.

PLACING THE MATERIAL WORKED ON

In cases where it is difficult to readjust the work place, much fatigue may often be eliminated by placing the work in a better position. In fact this aspect of the problem should always be considered along with the readjustment of the work itself. For example, in folding handkerchiefs, a folder may be seated at a table, folding directly on the table. The table may be too low for the work. If she is given a board upon which to fold, this may not only put her work itself at the proper height, but it is also possible, with trifling added expense, to provide her with a table in two adjoining sections at two different heights, and a sloping board that will make the work less fatiguing, as she can maintain a much better posture. She will also be enabled to put the finished product at a lower level. This will increase speed, while at the same time eliminating fatigue, which is, of course, an ideal condition.

In considering the placing of materials, we must consider also the manner in which the materials come to the worker and in which they leave him. Our later method study will make so many changes here that only very apparent, necessary, and inexpensive improvements should be made at this stage. Be sure, however, that you are using gravity wherever it can be used to advantage. Often we have found a small belt conveyor to be helpful in cutting down the hand transportation.

THE PLACING OF TOOLS AND DEVICES

Gravity and mechanical means can be of use here, especially in carrying working equipment back to the place where it remains when not in use. Many preliminary improvements can also be made by standardizing the place where the tool is to be left when not in use. There is not only the bodily fatigue of bringing the tool from a more distant place than is necessary, there is also the unconscious fatigue of constantly deciding such unimportant questions as where it is to be placed.

THE CLOTHING OF THE WORKER

In an excellent series of articles on dress, published some years ago, Miss Tarbell laid down the rule that "suitability" is the final test of a costume. It is with this in mind that the clothing worn by the members of the organization while at work should be examined. It must be said, in the first place, that there is no more reason for the common custom of the worker providing his special outer clothing while at work than there is for his providing his other tools and equipment. In other times, the workmen of many trades preferred to provide their own tools, and did so, but in a scientifically managed plant to-day, the workers are provided by the management with standard tools. The management has standardized the best in a tool, and keeps it in the best possible working condition. In the same way, it should be the duty of the management to provide special working clothes, when they have been standardized. This involves, of course, the problem of laundering, which may seem complicated to one who is not acquainted with what has been done in this field.

There has been very little done in most kinds of work to provide a costume, designed to conform to motion economy and least fatigue, that is, at the same time, useful, artistic, and pleasing. Progress has been rendered even slower by the fact that many workers have a prejudice against such garments, feeling that they show a class distinction. All that is necessary is to create a fashion of wearing such garments, like the fashion of wearing atelier or studio clothes. In no place can an example of unsuitable clothing be more clearly seen than in the laundry industry. Much of the work done in the typical laundry is done while standing, and the women who form a majority of the workers wear clothes, and particularly shoes that make the work far more fatiguing than it need be. Yet in this very industry some of the most progressive work to improve conditions is being done. In Europe a shoe with a thick wooden sole and a heavy leather upper over the front part of the foot only is considered the most comfortable and least fatiguing. It is also certainly the cheapest and most durable. But Americans will not wear such a shoe. The shoe furnishes the most difficult feature of the costume problem. Here again the most important thing is that the "fashion" of wearing comfortable and efficient garments shall be set. We have hoped for years that sensible fashions in workers' clothes might be set by patterning after tennis or other athletic costumes, but the time when this will become general seems as yet far distant, due to the necessity of the worker using his oldest and discarded "dress up" clothes, ultimately for his working clothes. Nevertheless, the great loss in efficiency, due to the general custom of wearing clothes that interfere with comfortable work, and that cause unnecessary fatigue, has caused us to start a campaign for the design and standardization of more suitable clothes. As yet we have had but few designs submitted in answer to our appeal to the worker to study the clothes problem for himself or herself. We are making the same appeal to the management to suggest costumes for the approval of the worker.

In order that there may be no duplication, that we may pass on good ideas, we have started a little museum where typical fatigue-eliminating devices of all sorts may be gathered, and studied by any one interested. We must next describe in some detail what is and what is not as yet there, in order to offer definite suggestions for preliminary fatigue-eliminating designs that can be used from the first day of making changes.

SUMMARY

Preliminary fatigue elimination consists of improving lighting, heating, ventilation, fire and safety protection. It also consists of improving work places and work tables, of providing and improving chairs, and rearranging materials and tools, and studying the clothing of the worker. It aims to make immediate inexpensive changes before entering into an intensive study of the problem.

Fatigue Measurement and Fatigue Elimination: How to Attack the Problem Scientifically

•••

HISTORY OF FATIGUE MEASUREMENT

Accurate fatigue measurement is in its infancy as applied to the industries. Such measurement can take place only where there is complete cooperation between the man measured and the man making the measurements. With the cooperation, that is the natural result of measured functional management, comes the possibility of making accurate measurements of fatigue under either laboratory or shop conditions. It is as easy to pretend to be tired as to pretend to be working. There is little or no profit in measuring pretended states. Under the scientific form of management there is no incentive to pretend anything. The incentive is, rather, to show exactly what one is doing and how one feels, in order that accurate records may be made, and that the offered rewards may be received. We have, then, at this stage, where every member of the organization realizes that cooperation is necessary for the good of all, the opportunity to measure fatigue with considerable accuracy.

We have also the means. The psychologists and physiologists who have measured fatigue rely almost solely upon output as the unit of measurement. Decrease in output in a comparable unit of time, and all other working conditions remaining the same, is taken as indicative of being the result of fatigue. The observed man who is measured may add introspections, he may tell how he feels while working and at the close of work; but this testimony of his, while interesting and worthy to be recorded with the other data, cannot be submitted to the accurate measurement of the observer. In applying fatigue measurement to the industries in the same way that we measure activity and what it produces, we try to discover at the same time the

325

condition of the worker by his own accounts as to how he feels. We have not only conditions under which scientific observations can be made and a method of making them, we have also devices for measuring both activity and output and relative rate of output.

FATIGUE, A TEST OF EFFICIENT ACTIVITY

As for the relation between fatigue and activity, practically all of our knowledge of fatigue is derived from our knowledge of the activity that produces it. We measure the activity itself, and its product. We then measure the interval of time that elapses before the organism has gained enough activity to perform the same work in the same amount of time and with the same results. A study such as this cannot extend over a short space of time only. It must be carried on until any fatigue that is accumulated shows itself; but it is simply a question of extending the time over which the experiment stretches, and of varying the length of rest periods until the desired information is recorded in the data. As we come to compare various activities and their results, we find that the fatigue is a measurement of the efficiency of the activity. If two methods of doing the same piece of work take the same amount of time and produce the same amount of output, and if the interval needed to recover from the second is longer than that needed to recover from the first, then, other conditions being equal, the first method is the more efficient. A close study of the variables that affect the two methods will be necessary to show exactly why the first method is more efficient than the second, but the excess fatigue certainly shows that it is more efficient.

Fatigue can, then, be looked at in two ways:
1. As a product of doing work.
2. As a test of efficiency in doing work.

The amount of work done and the product are affected by various elements which affect the activity.

THE ACTIVITY

The activity is affected by the amount of practice that one has had. It is affected by the extent to which the action has become a habit. It is affected by the degree with which one has got into the swing of the work. This may be an individual difference. Some workers find it possible to start at work at very much the pace that they will use when they are well into it. A large number of our records shows that most workers never get into the swing at the beginning of a work period. Not only the hour of the workday, but the time in the work period will have a strong effect upon the amount of work turned out. Again we have the question of spurt, when for some reason or other the activity is being performed at a pace that is above the normal pace. The effect of all these elements of the activity upon the fatigue itself depends upon the relation between mental fatigue and bodily fatigue. This relationship must be worked out by psychologists and physiologists. It is for the observer who measures fatigue in the industries to attempt to discover, as far as he can, what fatigue exists, and why it exists, and then to make both physical and mental conditions under which the activity is carried on as favorable to efficient activity as possible.

MOTION STUDY, MICROMOTION STUDY, THE CYCLE-GRAPH, AND THE CHRONOCYCLEGRAPH METHOD AS MEASURERS OF ACTIVITY

We measure activity in two ways:
1. By motion study, which records in great detail the methods used in doing the work.
2. By records of outputs when using the various methods.

Motion study consists of dividing the activity into the smallest units possible, measuring the variables of these units, studying the data, and deducing methods by which the activity may express itself more efficiently. Motion study, whatever its type, implies time study, in that the time the motion occupies is one test of the efficiency of the motion.

Micromotion study is the name we have given to our method of recording motions and their surrounding conditions by means of a cinematograph and one of our special clocks which registers extremely small intervals of time, smaller than the elapsed time between any two pictures of the cinematograph film. The micromotion method enables us to record easily motions down to less than a ten-thousandth of a minute. This gives us all the information we could desire for purposes of time study, and the record is absolutely free from the errors in time due to the personal element. Although many of the various elements, or units, that comprise the path of a complete motion, or cycle of activity, appear on different pictures in the film, it is difficult to visualize or measure the orbit or exact path of the motions by means of the film.

The cyclegraph method permits us to record, measure, and see this orbit or exact path of a motion or cycle of motions. Small electric lights are attached to the hands, or any other members of the body involved in the motion. A photographic plate or film is then exposed while the motion is made, with the result that a path of light, which resembles a white wire, is seen upon the developed plate, representing the path of the motion. The effect is best gained by a stereoscopic photograph, which shows this path in three dimensions.

The chronocyclegraph method enables us not only to see the path of the motion, but also its directions, and the duration of the entire motion and of its elements. These chronocyclegraphs are made by attaching lights to the moving parts of the body, or machine, as in the cyclegraph, and by introducing a properly timed, pulsating interrupter in the circuit, which may be adjusted not only to record the time and duration, but also to record these with different graphs, representing the paths of each of several motions made by various parts of the body and their exact distances, exact times, relative times, exact speeds, relative speeds, and directions.

By means of the "penetrating screen," it is possible to pass a cross-sectioned plane in any direction through any desired plane, or through any number of planes in the cubic space under observation. This makes it possible to record the data with great accuracy in three dimensions, and to read the information from the data easily.

These various types of motion study supplement rather than supplant one another. Motion study is primarily for the purpose of observing the variables that affect such study, and for arousing such co-operation between observed and observer, as will make possible the testing of the differences of the effects of the variables. Micromotion study provides for an accurate record of what happened, with all such attending circumstances as appeal to the eye. It is the greatest aid in transference of skill and experience from a worker who has it to one who does not possess such skill and experience. The cyclegraph is useful in providing a simple, easily understood record of the path that any activity followed. The chronocyclegraph is most valuable when the activity is complicated, and when the time and direction of the elements of the motion must be visualized continuously in order to analyze, measure, synthesize, and standardize the process. The penetrating screen, finally, is useful in recording the three dimensional paths and speeds of even the smallest unit of activity.

These methods of applying motion study have been patented, but have been for years freely at the disposal of the colleges, which have begun to use them as means for recording accurately scientific data of various kinds. They have justified themselves as more accurate than ordinary records of activity, and have within recent times been put on a basis which makes their cost compare favourably with less accurate methods of measurement. What is more, we have discovered in our data, especially in the chronocyclegraphs, direct records of fatigue, that we believe are the first records of fatigue ever made under industrial conditions. The micromotion films also show breaks in well established habits of several motions that are undoubtedly due to fatigue, but the irregularities in the orbit line, that appear in the cyclegraphs, and that must, because of close control of the variables, be due to the fatigue alone, are more impressive from the physiological viewpoint.

TESTING THE WORK BY MOTIONS REQUIRED

It is for motion study to explain the methods of deducing standard methods by using activity records obtained through the various types of motion study data. Many such standards have been derived. We have in our motion study data many elementary motions with records of the space they cover and the amount of time they require. With these we can test the given work to see which of these motions it includes. Having tabulated this, we can make an intensive study of the motions that remain. When this study has been made, we can combine the resulting elementary motions that have proven themselves most efficient into the working method, and classify the work as work of a type requiring a certain set combination of motions.

TESTING WORKERS BY MOTION CAPABILITIES

In the same way we may test a worker by motion learning capabilities, before assigning him to any kind of work. Having reduced activities to their motions, we can test the worker's physical capability; his mental capability we can test by determining his learning curve. To these results we add a record of his interest in various types of work. From the resulting three types of records, we can make placements that, we believe, are far in advance of any that have been made up to the present time.

THE USE OF ACTIVITY RECORDS AS DATA FOR ELIMINATING FATIGUE

The fact that activity records are made of extremely small elements moving through a short path in a small amount of time means that the fatigue records cover the same short periods. This is a great help in making fatigue study. A new combination of elements of activity will also mean a combination of concurrent, or included, elements of fatigue. The combination may have some effect on the activity. If so, it will also affect the fatigue, but at the present state of the art the most accurate and satisfying work can be done by making use of activity records to eliminate unnecessary fatigue, without waiting for some hypothetical, direct records of fatigue, that may be worked out in the future. In other words, if you have accurate records of fatigue included in your activity records, use them immediately, without attempting to make separate records of the fatigue, that, while valuable, will mean delaying fatigue elimination, perhaps indefinitely.

THE TIME ELEMENT

Too much credit can never be given to Dr. Taylor for his emphasis on the laws of the time element. He was the first to call to our attention the fact that operations should be divided into the smallest possible, timable units for setting tasks. In this way it is possible for timed elements to be used in many combinations, thus eliminating an enormous amount of unnecessary work. Dr. Taylor also recommended that work periods should be timed separately from the rest periods. Our new measuring devices for time study make it possible to record much shorter intervals of time than were heretofore known, and now the limiting factor in the problem is no longer the quickness with which we can use a stop-watch.

Our methods and devices have been criticised as being specially adapted to problems involving the minutia of motions, but too expensive for the general time study purposes. A moment's consideration will show that the turning of the crank of the cinematograph may be done as slowly as the requirements of the particular case of time study demand. In fact we have films that were taken at the rate of one picture every ten minutes. With the sixteen pictures to the foot, a foot will last one hundred and sixty minutes, or two hours and forty minutes, at a total maximum cost of six cents. If desired, the speed of the crank can be instantly changed to any desired speed to enable one to take pictures too quickly to be seen with the eye, and more accurately than the highest-priced time study man can take by means of a stop-watch.

Our methods, devices, and records of activity and of output fulfil every requirement, and are now perfectly satisfactory. Fatigue still remains the elusive factor. Nothing but long-continued observation, absolute accuracy and co-operation between all interested will reduce fatigue study to the science which motion study has become.

THE STANDARDIZATION OF WORK AND REST

Meantime, in standardizing work and rest periods, it is customary and proper to make a larger allowance for fatigue than the records show to be necessary. We cite as an example a case of folding handkerchiefs. The old method of folding was to have the workers seated at low tables in chairs of ordinary height, working throughout the entire day, with the only rest periods an hour at noon and such ceasing from folding as took place when the workers went for supplies, or took back finished product to be checked, or other rest periods that they took at will, as the work was piece work. After an intensive study of the problem, made not only to increase their output but to better their working conditions and allow them to earn more money with less fatigue, the following schedule of work and rest periods was adopted.

Each hour was divided into ten periods. The work was placed on a work table of the proper height. The handkerchiefs already folded, those being folded, and those to be folded were arranged in the most convenient and efficient manner. All variables of the work had been studied, and the results of the study standardized. The first four periods, that is, the first twenty-four minutes, the girl remained seated. She worked five minutes and rested one. That is to say, she had four minutes' rest out of the twenty-four, and spent this rest seated so that she might lose no time in getting back to the work. The next two periods, that is for twelve minutes, the girl was standing. Again she worked five minutes and rested one minute, and for the second time worked five minutes and rested one minute. That is, she rested two out of the twelve minutes in the same position in which she worked. The third group, a space of eighteen minutes, she spent either sitting or standing, as she pleased. Here also she worked five minutes, rested one minute; worked five minutes, rested one minute; worked five minutes, and rested one minute in the position, either standing or sitting, which she herself had chosen. The last period, which consisted also of six minutes, was spent by the girl walking about and talking, or amusing herself as she otherwise chose. With this might be combined the last rest minute or period No. 9, which thus gave her seven consecutive minutes for unrestricted rest activity.

This was the schedule for all hours of the day except the hour before noon and the hour before closing time at night. In these hours the first nine periods resembled the first nine periods of the other hours; but the tenth period was spent in work, as a long rest period was to follow.

At the end of the day's work under these conditions the girls accomplished more than three times the amount of their previous best work, with a greater amount of interest and with no more fatigue. It may be stated here that the primary aim in this investigation was not to eliminate fatigue, but to increase the wages of the girls by raising the output. The operators had not seemed overfatigued at the start. They maintained that they were less tired at the close of the day when using the new method, and certainly the amount of fatigue caused by producing an amount of output such as was made under the old method was reduced to an enormous extent. With further practice these preliminary results will be further improved.

It is of fundamental importance in making an investigation of this type that the allowance for fatigue be greater than the physical condition of the worker at the end of the day seems to indicate necessary. It is also fundamental that the results of the investigation be at once incorporated into actual shop practice. If each member of the organization is at once placed under such working conditions that he can enjoy the rest periods along with the high pay that comes from a large product, he will co-operate most fully in the progressive work of fatigue elimination. It is a fundamental rule of scientific management that the rate once set must never be cut. It should also be a fundamental principle of our management that rest periods once established should not be abolished or shortened. Let the error, if error there is, always result to the advantage of the worker, never to that of the employer. If you have not allowed enough rest, make the allowance larger, then reinvestigate. If you have allowed too much rest, let the job stand as one to be given for special merit, and attack some other problem. The result will be an increased co-operation which will more than compensate for the occasional over allowance for fatigue.

SUMMARY

Fatigue measurement, as applied to the industries, is a new science. It is being developed through a study of the data of activity. The methods of measurement of activity are motion study, micromotion study, the cyclegraph, the chronocyclegraph, and the penetrating screen. Through the data derived by these, we standardize motion paths, motion habits, and all other motion variables. These enable us to test and classify, select and place, both work and workers, and to eliminate unnecessary fatigue. Through the time element we compare our various data, and finally arrive at results that enable us to standardize work and rest periods. Any errors in length of rest periods must result to the advantage of the worker.

The Outcome: How Far Have We Attained Our Aim?

●●

THE TESTS OF GENERAL HEALTH

We will now assume that the reader has attacked the fatigue problem in his particular plant, and has applied either preliminary or more permanent fatigue elimination. There are various general measurement tests which he may apply to the results, in order to see how much better the working condition of his organization actually is than it was when he started in upon his fatigue-eliminating work.

The first of these is the test of general health. It is, of course, perfectly possible that an individual worker's general health may go down under far better working conditions; this, because of some home influence, or something in his general condition or his life away from work, which pulls down his health. It would not be fair to blame the work for any illness easily traceable to home conditions, to an epidemic prevalent, or to some certain outside source; but, if conditions away from work have remained fixed, there is every reason to expect that general health should improve with fatigue elimination. This we find in actual practice is the case. Even where fatigue is not materially cut down during working hours, because measurement shows that the worker is not getting over-fatigued, the general health is apt to improve because of greater regularity in habits of work, and because of better physical and mental habits, while doing the work. The path along this line is a continuous, never-ending, upward spiral. Fatigue is eliminated by establishing proper habits.

Proper habits improve health. The improved health allows of more work with less fatigue, etc.

THE TEST OF PROLONGED ACTIVITY

In order to be thoroughly satisfactory, observations of the effect of the changes upon the worker must be made during a long period. The worker's greatest asset is his ability to work. In order to prove its value, fatigue eliminating work must actually show results in prolonging the years that he is able to devote to his life work. This in practice it does. Not only does the average worker remain physically able to work more years than where no fatigue elimination has taken place, but also through the fatigue study and motion study, which he has co-operated to make, he learns to be able to teach that thing, or those things, at which he is most skilled, and thus to prolong his years of economic value. You must note how many of your workers are beyond the usual working age, and are still at work. Some of these will be working at the work itself; that is, in the performing department. Others will be planning or teaching the work in some way. The number of these and their condition will form an admirable unit of measurement of the success of your work.

THE TEST OF POSTURE

The third test is that of posture. Take another walk through your plant, and look at those workers to whom fatigue elimination work has been applied, and note how they are sitting, or standing, or walking.

The American Posture League, with headquarters at 30 Church Street, New York City, will gladly furnish standards for proper posture in various positions. It will be impossible, of course, to eradicate wrong habits of posture in a short time, no matter how radical the change may be, but you should note improvements. At least each worker should be so placed that he could work in the proper posture if he chose, and so that the proper posture will be the easiest for him. If the chairs, benches, levers, or devices force him to assume the proper posture, so much the better. Consideration of the devices shows, unfortunately, that few are designed for operation with least fatigue; more being designed to use the least quantity of material.

In the case of young workers, especially, it is surprising how quickly the proper devices will induce the correct posture, especially if the betterment staff co-operate to explain the correct posture, and its effect upon health. Where no betterment staff exists, the posters of the Posture League will serve as desirable examples and object lessons. Here again, as in so many other places, "fashion of work" is a most important element. Let correct posture become the fashion, and let the devices make the posture possible, and astonishing results will follow.

It is, of course, always a great aid to make anything that one desires the easiest thing to do. The proper chairs and work places make correct posture the easiest posture to hold. This is a great force towards maintaining it.

THE TEST OF BEHAVIOUR AND IMPLIED MENTAL ATTITUDE

The fourth test is to observe the behaviour of the workers. Do their actions, their resulting work, and whole attitude towards the work indicate that the fatigue eliminating work has been effective? There should be better "habits of work" than have ever existed before. More work should be turned over to the habit processes, and the formation and maintenance of good habits should become a part of the day's work. It should be noted just exactly what seems to be the kind and amount of incentive that keeps the workers at the work. If the fatigue elimination has done what it should along its line, the reason for doing the work as it is being done will be the belief that this way is the best way yet found, a belief that one is safe in following the method, since proper allowance for fatigue has been made. There should also be present a desire to contribute to the welfare of all by looking for easy ways, as well as scientifically-derived ways, to eliminate fatigue, while at the same time following the best method as yet available.

The question of motivation is one demanding understanding and serious consideration in every field of activity to-day. This is true in education. It is also true in the industries. The motive of getting all that one can for one's work must always exist, and is a perfectly justifiable motive, but the fatigue-eliminating work cannot be considered successfully, unless this motive of self interest has also with it the motive of interest in the welfare of others, and in cutting out all fatigue that can effect any member of the group in any way. This feeling should express itself in a social attitude, which is another behaviour test. If every member of the organization stands ready to endorse the fatigue elimination, and to co-operate in further fatigue elimination for the good of all, the social attitude shows that the work that has been done is worth while.

THE TEST OF TRANSFERENCE OF SKILL

The amount of skill that is successfully transferred may be used as a test of fatigue elimination. Each member of the organization is supposed to transfer skill, and also to acquire skill. He transfers to others the skill in the lines of work in which he is proficient, yet which are not the highest types of work that he can do. He learns from others such types of work as are of the highest type that it is possible for him to learn, that he has never had an opportunity to learn because of the time taken by work requiring less skill, that it was necessary under the old plan for him to do.

It is a fallacy to suppose that work which does not demand all the skill at one's disposal is less fatiguing than work which does. Work is not less fatiguing because it demands less skill. It is less fatiguing when it is done with ease and when there is a joy of achievement requiring skill; that is, when it is satisfying. Because of lack of opportunity, one may only perform with ease the work which does not demand much skill. As soon as he learns to perform the skilled work with ease, it causes even less fatigue, other things being equal, than does unskilled work, because it holds the interest, hence the attention, more easily.

We enjoy doing that which we can do well. Whether we improve in the doing because we take pleasure in doing it, or simply because the pleasure makes us do more, and we improve with the practice, is not of great importance. Psychologists are divided in their opinions as to the effect of pleasure upon work, but all agree that, directly or indirectly, pleasure in the work does affect the work favourably. Through the transference of skill this pleasure is given to the work, or increased in the work, and, therefore, the amount of skill transferred is a test of fatigue elimination.

TEST OF "HAPPINESS MINUTES," INDIVIDUAL
AND SOCIAL

The final test of fatigue elimination, as of every other change made in doing things, is its influence upon the total output of "Happiness Minutes." The aim of life is happiness, no matter how we differ as to what true happiness means. Fatigue elimination, starting as it does from a desire to conserve human life and to eliminate enormous waste, must increase "Happiness Minutes," no matter what else it does, or it has failed in its fundamental aim. Have you reason to believe that your workers are really happier because of the work that you have done on fatigue study? Do they look happier, and say they are happier? Then your fatigue eliminating work has been worth while in the highest sense of the term, no matter what the financial outcome. Naturally the savings that accrue must benefit every one, but saving lies at the root of fatigue elimination, and, if every member of the organization, including the manager and the stockholders, is getting more "Happiness Minutes," you surely are working along the right lines.

Social "Happiness Minutes" will consist of the sum of the individual "Happiness Minutes" plus that intangible thing called "social spirit." It is exemplified in a case like this: A certain group of workers had been studied from the motion study and the fatigue standpoint. The result of the work had been incorporated in their daily practice, and they had been working for a period of many months under the readjusted working conditions and with the new methods. At the end of this time they were gathered at a foremen's meeting, where a micromotion film, showing the development of the methods which they used, was presented. In discussing the film the speaker took the occasion to say that on observing the work in the plant he felt that some lapses from the method prescribed were in existence. The next morning, when he walked through the plant, he was stopped by a worker, who said, "See here! I don't believe we are falling away from that method a bit. If we are, just show us where, and we will go straight back to it. We want to play the game right." This is the test of the outcome. Is the organization lined up as one man back of the work? If so, the problem of maintenance and of automatic improvement is solved.

SUMMARY

At any stage in the process of fatigue elimination the results may be tested. The general health of the worker, his prolonged activity, his posture, his behaviour act as such tests. To these may be added the amount of skill transferred and being transferred, and the effect, in particular, on "Happiness Minutes." If the organization endorses the work and co-operates in it, the work may be rated successful.

The Future: What Each One of Us Can Do

••

THE WORK OF THE COLLEGES

It should be the work of the colleges to gather together what has been done in fatigue elimination, and to put it at the disposal of all interested. Each college should start a fatigue museum, and should invite its graduates first, and all those in its vicinity second, to cooperate and to send exhibits or pictures of exhibits to its museum. The colleges are recognized as not interested in any particular industry, as fair and impartial, and as standing for uplift in the community. It is, therefore, their duty to act as repositories for the data, at least until such times as the national government takes over the leadership in the entire fatigue question, and becomes the cutodian of the data.

The colleges can help in a second way by making fatigue study a subject in the curriculum. It is not necessary that this be a new subject. It should rather be a new aspect in which the old subjects are presented. Especially in the colleges of engineering and business administration great emphasis should be laid upon fatigue study, both the theory and the practice. It is not essential that the students be sent out into the shops for actual practice in such study, although anything like the half-time plan is to be commended. The student may well apply fatigue study to his own activities. This will present an admirable field and a splendid incentive. After such a study the fatigue problem will never again seem remote or vague to the student. Also the student may well be sent, or taken, on tours of inspection through neighbouring industries, or may be allowed to co-operate in preliminary fatigue surveys. They should learn the general principle of fatigue study, and should become fingerwise. This preparation is identical to that for making motion study, and, in fact, is prerequisite or first step for greatest success in any managerial work.

But the college should not confine its activity in fatigue elimination to the museum, and to training the student who expects to enter

338

the field. They should themselves become examples of successful fatigue elimination. In this way they can do most to cut down waste, and to train our young people to take an active part later in the waste elimination campaign being waged in the world's work.

THE WORK OF THE MANAGER

The fatigue study and the installation which must follow it to be done by the manager have been outlined in this book. The manager who has put his own plant at such a stage of improvement that unnecessary fatigue is cut out to a great extent, and that recovery from necessary fatigue is provided for, has contributed greatly to the cause, but his work should not end here. He should educate those with whom he comes in contact on the subject of fatigue elimination. He should co-operate with those in his own neighbourhood, and also with those in his own trade towards solving the fatigue problem peculiar to the locality or the trade.

The Home Reading Box has been successfully installed by a group of manufacturers engaged in the same trade. This particular work furnishes an admirable starting point, and is a great help in arousing local interest. If even a few interested in the same trade in various parts of the country will co-operate, it will soon be possible, through trade journals, and through a general demand for equipment designed from the fatigue standpoint, to revolutionize fatigue conditions in that industry. Editors and writers of papers of all types have been quick to see the benefits of fatigue elimination, and to offer to co-operate in a campaign for education. Manufacturers have been equally eager to satisfy any demands which may be made. The managers can have a large share in making such demands, and in encouraging the support of publications in which they are interested.

THE WORK OF THE WORKER

The worker has two chief ways in which he can help in fatigue elimination. The first is to co-operate with the management in installing fatigue elimination methods and devices in the particular plant in which they are both interested. The second is to help to make fatigue elimination fashionable. This latter duty lies with no one but the worker himself. No new methods spread more quickly than the "fashion of work." There is nothing of which a well run plant is more proud than the "way" it works, the work spirit. The whole idea must be that it is a disgrace to have causes of unnecessary fatigue existing. Overfatigue is a positive proof of inefficiency. There is no fear but that the workers will recognize these duties, and will perform them heartily and with good will, when they know that they are getting a square deal. It is right that they should make very sure that they are going to receive such treatment, and that fatigue study is not a new scheme for taking advantage of them, but they must be ready to listen to the proof and to accept it when they are convinced that it is true. Having accepted it, and thus made sure that they are safe in co-operating, the next step is to help actively in the good work.

THE WORK OF THE PUBLIC

The great work of the public is to demand fatigue elimination. The adoption of a few simple slogans, like "Buy of the seated worker," would help bring immediate results in fatigue elimination. Consider what the Consumers' League has done in securing better working conditions. Note how the "Safety First" movement has spread through the whole country. The "Fatigue Eliminating Movement" can spread in the same way, if only every one will do his part to demand that the fatigue be reduced and to help in the actual reduction.

The workers of the country have long recognized the need for fatigue elimination: the employers are coming to a realization that they are paying a large price for fatigue. Many employers have resolved that, so far as their plants are concerned, needless fatigue must be eliminated. They have resolved that the day is coming when every worker shall go home from work happy in what he has done, with the least amount of unnecessary fatigue, and prepared to go back in perfect condition on the morrow. How soon this much desired time will arrive depends upon the co-operation of the public, upon the public sentiment that can be aroused.

There is no reader of this book who does not belong to at least two groups that should be interested in fatigue elimination. Decide at once, then, in which group you belong, and set to work. Be you teacher, manager, worker, or simply a member of the great public to which we all belong, begin to work for fatigue elimination, and begin now.

The good in your life consists of the quantity of "Happiness Minutes" that you have created or caused. Increase your own record by eliminating unnecessary fatigue of the workers.

9

THE

PSYCHOLOGY

OF

MANAGEMENT*

* *The Psychology of Management,* by Lillian M. Gilbreth, was published by Sturgis and Walton Co., New York, in 1914.

Description and General Outline of the Psychology of Management

••

Definition of Psychology of Management.—The Psychology of Management, as here used, means,—the effect of the mind that is directing work upon that work which is directed, and the effect of this undirected and directed work upon the mind of the worker.

Importance of the Subject.—Before defining the terms that will be used more in detail, and outlining the method of treatment to be followed, it is well to consider the importance of the subject matter of this book, for upon the reader's interest in the subject, and his desire, from the outset, to follow what is said, and to respond to it, rests a large part of the value of this book.

Value of Psychology.—First of all, then, what is there in the subject of psychology to demand the attention of the manager?

Psychology, in the popular phrase, is "the study of the mind." It has for years been included in the training of all teachers, and has been one of the first steps for the student of philosophy; but it has not, usually, been included among the studies of the young scientific or engineering student, or of any students in other lines than Philosophy and Education. This, not because its value as a "culture subject" was not understood, but because the course of the average student is so crowded with technical preparation necessary to his life work, and because the practical value of psychology has not been recognized. It is well recognized that the teacher must understand the working of the mind in order best to impart his information in that way that will enable the student to grasp it most readily. It was not recognized that every man going out into the world needs all the knowledge that he can get as to the working of the human mind in order not only to give but to receive information with the least waste

343

and expenditure of energy, nor was it recognized that in the industrial, as well as the academic world, almost every man is a teacher.

Value of Management.—The second question demanding attention is;—Of what value is the study of management?

The study of management has been omitted from the student's training until comparatively recently, for a very different reason than was psychology. It was never doubted that a knowledge of management would be of great value to anyone and everyone, and many were the queer schemes for obtaining that knowledge after graduation. It was doubted that management could be studied otherwise than by observation and practice.[1] Few teachers, if any, believed in the existence, or possibility, of a teaching science of management. Management was assumed by many to be an art, by even more it was thought to be a divinely bestowed gift or talent, rather than an acquired accomplishment. It was common belief that one could learn to manage only by going out on the work and watching other managers, or by trying to manage, and not by studying about management in a class room or in a text book; that watching a good manager might help one, but no one could hope really to succeed who had not "the knack born in him."

With the advent of "Scientific Management," and its demonstration that the best management is founded on laws that have been determined, and can be taught, the study of management in the class room as well as on the work became possible and actual.[2]

Value of Psychology of Management.—Third, we must consider the value of the study of the psychology of management.[3]

This question, like the one that precedes it, is answered by Scientific Management. It has demonstrated that the emphasis in successful management lies on the *man,* not on the *work;* that efficiency is best secured by placing the emphasis on the man, and modifying the equipment, materials and methods to make the most of the man. It has, further, recognized that the man's mind is a controlling factor in his efficiency, and has, by teaching, enabled the man to make the most of his powers.[4] In order to understand this teaching element that is such a large part of management, a knowledge of psychology is imperative; and this study of psychology, as it applies to the work of

[1] Charles Babbage, *Economy of Manufacturers.* Preface, p. v.
[2] Halbert P. Gillette, Paper No. 1, American Society of Engineering Contractors.
[3] Gillette and Dana, *Cost Keeping and Management,* p. 5.
[4] F. B. Gilbreth, *Motion Study,* p. 98.

the manager or the managed, is exactly what the "psychology of management" is.

Five Indications of This Value.—In order to realize the importance of the psychology of management it is necessary to consider the following five points:—

1. Management is a life study of every man who works with other men. He must either manage, or be managed, or both; in any case, he can never work to best advantage until he understands both the psychological and managerial laws by which he governs or is governed.

2. A knowledge of the underlying laws of management is the most important asset that one can carry with him into his life work, even though he will never manage any but himself. It is useful, practical, commercially valuable.

3. This knowledge is to be had *now*. The men who have it are ready and glad to impart it to all who are interested and who will pass it on.[5] The text books are at hand now. The opportunities for practical experiences in Scientific Management will meet all demands as fast as they are made.

4. The psychology of, that is, the mind's place in management is only one part, element or variable of management; one of numerous, almost numberless, variables.

5. It is a division well fitted to occupy the attention of the beginner, as well as the more experienced, because it is a most excellent place to start the study of management. A careful study of the relations of psychology to management should develop in the student a method of attack in learning his selected life work that should help him to grasp quickly the orderly array of facts that the other variables, as treated by the great managers, bring to him.

Purpose of This Book.—It is scarcely necessary to mention that this book can hope to do little more than arouse an interest in the subject and point the way to the detailed books where such an interest can be more deeply aroused and more fully satisfied.

What This Book Will Not Do.—It is not the purpose of this book to give an exhaustive treatment of psychology. Neither is it possible in this book to attempt to give a detailed account of management in general, or of the Taylor plan of "Scientific Management" so-called, in particular. All of the literature on the subject has been carefully

[5] F. W. Taylor, *Principles of Scientific Management,* p. 144.

studied and reviewed for the purpose of writing this book,—not only what is in print, but considerable that is as yet in manuscript. No statement has been made that is not along the line of the accepted thought and standardized practice of the authorities. The foot notes have been prepared with great care. By reading the references there given one can verify statements in the text, and can also, if he desires, inform himself at length on any branch of the subject that especially interests him.

What This Book Will Do.—This book aims not so much to instruct as to arouse an interest in its subject, and to point the way whence instruction comes. If it can serve as an introduction to psychology and to management, can suggest the relation of these two fields of inquires and can ultimately enroll its readers as investigators in a resultant great field of inquiry, it will have accomplished its aim.

Definition of Management.—To discuss this subject more in detail—

First: What is "Management"?

"Management," as defined by the Century Dictionary, is "the art of managing by direction or regulation."

Successful management of the old type was an art based on no measurement. Scientific Management is an art based upon a science, —upon laws deducted from measurement. Management continues to be what it has always been,—the *art* of directing activity.

Change in the Accepted Meaning.—"Management," until recent years, and the emphasis placed on Scientific Management was undoubtedly associated, in the average mind, with the *managing* part of the organization only, neglecting that vital part—the best interests of the managed, almost entirely. Since we have come to realize that management signifies the relationship between the managing and the managed in doing work, a new realization of its importance has come about.[6]

Inadequacy of the Terms Used.—It is unfortunate that the English language is so poor in synonyms in this field that the same word must have two such different and conflicting meanings, for, though the new definition of management be accepted, the "Fringe" of associations that belong to the old are apt to remain.[7] The thoughts of "knack, aptitude, tact, adroitness,"—not to speak of the less desirable

[6] F. W. Taylor, *Shop Management,* para. 16, Am. Soc. M. E., Paper No. 1003.
[7] William James, *Psychology,* Vol. I, p. 258.

"brute force," "shrewdness, subtlety, cunning, artifice, deceit, duplicity," of the older idea of management remain the background of the mind and make it difficult, even when one is convinced that management is a science, to think and act as if it were.

It must be noticed and constantly remembered that one of the greatest difficulties to overcome in studying management and its development is the meaning of the terms used. It is most unfortunate that the new ideas have been forced to content themselves with old forms as best they may.

Psychological Interest of the Terms.—Psychology could ask no more interesting subject than a study of the mental processes that lie back of many of these terms. It is most unfortunate for the obtaining of clearness, that new terms were not invented for the new ideas. There is, however, an excellent reason for using the old terms. By their use it is emphasized that the new thought is a logical outgrowth of the old, and experience has proved that this close relationship to established ideas is a powerful argument for the new science; but such terms as "task," "foreman," "speed boss," "piece-rate" and "bonus," as used in the science of management, suffer from misunderstanding caused by old and now false associations. Furthermore, in order to compare old and new interpretations of the ideas of management, the older terms of management should have their traditional meanings only. The two sets of meanings are a source of endless confusion, unwarranted prejudice, and worse. This is well recognized by the authorities on Management.

The Three Types of Management.—We note this inadequacy of terms again when we discuss the various *types* of Management.

We may divide all management into three types—

    (1) Traditional
    (2) Transitory
    (3) Scientific, or measured functional.[8]

Traditional Management, the first, has been variously called "Military," "Driver," the "Marquis of Queensberry type," "Initiative and Incentive Management," as well as "Traditional" management.

Definition of the First Type.—In the first type, the power of managing lies, theoretically at least, in the hands of one man, a capable "all-around" manager. The line of authority and of responsibility is clear, fixed and single. Each man comes in direct contact with but one man above him. A man may or may not manage more than one

[8] F. B. Gilbreth, *Cost Reducing System*, Chap. I.

man beneath him, but, however this may be, he is managed by but one man above him.

Preferable Name for the First Type.—The names "Traditional," or "Initiative and Incentive," are the preferable titles for this form of management. It is true they lack in specificness, but the other names, while aiming to be descriptive, really emphasize one feature only, and in some cases with unfortunate results.

The Name "Military" Inadvisable.—The direct line of authority suggested the name "Military,"[9] and at the time of the adoption of that name it was probably appropriate as well as complimentary.[10] Appropriate in the respect referred to only, for the old type of management varied so widely in its manifestations that the comparison to the procedure of the Army was most inaccurate. "Military" has always been a synonym for "systematized," "orderly," "definite," while the old type of management was more often quite the opposite of the meaning of all these terms. The term "Military Management" though often used in an uncomplimentary sense would, today, if understood, be more complimentary than ever it was in the past. The introduction of various features of Scientific Management into the Army and Navy,—and such features are being incorporated steadily and constantly,—raising the standard of management there to a high degree. This but renders the name "Military" Management for the old type more inaccurate and misleading.

It is plain that the stirring associations of the word "military" makes its use for the old type, by advocates of the old type, a weapon against Scientific Management that only the careful thinker can turn aside.

The Names "Driver" and "Marquis of Queensberry" Unfortunate. —The name "Driver" suggests an opposition between the managers and the men, an opposition which the term "Marquis of Queensberry" emphasizes. This term "Marquis of Queensberry" has been given to that management which is thought of as a mental and physical contest, waged "according to the rules of the game." These two names are most valuable pictorially, or in furnishing oratorical material. They are constant reminders of the constant desire of the managers to get all the work that is possible out of the men, but they are

[9] Morris Llewellyn Cooke, *Bulletin No. 5 of the Carnegie Foundation for the Advancement of Teaching*, p. 17.

[10] F. W. Taylor, *Shop Management*, para. 234, Am. Soc. M. E., Paper No. 1003.

scarcely descriptive in any satisfactory sense, and the visions they summon, while they are perhaps definite, are certainly, for the inexperienced in management, inaccurate. In other words, they usually lead to imagination rather than to perception.

The Name "Initiative and Incentive" Authoritative.—The term "Initiative and Incentive," is used by Dr. Taylor, and is fully described by him.[11] The words themselves suggest, truly, that he gives the old form of management its due. He does more than this. He points out in his definition of the terms the likenesses between the old and new forms.

The Name "Traditional" Brief and Descriptive.—The only excuses for the term "Traditional," since Dr. Taylor's term is available, are its brevity and its descriptiveness. The fact that it is indefinite is really no fault in it, as the subject it describes is equally indefinite. The "fringe"[12] of this word is especially good. It calls up ideas of information handed down from generation to generation orally, the only way of teaching under the old type of management. It recalls the idea of the inaccurate perpetuation of unthinking custom, and the "myth" element always present in tradition,—again undeniable accusations against the old type of management. The fundamental idea of the tradition, that it is *oral,* is the essence of the difference of the old type of management from science, or even system, which must be written.

It is not necessary to make more definite here the content of this oldest type of management, rather being satisfied with the extent, and accepting for working use the name "Traditional" with the generally accepted definition of that name.

Definition of the Second Type of Management.—The second type of management is called "Interim" or "Transitory" management. It includes all management that is consciously passing into Scientific Management and embraces all stages, from management that has incorporated one scientifically derived principle, to management that has adopted all but one such principle.

Preferable Name for Second Type of Management.—Perhaps the name "Transitory" is slightly preferable in that, though the element of temporariness is present in both words, it is more strongly emphasized in the latter. The usual habit of associating with it the ideas

[11] F. W. Taylor, *Principles of Scientific Management,* pp. 33–38.
[12] The idea called to mind by the use of a given word.—*Ed.*

of "flitting, evanescent, ephemeral, momentary, short-lived," may have an influence on hastening the completion of the installing of Scientific Management.

Definition of the Third Type of Management.—The third form of management is called "Ultimate," "measured Functional," or "Scientific," management, and might also be called,—but for the objection of Dr. Taylor, the "Taylor Plan of Management." This differs from the first two types mentioned in that it is a definite plan of management synthesized from scientific analysis of the data of management. In other words, Scientific Management is that management which is a science, i. e., which operates according to known, formulated, and applied laws.[13]

Preferable Name of the Third Type of Management.—The name "Ultimate" as, especially to the person operating under the transitory stage, all the charm and inspiration of a goal. It has all the incentives to accomplishment of a clearly circumscribed task. Its very definiteness makes it seem possible of attainment. It is a great satisfaction to one who, during a lifetime of managing effort, has tried one offered improvement after another to be convinced that he has found the right road at last. The name is, perhaps, of greatest value in attracting the attention of the uninformed and, as the possibilities of the subject can fulfill the most exacting demands, the attention once secured can be held.

The name "measured functional" is the most descriptive, but demands the most explanation. The principle of functionalization is one of the underlying, fundamental principles of Scientific Management. It is not as necessary to stop to define it here, as it is necessary to discuss the definition, the principle, and the underlying psychology, at length later.

The name "scientific" while in some respects not so appropriate as are any of the other names, has already received the stamp of popular approval. In derivation it is beyond criticism. It also describes exactly, as has been said, the difference between the older forms of management and the new. Even its "fringe" of association is, or at least was when first used, all that could be desired; but the name is, unfortunately, occasionally used indiscriminately for any sort of system and for schemes of operation that are not based on time study. It has gradually become identified more or less closely with

13 Henry R. Towne, Introduction to *Shop Management*. (Harper & Bros.)

1. the Taylor Plan of Management
2. what we have defined as the "Transitory" plan of management
3. management which not only is not striving to be scientific, but which confounds "science" with "system." Both its advocates and opponents have been guilty of misuse of the word. Still, in spite of this, the very fact that the word has had a wide use, that it has become habitual to think of the new type of management as "Scientific," makes its choice advisable. We shall use it, but restrict its content. With us "Scientific Management" is used to mean the complete Taylor plan of management, with no modifications and no deviations.

We may summarize by saying that:

1. the popular name is Scientific Management,
2. the inspiring name is Ultimate management,
3. the descriptive name is measured Functional management,
4. the distinctive name is the Taylor Plan of Management.

For the purpose of this book, Scientific Management is, then, the most appropriate name. Through its use, the reader is enabled to utilize all his associations, and through his study he is able to restrict and order the content of the term.

Relationship Between the Three Types of Management.—From the foregoing definitions and descriptions it will be clear that the three types of management are closely related. Three of the names given bring out this relationship most clearly. These are Traditional (i. e., Primitive), Interim, and Ultimate. These show, also, that the relationship is genetic, i. e., that the second form grows out of the first, but passes through to the third. The growth is evolutional.

Under the first type, or in the first stage of management, the laws or principles underlying right management are usually unknown, hence disregarded.

In the second stage, the laws are known and installed as fast as functional foremen can be taught their new duties and the resistances of human nature can be overcome.[14]

In the third stage the managing is operated in accordance with the recognized laws of management.

Psychological Significance of This Relationship.—The importance of the knowledge and of the desire for it can scarcely be overestimated. This again makes plain the value of the psychological study of management.

[14] F. W. Taylor, *Principles of Scientific Management*, p. 123. (Harper & Bros.)

Possible Psychological Studies of Management.—In making this psychological study of management, it would be possible to take up the three types as defined above, separately and in order, and to discuss the place of the mind in each, at length; but such a method would not only result in needless repetition, but also in most difficult comparisons when final results were to be deduced and formulated.

It would, again, be possible to take up the various elements or divisions of psychological study as determined by a consensus of psychologists, and to illustrate each in turn from the three types of management; but the results from any such method would be apt to seem unrelated and impractical, i. e., it would be a lengthy process to get results that would be of immediate, practical use in managing.

Plan of Psychological Study Used Here.—It has, therefore, seemed best to base the discussion that is to follow upon arbitrary divisions of scientific management, that is—

1. To enumerate the underlying principles on which scientific management rests.

2. To show in how far the other two types of management vary from Scientific Management.

3. To discuss the psychological aspect of each principle.

Advantages of This Plan of Study.—In this way the reader can gain an idea of

1. The relation of Scientific Management to the other types of management.

2. The structure of Scientific Management.

3. The relation between the various elements of Scientific Management.

4. The psychology of management in general, and of the three types of management in particular.

Underlying Ideas and Divisions of Scientific Management.— These underlying ideas are grouped under nine divisions, as follows:—

1. Individuality.

2. Functionalization.

3. Measurement.

4. Analysis and Synthesis.

5. Standardization.

6. Records and Programmes.

7. Teaching.

8. Incentives.

9. Welfare.

It is here only necessary to enumerate these divisions. Each will be made the subject of a chapter.

Derivation of These Divisions.—These divisions lay no claim to being anything but underlying ideas of Scientific Management, that embrace varying numbers of established elements that can easily be subjected to the scrutiny of psychological investigation.

The discussion will be as little technical as is possible, will take nothing for granted and will cite references at every step. This is a new field of investigation, and the utmost care is necessary to avoid generalizing from insufficient data.

Derivation of Scientific Management.—There has been much speculation as to the age and origin of Scientific Management. The results of this are interesting, but are not of enough practical value to be repeated here. Many ideas of Scientific Management can be traced back, more or less clearly and directly, to thinkers of the past; but the Science of Management, as such, was discovered, and the deduction of its laws, or "principles," made possible when Dr. Frederick W. Taylor discovered and applied Time Study. Having discovered this, he constructed from · it and the other fundamental principles a complete whole.

Mr. George Iles in that most interesting and instructive of books, "Inventors at Work,"[15] has pointed out the importance, to development in any line of progress or science, of measuring devices and methods. Contemporaneous with, or previous to, the discovery of the device or method, must come the discovery or determination of the most profitable unit of measurement which will, of itself, best show the variations in efficiency from class. When Dr. Taylor discovered units of measurement of determining, *prior to performance,* the amount of any kind of work that a worker could do and the amount of rest he must have during the performance of that work, then, and not until then, did management become a science. On this hangs the science of management.[16]

Outline of Method of Investigation.—In the discussion of each of the nine divisions of Scientific Management, the following topics must be treated:

1. Definition of the division and its underlying idea.

---

[15] Doubleday, Page & Co.

[16] F. W. Taylor, *Principles of Scientific Management,* p. 137. (Harper & Bros.)

2. Appearance and importance of the idea in Traditional and Transitory Management.

3. Appearance and importance of the idea in Scientific Management.

4. Elements of Scientific Management which show the effects of the idea.

5. Results of the idea upon work and workers.

These topics will be discussed in such order as the particular division investigated demands. The psychological significance of the appearance or non-appearance of the idea, and of the effect of the idea, will be noted. The results will be summarized at the close of each chapter, in order to furnish data for drawing conclusions at the close of the discussion.

Conclusions to be Reached.—These conclusions will include the following:—

1. "Scientific Management" is a science.

2. It alone, of the Three Types of Management, is a science.

3. Contrary to a widespread belief that Scientific Management kills individuality, it is built on the basic principle of recognition of the individual, not only as an economic unit but also as a personality, with all the idiosyncrasies that distinguish a person.

4. Scientific Management fosters individuality by functionalizing work.

5. Measurement, in Scientific Management, is of ultimate units of subdivision.

6. These measured ultimate units are combined into methods of least waste.

7. Standardization under Scientific Management applies to all elements.

8. The accurate records of Scientific Management make accurate programmes possible of fulfillment.

9. Through the teaching of Scientific Management the management is unified and made self-perpetuating.

10. The method of teaching of Scientific Management is a distinct and valuable contribution to Education.

11. Incentives under Scientific Management not only stimulate but benefit the worker.

12. It is for the ultimate as well as immediate welfare of the worker to work under Scientific Management.

13. Scientific Management is applicable to all fields of activity,

and to mental as well as physical work.

14. Scientific Management is applicable to self-management as well as to managing others.

15. It teaches men to coöperate with the management as well as to manage.

16. It is a device capable of use by all.

17. The psychological element of Scientific Management is the most important element.

18. Because Scientific Management is psychologically right it is the ultimate form of management.

19. This psychological study of Scientific Management emphasizes especially the teaching features.

20. Scientific Management simultaneously
   a. increases output and wages and lowers costs.
   b. eliminates waste.
   c. turns unskilled labor into skilled.
   d. provides a system of self-perpetuating welfare.
   e. reduces the cost of living.
   f. bridges the gap between the college trained and the apprenticeship trained worker.
   g. forces capital and labor to coöperate and to promote industrial peace.

Individuality

••

Definition of Individuality.—"An individual is a single thing, a being that is, or is regarded as, a unit. An individual is opposed to a crowd. Individual action is opposed to associate action. Individual interests are opposed to common or community interests." These definitions give us some idea of the extent of individuality. Individuality is a particular or distinctive characteristic of an individual; "that quality or aggregate of qualities which distinguishes one person or thing from another, idiosyncrasy." This indicates the content.

For our purpose, we may define the study of individuality as a consideration of the individual as a unit with special characteristics. That it is a *unit* signifies that it is one of many and that it has likeness to the many. That it has *special characteristics* shows that it is one of many, but different from the many. This consideration of individuality emphasizes both the common element and the diverging characteristics.

Individuality as Treated in This Chapter.—The recognition of individuality is the subject of this chapter. The utilization of this individuality in its deviation from class, is the subject of the chapter that follows, Functionalization.

Individuality as Considered by Psychology.—Psychology has not always emphasized the importance of the individual as a unit for study. Prof. Ladd's definition of psychology, quoted and endorsed by Prof. James, is "the description and explanation of states of consciousness, as such."[1] "By states of consciousness," says James, "are meant such things as sensation, desires, emotions, cognitions, reasonings, decisions, volitions, and the like." This puts the emphasis on such divisions of consciousness as, "attention," "interest," and "will."

With the day of experimental psychology has come the importance of the individual self as a subject of study,[2] and psychology has come to be defined, as Calkins defines it, as a "science of the self as conscious."[3]

We hear much in the talk of today of the "psychology of the crowd," the "psychology of the mob," and the "psychology of the type," etc., but the mind that is being measured, and from whose measurements the laws are being deduced and formulated is, at the present the *individual* mind.[4]

The psychology which interested itself particularly in studying such divisions of mental activity as attention, will, habit, etc., emphasizes more particularly the likenesses of minds. It is necessary to understand thoroughly all of these likenesses before one can be sure what the differences, or idiosyncrasies, are, and how important they are, because, while the likenesses furnish the background, it is the differences that are most often actually utilized by management. These must be determined in order to compute and set the proper individual task for the given man from standard data of the standard, or first-class man.

[1] William James, *Psychology, Briefer Course*, p. 1.
[2] Hugo Münsterberg, *American Problems*, p. 34.
[3] Mary Whiton Calkins, *A First Book in Psychology*, p. 1.
[4] James Sully, *Teacher's Handbook of Psychology*, p. 14.

In any study of the individual, the following facts must be noted:—

1. The importance of the study of the individual, and the comparatively small amount of work that has as yet been done in that field.

2. The difficulty of the study, and the necessity for great care, not only in the study itself, but in deducing laws from it.

3. The necessity of considering any one individual trait as modified by all the other traits of the individual.

4. The importance of the individual as distinct from the type.

Many students are so interested in studying types and deducing laws which apply to types in general, that they lose sight of the fact that the individual is the basis of the study,—that individuality is that for which they must seek and for which they must constantly account. As Sully says, we must not emphasize *"typical developments* in a new individual," at the expense of "typical development *in a new individual."*[5] It is the fact that the development occurs in an individual, and not that the development is typical, that we should emphasize.

Individuality Seldom Recognized under Traditional Management.—Under Traditional Management there was little or no systematized method for the recognition of individuality or individual fitness.[6] The worker usually was, in the mind of the manager, one of a crowd, his only distinguishing mark being the amount of work which he was capable of performing.

Selecting Workers under Traditional Management.—In selecting men to do work, there was little or no attempt to study the individuals who applied for work. The matter of selection was more of a process of "guess work" than of exact measurement, and the highest form of test was considered to be that of having the man actually tried out by being given a chance at the work itself. There was not only a great waste of time on the work, because men unfitted to it could not turn it out so successfully, but there also was a waste of the worker, and many times a positive injury to the worker, by his being put at work which he was unfitted either to perform, to work at continuously, or both.

In the most progressive type of Traditional Management there was usually a feeling, however, that if the labor market offered even temporarily a greater supply than the work in hand demanded, it

[5] James Sully, *Teacher's Handbook of Psychology,* p. 577.
[6] H. L. Gantt, *Work, Wages and Profits,* p. 52.

was wise to choose those men to do the work who were best fitted for it, or who were willing to work for less wages. It is surprising to find in the traditional type, even up to the present day, how often men were selected for their strength and physique, rather than for any special capabilities fitting them for working in, or at, the particular line of work to be done.

Output Seldom Separated under Traditional Management.— Under Traditional Management especially on day work the output of the men was not usually separated, nor was the output recorded separately, as can be done even with the work of gangs.

Few Individual Tasks under Traditional Management.—Seldom, if ever, was an individual task set for a worker on day work, or piece work, and even if one were set, it was not scientifically determined. The men were simply set to work alone or in gangs, *as the work demanded,* and if the foreman was overworked or lazy, allowed to take practically their own time to do the work. If, on the other hand, the foreman was a "good driver," the men might be pushed to their utmost limit of their individual undirected speed, regardless of their welfare.

Little Individual Teaching under Traditional Management.— Not having a clear idea either of the present fitness and the future possibilities of the worker, or the requirements of the work, no intelligent attempt could be made at efficient individual teaching. What teaching was done was in the form of directions for all, concerning the work in general, the directions being given by an overworked foreman, the holding of whose position often depended more upon whether his employer made money than upon the way his men were taught, or worked.

Seldom an Individual Reward under Traditional Management.— As a typical example of disregard of individuality, the worker in the household may be cited, and especially the "general housework girl." Selected with no knowledge of her capabilities, and with little or no scientific or even systematized knowledge of the work that she is expected to do, there is little or no thought of a prescribed and definite task, no teaching specially adapted to the individual needs of the taught, and no reward in proportion to efficiency.

Cause of These Lacks under Traditional Management.—The fault lies not in any desire of the managers to do poor or wasteful work, or to treat their workers unfairly,—but in a lack of knowledge and of accurate methods for obtaining, conserving and transmitting knowledge. Under Traditional Management no one individual knows precisely what is to be done. Such management seldom knows how work could best be done;—never knows how much work each individual can do.[7] Understanding neither work nor workers, it can not adjust the one to the other so as to obtain least waste. Having no conception of the importance of accurate measurement, it has no thought of the individual as a unit.

Individuality Recognized under Transitory Management.—Recognition of individuality is one of the principles first apparent under Transitory Management.

This is apt to demonstrate itself first of all in causing the outputs of the workers to "show up" separately, rewarding these separated outputs, and rewarding each worker for his individual output.

Benefits of This Recognition.—The benefits of introducing these features first are that the worker, (1) seeing his individual output, is stimulated to measure it, and (2) receiving compensation in accordance with his output, is satisfied; and (3) observing that records are necessary to determine the amount of output and pay, is glad to have accurate measurement and the other features of Scientific Management introduced.

Individuality a Fundamental Principle of Scientific Management.—Under Scientific Management the individual is the unit to be measured. Functionalization is based upon utilizing the particular powers and special abilities of each man. Measurement is of the individual man and his work. Analysis and synthesis build up methods by which the individual can best do his work. Standards are of the work of an individual, a standard man, and the task is always for an individual, being that percentage of the standard man's task that the particular individual can do. Records are of individuals, and are made in order to show and reward individual effort. Specific individuals are taught those things that they, individually, require. Incentives are individual both in the cases of rewards and punishments, and, finally, it is the welfare of the individual worker that is considered, without the sacrifice of any for the good of the whole.

Individuality Considered in Selecting Workers.—Under Scientific Management individuality is considered in selecting workers as it could not be under either of the other two forms of management.

[7] F. W. Taylor, *Shop Management,* p. 25. (Harper & Bros.)

This for several reasons:

1. The work is more specialized, hence requires more carefully selected men.

2. With standardized methods comes a knowledge to the managers of the qualifications of the "standard men" who can best do the work and continuously thrive.

3. Motion study, in its investigation of the worker, supplies a list of variations in workers that can be utilized in selecting men.[8]

Variables of the Worker.—This list now includes at least 50 or 60 variables, and shows the possible elements which may demand consideration. When it is remembered that the individual selected may need a large or small proportion of most of the variables in order to do his particular work most successfully, and that every single one of these variables, as related to the others, may, in some way affect his output and his welfare in doing his assigned work, the importance of taking account of individuality in selection is apparent.

Scientific Management Needs Support in Studying Workers.— The best of management is by no means at its ultimate stage in practice in this field. This, not because of a lack in the laws of management, but because, so far, Scientific Management has not received proper support from other lines of activity.

Present Lack of Knowledge of Applicants.—At present, the men who apply to the Industries for positions have no scientifically determined idea of their own capabilities, neither has there been any effort in the training or experience of most of those who apply for work for the first time to show them how fit they really are to do the work which they wish to do.

Supplements Demanded by Scientific Management.—Before the worker can be scientifically selected so that his individuality can be appreciated, Scientific Management must be supplemented in two ways:—

1. By psychological and physiological study of workers under it. By such study of the effect of various kinds of standardized work upon the mind and body, standard requirements for men who desire to do the work can be made.

2. By scientific study of the worker made before he comes into the Industries, the results of which shall show his capabilities and possibilities.[9]

[8] F. B. Gilbreth, *Motion Study*, p. 7.
[9] L. B. Blan, *A Special Study of the Incidence of Retardation*, p. 80.

Whence This Help Must Come.—This study must be made

a. In the Vocational Guidance Work.

b. In the Academic Work,

and in both fields psychological and physiological investigations are called for.

Work of Vocational Guidance Bureaus.—Vocational Guidance Bureaus are, at present, doing a wonderful work in their line. This work divides itself into two parts:

1. Determining the capabilities of the boy, that is, seeing what he is, by nature and training, best fitted to do.

2. Determining the possibilities of his securing work in the line where he is best fitted to work, that is, studying the industrial opportunities that offer, and the "welfare" of the worker under each, using the word welfare in the broadest sense, of general wellbeing, mental, physical, moral and financial.

Work of Academic World.—The Academic World is also, wherever it is progressive, attempting to study the student, and to develop him so that he can be the most efficient individual. Progressive educators realize that schools and colleges must stand or fall, as efficient, as the men they train become successful or unsuccessful in their vocations, as well as in their personal culture.

Need for Psychological Study in All Fields.—In both these complementary lines of activity, as in Scientific Management itself, the need for psychological study is evident.[10] Through it, only, can scientific progress come. Here is emphasized again the importance of measurement. Through accurate measurement of the mind and the body only can individuality be recognized, conserved and developed as it should be.

Preparedness of Experimental Psychology.—Experimental psychology has instruments of precision with which to measure and test the minds and bodies brought to it, and its leading exponents are so broadening the scope of its activities that it is ready and glad to plan for investigations.

Method of Selection Under Ultimate Management.—Under Ultimate Management, the minds of the workers,—and of the managers too,—will have been studied, and the results recorded from earliest childhood. This record, made by trained investigators, will enable vocational guidance directors to tell the child what he is fitted to be, and thus to help the schools and colleges to know how best to train

[10] Hugo Münsterberg, *American Problems*, pp. 38–39.

him, that is to say, to provide what he will need to know to do his life work, and also those cultural studies that his vocational work may lack, and that may be required to build out his best development as an individual.

It is not always recognized that even the student who can afford to postpone his technical training until he has completed a general culture course, requires that his culture course be carefully planned. Not only must he choose those general courses that will serve as a foundation for his special study, and that will broaden and enrich his study, but also he must be provided with a counter-balance,—with interests that his special work might never arouse in him. Thus the field of Scientific Management can be narrowed to determining and preparing standard plans for standard specialized men, and selecting men to fill these places from competent applicants.

What part of the specialized training needed by the special work shall be given in schools and what in the industries themselves can be determined later. The "twin apprentice" plan offers one solution of the problem that has proved satisfactory in many places. The psychological study should determine through which agency knowledge can best come at any particular stage of mental growth.

Effect on Workers of Such Selection.—As will be shown at greater length under "Incentives," Scientific Management aims in every way to encourage initiative. The outline here given as to how men must, ultimately, under Scientific Management, be selected serves to show that, far from being "made machines of," men are selected to reach that special place where their individuality can be recognized and rewarded to the greatest extent.

Selection Under Scientific Management To-day.—At the present day, the most that Scientific Management can do, in the average case, is to determine the type of men needed for any particular kind of work, and then to select that man who seems, from such observations as can be made, best to conform to the type. The accurate knowledge of the requirements of the work, and the knowledge of variables of the worker make even a cursory observation more rich in results than it would otherwise be. Even such an apparently obvious observation, as that the very fact that a man claims that he can do the work implies desire and will on his part to do it that may overcome many natural lacks,—even this is an advance in recognizing individuality.

Effect of This Selection.—The result of this scientific selection of the workman is not only better work, but also, and more important from the psychological side, the development of his individuality. It is not always recognized that the work itself is a great educator, and that acute cleverness in the line of work to which he is fitted comes to the worker.

Individuality Developed by Separating Outputs.—Under Scientific Management the work of each man is arranged either so that his output shows up separately and on the individual records, or, if the work is such that it seems best to do it in gangs, the output can often be so recorded that the individual's output can be computed from the records.

Purpose of Separating Outputs.—The primary purpose of separating the output is to see what the man can do, to record this, and to reward the man according to his work, but this separating of output has also an individual result, which is even more important than the result aimed at, and that is the development of individuality.

Under Traditional Management and the usual "day work," much of the work is done by gangs and is observed or recorded as of gangs. Only now and then, when the work of some particular individual shows up decidedly better or worse than that of his fellows, and when the foreman or superintendent, or other onlooker, happens to observe this is the individual appreciated, and then only in the most inexact, unsystematic manner.

Under Scientific Management, making individual output show up separately allows of individual recording, tasks, teaching and rewards.

Effect on Athletic Contests.—Also, with this separation of the work of the individual under Scientific Management comes the possibility of a real, scientific, "athletic contest." This athletic contest, which proves itself so successful in Traditional Management, even when the men are grouped as gangs and their work is not recorded or thought of separately, proves itself quite as efficient or more efficient under Scientific Management, when the work of the man shows up separately. It might be objected that the old gang spirit, or it might be called "team" spirit, would disappear with the separation of the work. This is not so, as will be noted by a comparison to a baseball team, where each man has his separate place and his separate work and where his work shows up separately with separate records, such as "batting average" and "fielding average." Team spirit is the result of being grouped together against a common opponent, and it will be the same in any sort of work when the men are so grouped, or given to understand that they belong on the same side.

The following twelve rules for an Athletic Contest under Transitory System are quoted as exemplifying the benefits which accrue to Individuality.

1. Men must have square deal.
2. Conditions must be similar.
3. Men must be properly spaced and placed.
4. Output must show up separately.
5. Men must be properly started.
6. Causes for delay must be eliminated.
7. Pace maker must be provided.
8. Time for rest must be provided.
9. Individual scores must be kept and posted.
10. "Audience" must be provided.
11. Rewards must be prompt and provided for all good scores—not for winners only.
12. Appreciation must be shown.[11]

This list shows the effects of many fundamental principles of Scientific Management,—but we note particularly here that over half the rules demand that outputs be separated as a prerequisite.

None of the benefits of the Athletic Contest are lost under Scientific Management. The only restrictions placed are that the men shall not be grouped according to any distinction that would cause hatred or ill feeling, that the results shall be ultimately beneficial to the workers themselves, and that all high scores shall win high prizes.

As will be brought out later under "Incentives," no competition is approved under Scientific Management which speeds up the men uselessly, or which brings any ill feeling between the men or any feeling that the weaker ones have not a fair chance. All of these things are contrary to Scientific Management, as well as contrary to common sense, for it goes without saying that no man is capable of doing his best work permanently if he is worried by the idea that he will not receive the square deal, that someone stronger than he will be allowed to cheat or to domineer over him, or that he will be speeded up to such an extent that while his work will increase for one day, the next day his work will fall down because of the effect of the fatigue of the day before.

The field of the contests is widened, as separating of the work of the individual not only allows for competition between individuals, but for the competition of the individual with his own records. This

[11] F. B. Gilbreth, *Cost Reducing System,* Chap. III.

competition is not only a great, constant and helpful incentive to every worker, but it is also an excellent means of developing individuality.

Advantages to Managers of Separating Output.—The advantages to the managers of separating the work are that there is a chance to know exactly who is making the high output, and that the spirit of competition which prevails when men compare their outputs to their own former records or others, leads to increased effort.

Advantages to Workers of Separating Output.—As for advantages to the men:

By separation of the individual work, not only is the man's work itself shown, but at the same time the work of all other people is separated, cut away and put aside, and he can locate the man who is delaying him by, for example, not keeping him supplied with materials. The man has not only an opportunity to concentrate, but every possible incentive to exercise his will and his desire to do things. His attention is concentrated on the fact that he as an individual is expected to do his very best. He has the moral stimulus of responsibility. He has the emotional stimulus of competition. He has the mental stimulus of definiteness. He has, most valuable of all, a chance to be an entity rather than one of an undiscriminated gang. This chance to be an individual, or personality, is in great contradistinction to the popular opinion of Scientific Management, which thinks it turns men into machines. A very simple example of the effect of the worker's seeing his output show up separately in response to and in proportion to his effort and skill is that of boys in the lumber producing districts chopping edgings for fire wood. Here the chopping is so comparatively light that the output increased very rapidly, and the boy delights to "see his pile of fire wood grow."

With the separation of the work comes not only the opportunity for the men to see their own work, but also to see that of others, and there comes with this the spirit of imitation, or the spirit of friendly opposition, either of which, while valuable in itself is even more valuable as the by-product of being a life-giving thought, and of putting life into the work such as there never could be when the men were working together, more or less objectless, because they could not see plainly either what they were doing themselves, or what others were doing.

Separation of the output of the men gives them the greatest opportunity to develop. It gives them a chance to concentrate their attention at the work on which they are, because it is not necessary for them to waste any time to find out what that work is. Their work stands out by itself; they can put their whole minds to that work; they can become interested in that work and its outcome, and they can be positive that what they have done will be appreciated and recognized, and that it will have a good effect, with no possibility of evil effect, upon their chance for work and their chance for pay and promotion in the future. Definiteness of the boundaries, then, is not only good management in that it shows up the work and that it allows each man to see, and each man over him, or observing him to see exactly what has been done,—it has also an excellent effect upon the worker's mind.

Individuality Developed by Recording Output Separately.—The spirit of individuality is brought out still more clearly by the fact that under Scientific Management, output is recorded separately. This recording of the outputs separately is, usually, and very successfully, one of the first features installed in Transitory Management, and a feature very seldom introduced, even unconscious of its worth, in day work under Traditional Management. It is one of the great disadvantages of many kinds of work, especially in this day, that the worker does only a small part of the finished article and that he has a feeling that what he does is not identified permanently with the success of the completed whole. We may note that one of the great unsatisfying features to such arts as acting and music, is that no matter how wonderful the performer's efforts, there was no permanent record of them; that the work of the day dies with the day. He can expect to live only in the minds and hearts of the hearers, in the accounts of spectators, or in histories of the stage.

It is, therefore, not strange that the world's best actors and singers are now grasping the opportunity to make their best efforts permanent through the instrumentality of the motion picture films and the talking machine records. This same feeling, minus the glow of enthusiasm that at least attends the actor during the work, is present in more or less degree in the mind of the worker.

Records Make Work Seem Worth While.—With the feeling that his work is recorded comes the feeling that the work is really worth while, for even if the work itself does not last, the records of it are such as can go on.

Records Give Individuals a Feeling of Permanence.—With recorded individual output comes also the feeling of permanence, of credit for good performance. This desire for permanence shows itself all through the work of men in Traditional Management, for example—in the stone cutter's art where the man who had successfully dressed the stone from the rough block was delighted to put his own individual mark on it, even though he knew that that mark probably would seldom, if ever, be noticed again by anyone after the stone was set in the wall. It is an underlying trait of the human mind to desire this permanence of record of successful effort, and fulfilling and utilizing this desire is a great gain of Scientific Management.

Mental Development of Worker Through Records.—It is not only for his satisfaction that the worker should see his records and realize that his work has permanence, but also for comparison of his work not only with his own record, but with the work of others. The value of these comparisons, not only to the management but to the worker himself, must not be underestimated. The worker gains mental development and physical skill by studying these comparisons.

Advantages to Worker of Making his Own Records.—These possibilities of mental development are still further increased when the man makes his own records. This leads to closer attention, to more interest in the work, and to a realization of the man as to what the record really means, and what value it represents. Though even a record that is made for him and is posted where he can see it will probably result in a difference in his pay envelope, no such progress is likely to occur as when the man makes his own record, and must be conscious every moment of the time exactly where he stands.

Possibilities of Making Individual Records.—Records of individual efficiency are comparatively easy to make when output is separated. But even when work must be done by gangs or teams of men, there is provision made in Scientific Management for recording this gang work in such a way that either the output or the efficiency, or both, of each man shows up separately. This may be done in several ways, such as, for example, by recording the total time of delays avoidable and unavoidable, caused by each man, and from this computing individual records. This method of recording is psychologically right, because the recording of the delay will serve as a warning to the man, and as a spur to him not to cause delay to others again.

The forcefulness of the "don't" and the "never" have been investigated by education. Undoubtedly the "do" is far stronger, but in this particular case the command deduced from the records of delay to others is, necessarily, in the negative form, and a study of the psychological results proves most instructive.

Benefits to Managers of Individual Records.—The value of the training to the foremen, to the superintendents and to the managers higher up, who study these records, as well as to the timekeepers, recorders and clerks in the Time and Cost Department who make the records, is obvious. There is not only the possibility of appreciating and rewarding the worker, and thus stimulating him to further activity, there is also, especially in the Transitory stage, when men are to be chosen on whom to make Time Study observations, an excellent chance to compare various methods of doing work and their results.

Incentives with Individual Records.—The greatest value of recorded outputs is in the appreciation of the work of the individual that becomes possible. First of all, appreciation by the management, which to the worker must be the most important of all, as it means to him a greater chance for promotion and for more pay. This promotion and additional pay are amply provided for by Scientific Management, as will be shown later in discussing Incentives and Welfare.

Not only is the work appreciated by the management and by the man himself, but also the work becomes possible of appreciation by others. The form of the record as used in Scientific Management, and as introduced early in the transitory stage, makes it possible for many beside those working on the job, if they take the pains to consult the records, which are best posted in a conspicuous place on the work, to know and appreciate what the worker is doing. This can be best illustrated, perhaps, by various methods of recording output on contracting work,—out-of-door work.

The flag flown by the successful contestants in the athletic contests, showing which gang or which individual has made the largest output during the day previous, allows everyone who passes to appreciate the attainment of that particular worker, or that group of workers. The photographs of the "high priced men," copies of which may be given to the workers themselves, allow the worker to carry home a record and thus impress his family with what he has done. Too often the family is unable by themselves to understand the value of the worker's work, or to apreciate the effect of his home life, food, and rest conditions upon his life work, and this entire strong element of interest of the worker's family in his work is often lost.

Relation of Individual Records to Scientific Management in General.—Any study of Records of an individual's work again makes clear that no one topic of Scientific Management can be properly noted without a consideration of all other elements. The fact that under Scientific Management the record with which the man most surely and constantly competes is his own, as provided for by the individual instruction card and the individual task; the fact that under Scientific Management the man need be in no fear of losing his job if he does his best; the fact that Scientific Management is founded on the "square deal";—all of these facts must be kept constantly in mind when considering the advantages of recording individual output, for they all have a strong psychological effect on the man's mind. It is important to remember that not only does Scientific Management provide for certain directions and thoughts entering the man's mind, but that it also eliminates other thoughts which would surely have a tendency to retard his work. The result is output far exceeding what is usually possible under Traditional Management, because drawbacks are removed and impetuses added.

The outcome of the records, and their related elements in other branches of Scientific Management, is to arouse interest. Interest arouses abnormally concentrated attention, and this in turn is the cause of genius. This again answers the argument of those who claim that Scientific Management kills individuality and turns the worker into a machine.

Individual Task Under Scientific Management.—Individuality is also taken into consideration when preparing the task. This task would always be for an individual, even in the case of the gang instruction card. It usually recognizes individuality, in that,—

1. It is prepared for one individual only, when possible.
2. It is prepared for the particular individual who is to do it.

The working time, as will be shown later, is based upon time study observations on a standard man, but when a task is assigned for a certain individual, that proportion of the work of the standard or first class man is assigned to that particular given man who is actually to do it, which he is able to do. It is fundamental that the task must be such that the man who is actually put at it, when he obeys orders and works steadily, can do it; that is, the task must be achievable, and achievable without such effort as would do mental or physical injury to the worker. This not only gives the individual the proper amount of work to do, recognizes his particular capabilities and is particularly adapted to him, but it also eliminates all dread on the score of his not being appreciated, in that the worker knows that if he achieves or exceeds his task he will not only receive the wage for it, but will continue to receive that wage, or more, for like achievement. The rate is not cut. Under the "three-rate with increased rate system," which experience has shown to be a most advanced plan for compensating workmen, the worker receives one bonus for exactness as to methods, that is, he receives one bonus if he does the task exactly as he is instructed to do it as to methods; and a second bonus, or extra bonus, if he completes his task in the allotted time. This not only assures adequate pay to the man who is slow, but a good imitator, but also to the man who, perhaps, is not such a good imitator, and must put attention on the quality rather than the quantity of his performance.

Individuality Emphasized by Instruction Card.—This individual task is embodied in an individual instruction card.

In all work where it is possible to do so, the worker is given an individual instruction card, even though his operations and rest periods are also determined by a gang instruction card. This card not only tells the man what he is to do, how he can best do it, and the time that it is supposed to take him to do it,—but it bears also the signature of the man who made it. This in order that if the worker cannot fulfill the requirements of the card he may lose no time in determining who is to give him the necessary instructions or help that will result in his earning his large wages. More than this, he must call for help from his assigned teachers, as is stated in large type on a typical Instruction Card as follows: "When instructions cannot be carried out, foreman must at once report to man who signed this card."

The signature of the man who made the card not only develops his sense of individuality and responsibility, but helps create a feeling of inter-responsibility between the workers in various parts of the organization.

The Gang Instruction Card.—A gang instruction card is used for such work only as must be done by a group of men all engaged at the work at once, or who are working at a dependent sequence of operations, or both. This card contains but those portions of the instructions for each man which refer to those elements which must be completed before a following element, to be done by the next man in the sequence, can be completed. Because of the nature of the work, the gang instruction card must be put in the hands of a leader, or foreman, whether or not it is also in the hands of each of the individuals. The amount of work which can be required as a set task for each individual member of the gang, the allowance for rest for overcoming fatigue, the time that the rest periods must occur, and the proper pay, are fully stated on the Individual Instruction Cards.

Methods of Teaching Foster Individuality.—As will be shown at length in the Chapter on Teaching, under Scientific Management teaching is not only general, by "Systems," "Standing Orders," or "Standard Practice," but also specific. Specialized teachers, called, unfortunately for the emphasis desired to be put on teaching, "functional foremen," help the individual worker to overcome his peculiar difficulties.

This teaching not only allows every worker to supplement his deficiencies of disposition or experience, but the teachers' places give opportunities for those who have a talent for imparting knowledge to utilize and develop it.

Individual Incentive and Welfare.—Finally, individual incentive and individual welfare are not only both present, but interdependent. Desire for individual success, which might lead a worker to respond to the incentive till he held back perhaps the work of others, is held in balance by interdependence of bonuses. This will be explained in full in the Chapters on Incentives and Welfare.

SUMMARY

Result of Idea of Individuality upon Work.—To recapitulate;— Under Traditional Management, because of its frequent neglect of the idea of individuality, work is often unsystematized, and high output is usually the result of "speeding up" only, with constant danger of a falling off in quality over-balancing men and injury to men and machinery.

Under Transitory Management, as outputs are separated, separately recorded, and as the idea of Individuality is embodied in selecting men, setting tasks, the instruction cards, periods of rest, teaching, incentives and welfare, output increases without undue pressure on the worker.

Under Scientific Management—with various elements which embody individuality fully developed, output increases, to the welfare of worker, manager, employer and consumer and with no falling off in quality.

Effect Upon the Worker.—The question of the effect upon the worker of emphasis laid upon individuality, can perhaps best be answered by asking and answering the following questions:—

1. When, where, how, and how much is individuality considered?

2. What consideration is given to the relation of the mind to the body of the individual?

3. What is the relative emphasis on consideration of individual and class?

4. In how far is the individual the unit?

5. What consideration is given to idiosyncrasies?

6. What is the effect toward causing or bringing about development, that is, broadening, deepening and making the individual more progressive?

Extent of Consideration of Individuality.—1. Under Traditional Management consideration of individuality is seldom present, but those best forms of Traditional Management that are successful are so because it is present. This is not usually recognized, but investigation shows that the successful manager, or foreman, or boss, or superintendent succeeds either because of his own individuality or because he brings out to good advantage the individual possibilities of his men. The most successful workers under Traditional Management are those who are allowed to be individuals and to follow out their individual bents of greatest efficiency, instead of being crowded down to become mere members of gangs, with no chance to think, to do, or to be anything but parts of the gang.

Under Transitory Management, and most fully under Scientific Management, the spirit of individuality, far from being crowded out, is a basic principle, and everything possible is done to encourage the desire to be a personality.

Relation of Mind to Body.—Under Traditional Management, where men worked in the same employ for a long time, much consideration was given to the relation of the mind to the body. It was realized that men must not be speeded up beyond what they could do healthfully; they must have good sleeping quarters and good, savory and appetizing food to eat and not be fatigued unnecessarily, if they were to become successful workers. More than this, philanthropic employers often attempted to supply many kinds of comfort and amusement.

Under Transitory Management the physical and mental welfare are provided for more systematically.

Under Scientific Management consideration of the mind and body of the workman, and his health, and all that that includes, is a subject for scientific study and for scientific administration. As shown later, it eliminates all discussion and troubles of so-called "welfare work," because the interests of the employer and the worker become identical and everything that is done becomes the concern of both.

Scientific Management realizes that the condition of the body effects every possible mental process. It is one of the great advantages of a study of the psychology of management that the subject absolutely demands from the start, and insists in every stage of the work, on this relationship of the body to the mind, and of the surroundings, equipment, etc., of the worker to his work.

It is almost impossible, in management, to separate the subject of the worker from that of his work, or to think of the worker as not working except in such a sense as "ceasing-from-work," "about-to-work," "resting to overcome fatigue of work," or "resting during periods of unavoidable delays." The relation of the worker to his work is constantly in the mind of the manager. It is for this reason that not only does management owe much to psychology, but that psychology, as applied to any line of study, will, ultimately, be recognized as owing much to the science of management.

Relative Emphasis on Individual and Class.—Under Traditional Management the gang, or the class, usually receives the chief emphasis. If the individual developed, as he undoubtedly did, in many kinds of mechanical work, especially in small organizations, it was more or less because it was not possible for the managers to organize the various individuals into classes or gangs. In the transitory stage the emphasis is shifting. Under Scientific Management the emphasis is most decidedly and emphatically upon the individual as the unit to be managed, as has been shown.

Individual as the Unit.—Under Traditional Management the individual was seldom the unit. Under Transitory Management the individual is the unit, but there is not much emphasis in the early stages placed upon his peculiarities and personalities. Under Scientific Management the unit is always the individual, and the utilizing and strengthening of his personal traits, special ability and skill is a dominating feature.

Emphasis on Idiosyncrasies.—Under Traditional Management there is either no consideration given to idiosyncrasies, or too wide a latitude is allowed. In cases where no consideration is given, there is often either a pride in the managers in "treating all men alike," though they might respond better to different handling, or else the individual is undirected and his personality manifests itself in all sorts of unguided directions, many of which must necessarily be wasteful, unproductive, or incomplete in development. Under Scientific Management, functionalization, as will be shown, provides for the utilization of all idiosyncrasies and efficient deviations from class, and promotion is so planned that a man may develop along the line of his chief ability. Thus initiative is encouraged and developed constantly.

Development of Individuality.—The development of individuality is more sure under Scientific Management than it is under either of the other two forms of management, (a) because this development is recognized to be a benefit to the worker and to the employer and (b) because this development as a part of a definite plan is provided for and perfected scientifically.

Measurement

Definition of Measurement.—"Measurement," according to the Century Dictionary,—"is the act of measuring," and to measure is— "to ascertain the length, extent, dimensions, quantity or capacity of, by comparison with a standard; ascertain or determine a quantity by exact observation," or, again, "to estimate or determine the relative extent, greatness or value of, appraise by comparison with something else."

Measurement Important in Psychology.—Measurement has always been of importance in psychology; but it is only with the development of experimental psychology and its special apparatus, that methods of accurate measurements are available which make possible the measurement of extremely short periods of time, or measurements "quick as thought." These enable us to measure the variations of different workers as to their abilities and their mental and physical fatigue;[1] to study mental processes at different stages of mental and physical growth; to compare different people under the same conditions, and the same person under different conditions; to determine the personal coefficient of different workers, specialists and foremen, and to formulate resultant standards. As in all other branches of science, the progress comes with the development of measurement.

Methods of Measurement in Psychology.—No student of management and of measurement in the field of management can afford not to study carefully and at length methods of measurement under psychology. This for at least two most important reasons which will actually improve him as a measurer, i. e.—

1. The student will discover, in the books on experimental psychology and in the "Psychological Review," a marvelous array of results of scientific laboratory experiments in psychology, which will be of immediate use to him in his work.

2. He will receive priceless instruction in methods of measuring. No where better than in the field of psychology, can one learn to realize the importance of measurements, the necessity for determination of elements for study, and the necessity for accurate apparatus and accuracy in observation.

Prof. George M. Stratton, in his book "Experimental Psychology and Culture,"—says "In mental measurements, therefore, there is no pretense of taking the mind's measure as a whole, nor is there usually any immediate intention of testing even some special faculty or capacity of the individual. What is aimed at is the measurement of a limited event in consciousness, such as a particular perception or feeling. The experiments are addressed, of course, not to the weight or size of such phenomena, but usually to their duration and intensity."[2]

The emphasis laid on a study of elements is further shown in the same book by the following,—"The actual laboratory work in time-measurement, however, has been narrowed down to determining, not the time in general that is occupied by some mental action, but rather the shortest possible time in which a particular operation, like discrimination or choice or association or recognition, can be performed under the simplest and most favorable circumstances.[3] The experimental results here are something like speed or racing records,

---

[1] Hugo Münsterberg, *American Problems*, p. 34.
[2] G. M. Stratton, *Experimental Psychology and Its Bearing upon Culture*, p. 37.
[3] *Ibid.*, p. 38.

made under the best conditions of track and training. A delicate chronograph or chronoscope is used, which marks the time in thousandths of a second."

Measurement in Psychology Related to Measurement in Management.—Measurement in psychology is of importance to measurement in management not only as a source of information and instruction, but also as a justification and support. Scientific Management has suffered from being called absurd, impractical, impossible, overexact, because of the emphasis which it lays on measurement. Yet, to the psychologist, all present measurement in Scientific Management must appear coarse, inaccurate and of immediate and passing value only. With the knowledge that psychologists endorse accurate measurement, and will coöperate in discovering elements for study, instruments of precision and methods of investigation, the investigator in industrial fields must persist in his work with a new interest and confidence.[4]

Scientific Management cannot hope to furnish psychology with either data or methods of measurement. It can and does, however, open a new field for study to experimental psychology, and shows itself willing to furnish the actual working difficulties or problems, to do the preliminary investigation, and to utilize results as fast as they can be obtained.

Psychologists Appreciate Scientific Management.—The appreciation which psychologists have shown of work done by Scientific Management must be not only a matter of gratification, but of inspiration to all workers in Scientific Management.

So, also, must the new divisions of the Index to the Psychological Review relating to Activity and Fatigue, and the work being so extensively done in these lines by French, German, Italian and other nations, as well as by English and American psychologists.

Measurement Important in Management.—The study of individuality and of functionalization have made plain the necessity of measurement for successful management. Measurement furnishes the means for obtaining that accurate knowledge upon which the science of management rests, as do all sciences—exact and inexact.[5] Through measurement, methods of less waste are determined, standards are made possible, and management becomes a science, as it derives

---

[4] For apparatus for psychological experiment see Stratton, p. 38, p. 171, p. 265.
[5] H. L. Gantt, *Work, Wages and Profits,* p. 15.

standards, and progressively makes and improves them, and the comparisons from them, accurate.

Problem of Measurement in Management.—One of the important problems of measurement in management is determining how many hours should constitute the working day in each different kind of work and at what gait the men can work for greatest output and continuously thrive. The solution of this problem involves the study of the men, the work, and the methods, which study must become more and more specialized; but the underlying aim is to determine standards and individual capacity as exactly as is possible.[6]

Capacity.—There are at least four views of a worker's capacity.

1. What he thinks his capacity is.
2. What his associates think his capacity is.
3. What those over him think his capacity is.
4. What accurate measurement determines his actual capacity to be.

Ignorance of Real Capacity.—Dr. Taylor has emphasized the fact that the average workman does not know either his true efficiency or his true capacity.[7] The experience of others has also gone to show that even the skilled workman has little or inaccurate knowledge of the amount of output that a good worker can achieve at his chosen vocation in a given time.[8]

For example,—until a bricklayer has seen his output counted for several days, he has little idea of how many bricks he can lay, or has laid, in a day.[9]

The average manager is usually even more ignorant of the capacity of the workers than are the men themselves.[10] This is because of the prevalence of, and the actual necessity for the worker's best interest, under some forms of management, of "soldiering." Even when the manager realizes that soldiering is going on, he has no way, especially under ordinary management, of determining its extent.

Little Measurement in Traditional Management.—Under Traditional Management there was little measurement of a man's capacity. The emphasis was entirely on the results. There was, it is true, in

[6] Morris Llewellyn Cooke, Bulletin No. 5, *The Carnegie Foundation for the Advancement of Teaching*, p. 7.

[7] F. W. Taylor, *Shop Management*, para. 29. Harper Ed., p. 25.

[8] H. L. Gantt, Paper No. 928, A. S. M. E., para. 6.

[9] F. B. Gilbreth, *Cost Reducing System*.

[10] F. W. Taylor, *Shop Management*, para. 61. Harper Ed., p. 33.

everything beyond the most elementary of Traditional Management, a measurement of the result. The manager did know, at the end of certain periods of time, how much work had been done, and how much it had cost him. This was a very important thing for him to know. If his cost ran too high, and his output fell too low, he investigated. If he found a defect, he tried to remedy it; but much time had to be wasted in this investigation, because often he had no idea where to start in to look for the defects. The result of the defects was usually the cause for the inquiry as to their presence.

He might investigate the men, he might investigate the methods, he might investigate the equipment, he might investigate the surroundings, and so on,—and very often in the mind of the Traditional manager, there was not even this most elementary division. If things went wrong he simply knew,—"Something is wrong somewhere," and it was the work of the foremen to find out where the place was, or so to speed up the men that the output should be increased and the cost lowered. Whether the defects were really remedied, or simply concealed by temporarily speeding up, was not seriously questioned.

Moreover, until measuring devices are secured, the only standard is what someone thinks about things, and the pity of it is that even this condition does not remain staple.

Transitory Management Realizes Value of Measurement.—One of the first improvements introduced when Traditional Management gives place to the Transitory stage is the measurement of the separated output of individual workers. These outputs are measured and recorded. The records for extra high outputs are presented to the worker promptly, so that he may have a keen idea constantly of the relation of effort to output, while the fatigue and the effort of doing the work is still fresh in his mind.

The psychology of the prompt reward will be considered later at length, but it cannot be emphasized too often that the prompter the reward, the greater the stimulus. The reward will become associated with the fatigue in such a way that the worker will really get, at the time, more satisfaction out of his fatigue than he will discomfort; at the least, any dissatisfaction over his fatigue will be eliminated, by the constant and first thought of the reward which he has gotten through his efforts.

This record of efficiency is often so presented to the workers that they get an excellent idea of the numerical measure of their efficiency and its trend. This is best done by a graphical chart.

The records of the outputs of others on the same kind of work done concurrently, or a corresponding record on work done previously, will show the relative efficiency of any worker as compared with the rest. These standards of comparison are a strong incentive and, if they are shown at the time that such work is done, they also become so closely associated not only with the mental but the bodily feeling of the man that the next time the work is repeated, the thoughts that the same effort will probably bring greater results, and that it has done so in the past with others, will be immediately present in the mind.

Measurement Is Basic Under Scientific Management.—Under Scientific Management measurement is basic. Measurement is of the work, of outputs, of the methods, the tools, and of the worker, with the individual as a unit, and motion study, time study and micromotion study and the chrono-cyclegraph as the methods of measurement.

Measurement is a most necessary adjunct to selecting the workers and the managers and to assigning them to the proper functions and work. They cannot be selected to the greatest advantage and set to functionalized work until—

(a) the unit of measurement that will of itself tend to reduce costs has been determined.

(b) methods of measurement have been determined.

(c) measurement has been applied.

(d) standards for measurement have been derived.

(e) devices for cheapening the cost of measuring have been installed.

Under Scientific Management Measurement Determines the Task. —An important aim of measurement under Scientific Management is to determine the Task, or the standard amount of any kind of work that a first class man can do in a certain period of time. The "standard amount" is the largest amount that a first class man can do and continuously thrive.

The "first-class" man is the man who can eventually become best fitted, by means of natural and acquired capabilities, to do the work. The "certain period of time" is that which best suits the work and the man's thriving under the work. The amount of time allowed for a task consists of three parts—

1. time actually spent at work.

2. time for rest for overcoming fatigue.

3. time for overcoming delays.

Measurement must determine what percentage of the task time is to be spent at work and what at rest, and must also determine whether the rest period should all follow the completed work, or should be divided into parts, these parts to follow certain cycles through the entire work period.

The method of constructing the task is discussed under two chapters that follow, Analysis and Synthesis, and Standardization. Here we note only that the task is built up of elementary units measured by motion study, time study, and micro-motion study.

When this standard task has been determined the worker's efficiency can be measured by his performance of, or by the amount that he exceeds, the task.

Qualifications of the Observer or Measurer.—The position of observer, or as he has well been called, "trade revolutionizer," should be filled by a man specially selected for the position on account of his special natural fitness and previous experience. He also should be specially trained for his work. As in all other classes of work, the original selection of the man is of vital importance. The natural qualities of the successful hunter, fisherman, detective, reporter and woodsman for observation of minute details are extremely desirable. It is only by having intimate knowledge of such experiences as Agassiz had with his pupils, or with untrained "observers" of the trade, that one can realize the lack of powers of observation of detail in the average human being.

Other natural qualifications required to an efficient observer are that of being

(a) an "eye worker";
(b) able to concentrate attention for unusually long periods;
(c) able to get every thought out of a simple written sentence;
(d) keenly interested in his work;
(e) accurate;
(f) possessed of infinite patience;
(g) an enthusiastic photographer.

The measurer or observer should, preferably, have the intimate knowledge that comes from personal experience of the work to be observed, although such a man is often difficult if not impossible to obtain.

The position of observer illustrates another of the many opportunities of the workmen for promotion from the ranks to higher positions when they are capable of holding the promotion. Naturally, other things being equal, no man is so well acquainted with the work to be observed as he who has actually done it himself, and if he have also the qualifications of the worker at the work, which should, in the future, surely be determined by study of him and by vocational guidance, he will be able to go at once from his position in the ranks to that of observer, or time study man.

The observer must also familiarize himself with the literature regarding motion study and time study, and must form the habit of recording systematically the minutest details observable.

The effect upon the man making the observation of knowing that his data, even though at the time they may seem unimportant, can be used for the deduction of vital laws, is plain. He naturally feels that he is a part of a permanent scheme, and is ready and willing to put his best activity into the work. The benefits accruing from this fact have been so well recognized in making United States surveys and charts, that the practice has been to have the name of the man in charge of the work printed on them.

Anyone Interested May Become an Observer.—A review of the mental equipment needed by a measurer, or observer, will show that much may be done toward training oneself for such a position by practice. Much pleasure as well as profit can be obtained by acquiring the habit of observation, both in the regular working and in the non-working hours. Vocational Guidance Bureaus should see that this habit of observation is cultivated, not only for the æsthetic pleasure which it gives, but also for its permanent usefulness.

Unbiased Observation Necessary.—In order to take observations properly, the investigator should be absolutely impartial, unprejudiced, and unbiased by any preconceived notions. Otherwise, he will be likely to think that a certain thing ought to happen. Or he may have a keen desire to obtain a certain result to conform to a pet theory. In other words, the observer must be of a very stable disposition. He must not be carried away by his observations.

The elimination of any charting by the man who makes the observations, or at least its postponement until all observations are made, will tend to decrease the dangers of unconscious effect of what he considers the probable curve of the observations should be.

As has been well said, watching the curve to be charted before all of the data have been obtained develops a distinct theory in the mind of the investigator and is apt to "bend the curve" or, at least, to develop a feeling that if any new, or special, data do not agree with the tendency of the curve—so much the worse for the reputation of the data for reliability.

Observed Worker Should Realize the Purpose of the Measurement.—The observed worker should be made to realize the purpose and importance of the measurement. The observing should always be done with his full knowledge and hearty coöperation. He will attain much improvement by intelligent coöperation with the observer, and may, in turn, be able to be promoted to observing if he is interested enough to study and prepare himself after hours.

Worker Should Never Be Observed Surreptitiously.—No worker should ever be observed, timed and studied surreptitiously. In the first place, if the worker does not know that he is being observed, he cannot coöperate with the observer to see that the methods observed are methods of least waste. Therefore the motion study and time study records that result will not be fundamental standards in any case and will probably be worthless.

In the second place, if the worker discovers that he is being observed secretly, he will feel that he is being spied upon and is not being treated fairly. The stop watch has too long been associated with the idea of "taking the last drop of blood from the worker." Secret observations will tend strongly to lend credence to this idea. Even should the worker thus observed not think that he was being watched in order to force him, at a later time, to make higher outputs, after he has once learned that he is being watched secretly, his attention will constantly be distracted by the thought that perhaps he is being studied and timed again. He will be constantly on the alert to see possible observers. This may result in "speeding him up," but the speed will not be a legitimate speed, that results to his good as well as to that of his employer.

Worst of all, he will lose confidence in the "squareness" of his employer. Hence he will fail to cooperate, and one of the greatest advantages of Scientific Management will thus be lost.

It is a great advantage of micro-motion study that it demands coöperation of the man studied, and that its results are open to study by all.

An Expert Best Worker to Observe.—The best worker to observe for time study is he who is so skilled that he can perform a cycle of prescribed standard motions automatically, without mental concentration. This enables him to devote his entire mental activity to deviating the one desired variable from the accepted cycle of motions.

The difficulty in motion study and time study is not so often to vary the variable being observed and studied, as it is to maintain the other variables constant. Neither skill nor appreciation of what is wanted is enough alone. The worker who is to be measured successfully must

1. have the required skill.
2. understand the theory of what is being done.
3. be willing to coöperate.

Everyone Should Be Trained in Being Measured.—Accurate measurement of individuals, in actual practice, brings out the fact that lamentably few persons are accustomed to be, or can readily be, measured. It has been a great drawback to the advance of Scientific Management that the moment a measurer of any kind is put on the work, either a device to measure output or a man to measure or to time reactions, motions, or output, the majority of the workers become suspicious. Being unaccustomed to being measured, they think, as is usually the case with things to which we are unaccustomed, that there is something harmful to them in it. This feeling makes necessary much explanation which in reality should not be needed.

The remedy for this condition is a proper training in youth. A boy brought up with the fundamental idea of the importance of measurement to all modern science, for all progress, accustomed to being measured, understanding the "why" of the measuring, and the results from it, will not hesitate or object, when he comes to the work, to being measured in order that he may be put where it is best for himself, as well as for the work, that he be put.

The importance of human measurement to vocational guidance and to the training of the young for life work has never been properly realized. Few people understand the importance of psychological experiment as a factor in scientific vocational guidance. For this alone, it will probably in time be a general custom to record and keep as close track as possible of the psychological measurements of the child during the period of education, vocational guidance and apprenticeship. Not only this, but he also should be accustomed to being measured, physically and psychologically, from his first years, just as he is now accustomed to being weighed.

The child should be taught to measure himself, his faculties, his reactions, his capabilities as compared with his former self and as compared with the capabilities of others. It is most important that the child should form a habit not only of measuring, but of being measured.

Motion Study and Time Study Are the Method of Measurement Under Scientific Management.—Under Scientific Management, much measuring is done by motion study and time study, which measure the relative efficiency of various men, of various methods, or of various kinds of equipment, surroundings, tools, etc. Their most important use is as measuring devices of the men. They have great psychological value in that they are founded on the "square deal" and the men know this from the start. Being operated under laws, they are used the same way on all sorts of work and on all men. As soon as the men really understand this fact, and realize

1. that the results are applied to all men equally;
2. that all get an ample compensation for what they do;
3. that under them general welfare is considered; the objections to such study will vanish.

Motion Study Is Determining Methods of Least Waste.—Motion Study is the dividing of the elements of the work into the most fundamental sub-divisions possible; studying these fundamental units separately and in relation to one another; and from these studied, chosen units, when timed, building up methods of least waste.

Time Study Is Determining Standard Unit Times.—Time study consists of timing the elements of the best method known, and, from these elementary unit times, synthesizing a standard time in which a standard man can do a certain piece of work in accordance with the finally accepted method.

Micro-motion study is timing sub-divisions, or elements of motions by carrying out the principles of motion study to a greater degree of accuracy by means of a motion picture camera, a clock that will record different times of day in each picture of a moving picture film together with a cross sectioned background and other devices for assisting in measuring the relative efficiency and wastefulness of motions. It also is the cheapest, quickest and more accurate method of recording indisputable time study records. It has the further advantage of being most useful in assisting the instruction card man to devise methods of least waste.[11]

Motion Study and Time Study Measure Individual Efficiency.—Motion Study and Time Study measure individual capacity or effi-

[11] *Industrial Engineering,* Jan., 1913.

ciency by providing data from which standards can be made. These standards made, the degree to which the individual approaches or exceeds the standard can be determined.

Motion Study and Time Study Measure Methods.—Motion Study and Time Study are devices for measuring methods. By their use, old methods are "tried out," once and for all, and their relative value in efficiency, determined. By their use, also, new methods are "tried out." This is most important under Scientific Management.

Any new method suggested can be tested in a short time. Such elements of it as have already been tested, can be valued at the start, the new elements introduced can be motion studied and time studied, and waste eliminated to as great an extent as possible, with no loss of time or thought.

Under Scientific Management, the men who understand what motion study and time study mean, know that their suggested methods will be tested, not only fairly, but so effectively that they, and everyone else, can know at once exactly the worth of their suggestions.

Comparison of Methods Fosters Invention.—The value of such comparative study can be seen at a glance. When one such method after another is tried out, not only can one tell quickly what a new method is worth, but can also determine what it is worth compared to all others which have been considered. This is because the study is a study of elements, primarily, and not of methods as a whole. Not only can suggested methods be estimated, but also new methods which have never been suggested will become apparent themselves through this study. Common elements, being at once classified and set aside, the new ones will make themselves prominent, and better methods for doing work will suggest themselves, especially to the inventive mind.

Books of Preliminary Data Needed.—In order that this investigation may be best fostered, not only must books of standards be published, but also books of preliminary data, which other workers may attack if they desire, and where they can find common elements. Such books of preliminary data are needed on all subjects.[12]

Motion Study and Time Study Measure Equipment and Tools.— Time and motion study are measuring devices for ascertaining relative merits of different kinds of equipment, surroundings and tools.

---

[12] F. W. Taylor, *Shop Management*, pp. 398–391. Harper Ed., p. 179. Compare, U.S. Bulletin of Agriculture No. 208. *The Influence of Muscular and Mental Work on Metabolism.*

Through them, the exact capacities of equipment or of a tool or machine can be discovered at once, and also the relative value in efficiency. Also motion study and time study determine exactly how a tool or a piece of equipment can best be used.

In "On The Art of Cutting Metals" Dr. Taylor explains the effect of such study on determining the amount of time that tools should be used, the speed at which they should be used, the feed, and so on.[13] This paper exemplifies more thoroughly than does anything else ever written the value of Time Study, and the scientific manner in which it is applied.

The Scope of Time and Motion Study Is Unlimited.—It is a great misfortune that the worker does not understand, as he should, that motion study and time study apply not only to his work, but also to the work of the managers. In order to get results from the start, and paying results, it often happens that the work of the worker is the first to be so studied, but when Scientific Management is in full operation, the work of the managers is studied exactly to the same extent, and set down exactly as accurately, as the work of the worker himself. The worker should understand this from the start, that he may become ready and willing to coöperate.

Detailed Records Necessary.—Motion study and time study records must go into the greatest detail possible. If the observations are hasty, misdirected or incomplete they may be quite unusable and necessitate going through the expensive process of observation all over again. Dr. Taylor has stated that during his earlier experiences he was obliged to throw away a large quantity of time study data, because they were not in sufficient detail and not recorded completely enough to enable him to use them after a lapse of a long period from the time of their first use. No system of time study, and no individual piece of time study, can be considered a success unless by its use at any time, when new, or after a lapse of years, an accurate prediction of the amount of work a man can do can be made.

All results attained should invariably be preserved, whether they appear at the moment to be useful or valuable or not. In time study in the past it has been found, as in the investigations of all other sciences, that apparently unimportant details of today are of vital importance years after, as a necessary step to attain, or further proof of a discovery. This was exemplified in the case of the shoveling experiment of Dr. Taylor. The laws came from what was considered

[13] President's Annual Address, Dec., 1906. Vol. 28, Transactions A. S. M. E.

the unimportant portion of the data. There is little so unimportant that time and motion study would not be valuable. Just as it is a great help to the teacher to know the family history of the student, so it is to the one who has to use time and motion study data to know all possible of the hereditary traits, environment and habits of the worker who was observed.

Specialized Study Imperative.—As an illustration of the field for specialized investigation which motion study and time study present, we may take the subject of fatigue. Motion Study and Time Study aim to show,

1. the least fatiguing method of getting least waste.
2. the length of time required for a worker to do a certain thing.
3. the amount of rest and the time of rest required to overcome fatigue.

Dr. Taylor spent years in determining the percentage of rest that should be allowed in several of the trades, beginning with those where the making of output demands weight hanging on the arms; but there is still a great amount of investigation that could be done to advantage to determine the most advisable percentage of rest in the working day of different lengths of hours. Such investigation would probably show that many of our trades could do the same amount of work in fewer hours, if the quantity and time of rest periods were scientifically determined.

Again, there is a question of the length of each rest period. It has been proven that in many classes of work, and especially in those where the work is interrupted periodically by reason of its peculiar nature, or by reason of inefficient performance in one of the same sequence of dependent operations, alternate working and resting periods are best. There is to be considered in this connection, however, the recognized disadvantage of reconcentrating the attention after these rest periods. Another thing to be considered is that the rate of output does not decline from the beginning of the day, but rather the high point of the curve representing rate of production is at a time somewhat later than at the starting point. The period before the point of maximum efficiency is known as "warming up" among ball players, and is well recognized in all athletic sports.

As for the point of minimum efficiency, or of greatest fatigue, this varies for "morning workers," and "night workers." This exemplifies yet another variable.

The minuteness of the sub-fields that demand observation, is shown by an entry in the Psychological Index: "1202. Benedict, F. G. "Studies in Body—Temperature." 1. Influence of the Inversion of the Daily Routine; the Temperature of Night Workers."[14]

Selection of Best Unit of Measurement Necessary and Important. —Selecting the unit of measurement that will of itself reduce costs is a most important element in obtaining maximum efficiency.[15] This is seldom realized.[16] Where possible, several units of measurements should be used to check each other.[17] One alone may be misleading, or put an incentive on the workers to give an undesirable result.

The rule is,—always select that unit of output that will, of itself, cause a reduction in costs.

For example:—In measuring the output of a concrete gang, counting cement bags provides an incentive to use more cement than the instruction card calls for. Counting the batches of concrete dumped out of the mixer, provides an incentive to use rather smaller quantities of broken stone and sand than the proportions call for,—and, furthermore, does not put the incentive on the men to spill no concrete in transportation, neither does it put an incentive to use more lumps for Cyclopean concrete.

Measuring the quantity actually placed in the forms puts no incentive to watch bulging forms closely.

While measuring outputs by all these different units of measurements would be valuable to check up accuracy of proportions, accuracy of stores account, and output records, the most important unit of measurement for selection would be, "cubic feet of forms filled," the general dimensions to be taken from the latest revised engineer's drawings.

Necessity for Checking Errors.—Dr. Stratton says,—"No measurements, whether they be psychic or physical, are exact beyond a certain point, and the art of using them consists largely in checks and counter checks, and in knowing how far the measurement is reliable and where the doubtful zone begins."[18]

Capt. Metcalfe says,—"Errors of observation may be divided into two general classes; the instrumental and those due to the personal bias of the observer; the former referring to the standard itself, and

---

[14] *American Journal of Physiology,* 1904, XI, pp. 145–170.

[15] R. T. Dana, For Construction Service Co., *Handbook of Steam Shovel Work,* p. 161. H. P. Gillette, Vol. I, p. 71, A. S. E. C.

[16] F. W. Taylor, Vol. 28, A. S. M. E., Paper 1119, para. 68.

[17] Hugo Münsterberg, *American Problems,* p. 37.

[18] G. M. Stratton, *Experimental Psychology and Culture,* p. 59.

the latter to the application of the standard and the record of the measurement."[19]

The concrete illustration given above is an example of careful checking up. Under Scientific Management so many, and such careful records are kept that detecting errors becomes part of the daily routine.

SUMMARY

Results of Measurement to the Work.—Under Traditional Management, even the crudest measurement of output and cost usually resulted in an increase in output. But there was no accuracy of measurement of individual efficiency, nor was there provision made to conserve results and make them permanently useful.

Under Transitory Management and measurement of individual output, output increased and rewards for the higher output kept up the standard.

Under Scientific Management Better Methods and Better Work Results.—Under Scientific Measurement, measurement of the work itself determines

1. what kind of workers are needed.
2. how many workers are needed.
3. how best to use them.

Motion Study and Time Study measurement,—

1. divide the work into units.
2. measure each unit.
3. study the variables, or elements, one at a time.
4. furnish resulting timed elements to the synthesizer of methods of least waste.

Accurate Measuring Devices Prevent Breakdowns and Accidents.—The accurate measuring devices which accomplish measurement under Scientific Management prevent breakdowns and accidents to life and limb.

For example.—

1. The maintained tension on a belt bears a close relation to its delay periods.
2. The speed of a buzz planer determines its liability to shoot out pieces of wood to the injury of its operator, or to injure bystanders.

Scientific Management, by determining and standardizing methods and equipment both, provides for uninterrupted output.

[19] Henry Metcalfe, *Cost of Manufacturers.*

Effect on the Worker.—Under Traditional Management there is not enough accurate measurement done to make its effect on the worker of much value.

Under Transitory Management, as soon as individual outputs are measured, the worker takes more interest in his work, and endeavors to increase his output.

Under Scientific Management measurement of the worker tells

1. what the workers are capable of doing.
2. what function it will be best to assign them to and to cultivate in them.

Waste Eliminated by Accurate Measurement.—This accurate measurement increases the worker's efficiency in that it enables him to eliminate waste. "Cut and try" methods are eliminated. There is no need to test a dozen methods, a dozen men, a dozen systems of routing, or various kinds of equipment more than once,—that one time when they are scientifically tried out and measured. This accurate measurement also eliminates disputes between manager and worker as to what the latter's efficiency is.

Efficiency Measured by Time and Motion Study.—Time and Motion Study

    (a) measure the man by his work; that is, by the result of his activities;

    (b) measure him by his methods;

    (c) measure him by his capacity to learn;

    (d) measure him by his capacity to teach.

Now measurement by result alone is very stimulating to increasing activities, especially when it shows, as it does under Scientific Management, the relative results of various people doing the same kind of work. But it does not, itself, show the worker *how* to obtain greater results without putting on more speed or using up more activities. But when the worker's methods are measured, he begins to see, for himself, exactly why and where he has failed.

Scientific Management provides for him to be taught, and the fact that he sees through the measurements exactly what he needs to be taught will make him glad to have the teacher come and show him how to do better. Through this teaching, its results, and the speed with which the results come, the workers and the managers can see how fast the worker is capable of learning, and, at the same time, the worker, the teacher and the managers can see in how far the foreman is capable of instructing.

Final Outcome Beneficial to Managers and Men.—Through measurement in Scientific Management, managers acquire—

1. ability to select men, methods, equipment, etc.;

2. ability to assign men to the work which they should do, to prescribe the method which they shall use, and to reward them for their output suitably;

3. ability to predict. On this ability to predict rests the possibility of making calendars, chronological charts and schedules, and of planning determining sequence of events, etc., which will be discussed at length later.

Ability to predict allows the managers to state "premature truths," which the records show to be truths when the work has been done.

It must not be forgotten that the managers are enabled not only to predict what the men, equipment, machinery, etc., will do, but what they can do themselves.

The Effect on the Men Is That the Worker Cooperates.—1. The worker's interest is held. The men know that the methods they are using are the best. The exact measurements of efficiency of the learner,—and under Scientific Management a man never ceases to be a learner,—give him a continued interest in his work. It is impossible to hold the attention of the intelligent worker to a method or process that he does not believe to be the most efficient and least wasteful.

Motion study and time study are the most efficient measuring device of the relative qualities of differing methods. They furnish definite and exact proof to the worker as to the excellence of the method that he is told to use. When he is convinced, lack of interest due to his doubts and dissatisfaction is removed.

2. The worker's judgment is appealed to. The method that he uses is the outcome of coöperation between him and the management. His own judgment assures him that it is the best, up to that time, that they, working together, have been able to discover.

3. The worker's reasoning powers are developed. Continuous judging of records of efficiency develops high class, well developed reasoning powers.

4. The worker fits his task, therefore there is no need of adjustment, and his attitude toward his work is right.

5. There is elimination of soldiering, both natural and systematic.[20]

---

[20] F. W. Taylor, *Shop Management*, para. 46. Harper Ed., p. 30. F. W. Taylor, *A Piece Rate System*, Paper 647, A. S. M. E., para. 22.

All Knowledge Becomes the Knowledge of All.—Two outcomes may be confidently expected in the future, as they are already becoming apparent wherever Scientific Management is being introduced:

1. The worker will become more and more willing to impart his knowledge to others. When the worker realizes that passing on his trade secrets will not cause him to lose his position or, by raising up a crowd of competitors, lower his wages, but will, on the contrary, increase his wages and chances of promotion, he is ready and willing to have his excellent methods standardized.

Desire to keep one's own secret, or one's own method a secret is a very natural one. It stimulates interest, it stimulates pride. It is only when, as in Scientific Management, the possessor of such a secret may receive just compensation, recognition and honor for his skill, and receive a position where he can become an appreciated teacher of others that he is, or should be, willing to give up this secret. Scientific Management, however, provides this opportunity for him to teach, provides that he receives credit for what he has done, and receive that publicity and fame which is his due, and which will give him the same stimulus to work which the knowledge that he had a secret skill gave him in the past.

One method of securing this publicity is by naming the device or method after its inventor. This has been found to be successful not only in satisfying the inventor, but in stimulating others to invent.

Measurement of Individual Efficiency Will Be Endorsed by All.—2. The worker will, ultimately, realize that it is for the good of all, as well as for himself, that individual efficiency be measured and rewarded.

It has been advanced as an argument against measurement that it discriminates against the "weaker brother," who should have a right to obtain the same pay as the stronger, for the reason that he has equal needs for this pay to maintain life and for the support of his family.

Putting aside at the moment the emotional side of this argument, which is undoubtedly a strong side and a side worthy of consideration, with much truth in it, and looking solely at the logical side,— it cannot do the "weaker" brother any good in the long run, and it does the world much harm, to have his work overestimated. The day is coming, when the world will demand that the quantity of the day's work shall be measured as accurately where one sells labor, as where one sells sugar or flour. Then, pretending that one's output is greater than it really is will be classed with "divers weights and divers measures," with their false standards. The day will come when the public will insist that the "weaker brother's" output be measured to determine just how weak he is, and whether it is weakness, unfitness for that particular job, or laziness that is the cause of his output being low. When he reaches a certain degree of weakness, he will be assisted with a definite measured quantity of assistance. Thus the "weaker brother" may be readily distinguished from the lazy, strong brother, and the brother who is working at the wrong job. Measurement should certainly be insisted on, in order to determine whether these strong brothers are doing their full share, or whether they are causing the weaker brothers to over-exert themselves.

No one who has investigated the subject properly can doubt that it will be better for the world in general to have each man's output, weak and strong, properly measured and estimated regardless of whether the weak and strong are or are not paid the same wages. The reason why the unions have had to insist that the work shall not be measured and that the weaker brother's weakness shall not be realized is, that in the industrial world the only brotherhood that was recognized was the brotherhood between the workers, there being a distinct antagonism between the worker and the manager and little or no brotherhood of the public at large. When Scientific Management does away, as it surely will, with this antagonism, by reason of the coöperation which is its fundamental idea, then the workers will show themselves glad to be measured.

As for the "weaker" brother idea, it is a natural result of such ill treatment. It has become such a far-reaching emotion that even Scientific Management, with its remedy for many ills, cannot expect in a moment, or in a few years, to alter the emotional bias of the multitudes of people who have held it for good and sufficient reasons for generations.

The Government Should Conserve Measurement Data.—The one thing which can permanently alter this feeling forms the natural conclusion to this chapter. That is, measurements in general and motion study and time study in particular must become a matter of government investigation. When the government has taken over the investigation and established a bureau where such data as Scientific Management discovers is collected and kept on file for all who will to use, then the possessor of the secret will feel that it can safely place the welfare of its "weaker brothers" in the hands of a body which is founded and operates on the idea of the "square deal."

Appreciation of Time Study by Workers the First Step.—The first step of the workers in this direction must be the appreciation of time study, for on time study hangs the entire subject of Scientific Management. It is this great discovery by Dr. Taylor that makes the elimination of waste possible. It has come to stay. Many labor leaders are opposed to it, but the wise thing for them to do is to study, foster and cultivate it. They cannot stop its progress. There is no thing that can stop it. The modern managers will obtain it, and the only way to prevent it from being used by unscrupulous managers is for the workman also to learn the facts of time study. It is of the utmost importance to the workers of the country, for their own protection, that they be as familiar with time study data as the managers are. Time study is the foundation and frame work of rate setting and fixing, and certainly the subject of rate fixing is the most important subject there is to the workmen, whether they are working on day work, piece work, premium, differential rate piece, task with bonus, or three-rate system.

Dr. Taylor has proved by time study that many of the customary working days are too long, that the same amount of output can be achieved in fewer hours per day. Time study affords the means for the only scientific proof that many trades fatigue the workers beyond their endurance and strength. Time study is the one means by which the workers can prove the real facts of their unfortunate condition under the Traditional plan of management.

The workers of the country should be the very ones that should insist upon the government taking the matter in hand for scientific investigation. Knowledge is power,—a rule with no exception, and the knowledge of scientific time study would prepare the workers of any trade, and would provide their intelligent leaders with data for accurate decisions for legislation and other steps for their best interests. The national bodies should hire experts to represent them and to coöperate with the government bureau in applying science to their life work.

The day is fast approaching when makers of machinery will have the best method of operating their machines micro-motion studied and cyclegraphed and description of methods of operation in accordance with such records will be everywhere considered as a part of the "makers' directions for using."

Furthermore associations of manufacturers will establish laboratories for determining methods of least waste by means of motion study, time study and micro-motion study, and the findings of such laboratories will be put in standardized shape for use by all its members. The trend today shows that soon there will be hundreds of books of time study tables. The government must sooner or later save the waste resulting from this useless duplication of efforts.

Standardization

● ●

Definition of Standardization.—Standardization is "the act of standardizing, or the state of being standardized." "A standard," according to the Century Dictionary, "is that which is set up as a unit of reference; a form, type, example, incidence, or combination of conditions accepted as correct and perfect and hence as a basis of comparison. A criterion established by custom, public opinion or general consent; a model."[1]

We must note particularly that the standard is a "unit of reference," that it is a "basis of comparison," and that it is "a model." These three phrases describe the standard in management, and are particularly emphasized by the use of the standard in Scientific Management.

Standards Derived from Actual Practice.—Management derives its standards not from theories as to best methods, but from scientific study of actual practice.[2] As already shown, the method of deriving a standard is—

1. to analyze the best practice known into the smallest possible elements,

2. to measure these elements,

3. to adopt the least wasteful elements as standard elements,

4. to synthesize the necessary standard elements into the standard.

[1] Compare R. T. Dana and W. L. Sanders, *Rock Drilling*, chap. XVI.

[2] The idea of perfection is not involved in the standard of Scientific Management. Morris Llewellyn Cooke, Bulletin No. 5, of *The Carnegie Foundation for the Advancement of Teaching*, p. 6.

The Standard Is Progressive.—A standard remains fixed only until a more perfect standard displaces it. The data from which the standard was derived may be reviewed because of some error, because a further subdivision of the elements studied may prove possible, or because improvements in some factor of the work, i. e., the worker, material, tools, equipment, etc., may make a new standard desirable.

The fact that a standard is recognized as not being an ultimate standard in no wise detracts from its working value. As Captain Metcalfe has said: "Whatever be the standard of measurement, it suffices for comparison if it be generally accepted, if it be impartially applied, and if the results be fully recorded."[3]

Change in the Standard Demands Change in the Task and in the Incentive.—Necessarily, with the change in the standard comes a change in the task and in the reward. All parts of Scientific Management are so closely related that it is impossible to make a successful progressive step in one branch without simultaneously making all the related progressions in other branches that go with it.

For example,—if the material upon which a standard was based caused more care or effort, a smaller task must be set, and wages must be proportionately lowered. *Proportionately,* note, for determining that change would necessitate a review and a redistribution of the cost involved.

In the same way, if an improvement in equipment necessitated a new method, as does the packet in laying brick, a new task would become imperative, and a reconsideration of the wage. The wage might remain the same, it might go down, it might go up. In actual practice, in the case of bricklayers, it has gone up. But the point is, it *must* be restudied. This provides effectually against cutting the rate or increasing the task in any unjust manner.

Similarity Between the Standard and the "Judgment" of Psychology.—There are many points of similarity between the "Standard," of management, and the "judgment" of psychology. Sully says, in speaking of the judgment,[4]—"This process of judging illustrates the two fundamental elements in thought activity, viz., analysis and synthesis." "To judge is clearly to discern and to mark off as a special object of thought some connecting relation." "To begin with, before we can judge we must have the requisite materials for form-

---

[3] *Cost of Manufactures.*
[4] Sully, *The Teacher's Handbook of Psychology,* pp. 290–292.

ing a judgment." "In the second place, to judge is to carry out a process of reflection on given material." "In addition to clearness and accuracy, our judgments may have other perfections. So far as our statements accord with known facts, they should be adhered to, —at least, till new evidence proves them untrue."

Psychology a Final Appeal as to Permanent Value of Any Standard.—The standard under management, even under Scientific Management, can lay no claim to being perfect. It can never nearly approach perfection until the elements are so small that it is practicable to test them psychologically and physiologically. The time when this can be done in many lines, when the benefit that will directly accrue will justify the necessary expenditure, may seem far distant, but every analysis of operations, no matter how rudimentary, is hastening the day when the underlying, permanently valuable elements can be determined and their variations studied.

Coöperation Will Hasten the Day of Psychological and Physiological Study of Standards.—Coöperation in collecting and comparing the results of motion study and time study everywhere will do much to assist toward more ultimate determination of elements. At the present time the problems that management submits to psychology are too indefinite and cover too large a field to be attacked successfully. Coöperation between management standardizers would mean—

1. that all management data would be available to psychologists and physiologists.

2. that such data, being available also to all standardizers, would prevent reduplication of results.

3. that savings would result.

4. that, from a study and comparison of the collected data a trained synthetic mind could build up better standards than could be built from any set of individual data.

5. savings would result from this.

6. inventions would also result.

7. savings would again result from these.

8. all of these various savings could be invested in more intensive study of elements.

9. these more valuable results would again be available to psychologists and physiologists.

This cycle would go on indefinitely. Meantime, all would benefit with little added cost to any. For the results of the psychological and physiological study would be available to all, and investigators in those lines have shown themselves ready and glad to undertake investigations.

Purpose of Standardization.—The purpose of standardizing is the same under all types of management; that is, it is the elimination of waste.

Standardization Frequently Attempted Under Traditional Management.—In much progressive Traditional Management there is an appreciation of the necessity of standardizing tools and equipment, that is to say, of having these on the "duplicate part system," that assembling may be done quickly, and repairs made without delay.

The manager notices some particularly successful man, or method, or arrangement of tools, equipment, or the surroundings, and decides to have a record made thereof that the success may be repeated. These records, if made in sufficient detail, are very valuable. The difficulty is that so often the man making the records does not observe all the variables. Hence the very elements which caused the success may be overlooked entirely.

Value of Standardization Not Appreciated Under Traditional Management.—It is surprising, under Traditional Management, to note, in many cases, the years that elapse before any need for standardization is felt. It is also surprising that, even when some standardization has been done, its importance is seldom realized. The new standard becomes a matter of course, and the management fails to be impressed enough with its benefits to apply the principle of standardization to other fields.

Under Transitory Management Standardization Becomes Constantly More Important.—Not until Motion Study and Time Study have been introduced can the full benefits of standardization be attained. But as soon as the Transitory Stage of Management appears, the importance of standardization is realized. This is brought about largely through the records of individual outputs, which constantly call attention to the necessity of making available to all the methods, tools and equipment of the most successful workers.

Records of Successes Become More Profitable.—The rules which embody successful practice become more profitable as the necessity for more detailed recording of all the variables becomes possible. An appreciation of what scientific motion study and time study will ultimately do affects the minds of the management until the workers are given directions as to methods to be used, and the incentive of extra pay for following directions.

"Systems" Show an Appreciation of Psychology.—The "Systems," standing orders or collections of written directions, that are evolved at this stage have a permanent value. This is especially true when the directions, often called "rules," contain the reason for the rule. There is a decided awakening to the importance of Psychology in this appeal to the reason of the worker. He is not affronted by being forced to follow directions for which he is given no reason and which he has no reason to believe have been scientifically derived. These rules, in a certain typical case, are stated in simple language, some in the form of commands, some in the form of suggestions, and are obviously so prepared as to be understood and obeyed by the workers with the least possible amount of effort, opposition and time. As ample opportunity is given for suggestions, the worker's attention and interest are held, and any craving he may have for self-expression is gratified.

Systems Permanently Useful.—These systems, collections of rules, directions or standing orders are useful even when Ultimate Management is completely installed—

1. for use as records of successful methods which may be scientifically studied for elements.

2. for use by the instruction card clerk in explaining to the men why the rules on the instruction card are given.

Relation of Systems to Standards Should Be Emphasized.—The worker is too often not made to understand the relation of Systems to Standards. The average worker does not object to Systems, because he realizes that the System is a collection of his best, least wasteful methods of doing work. When he can be convinced that standards are only efficient elements of his own methods scientifically studied and combined, any opposition to them will disappear.

The Personal Note of the "System" Should Be Preserved.—Perhaps one thing that makes the typical "Systems" so attractive is the personal note that they contain. Illustrated with pictures of successful work that the workers themselves have done, often containing pictures of the men themselves that illustrate successful methods, with mention of the names of men who have offered valuable suggestions or inventions, they make the worker feel his part in successful results. They conserve the old spirit of coöperation between the master and his apprentices.

The conditions of modern industry make it extremely difficult to conserve this feeling. Scientific Management is successful not only because it makes possible a more effective coöperation than has ever existed since the old "master-and-apprentice" relation died out, but also because it conserves in the Systems the interim channel for personal communication between the various members of the organization.

Systems a Valuable Assistance in Transition to Scientific Management.—One great problem which those introducing Scientific Management have to face is exactly how to make the worker understand the relation of the new type of management to the old. The usefulness of the written system in use in most places where it is planned to introduce Scientific Management as a means of making the worker understand the transition has, perhaps, not been appreciated.

The development of the standard from the system is easy to explain. This being done, all parts of Scientific Management are so closely related that their interrelation can be readily made apparent.

It is the worker's right as well as privilege to understand the management under which he works, and he only truly coöperates, with his will and judgment as well as with his hands, when he feels that his mind is a part of the directing mind.

Standardization Under Scientific Management Eliminates Waste Scientifically.—Under Scientific Management the elimination of waste by the use of standards becomes a science. Standards are no longer based on opinions, as under Traditional Management, but are based upon scientific investigation of the elements of experience.

As James says, in the "Psychology, Briefer Course," page 156, paragraph 4,—"It is obvious and palpable that our state of mind is never precisely the same. Every thought we have of a given fact is, strictly speaking, unique and only bears a resemblance of kind with our other thoughts of the same facts. When the identical fact recurs we must think of it in a fresh manner, see it under a somewhat different angle, apprehend it in different relations from those in which it last appeared."

The Standard the Result of Measurement.—It is obvious, therefore, that a scientifically derived standard can never be the outcome of an opinion. Whenever the opinion returns, the different thoughts with which it would be accompanied would so color it as to change it, and the standard with it. It is obvious, therefore, that a standard must be the result of definite mathematical and other measured proof, and not of an opinion, and that the standard must be in such physical shape that the subject-matter will always be clearly defined, otherwise the ultimate losses resulting from dependent sequences of the standard schedule and time-tables would be enormous.

Successful Standardization Demands Complete Conformity to Standards.—The laws for establishment of standards; the laws of achieving them; the laws for preventing deviations from those paths that will permit of their achievement; the dependent sequences absolutely necessary to perform the complete whole: these have been worked out and given to the world by Dr. Taylor, who recognized, as James has said, page 157, that, "a permanently existing 'Idea' which makes its appearance before the footlights of consciousness at periodic intervals, is as mythological an entity as the Jack of Spades." The entire organization from the highest to the lowest must conform to these standards. It is out of the question to permit the deviations resulting from individual initiative. Individual initiative is quite as objectionable in obtaining the best results,—that is, high wages and low production cost,—as service would be on a railroad if each locomotive engineer were his own train despatcher, determining at what time and to what place he would go.

Initiative Provided For.—There is a distinct place for initiative in Scientific Management, but that place is not outside of the planning department, until the planning department's method has been proved to be fully understood by achieving it. The standards must be made by the men to whom this work is assigned, and they must be followed absolutely by the worker. He is willing to follow them, under Scientific Management, because he realizes that a place for his suggestions is supplied, and that, if his suggestions are accepted, they will be incorporated into the new standards which must then be followed by all thereafter.

Standardization Applies to the Work of All.—It is important to note that standardizing is applied to the work of all. This, if understood by all, will do away with all question of discrimination or the lack of a "square deal." It will make the worker feel ready to follow his standard exactly, just as he knows the manager is following his. So, also, the worker should be made to realize that the very fact that there is a standardization means, under Scientific Management, that that applies to every man, and that there is no discrimination against him in any possible way.

Standardization Conserves and Develops Individuality.—Standardization conserves individual capacity by doing away with the wasteful process of trial and error of the individual workman. It develops individuality by allowing the worker to concentrate his initiative upon work that has not before been done, and by providing incentive and reward for inventions.

Waste Eliminated Is Eliminated Permanently.—Scientific Management not only eliminates waste, but provides that waste shall be eliminated for all time in the future.

The standard once written down, there can be no slipping back into the old methods based upon opinions of the facts.

Standardization Under Scientific Management Resembles Standardization of Spelling.—The need for standardization has already been emphasized, but might further be illustrated by the discussions, pro and con, of the question of simplified spelling. Before the days of dictionaries, our spelling was not standardized—it was the privilege of any good writer to spell much as he desired; but the creation of written standards of spelling, that is to say the making of dictionaries, fixed the forms of spelling at that time, that is, created standards. The Simplified Spelling Board is now endeavoring to make some new standards, their action being based upon sufficient reasons for making a change, and also for not changing the spelling of any word until it is determined that the suggested spelling is more advisable than the old spelling.

Just so, under Scientific Management, the best known standards are used continuously until better ones have been discovered. The planning department, consisting of the best men available, whose special duty it is to create new standards, acts as does the Simplified Spelling Board, as a court of appeals for new standards, which must pass this court before they can hope to succeed the old, and which must, if they are to be accepted, possess many elements of the old and be changed only in such a way that the users can, without difficulty, shift to the new use.

Under Scientific Management Nomenclature Is Standardized.— Under Standardization in Scientific Management the standardization of the nomenclature, of the names and of the terms used must be noted. The effect of this upon the mind is excellent, because the use of a word very soon becomes a habit—its associations become fixed. If different names are used for the same thing,—that is to say, if different names are used indiscriminately, the thing itself becomes hazy, in just such a degree as it possesses many names. The use of the fixed term, the fixed word, leads to definiteness always. Just so, also, the Mnemonic Symbol system in use by Scientific Management, leads to swift identification of the subdivision of the classification to which it is applied, and to elimination of waste in finding and remembering where to find any particular thing or piece of information desired. By it may be identified "the various articles of manufacture and papers relating to it as well as the operations to be performed on each piece and the various charges of the establishment."

Mnemonic Symbols Save Time and Effort.—These Mnemonic Symbols save actual motions and time in speaking and writing, and save time in that they are so designed as to be readily remembered. They also save time and effort in that the mind accustomed to them works with them as collective groups of ideas, without stopping to elaborate them into their more detailed form.

Standard Phraseology Eliminates Waste.—As typical of the savings effected by standardization, we may cite a lineman talking to the Central Telephone Office:—

"John Doe—1234 L. Placing Extension Station." This signified— "My name is John Doe, I am telephoning from number 1234, party L. I have finished installing an extension station. Where shall I go next?"

In the same way standard signals are remembered best by the man who signals and are understood quickest by the man who receives them, with a direct increase in speed to the work done.

Standard Man Is the Man upon Whom Studies Are Made.—The standard man is the ideal man to observe and with whom to obtain the best Motion Study and Time Study data. He is the fastest worker, working under the direction of the man best informed in the particular trade as to the motions of best present practice, and being timed by a Time Study Expert.

Relation Between the Standard Man, the First-Class Man, the Given Man and the Task.—The "first-class man" under Scientific Management means the man who is best fitted by nature and by training to do the task permanently or until promoted.

The "given man" is the man who is actually put to work at the task, whether or not he is well fitted for its performance.

The "task" is that percentage of the standard man's achievement that the given man to whom the task is to be assigned can do continuously and thrive, that he can do easily enough to win his bonus without injuring himself, temporarily or permanently, in any way.

Writing the Standard Means for Conveying Information.—Under

Scientific Management, and even in the early stages of Transitory Management, writing is the standard means of conveying information.

All orders, without exception, should be in writing. This insures that the "eye workers" get their directions in the most impressive form; does away with the need of constant oral repetition; eliminates confusion; insures a clear impression in the mind of the giver as well as of the receiver of the order as to exactly what is wanted; and provides a record of all orders given. Putting the instructions in writing in no way precludes utilizing the worker's natural aptitude to learn by imitation, for he also always has the opportunity to watch and imitate the workings of the functional teachers as well as his scientifically taught fellow-workers.

The Instruction Card the Standard Method of Conveying Instructions as to the Task.—The records of the work of the standard man are contained in data of the Motion Study and Time Study department. These records, in the form in which they are to be used by the man who is to perform the task, are, for the benefit of that man, incorporated in what is known as the instruction card.

Definition of the Instruction Card.—The instruction card is a set of directions for the man, telling him what he is to do, how he is to do it, how long it should take him to do it, and what he will receive for doing it, and giving him an opportunity to call for, and obtain, assistance the instant that he finds he cannot do it, and to report back to the managers as to how he has succeeded in the performance.

The Instruction Card has been called "a self-producer of a predetermined product."

Comparative Definition of Instruction Cards, Under Scientific Management.—There are three types of Instruction Cards, which may be described as follows:

Type One:—Largely geographical, telling

1. Where to Work.
2. From Whom to Take Orders.
3. What to Do.

Type Two:—Typical engineer's specification,—telling

1. Results desired.
2. Qualities of Products.

Type Three:—A list of elementary, step-by-step instructions, subdivided into their motions, with time allowed for each timable element, preferably for each motion, and a division between

1. Getting ready.

2. Making or constructing.

3. Clearing up. This is the only type used by Scientific Management.

Directions, Pay Allowance and Time Allowance Essential.—The Instruction Card under Scientific Management must contain directions, and state the pay allowance and time allowance.

Directions as to how the work shall be done eliminate waste by cutting out all wrong methods and prescribing the right method exactly.

The setting of a time in which the work is to be done is a great stimulus to the worker, and is also necessary, because upon the attainment of this set time depends the ability of the managers to pay the bonus to the worker, and also to maintain a schedule, or time-table, that will make possible the maintaining of necessary conditions for others, in turn, to earn their bonuses. It cannot be too often emphasized that the extra wages are paid to the men out of the savings, and are absolutely dependent upon the fact of there being savings. It is only when the worker does the work within the time prescribed, that the managers do save enough to warrant the payment of the extra wages that compensate the man for doing the stipulated quantity of work.

The instruction card contains a statement of the wage or bonus that will be earned for the complete performance of the task set therein, thus furnishing an incentive at the time that the work is done.

Standard Division of Instruction Card Necessary.—There are many reasons for dividing an instruction card in the present standard way, namely,—

(a) to reduce the amount of time study observation necessary to be taken,

(b) to reduce the difficulties of synthesizing the time studied element,

(c) to locate quickly just where the worker needs help and instruction to enable him to achieve his task,

(d) to keep up the interest of the worker by having short time elements with which to measure his relative ability,

(e) to present the subject-matter of instruction in such natural subdivisions that resting places are automatically provided that allow the mind to recover from its absorption of each subdivision. This provides definite stopping places between co-related units of instruction holding the attention as a complete unit against distraction, and a complete resting place between subdivisions that permits the mind to relax and wander without losing complete grasp of each unit as a whole.

Detailed Instruction Educative.—The greater the perfection of the detail of the instruction card, the greater the educative value of this plan of management. The educative value of the instruction card will be discussed at length under Teaching.

Those inexperienced in Scientific Management have complained that the detail of Instruction Cards and other parts of Scientific Management is tiresome. Dr. Taylor has answered such objectors in Discussions, and also in his own directions for planning the Instruction Card, which are to be found in "Shop Management."

The advantages of the detailed instruction card are more than might appear on the surface. Not only does the man whose attention is easily distracted keep to his work better if he is told every possible detail, but also the cards when filed can be taken out again, and every detail and item of the method reviewed at length and revised if necessary.

The experienced worker who gets to know the instruction by rote is not bothered by extreme detail. On the contrary, he grasps it at a glance, and focuses his mind upon any new feature and upon the speed and exactness of muscular action needed for compliance with the card.

Language of Instruction Card Important.—The language in which instructions and commands are transmitted on the instruction card is of sufficient importance to warrant careful consideration. It would be helpful if the instruction card clerk and the man who is to use the instruction cards were both masters of English, but this is hardly to be expected. The best substitute for such special English training is a "System" for the use of the instruction card clerk that will give him some outline of English that will by degrees make his wording terse, simple and unambiguous.

He should be impressed with the value of short sentences, and of sentences that will require no punctuation other than a period at the end. The short sentence is the most important step toward brevity, terseness, conciseness and clear thinking.

The second most important feature is that the instruction card clerk always uses the same standard wording for the same instructions. Repetition of phrasing is a virtue, and the use of the same word for the same thing and the same meaning repeatedly is very desirable. The wording, phrasing and sentencing should be standard wherever possible.

Standard Phrasing Desirable.—After a short time a phrase or sentence that is often repeated will be recognized as quickly as will a word or a letter. Men who cannot read and write at all are comparatively few. Men who can read and write but little are many. It is entirely possible to teach such men standard groupings, which they can recognize on the Instruction Card and use in a very short time.

For example,—laborers who do not even know their alphabets will learn quickly to read setting marks on cut stone.

Just as mnemonic symbols save time and effort, so standard phrasing aids toward finding out what is to be done, and remembering how it is to be done.[5] Both of these can be accomplished if the standardization is so complete that directions can be read and remembered almost at a glance.[6]

Specific Terms Helpful.—To be most effective, directions should be in the imperative form, and in specific terms.

The history and growth of language shows that the language of the savage consisted of vague general terms as compared to the specific individual terms of the modern language of civilized man. There are examples to be seen on every hand to-day where the oral language of instructions and orders to proceed, that are given to the worker, are still more vague, comparatively, than the language between savages.

Similarity of Form and Shape Advisable.—As for the form and shape, as Dr. Taylor says, "anything that will transmit ideas by sketch or wording will serve as an instruction card." He advises, however, taking advantage of the saving in time to be gained by having the instruction cards as nearly alike as possible. They may, for convenience' sake, vary as to length, but in width, ruling, spacing and wording they should be as nearly alike as possible.

Standard Surroundings Valuable.—Standard environment, or surroundings, of the worker are valuable for two reasons:

1. Because they directly increase output by eliminating everything which might distract attention or cause needless fatigue, and by as-

---

[5] C. B. Going, *Methods of the Sante Fé,* p. 66.

[6] For desirability of standard signals see R. T. Dana, *Handbook of Steam Shovel Work,* p. 32.

sisting in the attainment of more output by having the best possible surroundings for greater output.

2. Because all surroundings suggest an easy achievement. Knowing that everything has been done to make his work possible and easy, the worker feels this atmosphere of possibility and ease around him, and the suggestive power of this is strong.

Unnecessary Fatigue Should Be Eliminated.—The walls, appliances and furniture, and the clothing of the worker should be of that color which will rest his eyes from the fatigue of the work. All unnecessary noise should be eliminated, and provision should be made, where possible, that the workers may enjoy their sleep or their rest hours in perfect quiet.

Records show the value of having quiet reign in and near the camp, that the workers may not be disturbed. Even though they are not disturbed enough to be waked up, every noise that is registered in the brain affects the body, for it is now conceded that the body reflects every phase of mental activity.

All Mental States Affect Bodily States.—Dr. Stratton says: "It is now generally accepted that the body reflects every shade of psychic operations; that in all manner of mental action there is some physical expression."[7] All consciousness is motor "is the brief expression of this important truth; every mental state somehow runs over into a corresponding bodily state."

Elimination of Worry Assists in Concentrating Attention.—The more fireproof the building, and the more stable the other conditions, the greater the efficiency of the inmate. Burglar-proof buildings not only actually induce better sleep, in that possible intrusions are eliminated, but give a state of mental peace by the removal of apprehension. So also, a "germ proof" house is not only really more healthful for an inmate, but eliminates worry over possible danger of ill health. The mental health of the worker not only controls, in a measure, his physical health, but also his desire to work. Having no distractions, he can put his mind upon that which is given him to do.

Distracted Attention Causes Fatigue.—The attention of the worker is apt to be distracted not only by recognized dangers, such as burglars, fires, and disease, but also by other transitory things that, involuntarily on his part, take his mind from the work in hand. A

[7] Stratton, *Experimental Psychology and Culture*, pp. 268–269.

flickering light distracts the attention and causes fatigue, whether we have consciously noticed it or not. Many things are recorded by the senses without one's being conscious of them; for example, the ceasing of a clock to tick, although we have not noticed that it was ticking. Another example is the effect upon the pulse or the brain of being spoken to when asleep.

The flickering lamp of the chronocyclegraph device is much more fatiguing than the steady lamp of plain cyclegraphs.

Proper Placing of Workers Eliminates Distracted Attention.— Workers must be placed so that they do not see intermittently moving objects out of the corners of their eyes. In the early history of man it was continuously necessary to watch for first evidence of things behind one, or at a distance, in order to be safe from an enemy. From generations of survival of the most fit there have developed human eyes most sensitive to moving objects that are seen out of the corner of the eye. Even civilized man has his attention distracted quickest, and most, by those moving objects that he sees the least distinctly, and furthest to one side from the direction in which he is looking.

The leaf that moves or the grass that trembles may attract the attention where seen "out of the corner of the eye" to a point where it will even cause a start and a great fear.

As an example of the distracting effect of moving objects seen "out of the corner of the eye," try reading a book facing a window in a car where the moving scenery can be seen on each side of the book. The flitting object will interrupt one, one cannot get the full meaning out of what one is reading—yet if one lays down the book and looks directly at the scenery, the mind can concentrate to a point where one does not see that moving scenery which is directly in front of the eyes.

There is a great difference in this power of sensitiveness of the corners of some workers' eyes from that of others. The first move of Scientific Management is to place and arrange all workers, as far as is possible, in such a position that nothing to distract them will be behind them, and later to see that the eyes of workers are tested, that those whose eyes are most sensitive may be placed accordingly.

This Elimination May Take Place in All Kinds of Work.—The necessity of removing all things which will distract the attention is as great for the brain worker as for the shop or construction worker. All papers that attract the eye, and hence the attention, should be cleaned from the desk, everything except that on which the worker is working. The capability of being distracted by the presence of other things varies in all workers.

In using the dictaphone, one can do much better work if one is in a room where there is little or nothing to distract attention. An outline of work ahead may tempt to study and planning of what is ahead, rather than to carrying out the task scheduled for immediate performance. The presence of a paper with an outline merely of what is being done is found to be a great help, as the eye can rest on that, and, after a few moments, will become so accustomed to it that the whole attention will be given to the dictating.

Benefits of Eliminating "Decision of Choice."—There is always time lost by "decision of choice." The elimination of this is well illustrated by the bricks that are piled on the packet, which decides for the bricklayer which brick is next, making an obvious sequence, hence the saving of time of decision regarding motions, also the saving coming from the play for position. Oftentimes a handicap of slow mental action can be compensated for, in a measure, by planning ahead in great detail. In this way, if the plan is made sufficiently in detail, there is absolutely no time possible left to be wasted in "decision of choice." The worker goes from one step to another, and as these steps are arranged logically, his mind does not tend to wander away, but to keep on in an uninterrupted sequence to the goal.

Standard Equipment Important.—As for equipment, the phenomena of habit are among the most important features of the psychology of management and the possibilities of the elimination of unnecessary waste resulting from taking advantage of this feature is possible only when the equipment, surroundings and methods of the worker are standardized. Therefore the insistence upon standardization, even down to the smallest things, is vital for achieving the greatest output.

For example,—suppose the keys of the monotype machine, piano or typewriter were not located permanently in the same relative position. Consider the loss of time in not being able to use habits in finding each key. Such an arrangement sounds ridiculous on the face of it, yet it is a common practice for many operators, especially of monotype machines, to make a complete mental decision as to the muscles and fingers with which they will strike the desired key.

Imagine the records of output of a typist who was using a different keyboard every day, if there were that many kinds of keyboards. It is easy for anyone to conceive the great advantages of standard keyboards for such machines, but only those who have made a study of output of all kinds of workers can fully realize that similar differences in sizes of output are being produced by the workers of the country for lack of similar standardization of working conditions and equipment.

Utmost Standardization Does Not Make "Machines" of the Workers Operating Under It.—The attention of those who believe that standardization makes machines out of the workers themselves, is called to the absence of such effect upon the typist as compared with the scribe, the monotype and linotype operator as compared with the compositor, and the mechanical computing machine operator as compared with the arithmetician.

Standard Methods Demand Standard Tools and Devices.—Habits cannot be standardized until the devices and tools used are of standard pattern. It is not nearly so essential to have the best tools as it is to have standard tools.[8] Experience in the hospitals points to the importance of this fact in surgery. Tools once adopted as standard should not be changed until the improvement or greater efficiency from their use will compensate for the loss during the period of "breaking in" the user, that is, of forming new habits in order to handle strange tools. As will be brought out more fully under "Teaching," good habits are as difficult to break as bad ones, the only difference being that one does not usually desire to break good ones. Naturally, if a new device is introduced, what was an excellent habit for the old device becomes, perhaps, a very bad habit for the new device. There must come a time before the manipulation of the new device has become a habit when output will go down and costs will go up. It is necessary, before introducing this device, to investigate whether the ultimate reduction of costs will be sufficient to allow for this period of lower production. It is not fair, however, to the new device or method really to consider its record until the use of it has become such a habit with the workers as was the use of the old device.

No one who has not made a study of cutting tools can realize the crying need for standardizing in that field. Dr. Taylor says, writing in the Revised "Shop Management" of 1911,—"Hardly a shop can be found in which tools made from a dozen different qualities of steel are not used side by side, in many cases with little or no means of tell-

[8] F. W. Taylor, *Shop Management,* para. 285. Harper Ed., pp. 123–124.

ing one make from another."[9] The effect of the slighest variation in
the shape or the method of handling the tool upon the three dimensions of the work that the tool can do in a given time, is astounding.[10]
More important, from the psychological point of view, is the effect
upon the mind of the worker of seeing such unstandardized equipment; of having to stop to select the particular tool that he desires,
and thus having his attention distracted from his work; and of knowing that his act of judgment in so selecting is of no permanent value,
as the next time he needs a similar tool he will probably have to
reselect.

Standard Clothing a Crying Need.—There is a great need today
for standardization in the field of clothing. The idea prevalent that
wearing apparel is attractive only when it is "different" is unfortunate in its influence upon the cost of living. How much more unfortunate is it, when it affects the mind of the worker, and leads him
to look upon standard working clothes with distaste.

To a careful observer, there is nothing more disheartening than a
study of workers' clothes, especially the clothes of women workers.
Too warm clothes where work requiring high temperature is done,
with no provision for adding needed wraps for the trip home; high-
heeled shoes where the worker must stand at her task for hours at a
time; tight waists and ill fitting skirts, where every muscle should
have free play,—these are but examples of hundreds of places where
reforms are needed.

Little or no blame attaches to the worker for this state of affairs.
Seldom, if ever, does the management attempt to standardize working clothes. Moreover, the underlying idea is not made clear that
such clothes bear no resemblance to the meaningless uniforms which
are badge and symbol of service. They resemble rather the blouse or
pinafore of the artist, the outfit of the submarine diver or the fire-
man.

The Sports Present a Fine Example of This.—The greatest advance toward standardizing clothing has come in the sports, which, in
many respects, present admirable object-lessons. In the tennis court,
on the links, on the gridiron, the diamond, or track, the garment
worn of itself does not increase fatigue. On the contrary, it is so designed as not to interfere with the efficiency of the wearer.

Management Should Provide Clothing Standards.—Under Ulti-

[9] F. W. Taylor, *Shop Management*, revised 1911, pp. 124–125.
[10] F. W. Taylor, *On the Art of Cutting Metals*, A. S. M. E., No. 1119.

mate Management the most efficient clothing for any kind of work will be standardized. The expense of such articles of clothing as will add to the quantity or quality of output will, directly or indirectly, be borne by the management, just as it now bears the expense for equipment and tools. These essentials being supplied, and the underlying dignity and importance of standardization understood, the worker will gladly conform, and supply the minor accessories.

Such Standards Must Apply to All.—It is of the utmost importance that such standardization, when adopted, should apply to the clothing of all, managers as well as employés. When the old pride in the "crafts" returns, or when efficiency is as universal in the industrial world as it is in the world of sport,—then one may look for results.

Effects of Such Standards Enormous.—The effect which such standardized clothing would have on the physical and mental well-being of the wearers can scarcely be overestimated. Fatigue would be eliminated, and the old "joy in working" might return. Not being based upon looks alone,—though the æsthetic appeal should not be neglected,—the worker's ability to work more and better with greater content of mind would be the criterion. The success of the clothing would be scientifically measured, the standards improved, and progress itself become standardized.

Standard Methods Eliminate Fatigue.—There is no doubt in the minds of those who have made it a study, that the constant receipt of the same kind of impressions, caused by the same kind of stimulation of the same terminal sense organs, causes semi-automatic response with less resulting fatigue, corresponding to the lessened effort. All methods should, therefore, as far as possible, be made up of standard elements under standard conditions, with standard devices and appliances, and they should be standardized from the standpoint of all of our senses as to color, shape, size, weight, location, position and surface texture, that the worker may grasp at a single thought by means of each or all his senses, that no special muscles or other fatiguing processes need be operated to achieve the standard result desired.

Muscles That Tire Easily Should Be Saved.—It must be remembered that all work should be so arranged that the muscles that changes the position or shape of the eye or the size of its pupil should not be operated except when necessary. Care in planning can oftentimes standardize conditions so as to relieve these and other muscles, which grow tired easily, or transfer this work to other muscles which are not so easily tired.

Not only do the reactions from such standards require less bodily effort, but it also requires less mental effort to work under methods that are standardized. Therefore, both directly and indirectly, the worker benefits by the standardization.

Rest from Fatigue Is Provided for Scientifically.—Scientific Management provides and prescribes rest for overcoming fatigue of the worker more scientifically and economically than he could possibly provide it for himself. Weber's law is that "our power of detecting differences between sensations does not depend on the absolute amount of difference in the stimuli, but on the relative amount."[11] The additional fatigue from handling additional weights causes fatigue to increase with the weight, but not in direct proportion to the extra weight handled. When the correct weight of the unit to be handled has been determined, the additional weight will cause fatigue in quantities greater in proportion than the extra weight handled.

Rest Periods Arranged for Best Good of Work and Worker.—If possible, rest from fatigue is so arranged as to interfere with work the least. The necessary rest periods of the individuals of a gang should come at that period of the cycle that does not cause any allowance to be made for rest in between the performance of the dependent operations of different members of the gang. Such an arrangement will enable the worker to keep a sustained interest in the work.

Work with Animals Should Be Standardized.—The necessity for standardizing work with animals has been greatly underestimated, although it has been done more or less successfully in systems for construction work. For work with horses and carts, the harnesses and the carts should be standardized and standards only should be used. The instruction card dealing with the action, motions and their sequence should be standard to save time in changing teams from the full to the empty cart and *vice versa*. While standardized action is necessary with men, it is even more necessary for men in connection with the work of animals, such as horses, mules and oxen. The instruction card for the act of changing of teams from an empty cart to a full cart should state the side that the driver gets down from his seat to the ground, the sequence in which he unhooks the harness and hooks it up again, and the side on which he gets up to his seat in the cart. Even the wording of his orders to his horse should be standardized.

[11] Stratton, *Experimental Psychology and Culture*, p. 11.

While this book will deal with the human mind only, it is in order to state that a book could be written to advantage on training the horse by means of a standard man-horse language and a standard practice of their combined action.

Animals have not the capacity for forming new habits that they have for remembering the sequence of former acts. They have little ability to adapt themselves to a sequence of motions caused by unexpected conditions, unless those conditions suggest the opportunity of revenge, or the necessity of self-preservation, or immediate welfare. This is only touched upon here from the man side.

Naturally, the output earning power of a man working with animals depends largely upon the handling of the animal, and the man can never attain his full output, or the managers get what they might expect to get from the man-horse combination, until the psychology of the horse, or mule, or elephant, or whatever animal is used, is also studied and combined with the other studies on Scientific Management.

An example of the benefits of standardized work with animals:— The standard fire signals in the Fire House cause such perfect horse action that the fire horses always have a reputation for superior intelligence.

The Worker Who Is Best Suited for His Work in the Performing Department Is Incapable of Discovering the Best Method.—An exaggerated case of the result of leaving the selection of the method to the worker is that of the West Indian negro who carried the wheelbarrow on his head.[12] This well-known example, though it seems impossible and absurd, is no more inefficient than are hundreds of methods in use in the industrial world to-day.

Under Scientific Management Quality Is Standardized.—Scientific Management determines exactly what quality as well as what quantity of work is needed, and the method prescribed is that one not only of lower costs, but which fits the particular need of the particular occasion most accurately.

Workers are kept under pressure for quality, yet the pressure is not irksome, because the worker understands exactly what quality is desired, and what variations from exactness are permitted.

Variations in Quality or Exactness Indicated by Standard Signs.— All dimensions on the drawings of work have either a letter or sym-

---

[12] Mary Whiton Calkins, *A First Book in Psychology*, p. 65.

bol or plus or minus signs. There is much to be said about the effect this has on the worker.

1. It gives the worker immediate knowledge of the prescribed quality demanded.

2. He does not have to worry as to the maximum variation that he can make without interfering with his bonus.

3. There is no fear of criticism or discharge for using his own faulty judgment.

Scientific Management Has a Standard "Method of Attack."— We must note next the standard "method of attack" in Scientific Management. It is recognized that sensations are modified by those that come before, by those that come simultaneously, and by those that follow. The psychic effect of each and every kind of sensation depends upon what other sensations have been experienced, are being experienced at that time, or will presently be experienced. The scientific manager realizes this, and provides for the most desirable sequence of sensation; then, having seen, to the best of his ability, that the sensation occurs at the time which he desires it to occur, he provides for concentration upon that one sensation and elimination of all other thoughts or desires.

Professor Faraday says: "That part of self-education which consists in teaching the mind to resist the desires and inclinations until they are proved to be right is the most important of all." How this is shown under Scientific Management will be shown in "Teaching." It is sufficient to say here that the method of attack of Scientific Management is to eliminate all possible bodily as well as mental exertion,—to cut down motions, to cut down even sensations and such mental acts as visualizing. The object is, not so much to eliminate these motions and these sensations, and this visualizing from the life of the worker, as simply to use up less energy in producing the output. This allows the worker an extra supply of energy upon which to fall back to produce greater output and to get greater wages. If his energy is not all utilized in his working hours, then, as will be shown more clearly under "Welfare," there is that much more left for him to enjoy in his own leisure time.

SUMMARY

Result to the Work.—Under Traditional Management, where standards are not established, the worker is constantly delayed by the necessity for decision of choice, by the lack of knowing what should be chosen, and by a dearth of standard equipment, materials and tools from which to choose.

Under Transitory Management, with the introduction of standards, the elimination of delays and the provision for standard surroundings and supplies of all kinds, comes increased output of the desired quality.

Under Scientific Management, not only is output increased and quality assured, but results of work can be predicted.[13]

Results to the Worker.—Results from standardization to the worker under Traditional and Transitory Management are the same as, and are included in, results under Scientific Management.

State of Worker's Feelings Improved.—Under Scientific Management the state of the employé's feelings is improved by the standardization. It is a recognized fact that mental disturbance from such causes as fear of losing his job will sometimes have the same ill effect upon a workman as does overwork, or insufficient rest for overcoming fatigue. It will occasionally wear upon the nervous system and the digestive organs. Now Scientific Management by standardization removes from the workman this fear of losing his job, for the worker knows that if he conforms to the standard instructions he certainly will not lose his position unless the business as a whole is unsuccessful.

On the other hand, feelings, such as happiness and contentment, and even hearing rhythmic sounds, music, etc., are an aid toward increasing output. For the best results, therefore, under Scientific Management the worker is furnished with standard conditions; his train of ideas is held upon the work in hand without interruption, and the working conditions are such that the managers furnish the worker with inducements to conform to the standard conditions happily.

Worker's Retentive Power Increased.—We note in the second place, the increased retentive power of anyone who is working with standards. There is great difference between different people of the same degree of intelligence as to their ability to memorize certain things, especially such as sequences of the elements of a process. This lack of retentive power is illustrated particularly well in the cases often found where the student has difficulty in learning to spell. It is here that the standard instruction card comes into play to good effect. Its great detail remedies the defect in memorizing of certain other-

[13] C. G. Barth, A. S. M. E., Vol. 25, Paper 1010, p. 46.

wise brilliant workers, and its standard form and repetition of standard phrases aid the retentive power of the man who has a good memory.

Standard Elements Serve as Memory Drills.—This use of standardized elements makes the time elapsing between repetitions shorter, for, while it may be a long time before the worker again encounters the identical work or method, still, the fact that elements are standard means that he will have occasion to repeat elements frequently, and that his memory will each time be further drilled by these repetitions.

Gang Instruction Card an Aid to Memory.—The gang instruction card has been used with good effect at the beginning of unfamiliar repetitive cycles of work to train the memory of whole gangs of men at once, and to cut down the elapsed time from the time when one man's operation is sufficiently completed to permit the next man to commence his. It has been found, in the case of setting timbers in mill construction for example, that to have one man call out the next act in the sequence as fast as the preceding one is finished, until all have committed the sequence to memory, will materially decrease the time necessary for the entire sequence of elements in a cycle of work.

Individual Instruction Card an Inanimate Memory.—The instruction card supplies a most accurate memory in inanimate form, that neither blurs nor distorts with age.

The ranter against this standard memory is no more sensible than a man who would advocate the worker's forgetting the result of his best experience, that his mind might be periodically exercised by rediscovering the method of least waste anew with each problem.

Other things being equal, that worker has the longest number of years of earning power who remembers the largest number of right methods; or at least remembers where to find them described in detail; and, conversely, those who have no memory, and know not where to look for or to lay their hand on the method of least waste, remain at the beginning of their industrial education. "Experience," from an earning standpoint, does not exist when the mind does not retain a memory of the method. The instruction card, then, acts as a form of transferable memory—it conserves memory. Once it is made, it furnishes the earning power without the necessity of the former experience having been had more than once.

Plans, details, free-hand sketches, and two-dimension photographs surpass the highest form of mental imagery, and such cultivated imagery is undoubtedly a high achievement. There is no kind of memory, visualization, nor constructive imagination that can equal the stereoscopic or three-dimension photographs that may accompany the instruction card for enabling the worker to "see the completed work before it is begun." Probably the greatest hindrance to development of lower forms of animal life is their inability to picture past experiences, and the reason for the intellectual strides made by the worker under Scientific Management is the development of this faculty.

A Conserver of Individual Memories.—Many people believe that the memory of a person ceases at his death. Whether this is so or not, the loss to the world, and particularly the industrial world, of not having the instruction card for the passing on of the worker's experience to the workers who follow is stupendous and incalculable, and this loss, like so many other losses, can be eliminated by the process of making written standards.

Motor Memory Improved by Standardization.—Not only are the retentive powers of the brain improved, but also the brain centers, and the muscles, etc., become trained through standardization. With standardization a long sequence of muscular motions or operations can be noted at a glance, and can be remembered without difficulty.

Standards Prevent Men from Becoming Machines.—Those who object to the worker taking advantage of these scientifically derived standards which aid the memory, can only be compared to such people as desire the workers to turn into unthinking animals. Psychologists believe that some of the lower animals have no memory. Turning the workers into machines which do not in any way utilize thought-saving devices is simply putting them but little above the class of these lower, memory-less, animals.

Through Standards the Worker's Attention Is Gained at the Start.—The general act of attention plays an important part in Scientific Management. The insistence upon standardized performance requires the utmost attention at the beginning of learning a new method of performance. This extra output of mental activity, which is always required for accomplishing new methods of work, could not be continuously maintained, but after the new method has once been learned, its repetition requires less attention, consequently less fatigue. The attention of the worker is, therefore, strongly demanded at the beginning and when, later, it is not needed except for new and unfamiliar work, an opportunity arises for invention and mental advancement.

Attention Allowed to Lapse and Then Recalled.—Standardization shifts the objects of attention and eliminates the need for constant concentration. The standardization of processes relieves the worker to a marked extent from the extremely fatiguing mental effort of unproductive fixed, valueless, and unnecessary attention on the stream of consciousness. The repeated elements which form a part of all standards reconcentrates the attention if it is allowed to lapse.

Standardization Eliminates the Shifting Viewpoint.—Under old-time Traditional Management the way that the man happened to feel at the particular time made a great difference, not only in his work, but in his relations with other men. The standardization not only of the relationship between the men, but of the relationships between the foreman, the manager, and the worker, the fact that the disciplining is put in the hands of a man who is not biased by his personal feelings in his dealings with the men;—all of these things mean that the viewpoint of the men as to their work and their relationship remains fixed. This standardizing of the viewpoint is an enormous help toward increasing output.

The Common Viewpoint Is an Impetus.—There are those who believe that the concerted standard process of thought of the many minds assists the operation of any one mind. However this may be, there is no doubt that the fact that the standard thought is present in all minds at one time at least eliminates some cause for discussion and leads to unity and consequent success in the work.

Invention Is Stimulated.—Chances for invention and construction are provided by standardization.[14] By having a scientifically derived standard method as a starter, the worker can exert much of his mental power toward improvement from that point upward, instead of being occupied with methods below it and in wasting, perhaps, a lifetime in striving to get up to it,[15] this in distinction to the old plan, where a worker knew only what he could personally remember of what had been handed down by tradition, tradition being the memory of society. Under Scientific Management a worker has many repetitions of experience, some of which he does not always recognize as such. When he does recognize them, he has the power and daring for

---

[14] Charles Babbage, *On the Economy of Machinery and Manufactures,* Secs. 224–225. Adam Smith, *Wealth of Nations,* Book I, chap. I, p. 4.

[15] F. W. Taylor, paper 1119, A. S. M. E., para. 51; para. 98–100.

rapid construction that come to those only who "know that they know."

Standardization of ultimate subdivisions, as such, brings that power to the worker sooner. The conscious knowledge of familiarity of process is an essential for attaining the complete benefits of experience.

Far from making machines out of the men, standardization causes a mental state that leads to invention, for the reason that the worker's brain is in most intimate contact with the work, and yet has not been unnecessarily fatigued by the work itself. No more monotonous work could be cited than that of that boy whose sole duty was to operate by hand the valve to the engine, yet he invented the automatic control of the slide valve used throughout the world to-day.

Standardization Prevents Accidents.—The results of standardization so far given, concern changes in the worker's mental capacity, or attitude. Such changes, and other changes, will be discussed from a different viewpoint under "Teaching." As for results to the worker's body, one of the most important is the elimination of causes for accidents.

The rigid inspection, testing, and repairing provided for by Scientific Management provides against accidents from defects in equipment, tools, or material. The fact that instructions are written, provides against wrong methods of handling work.[16] The concentrated attention caused by standardization, is a safeguard against accidents that occur from the worker's carelessness.[17] The proper allowance of rest for overcoming fatigue, insures that the worker's mind is fresh enough to enable him to comply with standards, and, finally, the spirit of coöperation that underlies Scientific Management is an added check against accidents, in that everyone is guarding his fellows as well as himself.

Progress of Standardization Assured.—As Scientific Management becomes older, progress will be faster, because up to this time there has been a hindrance standing in the way of rapid advancement of the best standards. This hindrance has been the tendency of habits of thought coinciding with former practice. For example, the design of concrete building for years followed the habit of thinking in terms of brick, or wood, or steel, and then attempting to design and con-

---

[16] F. A. Parkhurst, *Applied Methods of Scientific Management, Industrial Engineering,* Oct. 1911, p. 251.

[17] H. L. Gantt, paper 928, A. S. M. E., para. 15.

struct in reinforced concrete. Again, in the case of the motor car, habits of thinking in vehicles drawn by animals for years kept the design unnecessarily leaning toward that of horse vehicles. As soon as thought was in terms of power vehicles, the efficient motor truck of to-day was made, using the power also for power loading and power hoisting, as is now done in motor trucks specially designed for transporting and handling pianos and safes. So, also, while the thought was of traditional practice, standard practice was held back. Now that the theories of standardization are well understood, standardization and standards in general can advance with great rapidity.

Teaching

●●

Definition of Teaching.—The Century Dictionary defines "teaching" as "the act or business of instructing," with synonyms: "training" and "education;" and "to teach" is defined:—

1. "to point out, direct, show;" "to tell, inform, instruct, explain;"
2. "to show how (to do something); hence, to train;"
3. "to impart knowledge or practical skill to;" "to guide in learning, educate."

"Educate," we find meaning "to instruct, to teach methodically, to prescribe to; to indoctrinate;" and by "indoctrinate" is meant "to cause to hold as a doctrine or belief." "To educate," says the same authority, "is to develop mentally or morally by instruction; to qualify by instruction and training for the business and duty of life."

Under Traditional Management No Definite Plan of Teaching.—Under Traditional Management there is either no definite scheme of teaching by the management itself, or practically none; at least, this is usually the condition under the most elementary types of Traditional Management. In the very highest examples of the traditional plan the learner may be shown how, but this showing is not usually done in a systematic way, and under so-called Traditional Management is seldom in the form of written instructions.

No Specified Time for or Source of the Teaching.—Under Traditional Management there is no particular time in which this teaching goes on, no particular time allowed for the worker to ask for the instruction, nor is there any particular source from which he obtains the instructions. There is, moreover, almost every hindrance against his getting any more instruction than he absolutely must have in order to get the work done. The persons to whom he can possibly appeal for further information might discharge him for not already knowing. These persons are, if he is an apprentice, an older worker; if he is a journeyman, the worker next to him, or the foreman, or someone over him. An important fact bearing on this subject is that it is not to the pecuniary advantage of any particular person to give this teaching. In the first place, if the man be a fellow-worker, he will want to do his own work without interruption, he will not want to take the time off; moreover, he regards his particular skill as more or less of a trade secret, and desires to educate no more people than necessary, to be as clever as he is. In the third place, there is no possible reward for giving this instruction. Of course, the worker necessarily improves under any sort of teaching, and if he has a receptive mind, or an inventive mind, he must progress constantly, either by teaching himself or by the instruction, no matter how haphazard.

Great Variation Under Traditional Management.—Only discussion of teaching under this type of management with many men who have learned under it, can sufficiently emphasize the variations to be found. But the consensus of opinion would seem to prove that an apprentice of only a generation ago was too often hazed, was discouraged from appealing for assistance or advice to the workers near him, or to his foreman; was unable to find valuable literature for home-study on the subject of his trade. The experience of many an apprentice was, doubtless, different from this, but surely the mental attitude of the journeymen who were the only teachers must have tended toward some such resulting attitude of doubt or hesitancy in the apprentice.

Mental Attitude of the Worker-Teacher.—Under the old plan of management, the apprentice must appear to the journeyman more or less of a supplanter. From the employee's standpoint it was most desirable that the number of apprentices be kept down, as an oversupply of labor almost invariably resulted in a lowering of wages. The quicker and better the apprentice was taught, the sooner he became an active competitor. There seldom existed under this type of management many staff positions to which the workers could hope to be promoted, certainly none where they could utilize to the fullest extent their teaching ability. There was thus every reason for a journeyman to regard the teaching of apprentices as unremunerative, irksome, and annoying.

Worker Not to Blame for This.—The worker is not to be blamed for this attitude. The conditions under which he worked made it almost inevitable. Not only could he gain little or nothing by being a successful teacher, but also the bullying instinct was appealed to constantly, and the desire of the upper classmen in hazing days to make the next class "pay up" for the hazing that they were obliged to endure in their Freshman year.

Attitude of the Learner.—The attitude of the typical learner must frequently be one of hesitancy and self-distrust if not of fear, though conditions were so varied as almost to defy classification. One type of apprentice was expected to learn merely by observation and imitation. Another was practically the chore boy of the worker who was assigned to teach him. A third was under no direct supervision at all, but was expected to "keep busy," finding his work by himself. A fourth was put through a severe and valuable training by a martinet teacher,—and so on.

Teaching Often Painstaking.—It is greatly to the credit of the worker under this type of management that he was, in spite of all drawbacks, occasionally a painstaking teacher, to the best of his lights. He insisted on application, and especially on quality of work. He unselfishly gave of his own time and skill to help the apprentice under him.

Methods of Teaching Usually Wrong.—Unfortunately, through no fault of the worker-teacher the teaching was usually done according to wrong methods. Quality of resulting output was so emphasized that neither speed nor correct motions were given proper consideration.

Teacher Not Trained To Teach.—The reason for this was that the worker had no training to be a teacher. In the first place, he had no adequate idea of his own capabilities, and of which parts of his own method were fit to be taught. In the second place, he did not know that right motions must be insisted on first, speed next, and quality of output third; or in other words that if the motions were precise enough, the quality would be first. In the fourth place he had no pedagogical training.

Lack of Standards an Underlying Lack.—All shortcoming in the old time teaching may be traced to lack of standards. The worker had never been measured, hence had no idea of his efficiency, or of possible efficiency. No standard methods made plain the manner in which the work should be done. Moreover, no standard division and assignment of work allowed for placing apprentices at such parts of the work that quality could be given third place. No standard requirements had determined his fitness as a teacher, nor the specialty that he should teach, and no incentive held his interest to the teaching. These standards the worker-teacher could not provide for himself, and the wonder is that the teaching was of such a high character as it was.

Very Little Teaching of Adults.—Under Traditional Management, teaching of adults was slight,—there being little incentive either to teacher or to learner, and it being always difficult for an adult to change his method.[1] Moreover, it would be difficult for a worker using one method to persuade one using another that his was the better, there being no standard. Even if the user of the better did persuade the other to follow his method, the final result might be the loss of some valuable elements of the poorer method that did not appear in the better.

Failure to Appreciate the Importance of Teaching.—An underestimation of the importance of teaching lay at the root of the lack of progress. This is so directly connected with all the other lacks of Traditional Management,—provision for adequate promotion and pay, standards, and the other underlying principles of Scientific Management, especially the appreciation of coöperation,—that it is almost impossible to disentangle the reasons for it. Nor would it be profitable to attempt to do so here. In considering teaching under Scientific Management we shall show the influence of the appreciation of teaching,—and may deduce the lacks from its nonappreciation, from that discussion.

Under Transitory System Teaching Becomes More Important.— Under Transitory Management the importance of teaching becomes at once more apparent. This, both by providing for the teaching of foremen and journeymen as well as apprentices, and by the providing of written systems of instructions as to best practice. The worker has access to all the sources of information of Traditional Management, and has, besides these, in effect, unsystematically derived standards to direct him.

---

[1] F. B. Gilbreth, *Bricklaying System,* para. 541–545.

Systems Make Instruction Always Available.—The use of written systems enables every worker to receive instruction at any time, to feel free to ask it, and to follow it without feeling in any way humiliated.

The result of the teaching of these systems is a decided improvement in methods. If the written systems are used exclusively as a source of teaching, except for the indefinite teachers of the Traditional Management, the improvement becomes definitely proportioned to the time which the man spends upon the studying and to the amount of receptive power which he naturally has.

Incentives to Conform to System.—The worker has incentives to follow the systems—

1. In that he is required to render reasons in writing for permanent filing, for every disobedience of system.

2. That, as soon as work is placed on the bonus basis, the first bonus that is given is for doing work in accordance with the prescribed method.

Even before the bonus is paid, the worker will not vary for any slight reasons, if he positively knows at the time that he must account for so doing, and that he will be considered to have "stacked his judgment" against that of the manager. Being called to account for deviations gives the man a feeling of responsibility for his act, and also makes him feel his close relationship with the managers.

No Set Time for Using Systems.—There is, under this type of management, no set time for the study of the systems.

Systems Inelastic.—Being written, these systems have all the disadvantages of anything that is written. That is to say, they require considerable adaptability on the part of the man who is using them. He must consider his own mind, and the amount of time which he must put on studying; he must consider his own work, and adapting that method to his work while still obeying instructions. In the case of the system being in great detail, he can usually find a fairly detailed description of what he is going to do, and can use that. In the case of the system being not so complete, if his work varies, he must show intelligence in varying the system, and this intelligence often demands a knowledge which he has not, and knows not where to obtain.

Waste of Time from Unstandardized Systems.—The time necessitated by the worker's laying out details of his method is taken from the total time of his working day, hence in so far cuts down his total product. Moreover, if no record is kept of the details of his planning the next worker on the same kind of work must repeat the investigation.

Later Transitional Management Emphasizes Use of Standards.—Later Transitional Management eliminates this waste of time by standardizing methods composed of standardized timed units, thus both rendering standards elastic, and furnishing details.

Teaching Most Important Under Scientific Management.—Teaching is a most important element under Scientific Management not only because it increases industrial efficiency, but also because it fosters industrial peace.[2]

Importance Depends on Other Elements of Scientific Management.—As we have seen, Scientific Management has as a basic idea the necessity of divided responsibility, or functionalization. This, when accompanied by the interdependent bonus, creates an incentive to teach and an incentive to learn. Scientific Management divides the planning from the performing in order to centralize and standardize knowledge in the planning department, thus making all knowledge of each available to all. This puts at the disposal of all more than any could have alone. The importance of having this collected and standardized knowledge conveyed best to the worker cannot be overestimated. Through this knowledge, the worker is able to increase his output, and thus insure the lowered costs, that provide the funds with which to pay his higher wages,—to increase his potential as well as actual efficiency, and best to coöperate with other workers and with the management.

Importance of Teaching Element Best Claim to Permanence of Scientific Management.—Upon the emphasis which it places on teaching rests a large part of the claim of Scientific Management for permanence.[3] We have already shown the derivation of the standards which are taught. We have shown that the relation between the planning and performing departments is based largely on means and methods for teaching. We have only to show here that the teaching is done in accordance with those laws of Psychology that are the laws of Pedagogy.

Teaching in Scientific Management Not the Result of Theory Only.—The methods of teaching under Scientific Management were

[2] H. K. Hathaway, *Prerequisites to the Introduction of Scientific Management, Engineering Magazine*, April, 1911, p. 141.

[3] H. L. Gantt, paper 928, A. S. M. E., p. 372.

not devised in response to theories of education. They are the result of actual experience in getting work done most successfully. The teachers, the methods, the devices for teaching,—all these grew up to meet needs, as did the other elements of Scientific Management.

Conformity of Teaching to Psychological Laws Proof of Worth of Scientific Management.—The fact that teaching under Scientific Management does conform, as will be shown, to the laws of Psychology, is an added proof of the value of Scientific Management.

Change from Teaching Under Traditional Management.—Mr. Gantt says, "The general policy of the past has been to drive; but the era of force must give way to that of knowledge, and the policy of the future will be to teach and to lead, to the advantage of all concerned."[4] This "driving" element of Traditional Management is eliminated by Scientific Management.

Necessity for Personally Derived Judgment Eliminated.—So also is eliminated the old belief that the worker must go through all possible experiences in order to acquire "judgment" as to best methods. If the worker must pass through all the stages of the training of the old-fashioned mechanic, and this is seriously advocated by some, he may fail to reach the higher planes of knowledge afforded by training under Scientific Management, by reason of sheer lack of time. If, therefore, by artificial conditions caused by united agreement and collective bargaining, workmen insist upon forcing upon the new learners the old-school training, they will lose just so much of the benefits of training under those carefully arranged and carefully safe-guarded processes of industrial investigation in which modern science has been successful. To refuse to start in where others have left off, is really as wasteful as it would be to refuse to use mathematical formulas because they have been worked out by others. It might be advocated that the mind would grow by working out every possible mathematical formula before using it, but the result would be that the student would be held back from any further original investigation. Duplicating primary investigations might be original work for him, but it would be worthless as far as the world is concerned. The same is absolutely true in management. If the worker is held back by acquiring every bit of knowledge for himself instead of taking the work of others as the starting point, the most valuable initiative will be lost to the world.

[4] H. L. Gantt, *Work, Wages and Profits,* p. 116.

Bad Habits the Result of Undirected Learning.—Even worse than the waste of time would be the danger of acquiring habits of bad methods, habits of unnecessary motions, habits of inaccurate work; habits of inattention. Any or all of these might develop. These are all prevented under Scientific Management by the improved methods of teaching.

Valuable Elements of Traditional Management Conserved.— There are, however, many valuable elements of the old Traditional system of teaching and of management which should be retained and not be lost in the new.

For example,—the greatest single cause of making men capable under the old plan was the foreman's unconscious ability to make his men believe, before they started a task, that they could achieve it.

It must not be thought that because of the aids to the teacher under Scientific Management the old thought of personality is lost. The old ability to convert a man to the belief that he could do a thing, to inspire him with confidence in his foreman, with confidence in himself, and a desire to do things, is by no means lost, on the contrary it is carefully preserved under Scientific Management.

Teaching of Transitory Management Supplemented.—In the transforming of Transitory into Scientific Management, we note that the process is one of supplementing, not of discarding. Written system, which is the distinguishing characteristic of Transitory Management, is somewhat limited in its scope, but its usefulness is by no means impaired.

Scope of Teaching Under Scientific Management.—Under Scientific Management teaching must cover

1. Teaching of right methods of doing work,
2. Teaching of right habits of doing the right methods.

The teacher must so impart the knowledge that judgment can be acquired without the learner being obliged himself to experience all the elements of the judgment.

Needs for Teaching Under Scientific Management.—The needs for this teaching have been stated, but may be recapitulated here.

1. Worker may not observe his own mistakes.
2. Worker has no opportunity under the old industrial conditions to standardize his own methods.
3. Worker must know standard practice.
4. Waste can be eliminated by the teaching.
5. Right habits can be instilled.

Sources of Teaching Under Scientific Management.—The sources of teaching under Scientific Management are

1. Friends or Relatives ⎫
2. Fellow workers ⎪
3. Literature of the Trade ⎬ If the worker chooses to use them.
4. Night schools and study ⎪
5. The Management. ⎭

Methods of Teaching Under Scientific Management.—The Methods of Teaching under Scientific Management are

1. Written, by means of
    (a) Instruction Cards telling *what* is to be done and *how*.
    (b) Systems, explaining the *why*.
    (c) Drawings, charts, plans, photographs, illustrating methods.
    (d) Records made by the worker himself.
2. Oral, the teaching of the Functional Foremen.
3. Object-lessons:
    (a) Exhibits.
    (b) Working models.
    (c) Demonstrations by the Teacher.
    (d) Demonstrations by the worker under Supervision.

Worker a Source of These Methods.—It should be often stated that, ultimately, the elements of all methods are derived from a study of workers, and that the worker should be enabled to realize this. Only when he feels that he is a part of what is taught, and that the teachers are a *means* of presenting to him the underlying principles of his own experience, will the worker be able to coöperate with all his energy.

Instruction Cards Are Directions.—Instruction Cards are direct instructions for each piece of work, giving, in most concise form, closely defined description of standard practice and directions as to how each element of the standardized task is to be performed. The makers know that they must make their directions clear ultimately, therefore they strive constantly for clearness.

Instruction Cards Teach Directly and Indirectly.—These Instruction Cards not only teach the worker directly best to do his work, but also teach him indirectly how to become a leader, demonstrator, teacher and functional foreman. Study of them may lead to an interest in, and a study of, elements, and to preparation for becoming one of the planning department. The excellent method of attack of the Instruction Card cannot fail to have some good effect, even upon such workers as do not consciously note it.[5]

Systems Are Reasons and Explanations.—"Systems" or standing orders are collections of detailed reasons for, and explanations of, the decisions embodied in the directions of the Instruction Cards. There is a system showing the standard practice of each kind of work.

They Enlist the Judgment of the Worker.—Under really successful management, it is realized that the worker is of an inquiring mind, and that, unless this inquiring tendency of his is recognized, and his curiosity is satisfied, he can never do his best work. Unless the man knows why he is doing the thing, his judgment will never re-enforce his work. He may conform to the method absolutely, but his work will not enlist his zeal unless he knows just exactly why he is made to work in the particular manner prescribed. This giving of the "why" to the worker through the system, and thus allowing his reason to follow through all the details, and his judgment to conform absolutely, should silence the objections of those who claim that the worker becomes a machine, and that he has no incentive to think at his work. On the contrary, it will be seen that this method furnishes him with more viewpoints from which he can consider his work.

Drawings, Charts, Plans and Photographs Means of Making Directions Clearer.—The Instruction Cards are supplemented with drawings, charts, plans and stereoscopic and timed motion photographs,—any or all,—in order to make the directions of the Instruction Cards plainer.

Stereoscopic and Micro-Motion Study Photographs Particularly Useful.—Stereoscopic photographs are especially useful in helping non-visualizers, and in presenting absolutely new work. The value as an educator of stereoscopic and synthesized micro-motion photographs of right methods is as yet but faintly appreciated.

The "timed motion picture," or "micro-motion study photograph" as it is called, consists of rapidly photographing workers in action accompanied by a specially constructed chronometer that shows such minute divisions of time that motion pictures taken at a speed that will catch the most rapid of human motions without a blur, will show a different time of day in each photograph. The difference in the time in any two pictures gives the elapsed time of the desired motion operation or time unit.

[5] H. L. Gantt, paper 928, A. S. M. E., p. 342.

Self-Made Records Educative.—The educative value of the worker's making his own records has never been sufficiently appreciated. Dr. Taylor insists upon this procedure wherever possible.[6] Not only does the worker learn from the actual marking in of the spaces reserved for him, but also he learns to feel himself a part of the record making division of the management. This proof of the "square deal," in recording his output, and of the confidence in him, cannot fail to enlist his coöperation.

Oral Instruction Comes from the Functional Foremen.—The Functional Foremen are teachers whose business it is to explain, translate and supplement the various written instructions when the worker either does not understand them, does not know how to follow them, or makes a mistake in following them.

Oral Instruction Has Its Fitting Place Under Scientific Management.—Oral instruction under Scientific Management has at least four advantages over such instruction under Traditional Management.

1. The Instructor is capable of giving instruction.
2. The Instructor's specialty is giving instruction.
3. The instruction is a supplement to written instructions.
4. The instruction comes at the exact time that the learner needs it.

Teacher, or Functional Foreman, Should Understand Psychology and Pedagogy.—The successful teacher must understand the minds of his men, and must be able to present his information in such a way that it will be grasped readily. Such knowledge of psychology and pedagogy as he possesses he may acquire almost unconsciously

1. from the teaching of others,
2. from his study of Instruction Cards and Systems,
3. from actual practice in teaching.

The advantages of a study of psychology itself, as it applies to the field of teaching in general, and of teaching in the industries in particular, are apparent. Such study must, in the future, become more and more prevalent.

Advantage of Functional Foreman-Teacher Over Teacher in the Schools.—The Functional Foreman-teacher has an advantage over the teacher in the school in that the gap between him and those he teaches is not so great. He knows, because he remembers, exactly how the worker must have his information presented to him. This gap is

---

[6] F. W. Taylor, *Shop Management,* para. 289, Harper Ed., pp. 127–128.

narrowed by functionalizing the oral teaching, by using it merely as a supplement to the written teaching, and by supplementing it with object-lessons.

Teacher Must Have Practical Knowledge of the Trade He Is to Teach.—The teacher must have an intimate practical knowledge of the art or trade that he is to teach. The most profound knowledge of Psychology will never be a substitute for the mastery of the trade, as a condition precedent to turning out the best craftsmen. This is provided for by securing teachers from the ranks of the workers.[7]

He Must Have a Thorough Knowledge of the Standards.—He must have more than the traditional knowledge of the trade that he is to teach; he must have also the knowledge that comes only from scientific investigation of his trade. This knowledge is ready and at hand, in the standards of Scientific Management that are available to all for study.

He Must Be Convinced of the Value of the Methods He Teaches. —The teacher must also have an intimate acquaintance with the records of output of the method he is to teach as compared with those of methods held in high esteem by the believer in the old methods; for it is a law that no teacher can be efficient in teaching any method in which he does not believe, any more than a salesman can do his best work when he does not implicitly believe in the goods that he is selling.

He Must Be an Enthusiast.—The best teacher is the one who is an enthusiast on the subject of the work itself, who can cause contagion or imitation of his state of mind, by love of the problems themselves.

Such Enthusiasm Contagious.—It is the contagion of this enthusiasm that will always create a demand for teachers, no matter how perfect instruction cards may become. There is no form or device of management that does away with good men, and in the teacher, as here described, is conserved the personal element of the successful, popular Traditional foreman.

Valuable Teacher Interests Men in the Economic Value of Scientific Management.—The most valuable teacher is one who can arouse his pupils to such a state of interest in the economic values of the methods of Scientific Management, that all other objects that would ordinarily distract or hold their attention will be banished from their minds. They will then remember each step as it is introduced, and

[7] H. K. Hathaway, *Engineering Magazine,* April, 1911, p. 144.

they will be consumed with interest and curiosity to know what
further steps can be introduced, that will still further eliminate
waste.

Object-lesson May Be "Working Models."—The object-lesson may
be a "fixed exhibit" or a "working model," "a process in different
stages," or "a micro-motion study film" of the work that is to be done.
Successful and economical teaching may be done with such models,
which are especially valuable where the workers do not speak the
same language as the teacher, where many workers are to perform
exactly similar work, or where the memory, the visualizing and the
constructive imagination, are so poor that the models must be referred to constantly. Models naturally appeal best to those who take
in information easiest through the eyes.

Object-lessons May Be Demonstrations by the Teacher.—The
teacher may demonstrate the method manually to the worker, or by
means of films showing synthesized right methods on the motion-
picture screen. This, also, is a successful method of teaching those
who speak a different language, or of explaining new work,—though
it calls for a better memory than does the "working model." The
model, however, shows desired results; the demonstration, desired
methods.

Demonstration Method Chief Method of Teaching by Foremen.
—The manual demonstration method is the chief method of teaching the workmen by the foremen under Scientific Management, and
no method is rated as standard that cannot be successfully demonstrated by the teacher, at any time, on request.

Worker may Demonstrate Under Supervision.—If the worker is
of that type that can learn only by actually doing the work himself,
he is allowed to demonstrate the method under supervision of the
teacher.[8]

Teaching Always Available Under Scientific Management.—
Under Scientific Management all of these forms of teaching are available constantly. The instruction card and accompanying illustrations
are given to the worker before he starts to work, and are so placed
that he can consult them easily at any time during the work. As, also,
if object-lessons are used, they are given before work commences, and
repeated when necessary.

[8] W. D. Ennis, *An Experiment in Motion Study, Industrial Engineering*, June, 1911,
p. 462.

The teacher is constantly available for oral instruction, and the systems are constantly available for consultation.

Methods of Teaching Under Scientific Management Psychologically Right.—In order to prove that teaching under Scientific Management is most valuable, it is necessary to show that it is psychologically right, that it leads to mental development and improvement. Under Scientific Management, teaching,—

1. uses and trains the senses.
2. induces good habits of thinking and acting.
3. stimulates attention.
4. provides for valuable associations.
5. assists and strengthens the memory.
6. develops the imagination.
7. develops judgment.
8. utilizes suggestion.
9. utilizes "native reactions."
10. develops the will.

Teaching Under Scientific Management Trains the Senses.— Scientific Management, in teaching the man, aims to train all of his senses possible. Not only does each man show an aptitude for some special sense training,[9] but at certain times one sense may be stronger than another; for example, the sense of hearing, as is illustrated by the saying, "The patient in the hospital knoweth when his doctor cometh by the fall of his footsteps, yet when he recovereth he knoweth not even his face." At the time that a certain thing becomes of interest, and becomes particularly interesting to one sense, that sense is particularly keen and developed.

Scientific Management cannot expect, without more detailed psychological data than is as yet available, to utilize these periods of sense predominance adequately. It can, and does, aim to utilize such senses as are trained, and to supply defects of training of the other senses.

Such Training Partially Determines the Quality of the Work.— The importance of sense training can scarcely be overestimated. Through his senses, the worker takes in the directions as to what he is to do, and on the accuracy with which his senses record the impressions made upon them, depends the mental model which he ultimately follows, and the accuracy of his criticism of the resulting

[9] C. S. Myers, M.D., *An Introduction to Experimental Psychology,* chap. V, p. 73.

physical object of his work. Through the senses, the worker sets his own task, and inspects his work.

Sense Training Influences Increase of Efficiency.—With the training of the senses the possibility of increased efficiency increases. As any sense becomes trained, the minimum visable is reduced, and more accurate impressions become possible.[10] They lead to more rapid work, by eliminating time necessary for judgment. The bricklayer develops a fineness of touch that allows him to dispense with sight in some parts of his work.

Selective Power of Senses Developed.—James defines the sense organs as "organs of selection."[11] Scientific Management so trains them that they can select what is of most value to the worker.

Methods of Sense Training Under Scientific Management.—The senses are trained under Scientific Management by means of the various sources of teaching. The instruction card, with its detailed descriptions of operations, and its accompanying illustrations, not only tends to increase powers of visualization, but also, by the close observation it demands, it reduces the minimum visible. The "visible instruction card," or working model, is an example of supplementing weak power of visualization. The most available simple, inexpensive and easily handled device to assist visualizing is the stereo or three-dimension photograph, which not only serves its purpose at the time of its use, but trains the eye to see the third dimension always.

Much training is given to the eye in Scientific Management by the constant insistence on inspection. This inspection is not confined to the inspector, but is the constant practice of worker and foremen, in order that work may be of such a quality as will merit a bonus.

Senses That Are Most Utilized Best Trained.—The relative training given to the various senses depends on the nature of the work. When the ear is the tester of efficiency, as it often is with an engineer watching machinery in action, emphasis is laid on training the hearing. In work where touch is important, emphasis is on such training as will develop that sense.[12]

Variations in Sense Power Should Be Utilized.—Investigations are constantly going to prove that each sense has a predominance at a different time in the age of the child or man. Dottoressa Montessori's experience with teaching very young children by touch shows that

[10] G. M. Stratton, *Experimental Psychology and Culture*, p. 125.
[11] William James, *Psychology, Briefer Course*, p. 171.
[12] F. B. Gilbreth, *Bricklaying System*, chap. I, *Training of Apprentices*.

that sense is able to discriminate to an extraordinary extent for the first six years of life.[13]

So, also, acute keenness of any sense, by reason of age or experience should be conserved.[14] Such acuteness is often the result of some need, and, unless consciously preserved, will vanish with the need.

Progress in Such Training.—The elementary sense experiences are defined and described by Calkins.[15] Only through a psychological study can one realize the numerous elements and the possibility of study. As yet, doubtless, Scientific Management misses many opportunities for training and utilizing the senses. But the standardizing of elements, and the realization of the importance of more and more intensive study of the elements lends assurance that ultimately all possibilities will be utilized.

As Many Senses as Possible Appealed To.—Scientific Management has made great progress in appealing to as many senses as possible in its teaching. The importance of the relation between the senses is brought out by Prof. Stratton.[16]

In teaching, Scientific Management has, in its teachers, animate and inanimate, great possibilities of appealing to many senses simultaneously. The instruction card may be

1. read to oneself silently—eyes appealed to

2. read to oneself aloud—eyes and ears appealed to, also muscles used trained to repeat

3. read aloud to one—ears

4. read aloud to one and also read silently by one,—eyes and ears

5. read aloud, and at the same time copied—eyes, ears, muscles of mouth, muscles of hand

6. read to one, while process described is demonstrated

7. read to one while process is performed by oneself

There are only a few of the possible combinations, any of which are used, as best suits the worker and the work.[17]

Untrained Worker Requires Appeal to Most Senses.—The value of appeal to many senses is best realized in teaching an inexperienced worker. His senses help to remind him what to do, and to "check up" his results.

At Times Appeal to But One Sense Preferable.—In the case of

---

[13] *McClure's Magazine*, May, 1911, Dec., 1911, Jan., 1912.

[14] As a woodman's keenness of hearing.

[15] M. W. Calkins, *A First Book in Psychology*, chap. III.

[16] Stratton, *Experimental Psychology and Culture*, chap. VII.

[17] Compare with an actor's learning a part.

work that must be watched constantly, and that involves continuous processes, it may prove best to have directions read to the worker. So also, the Gang Instruction Card may often be read to advantage to the gang, thus allowing the next member of a group of members to rest, or to observe, while directions are taken in through the ears only. In this way time is allowed to overcome fatigue, yet the work is not halted.

At Times One Sense Is Best Not Utilized.—At times teaching may well omit one sense in its appeal, because that sense will tend to confuse the learning, and will, when the method is learned, be otherwise utilized than it could be during the learning process. In teaching the "touch system" of typewriting,[18] the position of the keys is quickly remembered by having the key named aloud and at the same time struck with the assigned finger, the eyes being blindfolded. Thus hearing is utilized, also mouth muscles and finger muscles, but *not* sight.

Importance of Fatigue Recognized.—A large part of the success of sense appeal and sense training of Scientific Management is in the appreciation of the importance of fatigue. This was early recognized by Dr. Taylor, and is constantly receiving study from all those interested in Scientific Management.

Psychology Already Aiding the Industries in Such Study.—Study of the *Psychological Review* will demonstrate the deep and increasing interest of psychologists in the subject of fatigue. The importance of such stimulating and helpful work as that done by Doctor A. Imbert of the University of Montpellier, France, is great.[19] Not only are the results of his investigations commercially valuable, but also they are valuable as indicating the close connection between Psychology and Industrial Efficiency.

Importance of Habits.[20]—Prof. William James says "an acquired habit, from the psychological point of view, is nothing but a new pathway of discharge formed in the brain, by which certain incoming currents ever after tend to escape."

And again,—"First, habit simplifies our movements, makes them accurate, and diminishes fatigue,"[21] and habit diminishes the conscious attention with which our acts are performed. Again he says,

---

[18] As proved by experimenting with a six-year-old child.

[19] Imbert, *Etudes experimentales de travail professional ouvrier, Sur la fatigue engendree par les mouvements rapides.*

[20] William James, *Psychology, Briefer Course,* p. 134.

[21] *Ibid.,* p. 138. William James, Psychology, Advanced Course. p. 112.

page 144, "The great thing, then, in all education, is to make our nervous system our ally instead of an enemy; as it is to fund and capitalize our acquisitions, and live at ease upon the interest of the fund. For this we must make automatic and habitual, as early as possible, as many useful actions as we can, and guard against the growing into ways that are likely to be disadvantageous to us, as we should guard against the plague."

These quotations demonstrate the importance of habit.

How deep these paths of discharge are, is illustrated by the fact that often a German, having spent the early years of his school life in Germany, will, even after learning to speak, read, write and think in English, find it difficult to figure in anything but German.

Habit Easily Becomes the Master.—Another illustration of the power of habit is exhibited by the bricklayer, who has been trained under old-time methods, and who attempts to follow the packet method. The standard motions for picking up the upper row of bricks from the packet are entirely different from those for picking up the lower row. The bricklayers were taught this, yet invariably used the old-time motions for picking up the bricks, in spite of the waste involved.[22]

Wrong Preconceived Ideas Hamper Development.—Wrong habits or ideas often retard development. For example, it took centuries for artists to see the colors of shadows correctly, because they were sure that such shadows were a darker tone of the color itself.[23]

Teaching Under Scientific Management Results in Good Habits. —The aim of teaching under Scientific Management, as has been said, is to create good habits of thinking and good habits of doing.

Standards Lead to Right Methods of Thinking and Acting.—The standards of Scientific Management, as presented to the worker in the instruction card, lead to good habits, in that they present the best known method of doing the work. They thus aid the beginner, in that he need waste no time searching for right methods, but can acquire right habits at once. They aid the worker trained under an older, supplanted method, in that they wage a winning war against old-time, worn-out methods and traditions. Old motor images, which tend to cause motions, are overcome by standard images, which suggest, and pass into, standard motions. The spontaneous recurring of images under the old method is the familiar cause of inattention and

[22] F. B. Gilbreth, *Bricklaying System,* p. 142.
[23] Stratton, *Experimental Psychology and Culture,* p. 214.

being unable to get down to business, and the real cause of the expression, "You can't teach old dogs new tricks." On the other hand, the spontaneous recurrence of the images of the standard method is the cause of greater speed of movement of the experienced man, and these images of the standard methods do recur often enough to drive down the old images and to enable all men who desire, to settle down and concentrate upon what they are doing.

Through Standards Bad Habits Are Quickest Broken.—Through the standards the bad habit is broken by the abrupt acquisition of a new habit. This is at once practiced, is practiced without exception, and is continually practiced until the new habit is in control.[24]

Through Standards New Habits Are Quickest Formed.—These same standards, as presented in teaching, allow for the speediest forming of habits, in that repetition is exact and frequent, and is kept so by the fact that the worker's judgment seconds that of the teacher.

Habits Are Instilled by Teaching.—The chief function of the teacher during the stage that habits are being formed is the instilling of good habits.

Methods of Instilling Good Habits.—This he does by insisting on

1. right motions first, that is to say,—the right number of right motions in the right sequence.

2. speed of motions second, that is to say, constantly increasing speed.

3. constantly improving quality.[25]

This Method Is Contrary to Most Old-time Practice.—Under most old-time practice the quality of the work was the first consideration, the quantity of work the second, and the methods of achieving the results the third.

Results of Old-time Practice.—As a result, the mechanical reactions, which were expected constantly to follow the improved habits of work, were constantly hindered by an involuntary impulse of the muscles to follow the old methods. Waste time and low output followed.

Some Early Recognition of "Right Motions First."—The necessity of teaching the right motions first was early recognized by a few progressive spirits, as is shown in military tactics; for example, see pages 6 and 7, "Cavalry Tactics of U.S.A." 1879, D. Appleton, also page 51.

[24] Prof. Bain, quoted in William James' *Psychology, Briefer Course*, pp. 145–147.
[25] F. B. Gilbreth, *Bricklaying System*, para. 18–19.

Note also motions for grooming the horse, page 473. These directions not only teach the man how, but accustoms the horse to the sequence and location of motions that he may expect.

Benefits of Teaching Right Motions First.—Through teaching right motions first reactions to stimuli gain in speed. The right habit is formed at the outset. With the constant insistence on these right habits that result from right motions, will come, naturally, an increase in speed, which should be fostered until the desired ultimate speed is reached.

Ultimately, Standard Quality Will Result.—The result of absolute insistence on right motions will be prescribed quality, because the standard motions prescribed were chosen because they best produced the desired result.

Under Scientific Management No Loss from Quality During Learning.—As will be shown later, Scientific Management provides that there shall be little or no loss from the quality of the work during the learning period. The delay in time before the learner can be said to produce such work as could a learner taught where quality was insisted upon first of all, is more than compensated for by the ultimate combination of speed and quality gained.

Results of Teaching the Right Motions First Are Far-reaching.— There is no more important subject in this book on the Psychology of Management than this of teaching right motions first. The most important results of Scientific Management can all, in the last analysis, be formulated in terms of habits, even to the underlying spirit of coöperation which, as we shall show in "Welfare," is one of the most important ideas of Scientific Management. These right habits of Scientific Management are the cause, as well as the result, of progress, and the right habits, which have such a tremendous psychological importance, are the result of insisting that right motions be used from the very beginning of the first day.

From Right Habits of Motion Comes Speed of Motions.—Concentrating the mind on the next motion causes speed of motion. Under Scientific Management, the underlying thought of sequence of motions is so presented that the worker can remember them, and make them in the shortest time possible.

Response to Standards Becomes Almost Automatic.—The standard methods, being associated from the start with right habits of motions only, cause an almost automatic response. There are no discarded habits to delay response.

Steady Nerves Result.—Oftentimes the power to refrain from action is quite as much a sign of education and training as the power to react quickly from a sensation. Such conduct is called, in some cases, "steady nerves." The forming of right habits is a great aid toward these steady nerves. The man who knows that he is taught the right way, is able almost automatically to resist any suggestions which come to him to carry out wrong ways. So the man who is absolutely sure of his method, for example, in laying brick, will not be tempted to make those extra motions which, after all, are merely an exhibition in his hand of the vacillation that is going on in his brain, as to whether he really is handling that brick in exactly the most efficient manner, or not.

Reason and Will Are Educated.—"The education of hand and muscle implies a corresponding training of reasoning and will; and the coördination of movements accompanies the coördination of thoughts."[26]

The standards of Scientific Management educate hand and muscle; the education of hand and muscle train the mind; the mind improves the standards. Thus we have a continuous cycle.

Judgment Results with No Waste of Time.—Judgment is the outcome of learning the right way, and knowing that it is the right way. There is none of the lost time of "trying out" various methods that exists under Traditional Management.

This power of judgment will not only enable the possessor to decide correctly as to the relative merits of different methods, but also somewhat as to the past history and possibilities of different workers.

This, again, illustrates the wisdom of Scientific Management in promoting from the ranks, and thus providing that every member of the organization shall, ultimately, know from experience how to estimate and judge the work of others.

Habits of Attention Formed by Scientific Management.—The good habits which result from teaching standard methods result in habits of attention. The standards aid the mind in holding a "selective attitude,"[27] by presenting events in an orderly sequence. The conditions under which the work is done, and the incentives for doing it, provide that the attention shall be "lively and prolonged."

Prescribed Motions Afford Rhythm and Æsthetic Pleasure.—The

---

[26] M. W. Calkins, *A First Book in Psychology*, p. 354.
[27] James Sully, *The Teacher's Handbook of Psychology*, p. 119.

prescribed motions that result from motion study and time study, and that are arranged in cycles, afford a rhythm that allows the attention to "glide over some beats and linger on others," as Prof. Stratton describes it, in a different connection.[28] So also the "perfectly controlled" movements, which fall under the direction of a guiding law, and which "obey the will absolutely,"[29] give an æsthetic pleasure and afford less of a tax upon the attention.

Instruction Card Creates and Holds Attention.—As has been already said in describing the instruction card under standardization, it was designed as a result of investigations as to what would best secure output,—to attract and hold the attention.[30] Providing, as it does, all directions that an experienced worker is likely to need, he can confine his attention solely to his worker and his card; usually, after the card is once studied, to his work alone. The close relation of the elements of the instruction card affords a field for attention to lapse, and be recalled in the new elements that are constantly made apparent.

Oral Individual Teaching Fosters Concentrated Attention.—The fact that under Scientific Management oral teaching is individual, not only directly concentrates the attention of the learner upon what he is being taught, but also indirectly prevents distraction from fear of ridicule of others over the question, or embarrassment in talking before a crowd.

The Bulletin Board Furnishes the Element of Change.—In order that interest or attention may be held, there must be provision for allied subjects on which the mind is to wander. This, under Scientific Management, is constantly furnished by the collection of jobs ahead on the bulletin board. The tasks piled up ahead upon this bulletin board provide a needed and ready change for the subject of attention or interest, which conserves the economic value of concentrated attention of the worker upon his work. Such future tasks furnish sufficient range of subject for wandering attention to rest the mind from the wearying effect of overconcentration or forced attention. The assigned task of the future systematizes the "stream of attention," and an orderly scheme of habits of thought is installed. When the scheme is an orderly shifting of attention, the mind is doing its best work, for, while the standardized extreme subdivision of Taylor's

---

[28] Stratton, *Experimental Psychology and Culture*, p. 99.

[29] Stratton, *Experimental Psychology and Culture*, p. 240.

[30] Attracting the attention is largely a matter of appealing to what is known to interest, for example, to a known ambition.

plan, the comparison of the ultimate unit, and groupings of units of future tasks are often helps in achieving the present tasks, without such a definite orderly scheme for shifting the attention and interest, the attention will shift to useless subjects, and the result will be scattered.

Incentives Maintain Interest.—The knowledge that a prompt reward will follow success stimulates interest. The knowledge that this reward is sure concentrates attention and thus maintains interest.

In the same way, the assurance of promotion, and the fact that the worker sees those of his own trade promoted, and knows it is to the advantage of the management, as well as to his advantage, that he also be promoted,—this also maintains interest in the work.

This Interest Extends to the Work of Others.—The interest is extended to the work of others, not only by the interrelated bonuses, but also by the fact that every man is expected to train up a man to take his place, before he is promoted.

Close Relationship of All Parts of Scientific Management Holds Interest.—The attention of the entire organization, as well as of the individual worker, is held by Scientific Management and its teaching, because all parts of Scientific Management are related, and because Scientific Management provides for scientifically directed progression. Every member of the organization knows that the standards which are taught by Scientific Management contain the permanent elements of past successes, and provide for such development as will assure progress and success in the future. Every member of the organization realizes that upon his individual coöperation depends, in part, the stability of Scientific Management, because it is based on universal coöperation. This provides an intensity and a continuity of interest that would still hold, even though some particular element might lose its interest.

This Relationship Also Provides for Associations.—The close relationship of all parts of Scientific Management provides that all ideas are associated, and are so closely connected that they can act as a single group, or any selected number of elements can act as a group.

Scientific Management Establishes Brain Groups That Habitually Act in Unison.—Professor Read, in describing the general mental principle of association says, "When any number of brain cells have been in action together, they form a habit of acting in unison, so that when one of them is stimulated in a certain way, the others will also behave in the way established by the habit."[31] This working of the brain is recognized in grouping of motions, such as "playing for position."[32] Scientific Management provides the groups, the habit, and the stimulus, all according to standard methods, so that the result is largely predictable.

Method of Establishing Such Groups in the Worker's Brain.—The standard elements of Scientific Management afford units for such groups. Eventually, with the use of such elements in instruction cards, would be formed, in the minds of the worker, such groups of units as would aid in foreseeing results, just as the foreseeing of groups of moves aids the expert chess or checker player. The size and number of such groups would indicate the skill of the worker.

That such skill may be gained quickest, Scientific Management synthesizes the units into definite groups, and teaches these to the workers as groups.

Teaching Done by Means of Motion Cycles.—The best group is that which completes the simplest cycle of performance. This enables the worker to associate certain definite motions, to make these into a habit, and to concentrate his attention upon the cycle as a whole, and not upon the elementary motions of which it is composed.

For example—The cycle of the pick and dip process of bricklaying is to pick up a brick and a trowel full of mortar simultaneously and deposit them on the wall simultaneously.[33] The string mortar method has two cycles, which are, first to pick a certain number of trowelfuls of mortar and deposit them on the wall, and then to pick up a corresponding number of bricks and deposit them on the wall.[34] Each cycle of these two methods consists of an association of units that can be remembered as a group.

Such Cycles Induce Speed.—The worker who has been taught thus to associate the units of attention and action into definite rhythmic cycles, is the one who is most efficient, and least fatigued by a given output. The nerves acquire the habit, as does the brain, and the resulting swift response to stimulus characterizes the efficiency of the specialist.[35]

Scientific Management Restricts Associations.—By its teaching of

[31] M. S. Read, *An Introductory Psychology*, p. 183.
[32] F. B. Gilbreth, *Motion Study*, p. 83.
[33] *Ibid., Bricklaying System.*
[34] F. B. Gilbreth, *Bricklaying System*, p. 150.
[35] M. S. Read, *An Introductory Psychology*, pp. 179–194.

standard methods, Scientific Management restricts association, and thus gains in the speed with which associated ideas arise.[36] Insistence on casual sequence is a great aid. This is rendered by the Systems, which give the reasons, and make the standard method easy to remember.

Scientific Management Presents Scientifically Derived Knowledge to the Memory.—Industrial memory is founded on experience, and that experience that is submitted by teaching under Scientific Management to the mind is in the form of scientifically derived standards. These furnish

(a) data that are correct.

(b) images that are an aid in acquiring new habits of forming efficient images.

(c) standards of comparison, and constant demands for comparison.

(d) such arrangement of elements that reasoning processes are stimulated.

(e) conscious, efficient grouping.

(f) logical association of ideas.

Provision for Repetition of Important Ideas.—Professor Ebbinghaur says, "Associations that have equal reproductive power lapse the more slowly, the older they are, and the oftener they have been reviewed by renewed memorizing." Scientific Management provides for utilizing this law by teaching right motions first, and by so minutely dividing the elements of such motions that the smallest units discovered are found frequently, in similar and different operations.

Best Periods for Memorizing Utilized.—As for education of the memory, there is a wide difference of opinion among leading psychologists in regard to whether or not the memorizing faculty, as the whole, can be improved by training; but all agree that those things which are specially desired to be memorized can be learned more easily, and more quickly, under some conditions than under others:

For example, there is a certain time of day, for each person, when the memory is more efficient than at other times. This is usually in the morning, but is not always so. The period when memorizing is easiest is taken advantage of, and, as far as possible, new methods and new instruction cards are passed out at that time when the worker is naturally best fitted to remember what is to be done.

Individual Differences Respected.—It is a question that varies

[36] G. M. Stratton, *Experimental Psychology and Culture*, p. 42.

with different conditions, whether the several instruction cards beyond the one he is working on shall be given to the worker ahead of time, that he may use his own judgment as to when is the best time to learn, or whether he shall have but one at a time, and concentrate on that. For certain dispositions, it is a great help to see a long line of work ahead. They enjoy getting the work done, and feeling that they are more or less ahead of record. Others become confused if they see too much ahead, and would rather attack but one problem at a time. This fundamental difference in types of mind should be taken advantage of when laying out material to be memorized.

Aid of Mnemonic Symbols to the Memory.—The mnemonic classifications furnish a place where the worker who remembers but little of a method or process can go, and recover the full knowledge of that which he has forgotten. Better still, they furnish him the equivalent of memory of other experiences that he has never had, and that are in such form that he can connect this with his memory of his own personal experience.

The ease with which a learner or skilled mechanic can associate new, scientifically derived data with his memory, because of the classifications of Scientific Management, is a most important cause of workers being taught quicker, and being more intelligent, under Scientific Management, than under any other type of management.

Proper Learning Insures Proper Remembering.—Professor Read says, "Take care of the learning and the remembering will take care of itself."[37] Scientific Management both provides proper knowledge, and provides that this shall be utilized in such a manner that proper remembering will ensue.

Better Habits of Remembering Result.—The results of cultivating the memory under Scientific Management are cumulative. Ultimately, right habits of remembering result that aid the worker automatically so to arrange his memory material as to utilize it better.[38]

"Imagination" Has Two Definitions.—Professor Read gives definitions for two distinct means of Imagination.

1. "The general function of the having of images."

2. "The particular one of having images which are not consciously memories or the reproduction of the facts of experience as they were originally presented to consciousness."[39]

Scientific Management Provides Material for Images.—As was

[37] M. S. Read, *An Introductory Psychology*, p. 208.
[38] William James, *Psychology, Advanced Course*, Vol. I, p. 667.
[39] M. S. Read, *An Introductory Psychology*, pp. 212–213. William James, *Psychology, Briefer Course*, p. 302.

shown under the discussion of the appeals of the various teaching devices of Scientific Management,—provision is made for the four classes of imagination of Calkins[40]—

1. visual,
2. auditory,
3. tactual, and
4. mixed.

It Also Realizes the Importance of Productive Imagination.— Scientific Management realizes that one of the special functions of teaching the trades is systematic exercising and guiding of imaginations of apprentices and learners. As Professor Ennis says,—"Any kind of planning ahead will result in some good," but to plan ahead most effectively it is necessary to have a well-developed power of constructive imagination. This consists of being able to construct new mental images from old memory images; of being able to modify and group images of past experiences, or thoughts, in combination with new images based on imagination, and not on experience. The excellence of the image arrived at in the complete work is dependent wholly upon the training in image forming in the past. If there has not been a complete economic system of forming standard habits of thought, the worker may have difficulty in controlling the trend of associations of thought images, and difficulty in adding entirely new images to the groups of experienced images, and the problem to be thought out will suffer from wandering of the mind. The result will be more like a dream than a well balanced mental planning. It is well known that those apprentices, and journeymen as well, are the quickest to learn, and are better learners, who have the most vivid imagination. The best method of teaching the trade, therefore, is the one that also develops the power of imagination.

Scientific Management Assists Productive Imagination.—Scientific Management assists productive, or constructive, imagination, not only by providing standard units, or images, from which the results may be synthesized, but also, through the unity of the instruction card, allows of imagination of the outcome, from the start.

For example,—in performing a prescribed cycle of motions, the worker has his memory images grouped in such a figure, form, or sequence,—often geometrical,—that each motion is a part of a growing, clearly imagined whole.

The elements of the cycle may be utilized in other entirely new

[40] M. W. Calkins, *A First Book in Psychology*, p. 25.

cycles, and are, as provided for in the opportunities for invention that are a part of Scientific Management.

Judgment the Result of Faithful Endeavor.—Judgment, or the "mental process which ends in an affirmation or negation of something,"[41] comes as the result of experience, as is admirably expressed by Prof. James,—"Let no youth have any anxiety about the upshot of his education whatever the line of it may be. If he keeps faithfully busy each hour of the working day, he may safely leave the final result to itself. He can with perfect certainty count on waking up some fine morning, to find himself one of the competent ones of his generation, in whatever pursuit he may have singled out. Silently, between all the details of his business, the *power of judging* in all that class of matter will have built itself up within him as a possession that will never pass away. Young people should know this truth in advance.[42] The ignorance of it has probably engendered more discouragement and faint-heartedness in youths embarking on arduous careers than all other causes put together."[43]

Teaching Supplies This Judgment Under Scientific Management. —Under Scientific Management this judgment is the result of teaching of standards that are recognized as such by the learner. Thus, much time is eliminated, and the apprentice under Scientific Management can work with all the assurance as to the value of his methods that characterized the seasoned veterans of older types of management.

Teaching Also Utilizes the Judgment.—The judgment that is supplied by Scientific Management is also used as a spring toward action.[44] Scientific Management appeals to the reason, and workers perform work as they do because, through the Systems and otherwise, they are persuaded that the method they employ is the best.

The Power of Suggestion Is Also Utilized.[45]—The dynamic power of ideas is recognized by Scientific Management, in that the instruction card is put in the form of direct commands, which, naturally, lead to immediate action. So, also, the teaching written, oral and object, as such, can be directly imitated by the learner.[46]

Imitation, which Dr. Stratton says "may well be counted a special

[41] James Sully, *The Teacher's Handbook of Psychology*, p. 290.
[42] William James, *Psychology, Briefer Course*, p. 150.
[43] W. D. Scott, *Influencing Men in Business*, chap. II.
[44] *Ibid.*, chap. III.
[45] W. D. Scott, *The Theory of Advertising*, p. 71.
[46] W. D. Scott, *Increasing Human Efficiency in Business*, p. 41.

form of suggestion," will be discussed later in this chapter at length.[47]

Worker Always Has Opportunity to Criticise the Suggestion.—
The worker is expected to follow the suggestion of Scientific Management without delay, because he believes in the standardization on which it is made, and in the management that makes it. But the Systems afford him an opportunity of reviewing the reasonableness of the suggestion at any time, and his constructive criticism is invited and rewarded.

Suggestion Must Be Followed at the Time.—The suggestion must be followed at the time it is given, or its value as a suggestion is impaired. This is provided for by the underlying idea of coöperation on which Scientific Management rests, which molds the mental attitude of the worker into that form where suggestions are quickest grasped and followed.[48]

"Native Reactions" Enumerated by Prof. James.—Prof. James enumerates the "native reactions" as (1) fear, (2) love, (3) curiosity, (4) imitation, (5) emulation, (6) ambition, (7) pugnacity, (8) pride, (9) ownership, (10) constructiveness.[49] These are all considered by Scientific Management. Such as might have a harmful effect are supplanted, others are utilized.

Fear Utilized by Ancient Managers.—The native reaction most utilized by the first managers of armies and ancient works of construction was that of fear. This is shown by the ancient rock carvings, which portray what happened to those who disobeyed.[50]

Fear Still Used by Traditional Management.—Fear of personal bodily injury is not usual under modern Traditional Management, but fear of less progress, less promotion, less remuneration, or of discharge, or of other penalties for inferior effort or efficiency is still prevalent.

Fear Transformed Under Scientific Management.—Under Scientific Management the worker may still fear that he will incur a penalty, or fail to deserve a reward, but the honest, industrious worker experiences no such horror as the old-time fear included. This is removed by his knowledge.

1. that his task is achievable.
2. that his work will not injure his health.

[47] G. M. Stratton, *Experimental Psychology and Culture,* p. 200.
[48] F. W. Taylor, *The Principles of Scientific Management,* p. 36.
[49] William James, *Talks to Teachers,* chap. III.
[50] Knight's *Mechanical Dictionary,* Vol. III, p. 2204.

3. that he may be sure of advancement with age and experience.

4. that he is sure of the "square deal."

Thus such fear as he has, has a good and not an evil effect upon him. It is an incentive to coöperate willingly. Its immediate and ultimate effects are advantageous.

Love, or Loyalty, Fostered by Scientific Management.—The worker's knowledge that the management plans to maintain such conditions as will enable him to have the four assurances enumerated above leads to love, or loyalty, between workers and employers.[51]

Far from Scientific Management abolishing the old personal and sympathetic relations between employers and workers, it gives opportunities for such relations as have not existed since the days of the guilds, and the old apprenticeship.[52]

The coöperation upon which Scientific Management rests does away with the traditional "warfare" between employer and workers that made permanent friendliness almost impossible. Coöperation induces friendliness and loyalty of each member in the organization to all the others.

Mr. Wilfred Lewis says, in describing the installation of Scientific Management in his plant, "We had, in effect, been installing at great expense a new and wonderful means for increasing the efficiency of labor, in the benefits of which the workman himself shared, and we have today an organization second, I believe, to none in its loyalty, efficiency and steadfastness of purpose."[53] This same loyalty of the workers is plain in an article in *Industrial Engineering*, on "Scientific Management as Viewed from the Workman's Standpoint," where various men in a shop having Scientific Management were interviewed.[54] After quoting various workers' opinions of Scientific Management and their own particular shop, the writer says: "Conversations with other men brought out practically the same facts. They are all contented. They took pride in their work, and seemed to be especially proud of the fact that they were employed in the Link-Belt shops."[55]

Teaching Under Scientific Management Develops Such Loyalty.—The manner of teaching under Scientific Management fosters such

[51] For example, see W. D. Scott's *Increasing Efficiency in Business,* chap. IV.
[52] R. A. Bray, *Boy Labor and Apprenticeship,* chap. II, especially p. 8.
[53] Wilfred Lewis, *Proceedings of the Congress of Technology,* 1911, p. 175.
[54] November, 1910.
[55] The Link-Belt Co., Philadelphia, Pa.

loyalty. Only through friendly aid can both teacher and taught prosper. Also, the perfection of the actual workings of this plan of management inspires regard as well as respect for the employer.

Value of Personality Not Eliminated.—It is a great mistake to think that Scientific Management under-estimates the value of personality.[56] Rather, Scientific Management enhances the value of an admirable personality. This is well exemplified in the Link-Belt Co.,[57] and in the Tabor Manufacturing Co. of Philadelphia, as well as on other work where Scientific Management has been installed a period of several years.

Curiosity Aroused by Scientific Management.—Scientific Management arouses the curiosity of the worker, by showing, through its teaching, glimpses of the possibility that exist for further scientific investigation. The insistence on standard methods of less waste arouses a curiosity as to whether still less wasteful methods cannot be found.

Curiosity Utilized by Scientific Management.—The curiosity is very useful as a trait of the learner, the planner and the investigator. It can be well utilized by the teacher who recognizes it in the learner, by an adaptation of methods of interpreting the instruction card, that will allow of partially satisfying, and at the same time further exciting, the curiosity.

In selecting men for higher positions, and for special work, curiosity as to the work, with the interest that is its result, may serve as an admirable indication of one sort of fitness. This curiosity, or general interest, is usually associated with a personal interest that makes it more intense, and more easy to utilize.

Scientific Management Places a High Value on Imitation.—It was a popular custom of the past to look down with scorn on the individual or organization that imitated others. Scientific Management believes that to imitate with great precision the best, is a work of high intelligence and industrial efficiency.

Scientific Management Uses Both Spontaneous and Deliberate Imitation.—Teaching under Scientific Management induces both spontaneous and deliberate imitation. The standardization prevalent, and the conformity to standards exacted, provide that this imitation shall follow directed lines.

[56] For value of personality see J. W. Jenks's *Governmental Action for Social Welfare*, p. 226.

[57] F. W. Taylor, *Shop Management*, para. 311, Harper Ed., p. 143.

Spontaneous Imitation Under Scientific Management Has Valuable Results.—Under Scientific Management, the worker will spontaneously imitate the teacher, when the latter has been demonstrating. This leads to desired results. So, also, the worker imitates, more or less spontaneously, his own past methods of doing work. The right habits early formed by Scientific Management insure that the results of such imitation shall be profitable.

Deliberate Imitation Constantly Encouraged.—Deliberate imitation is caused more than anything else by the fact that the man knows, if he does the thing in the way directed, his pay will be increased.

Such imitation is also encouraged by the fact that the worker is made to believe that he is capable, and has the will to overcome obstacles. He knows that the management believes he can do the work, or the instruction card would not have been issued to him. Moreover, he sees that the teacher and demonstrator is a man promoted from his rank, and he is convinced, therefore, that what the teacher can do he also can do.

Scientific Management Provides Standards for Imitation.—It is of immense value in obtaining valuable results from imitation, that Scientific Management provides standards. Under Traditional Management, it was almost impossible for a worker to decide which man he should imitate. Even though he might come to determine, by constant observation, after a time, which man he desired to imitate, he would not know in how far he would do well to copy any particular method. Recording individually measured output under Transitory Management allows of determining the man of high score, and either using him as a model, or formulating his method into rules. Under Scientific Management, the instruction card furnishes a method which the worker knows that he can imitate exactly, with predetermined results.

Imitation Is Expected of All.—As standardization applies to the work of all, so imitation of standards is expected of all. This fact the teacher under Scientific Management can use to advantage, as an added incentive to imitation. Any dislike of imitation is further decreased, by making clear to every worker that those who are under him are expected to imitate him,—and that he must, himself, imitate his teachers, in order to set a worthy example.

Imitation Leads to Emulation.—Imitation, as provided for by teaching under Scientific Management, and admiration for the skillful teacher, or the standard imitated, naturally stimulate emulation. This emulation takes three forms:

1. Competition with the records of others.
2. Competition with one's own record.
3. Competition with the standard record.

No Hard Feeling Aroused.—In the first sort of competition only is there a possibility of hard feeling being aroused, but danger of this is practically eliminated by the fact that rewards are provided for all who are successful. In the second sort of competition, the worker, by matching himself against what he has done, measures his own increased efficiency. In the third sort of competition, there is the added stimulus of surprising the management by exceeding the task expected. The incentive in all three cases is not only more pay and a chance for promotion, but also the opportunity to win appreciation and publicity for successful performance.

Ambition Is Aroused.—The outcome of emulation is ambition. This ambition is stimulated by the fact that promotion is so rapid, and so outlined before the worker, that he sees the chance for advancement himself, and not only advancement that means more pay, but advancement also that means a chance to specialize on that work which he particularly likes.

Pugnacity Utilized.—Pugnacity can never be entirely absent where there is emulation. Under Scientific Management it is used to overcome not persons, but things. Pugnacity is a great driving force. It is a wonderful thing that under Scientific Management this force is aroused not against one's fellow-workers, but against one's work. The desire to win out, to fight it out, is aroused against a large task, which the man desires to put behind him. Moreover, there is nothing under Scientific Management which forbids an athletic contest. While the workers would not, under the ultimate form, be allowed to injure themselves by overspeeding, a friendly race with a demonstration of pugnacity which harms no one is not frowned upon.

Pride Is Stimulated.—Pride in one's work is aroused as soon as work is functionalized. The moment a man has something to do that he likes to do, and can do well, he takes pride in it. So, also, the fact that individuality, and personality, are recognized, and that his records are shown, makes pride serve as a stimulus. The outcome of the worker's pride in his work is pride in himself. He finds that he is part of a great whole, and he learns to take pride in the entire management,—in both himself and the managers, as well as in his own work.

Feeling of Ownership Provided For.—It may seem at first glance that the instinct of ownership is neglected, and becomes stunted, under Scientific Management, in that all tools become more or less standardized, and the man is discouraged from having tools peculiar in shape, or size, for whose use he has no warrant except long time of use.

Careful consideration shows that Scientific Management provides two opportunities for the worker to conserve his instinct for ownership,—

1. During working hours, where the recognition of his personality allows the worker to identify himself with his work, and where his coöperation with the management makes him identified with its activities.

2. Outside the work. He has, under Scientific Management, more hours away from work to enjoy ownership, and more money with which to acquire those things that he desires to own.

The teacher must make clear to him both these opportunities, as he readily can, since the instinct of ownership is conserved in him in an identical manner.

Constructiveness a Part of Scientific Management.—Every act that the worker performs is constructive, because waste has been eliminated, and everything that is done is upbuilding. Teaching makes this clear to the worker. Constructiveness is also utilized in that exercise of initiative is provided for. Thus the instinct, instead of being weakened, is strengthened and directed.

Progress in Utilizing Instincts Demands Psychological Study.—Teaching under Scientific Management can never hope fully to understand and utilize native reactions, until more assistance has been given by psychology. At the present time, Scientific Management labors under disadvantages that must, ultimately, be removed. Psychologists must, by experiments, determine more accurately the reactions and their controlability. More thorough study must be made of children that Scientific Management may understand more of the nature of the reactions of the young workers who come for industrial training. Psychology must give its help in this training. Then only, can teaching under Scientific Management become truly efficient.

Scientific Management Realizes the Importance of Training the Will.—The most necessary, and most complex and difficult part of Scientific Management, is the training of the will of all members of the organization. Prof. Read states in his "Psychology" five means of training or influencing the will. These are[58]

"1. The first important feature in training the will is the help furnished by supplying the mind with a useful body of ideas,"

"2. The second great feature of the training of the will is the building up in the mind of the proper interests, and the habit of giving the attention to useful and worthy purposes."

"3. Another important feature of the training of the will is the establishing of a firm association between ideas and actions, or, in other words, the forming of a good set of habits."

"4. Another very important feature of the training of the will has reference to its strength of purpose or power of imitation."

"5. The matter of discipline."

Teaching under Scientific Management does supply these five functions, and thus provide for the strengthening and development of the will.

Variations in Teaching of Apprentices and Journeymen.—Scientific Management must not only be prepared to teach apprentices, as must all types of management, it must also teach journeymen who have not acquired standard methods.

Apprentices Are Easily Handled.—Teaching apprentices is a comparatively simple proposition, far simpler than under any other type of management. Standard methods enable the apprentice to become proficient long before his brother could, under the old type of teaching. The length of training required depends largely on how fingerwise the apprentice is.

Older Workers Must Be Handled with Tact.—With adult workers, the problem is not so simple. Old wrong habits, such as the use of ineffective motions, must be eliminated. Physically, it is difficult for the adult worker to alter his methods. Moreover, it may be most difficult to change his mental attitude, to convince him that the methods of Scientific Management are correct.

A successful worker under Traditional Management, who is proud of his work, will often be extremely sensitive to what he is prone to regard as the "criticism" of Scientific Management with regard to him.

[58] M. S. Read, *An Introductory Psychology*, pp. 297–303.

Appreciation of Varying Viewpoints Necessary.—No management can consider itself adequate that does not try to enter into the mental attitude of its workers. Actual practice shows that, with time and tact, almost any worker can be convinced that all criticism of him is constructive, and that for him to conform to the new standards is a mark of added proficiency, not an acknowledgment of ill-preparedness. The "Systems" do much toward this work of reconciling the older workers to the new methods, but most of all can be done by such teachers as can demonstrate their own change from old to standard methods, and the consequent promotion and success. This is, again, an opportunity for the exercise of personality.

Scientific Management Provides Places for Such Teaching.— Under the methods of teaching employed by Scientific Management, —right motions first, next speed, with quality as a resultant product, —it is most necessary to provide a place where learners can work. The standard planning of quality provides such a place. The plus and minus signs automatically divide labor so that the worker can be taught by degrees, being set at first where great accuracy is not demanded by the work, and being shifted to work requiring more accuracy as he becomes more proficient. In this way even the most untrained worker becomes efficient, and is engaged in actual productive work.

Measurement of Teaching and Learning.—Under Scientific Management the results of teaching and learning become apparent automatically in records of output. The learner's record of output of proper prescribed quality determines what pay he shall receive, and also has a proportionate effect on the teacher's pay. Such a system of measurement may not be accurate as a report of the learner's gain,— for he doubtless gains mental results that cannot be seen in his output,—but it certainly does serve as an incentive to teaching and to learning.

Relation of Teaching in Scientific Management to Academic Training and Vocational Guidance.[59]—Teaching under Scientific Management can never be most efficient until the field of such teaching is restricted to training learners who are properly prepared to receive industrial training.[60] This preparedness implies fitting school and academic training, and Vocational Guidance.

[59] Hugo Münsterberg, *American Problems,* p. 29.
[60] Morris Llewellyn Cooke, *Bulletin No. 5 of The Carnegie Foundation for the Advancement of Teaching,* p. 70. William Kent, *Discussion of Paper 647,* A. S. M. E., p. 891.

Learner Should Be Manually Adept.—The learner should, before entering the industrial world, be taught to be manually adept, or fingerwise, to have such control over his trained muscles that they will respond quickly and accurately to orders. Such training should be started in infancy,[61] in the form of guided play, as, for example, whittling, sewing, knitting, handling mechanical toys and tools, and playing musical instruments, and continued up to, and into, the period of entering a trade.

Schools Should Provide Mental Preparedness.—The schools should render every student capable of filling some place worthily in the industries. The longer the student remains in school, the higher the position for which he should be prepared. The amount and nature of the training in the schools depends largely on the industrial work to be done, and will be possible of more accurate estimation constantly, as Scientific Management standardizes work and shows what the worker must be to be most efficient.

Vocational Guidance Must Provide Direction.—As made most clear in Mr. Meyer Bloomfield's book, "Vocational Guidance,"[62] bureaus of competent directors stand ready to help the youth find that line of activity which he can follow best and with greatest satisfaction to himself. At present, such bureaus are seriously handicapped by the fact that little data of the industries are at hand, but this lack the bureaus are rapidly supplying by gathering such data as are available. Most valuable data will not be available until Scientific Management has been introduced into all lines.

Progress Demands Coöperation.—Progress here, as everywhere, demands coöperation.[63] The three sets of educators,—the teachers in the school, in the Vocational Guidance Bureaus, and in Scientific Management, must recognize their common work, and must coöperate to do it. There is absolutely no cause for conflict between the three; their fields are distinct, but supplementary. Vocational Guidance is the intermediary between the other two.

SUMMARY

Results to the Work.—Under the teaching of Traditional Management, the learner may or may not improve the quantity and quality

---

[61] A well known athlete started throwing a ball at his son in infancy, to prepare him to be an athlete, thus practically sure of a college education.

[62] Meyer Bloomfield, *The Vocational Guidance of Youth*, Houghton Mifflin & Co.

[63] A. Pimloche, *Pestalozzi and the Foundation of the Modern Elementary School*, p. 139.

of his work. This depends almost entirely on the particular teacher whom the learner happens to have. There is no standard improvement to the work.

Under the teaching of Transitory Management, the work gains in quantity as the methods become standardized, and quality is maintained or improved.

Under the teaching of Scientific Management, work, the quantity of work, increases enormously through the use of standards of all kinds; quantity is oftentimes tripled.

Under the teaching of Scientific Management, when the schools and Vocational Guidance movement coöperate, high output of required quality will be obtained at a far earlier stage of the worker's industrial life than is now possible, even under Scientific Management.

Results to the Worker.—Under Traditional Management, the worker gains a knowledge of how his work can be done, but the method by which he is taught is seldom, of itself, helpful to him. Not being sure that he has learned the best way to do his work, he gains no method of attack. The result of the teaching is a habit of doing work which is good, or bad, as chance may direct.

Under Transitory Management, with the use of Systems as teachers, the worker gains a better method of attack, as he knows the reason why the prescribed method is prescribed. He begins to appreciate the possibilities and benefits of standardized teaching.

The method laid down under Scientific Management is devised to further the forming of an accurate accumulation of concepts, which results in a proper method of attack. The method of instruction under Scientific Management is devised to furnish two things:

1. A collection of knowledge relating in its entirety to the future work of the learner.

2. A definite procedure, that will enable the learner to apply the same process to acquiring knowledge of other subjects in the most economical and efficient way.

It teaches the learner to be observant of details, which is the surest method for further development of general truths and concepts.

The method of attack of the methods provided for in Scientific Management results, naturally, in a comparison of true data. This is the most efficient method of causing the learner to think for himself.

Processes differing but little, apparently, give vastly different results, and the trained habits of observation quickly analyze and determine wherein the one process is more efficient than the other.

This result is, of course, the one most desired for causing quick and intelligent learning.

The most valuable education is that which enables the learner to make correct judgments. The teaching under Scientific Management leads to the acquisition of such judgment, plus an all-around sense training, a training in habits of work, and a progressive development.

A partial topic list of the results may make more clear their importance.

1. Worker better trained for all work.
2. Habits of correct thinking instilled.
3. Preparedness provided for.
4. Productive and repetitive powers increased.
5. Sense powers increased.
6. Habits of proper reaction established.
7. "Guided original work" established.
8. System of waste elimination provided.
9. Method of attack taught.
10. Brain fully developed.
11. "Standard response" developed.
12. Opportunities and demands for "thinking" provided.
13. Self-reliance developed.
14. Love of truth fostered.
15. Moral sentiment developed.
16. Resultant happiness of worker.

Results To Be Expected in the Future.—When the schools, vocational guidance and teaching under Scientific Management coöperate, the worker will not only receive the benefits now obtained from Scientific Management, but many more. There will be nothing to unlearn, and each thing that is learned will be taught by those best fitted to teach it. The collection of vocational guidance data will begin with a child at birth, and a record of his inheritance will be kept. This will be added to as he is educated, and as various traits and tendencies appear. From this scientifically derived record will accrue such data as will assist in making clear exactly in what place the worker will be most efficient, and in what sphere he will be able to be most helpful to the world, as well as to himself. All early training will be planned to make the youth adept with his muscles, and alert, with a mind so trained that related knowledge is easily acquired.

When the vocation for which he is naturally best fitted becomes apparent, as it must from the study of the development of the youth and his desires, the school will know, and can give exactly, that training that is necessary for the vocation. It can also supplement his limitations intelligently, in case he decides to follow a vocation for which he is naturally handicapped.

This will bring to the industry learners prepared to be taught those things that characterize the industry, the "tricks of the trade," and the "secrets of the craft," now become standard, and free to all. Such teaching Scientific Management is prepared to give. The results of such teaching of Scientific Management will be a worker prepared in a short time to fill efficiently a position which will allow of promotion to the limit of his possibilities.

The result of such teaching will be truly educated workers, equipped to work, and to live,[64] and to share the world's permanent satisfactions.

The effect of such education on industrial peace must not be underestimated. With education, including in education learning and culture,—prejudice will disappear. The fact that all men, those going into industries and those not, will be taught alike to be finger wise as well as book wise, up to the time of entering the industries, will lead to a better understanding of each other all through life.

The entire bearing of Scientific Management on industrial peace cannot be here fully discussed. We must note here the strong effect that teaching under Scientific Management will ultimately have on doing away with industrial warfare,—the great warfare of ignorance, where neither side understands the other, and where each side should realize that large immediate sacrifices should be made if necessary, that there may be obtained the great permanent benefit and savings that can be obtained only by means of the heartiest coöperation.

---

[64] Friedrich Froebel, *Education of Man,* "To secure for this ability skill and directness, to lift it into full consciousness, to give it insight and clearness, and to exalt it into a life of creative freedom, is the business of the subsequent life of man in successive stages of development and cultivation."

Incentives

●●●

Definition of Incentive.—An "incentive" is defined by the Century Dictionary as "that which moves the mind or stirs the passions; that which incites or tends to incite to action; motive, spur." Synonyms—"impulse, stimulus, incitement, encouragement, goad."

Importance of the Incentive.—The part that the incentive plays in the doing of all work is enormous. This is true in learning, and also in the performance of work which is the result of this learning: manual work and mental work as well. The business man finishing his work early that he may go to the baseball game; the boy at school rushing through his arithmetic that he may not be kept after school; the piece-worker, the amount of whose day's pay depends upon the quantity and quality he can produce; the student of a foreign language preparing for a trip abroad,—these all illustrate the importance of the incentive as an element in the amount which is to be accomplished.

Two Kinds of Incentives.—The incentive may be of two kinds: it may be first of all, a return, definite or indefinite, which is to be received when a certain portion of the work is done, or it may be an incentive due to the working conditions themselves. The latter case is exemplified where two people are engaged in the same sort of work and start in to race one another to see who can accomplish the most, who can finish the fixed amount in the shortest space of time, or who can produce the best quality. The incentive may be in the form of some definite aim or goal which is understood by the worker himself, or it may be in some natural instinct which is roused by the work, either consciously to the worker, or consciously to the man who is assigning the work, or consciously to both, or consciously to neither one. In any of these cases it is a natural instinct that is being appealed to and that induces the man to do more work, whether he sees any material reward for that work or not.

462

Definitions of Two Types.—We may call the incentive which utilizes the natural instinct, "direct incentive," and the incentive which utilizes these secondarily, through some set reward or punishment, "indirect incentive." This, at first sight, may seem a contradictory use of terms—it may seem that the reward would be the most direct of incentives; yet a moment's thought will cause one to realize that all the reward can possibly do is to arouse in the individual a natural instinct which will lead him to increase his work.

Indirect Incentives Include Two Classes.—We will discuss the indirect incentives first as, contrary to the usual use of the word "indirect," they are most easy to estimate and to describe. They divide themselves into two classes, reward and punishment.

Definition of Reward.—Reward is defined by the Century Dictionary as—"return, recompense, the fruit of one's labor or works; profit," with synonyms, "pay, compensation, remuneration, requital and retribution." Note particularly the word "retribution," for it is this aspect of reward, that is, the just outcome of one's act, that makes the reward justly include punishment. The word "reward" exactly expresses what management would wish to be understood by the incentive that it gives its men to increase their work.

Definition of Punishment.—The word "punishment" is defined as—"pain, suffering, loss, confinement, or other penalty inflicted on a person for a crime or offense by the authority to which the offender is subject," with synonyms, "chastisement, correction, discipline."

The word punishment, as will be noted later, is most unfortunate when applied to what Scientific Management would mean by a penalty, though this word also is unfortunate; but, in the first place, there is no better word to cover the general meaning; and in the second place, the idea of pain and suffering, which Scientific Management aims to and does eliminate, is present in some of the older forms of management. Therefore the word punishment must stand.

Rewards and Punishments Result in Action.—There can be no doubt that a reward is an incentive. There may well be doubt as to whether a punishment is an incentive to action or not. This, however, is only at first glance, and the whole thing rests on the meaning of the word "action." To be active is certainly the opposite of being at rest. This being true, punishment is just as surely an incentive to action as is reward. The man who is punished in every case will be led to some sort of action. Whether this really results in an increase of output or not simply determines whether the punishment is a scientifically prescribed punishment or not. If the punishment is of such a nature that the output ceases because of it, or that it incites the man punished against the general good, then it does not in any wise cease to be an active thing, but it is simply a wrong, and unscientifically assigned punishment, that acts in a detrimental way.

Soldiering Alone Cuts Down Activity.—It is interesting to note that the greatest cause for cutting down output is related more closely to a reward than a punishment. Under such managements as provide no adequate reward for all, and no adequate assurance that all can receive extra rewards permanently without a cut in the rate, it may be advisable, for the worker's best interests, to limit output in order to keep the wages, or reward, up, and soldiering results. The evils of soldiering will be discussed more at length under the "Systems of Pay." It is plain, however, here that soldiering is the result of a cutting down of action, and it is self-evident that anything which cuts down action is harmful, not only to the individual himself, but to society at large.

Nature of Rewards and Punishments.—Under all types of management, the principal rewards consist of promotion and pay, pay being a broad word used here to include regular wages, a bonus, shorter hours, other forms of remuneration or recompense; anything which can be given to the man who does the work to benefit him and increase his desire to continue doing the work. Punishments may be negative, that is, they may simply take the form of no reward; or they may be positive, that is, they may include fines, discharge, assignment to less remunerative or less desirable work, or any other thing which can be given to the man to show him that he has not done what is expected of him and, in theory at least, to lead him to do better.

Nature of Direct Incentives.—Direct incentives will be such native reaction as ambition, pride and pugnacity; will be love of racing, love of play; love of personal recognition; will be the outcome of self-confidence and interest, and so on.

The Reward Under Traditional Management Unstandardized.—As with all other discussion of any part or form of Traditional Management, the discussion of the incentive under Traditional Management is vague from the very nature of the subject. "Traditional" stands for vagueness and for variation, for the lack of standardization, for the lack of definiteness in knowledge, in process, in results. The rewards under Traditional Management, as under all types of management, are promotion and pay. It must be an almost unthinkably poor system of management, even under Traditional Management, which did not attempt to provide for some sort of promotion of the man who did the most and best work; but the lack of standardization of conditions, of instructions, of the work itself, and of reward, makes it almost impossible not only to give the reward, but even to determine who deserves the reward. Under Traditional Management, the reward need not be positive, that is, it might simply consist in the negation of some previously existing disadvantage. It need not be predetermined. It might be nothing definite. It might not be so set ahead that the man might look forward to it. In other words it might simply be the outcome of the good, and in no wise the incentive for the good. It need not necessarily be personal. It could be shared with a group, or gang, and lose all feeling of personality. It need not be a fixed reward or a fixed performance; in fact, if the management were Traditional it would be almost impossible that it would be a fixed reward. It might not be an assured reward, and in most cases it was not a prompt reward. These fixed adjectives describe the reward of Scientific Management,—positive, predetermined, personal, fixed, assured and prompt. A few of these might apply, or none might apply to the reward under Traditional Management.

Reward a Prize Won by One Only.—If this reward, whether promotion or pay, was given to someone under Traditional Management, this usually meant that others thereby lost it; it was in the nature of a prize which one only could attain, and which the others, therefore, would lose, and such a lost prize is, to the average man, for the time at least, a dampener on action. The rewarding of the winner, to the loss of all of the losers, has been met by the workmen getting together secretly, and selecting the winners for a week or more ahead, thus getting the same reward out of the employer without the extra effort.

Punishment Under Traditional Management Wrong in Theory.—The punishment, under Traditional Management, was usually much more than negative punishment; that is to say, the man who was punished usually received much more than simply the negative return of getting no reward. The days of bodily punishment have long passed, yet the account of the beatings given to the galley slaves and to other workers in the past are too vividly described in authentic accounts to be lost from memory. To-day, under Traditional Management, punishment consists of

1. fines, which are usually simply a cutting down of wages, the part deducted remaining with the company,

2. discharge, or

3. assignment to less pleasant or less desirable work.

This assignment is done on an unscientific basis, the man being simply put at something which he dislikes, with no regard as to whether his efficiency at that particular work will be high or not.

Results Are Unfortunate.—The punishment, under Traditional Management, is usually meted out by the foreman, simply as one of his many duties. He is apt to be so personally interested, and perhaps involved, in the case that his punishment will satisfy some wrong notions, impulse of anger, hate, or envy in him, and will arouse a feeling of shame or wounded pride, or unappreciation, in the man to whom punishment is awarded.

Direct Incentives Not Scientifically Utilized.—As for what we have called direct incentive, the love of racing was often used under Traditional Management through Athletic Contests, the faults in these being that the men were not properly studied, so that they could be properly assigned and grouped; care was not always exercised that hate should not be the result of the contest; the contest was not always conducted according to the rules of clean sport; the men slighted quality in hastening the work, and the results of the athletic contests were not so written down as to be thereafter utilized. Love of play may have been developed unconsciously, but was certainly not often studied. Love of personal recognition was probably often utilized, but in no scientific way. Neither was there anything in Traditional Management to develop self-confidence, or to arouse and maintain interest in any set fashion. Naturally, if the man were in a work which he particularly liked, which under Traditional Management was a matter of luck, he would be more or less interested in it, but there was no scientific way of arousing or holding his interest. Under Traditional Management, a man might take pride in his work, as did many of the old bricklayers and masons, who would set themselves apart after hours if necessary, lock themselves in, and cut bricks for a complicated arch or fancy pattern, but such pride was in no way fostered through the efforts of the management. Pugnacity was aroused, but it might have an evil effect as well as a good, so far as the management had any control. Ambition, in the same way, might be stimulated, and might not. There is absolutely nothing under Traditional Management to prevent a man being ambitious, gratifying his pride, and gratifying his pugnacity in a right way, and at the same time being interested in his work, but there was nothing under Traditional Management which provided for definite and exact methods for encouraging these good qualities, seeing that they developed in a proper channel, and scientifically utilizing the outcome again and again.

Pay for Performance Provided for by Transitory Management.—Under Transitory Management, as soon as practicable, one bonus is paid for doing work according to the method prescribed. As standardization takes place, the second bonus for completing the task in the time set can be paid. As each element of Scientific Management is introduced, incentives become more apparent, more powerful, and more assured.

Direct Incentives More Skillfully Used.—With the separating of output, and recording of output separately, love of personal recognition grew, self-confidence grew, interest in one's work grew. The Athletic Contest is so conducted that love of speed, love of play, and love of competition are encouraged, the worker constantly feeling that he can indulge in these, as he is assured of "fair play."

Incentives Under Scientific Management Constructive.—It is most important, psychologically and ethically, that it be understood that Scientific Management is not in any sense a destructive power. That only is eliminated that is harmful, or wasteful, or futile; everything that is good is conserved, and is utilized as much as it has ever been before, often much more than it has ever been utilized. The constructive force, under Scientific Management, is one of its great life principles. This is brought out very plainly in considering incentives under Scientific Management. With the scientifically determined wage, and the more direct and more sure plan of promotion, comes no discard of the well-grounded incentives of older types of management. The value of a fine personality in all who are to be imitated is not forgotten; the importance of using all natural stimuli to healthful activity is appreciated. Scientific Management uses all these, in so far as they can be used to the best outcome for workers and work, and supplements them by such scientifically derived additions as could never have been derived under the older types.

Characteristics of the Reward.—Rewards, under Scientific Management are—

(a) positive; that is to say, the reward must be a definite, posi-

tive gain to the man, and not simply a taking away of some
thing which may have been a drawback.

(b) predetermined; that is to say, before the man begins to work
it must be determined exactly what reward he is to get for
doing the work.

(c) personal; that is, individual, a reward for that particular
man for that particular work.

(d) fixed, unchanged. He must get exactly what it has been determined beforehand that he shall get.

(e) assured; that is to say, there must be provision made for this
reward before the man begins to work, so that he may be
positive that he will get the reward if he does the work. The
record of the organization must be that rewards have always
been paid in the past, therefore probably will be in the
future.

(f) the reward must be prompt; that is to say, as soon as the work
has been done, the man must get the reward. This promptness applies to the announcement of the reward; that is to
say, the man must know at once that he has gotten the reward, and also to the receipt of the reward by the man.

Positive Reward Arouses Interest and Holds Attention.—The
benefit of the positive reward is that it arouses and holds attention. A
fine example of a reward that is not positive is that type of "welfare
work" which consists of simply providing the worker with such surroundings as will enable him to work decently and without actual
discomfort. The worker, naturally, feels that such surroundings are
his right, and in no sense a reward and incentive to added activity.
The reward must actually offer to the worker something which he has
a right to expect only if he earns it; something which will be a positive addition to his life.

Predetermined Reward Concentrates Attention.—The predetermined reward allows both manager and man to concentrate their
minds upon the work. There is no shifting of the attention, while
the worker wonders what the reward that he is to receive will be.
It is also a strong factor for industrial peace, and for all the extra activities which will come when industrial conditions are peaceful.

Personal Reward Conserves Individuality.—The personal reward
is a strong incentive toward initiative, towards the desire to make the
most of one's individuality. It is an aid toward the feeling of personal

recognition. From this personal reward come all the benefits which have been considered under individuality.[1]

Fixed Reward Eliminates Waste Time.—The fact that the reward is fixed is a great eliminater of waste to the man and to the manager both. Not only does the man concentrate better under the fixed reward, but the reward, being fixed, need not be determined anew, over and over again; that is to say, every time that that kind of work is done, simultaneous with the arising of the work comes the reward that is to be paid for it. All the time that would be given to determining the reward, satisfying the men and arguing the case, is saved and utilized.

Assured Reward Aids Concentration.—The assured reward leads to concentration,—even perhaps more so than the fact that the reward is determined. In case the man was not sure that he would get the reward in the end, he would naturally spend a great deal of time wondering whether he would or not. Moreover, no immediate good fortune counts for much as an incentive if there is a prospect of bad luck following in the immediate future.

Needs for Promptness Varies.—The need for promptness of the reward varies. If the reward is to be given to a man of an elementary type of mind, the reward must be immediately announced and must be actually given very promptly, as it is impossible for anyone of such a type of intellect to look forward very far.[2] A man of a high type of intellectual development is able to wait a longer time for his reward, and the element of promptness, while acting somewhat as an incentive, is not so necessary.

Under Scientific Management, with the ordinary type of worker on manual work, it has been found most satisfactory to pay the reward every day, or at the end of the week, and to announce the score of output as often as every hour. This not only satisfies the longing of the normal mind to know exactly where it stands, but also lends a fresh impetus to repeat the high record. There is also, through the prompt reward, the elimination of time wasted in wondering what the result will be, and in allaying suspense. Suspense is not a stimulus to great activity, as anyone who has waited for the result of a doubtful examination can testify, it being almost impossible to concentrate the mind on any other work until one knows whether the work which has been done has been completed satisfactorily or not.

[1] W. P. Gillette, *Cost Analysis Engineering*, p. 3.
[2] F. W. Taylor, Paper 647, A. S. M. E., para, 33, para. 59.

Promptness Always an Added Incentive.—There are many kinds of life work and modes of living so terrible as to make one shudder at the thoughts of the certain sickness, death, or disaster that are almost absolutely sure to follow such a vocation. Men continue to work for those wages that lead positively to certain death, because of the immediateness of the sufficient wages, or reward. This takes their attention from their ultimate end. Much more money would be required if payment were postponed, say, five years after the act, to obtain the services of the air-man, or the worker subject to the poisoning of some branches of the lead and mercury industries.

If the prompt reward is incentive enough to make men forget danger and threatened death, how much more efficient is it in increasing output where there is no such danger.

Immediate Reward Not Always Preferable.—There are cases where the prompt reward is not to be preferred, because the delayed reward will be greater, or will be available to more people. Such is the case with the reward that comes from unrestricted output.

For example,—the immediacy of the temporarily increased reward caused by restricting output has often led the combinations of working men to such restriction, with an ultimate loss of reward to worker, to employer, and to the consumer.

Rewards Possible of Attainment by All.—Every man working under Scientific Management has a chance to win a reward. This means not only that the man has a "square deal," for the man may have a square deal under Traditional Management in that he may have a fair chance to try for all existing rewards. There is more than this under Scientific Management. By the very nature of the plan itself, the rewards are possible of achievement by all; any one man, by winning, in no way diminishes the chances of the others.

Rewards of Management Resemble Rewards of Workers.—So far the emphasis, in the discussion of reward, has been on the reward as given to the worker, and his feeling toward it. The reward to the management is just as sure. It lies in the increased output and therefore the possibility of lower costs and of greater financial gain. It is as positive; it is as predetermined, because before the reward to the men is fixed the management realizes what proportion that reward will bear to the entire undertaking, and exactly what profits can be obtained. It is a fundamental of Scientific Management that the management shall be able to prophesy the outputs ahead. It will certainly be as personal, if the management side is as thoroughly systematized as is the managed; it will be as fixed and as assured, and it certainly is as prompt, as the cost records can be arranged to come to the management every day, if that is desired.

Results of Such Rewards.—There are three other advantages to management which might well be added here. First, that a reward such as this attracts the best men to the work; second, that the reward, and the stability of it, indicates the stabiliy of the entire institution, and thus raises its standing in the eyes of the community as well as in its own eyes; and third, that it leads the entire organization, both managed and managing, to look favorably at all standardization. The standardized reward is sure to be attractive to all members. As soon as it is realized that the reason that it is attractive is because it is *standardized,* the entire subject of standardization rises in the estimation of every one, and the introduction of standards can be carried on more rapidly, and with greater success.

Rewards Divided into Promotion and Pay.—Rewards may be divided into two kinds; first, promotion and, second, pay. Under Scientific Management promotion is assured for every man and, as has been said, this promotion does not thereby hold back others from having the same sort of promotion. There is an ample place, under Scientific Management, for every man to advance.[3] Not only is the promotion sure, thus giving the man absolute assurance that he will advance as his work is satisfactory, but it is also gradual.[4] The promotion must be by degrees, otherwise the workers may get discouraged, from finding their promotion has come faster than has their ability to achieve, and the lack of attention, due to being discouraged, may be contagious. It is, therefore, of vital importace that the worker be properly selected, in order that, in his advancement and promotion, he shall be able to achieve his task after having been put at the new work. He must be advanced and promoted in a definite line of gradual development, in accordance with a fully conceived plan. This should be worked out and set down in writing as a definite plan, similar to the plan on the instruction card of one of his tasks.

Promotion May Be to Places Within or Without the Business.— In many lines of business, the business itself offers ample opportunity for promoting all men who can "make good" as rapidly as they can prepare themselves for positions over others, and for advancement; but under Scientific Management provision is made even in case the

---

[3] Hugo Diemer, *Factory Organization and Administration,* p. 5.
[4] James M. Dodge, Paper 1115, A. S. M. E., p. 723.

business does not offer such opportunities.[5] This is done by the management finding places outside their own organization for the men who are so trained that they can be advanced.

Such Promotion Attracts Workers.—While at first glance it might seem a most unfortunate thing for the management to have to let its men go, and while, as Dr. Taylor says, it is unfortunate for a business to get the reputation of being nothing but a training school, on the other hand, it has a very salutary effect upon the men to know that their employers are so disinterestedly interested in them that they will provide for their future, even at the risk of the individual business at which they have started having to lose their services. This will not only, as Dr. Taylor makes clear, stimulate many men in the establishment whose men go on to take the places of those who are promoted, but will also be a great inducement to other men to come into a place that they feel is unselfish and generous.

Subdivisions of "Pay."—Under "Pay" we have included eight headings:

1. Wages
2. Bonus
3. Shorter hours
4. Prizes other than money
5. Extra knowledge
6. Method of attack
7. Good opinion of others
8. Professional standing.

Relation Between Wages and Bonus.—Wages and bonus are closely related. By wages we mean a fixed sum, or minimum hourly rate, that the man gets in any case for his time, and by bonus we mean additional money that he receives for achievement of method, quantity or quality. Both might very properly be included under wages, or under money received for the work, or opportunities for receiving money for work, as the case might be. In the discussion of the different ways of paying wages under Scientific Management, there will be no attempt to discuss the economic value of the various means; the different methods will simply be stated, and the psychological significance will be, as far as possible, given.

Before discussing the various kinds of wages advised by the experts in Scientific Management, it is well to pause a moment to name the various sorts of methods of compensation recognized by authorities.

[5] F. W. Taylor, *Shop Management,* para. 310–311, Harper Ed., pp. 142–143.

David F. Schloss in his "Method of Industrial Remuneration" divides all possible ways of gaining remuneration into three—

1. the different kinds of wages
   1. time wage
   2. piece wage
   3. task wage
   4. progressive wage
   5. collective piece wage
   6. collective task wage
   7. collective progressive wage
   8. contract work
   9. coöperative work

with

2. profit sharing, and
3. industrial coöperation. These are defined and discussed at length in his book in a lucid and simple manner.

It is only necessary to quote him here as to the relationship between these different forms, where he says, page 11,—"The two leading forms of industrial remuneration under the Wages System are time wages, and piece wages. Intermediate between these principal forms, stands that known as task wage, while supplemental to these two named methods, we find those various systems which will here be designated by the name of Progressive Wages."[6]

Day Work Never Scientific.—The simplest of all systems, says Dr. Taylor in "A Piece Rate System," paragraph 10, in discussing the various forms of compensation "is the Day Work plan, in which the employés are divided into certain classes, and a standard rate of wages is paid to each class of men." He adds—"The men are paid according to the position which they fill, and not according to their individual character, energy, skill and reliability." The psychological objection to day work is that it does not arouse interest or effort or hold attention, nor does it inspire to memorizing or to learning.

It will be apparent that there is no inducement whatever for the man to do more than just enough to retain his job, for he in no wise shares in the reward for an extra effort, which goes entirely to his employer. "Reward," in this case, is usually simply a living wage,— enough to inspire the man, if he needs the money enough to work to

---

[6] See also C. U. Carpenter, *Profit Making in Shop and Factory Management*, pp. 113–115. For an extended and excellent account of the theory of well-known methods of compensating workmen, see C. B. Going, *Principles of Industrial Engineering*, chap. VIII.

hold his position, but not enough to incite him to any extra effort.

It is true that, in actual practice, through the foreman or some man in authority, the workers on day work may be "speeded up" to a point where they will do a great deal of work; the foreman being inspired, of course, by a reward for the extra output, but, as Dr. Taylor says, paragraph 17—"A Piece Rate System," this sort of speeding up is absolutely lacking in self-sustaining power. The moment that this rewarded foreman is removed, the work will again fall down. Therefore, day wage has almost no place in ultimate, scientifically managed work.

Piece Work Provides Pay in Proportion to Work Done.—Piece Work is the opposite of time work, in that under it the man is paid not for the time he spends at the work, but for the amount of work which he accomplishes. Under this system, as long as the man is paid a proper piece rate, and a rate high enough to keep him interested, he will have great inducements to work. He will have a chance to develop individuality, a chance for competition, a chance for personal recognition. His love of reasonable racing will be cultivated. His love of play may be cultivated.

All of these incentives arise because the man feels that his sense of justice is being considered; that if the task is properly laid out, and the price per piece is properly determined, he is given a "square deal" in being allowed to accomplish as great an amount of work as he can, with the assurance that his reward will be promptly coming to him.

Danger of Rate Being Cut.—Piece work becomes objectionable only when the rate is cut. The moment the rate is cut the first time, the man begins to wonder whether it is going to be cut again, and his attention is distracted from the work by his debating this question constantly. At best, his attention wanders from one subject to the other, and back again. It cannot be concentrated on his work. After the rate has been cut once or twice,—and it is sure to be cut unless it has been set from scientifically derived elementary time units,—the man loses his entire confidence in the stability of the rate, and, naturally, when he loses this confidence, his work is done more slowly, due to lack of further enthusiasm. On the contrary, as long as it is to his advantage to do the work and he is sure that his reward will be prompt, and that he will always get the price that has been determined as right by him and by the employers for his work, he can do this work easily in the time set. As soon as he feels that he will not get it, he will naturally begin to do less, as it will be not only to his personal advantage to do as little as possible, but also very much to the advantage of his fellows, for whom the rate will also be cut.

Task Wage Contains No Incentive to Additional Work.—What Schloss calls the Task Wage would, as he well says, be the intermediate between time or day wage and piece wage; that is, it would be the assigning of a definite amount of work to be done in definite time, and to be paid for by a definite sum. If the task were set scientifically, and the time scientifically determined, as it must naturally be for a scientific task, and the wage adequate for that work, there would seem to be nothing about this form of remuneration which could be a cause of dissatisfaction to the worker. Naturally, however, there would be absolutely no chance for him to desire to go any faster than the time set, or to accomplish any more work in the time set than that which he was obliged to, in that he could not possibly get anything for the extra work done.

Worth of Previous Methods in the Handling.—It will be noted in the discussion of the three types of compensation so far discussed, that there is nothing in them that renders them unscientific. Any one of the three may be used, and doubtless all are used, on works which are attempting to operate under Scientific Management. Whether they really are scientific methods of compensation or not, is determined by the way that they are handled. Certainly, however, all that any of these three can expect to do is to convince the man that he is being treated justly; that is to say, if he knows what sort of a contract he is entering into, the contract is perfectly fair, provided that the management keeps its part of the contract, pays the agreed-upon wage.

In proceeding, instead of following the order of Schloss we will follow the order, at least for a time, of Dr. Taylor in "A Piece Rate System"; this for two reasons:

First, for the reason that the "Piece Rate System" is later than Schloss' book, Schloss being 1891, and the "Piece Rate" being 1895; in the second place that we are following the Scientific Management side in distinction to the general economic side, laid down by Schloss. There is, however, nothing in our plan of discussion here to prevent one's following fairly closely in the Schloss also.

The Gain-sharing Plan.—We take up, then, the Gain-sharing Plan which was invented by Mr. Henry R. Towne and used by him with success in the Yale & Towne works. This is described in a paper read before the American Society of Mechanical Engineers, in professional paper No. 341, in 1888 and also in the Premium Plan, Mr. Halsey's modification of it, described by him in a paper entitled the "Premium Plan of Paying for Labor," American Society of Mechanical Engineers, 1891, Paper 449. In this, in describing the Profit-sharing Plan, Mr. Halsey says—"Under it, in addition to regular wages, the employés were offered a certain percentage of the final profits of the business. It thus divides the savings due to increased production between employer and employé."

Objections to This Plan.—We note here the objection to this plan: First,—"The workmen are given a share in what they do not earn; second, the workmen share regardless of individual deserts; third, the promised rewards are remote; fourth, the plan makes no provision for bad years; fifth, the workmen have no means of knowing if the agreement is carried out." Without discussing any farther whether these are worded exactly as all who have tried the plan might have found them, we may take these on Mr. Halsey's authority and discuss the psychology of them. If the workmen are given a share in what they do not earn, they have absolutely no feeling that they are being treated justly. This extra reward which is given to them, if in the nature of a present, might much better be a present out and out. If it has no scientific relation to what they have gotten, if the workmen share regardless of individual deserts, this, as Dr. Taylor says, paragraph 27 in the "Piece Rate System," is the most serious defect of all, in that it does not allow for recognition of the personal merits of each workman. If the rewards are remote, the interest is diminished. If the plan makes no provision for bad years, it cannot be self-perpetuating. If the workmen have no means of knowing if the agreement will be carried out or not, they will be constantly wondering whether it is being carried out or not, and their attention will wander.

The Premium Plan.—The Premium Plan is thus described by Mr. Halsey—"The time required to do a given piece of work is determined from previous experience, and the workman, in addition to his usual daily wages, is offered a premium for every hour by which he reduces that time on future work, the amount of the premium being less than his rate of wages. Making the hourly premium less than the hourly wages is the foundation stone upon which rest all the merits of the system."

Dr. Taylor's Description of This Plan.—Dr. Taylor comments upon this plan as follows:

"The Towne-Halsey plan consists in recording the quickest time in which a job has been done, and fixing this as a standard. If the workman succeeds in doing the job in a shorter time, he is still paid his same wages per hour for the time he works on the job, and, in addition, is given a premium for having worked faster, consisting of from one-quarter to one-half the difference between the wages earned and the wages originally paid when the job was done in standard time." Dr. Taylor's discussion of this plan will be found in "Shop Management," paragraphs 79 to 91.

Psychologically, the defect of this system undoubtedly is that it does not rest upon accurate scientific time study, therefore neither management nor men can predict accurately what is going to happen. Not being able to predict, they are unable to devote their entire attention to the work in hand, and the result cannot be as satisfactory as under an assigned task, based upon time study. The discussion of this is so thorough in Dr. Taylor's work, and in Mr. Halsey's work, that it is unnecessary to introduce more here.

Profit-sharing.—Before turning to the methods of compensation which are based upon the task, it might be well to introduce here mention of "Coöperation," or "Profit-sharing," which, in its extreme form, usually means the sharing of the profits from the business as a whole, among the men who do the work. This is further discussed by Schloss, and also by Dr. Taylor in paragraphs 32 to 35, in "A Piece Rate System"; also in "Shop Management," quoting from the "Piece Rate System," paragraphs 73 to 77.

Objections to Profit-sharing.—The objections, Dr. Taylor says, to coöperation are, first in the fact that no form of coöperation has been devised in which each individual is allowed free scope for his personal ambition; second, in the remoteness of the reward; third, in the unequitable division of the profits. If each individual is not allowed free scope, one sees at once that the entire advantage of individuality, and of personal recognition, is omitted. If the reward is remote, we recognize that its power diminishes very rapidly; and if there cannot be equitable division of the profits, not only will the men ultimately not be satisfied, but they will, after a short time, not even be satisfied while they are working, because their minds will constantly be distracted by the fact that the division will probably not be equitable, and also by the fact that they will be trying to plan ways in which they can get their proper share. Thus, not only in the ultimate outcome, but also during the entire process, the work will slow up necessarily, because the men can have no assurance either that the work itself, or the output, have been scientifically determined.

Scientific Management Embodies Valuable Elements of Profit-sharing.—Scientific Management embodies the valuable elements of profit-sharing, namely, the idea of coöperation, and the idea that the workers should share in the profit.

That the latter of these two is properly emphasized by Scientific Management is not always understood by the workers. When a worker is enabled to make three or four times as much output in a day as he has been accustomed to, he may think that he is not getting his full share of the "spoils" of increased efficiency, unless he gets a proportionately increased rate of pay. It should, therefore, be early made clear to him that the saving has been caused by the actions of the management, quite as much as by the increased efforts for productivity of the men. Furthermore, a part of the savings must go to pay for the extra cost of maintaining the standard conditions that make such output possible. The necessary planners and teachers usually are sufficient as object-lessons to convince the workers of the necessity of not giving all the extra savings to the workers.

It is realized that approximately one third of the extra profits from the savings must go to the employer, about one third to the employés, and the remainder for maintaining the system and carrying out further investigations.

This once understood, the satisfaction that results from a coöperative, profit-sharing type of management will be enjoyed.

The five methods of compensation which are to follow are all based upon the task, as laid down by Dr. Taylor; that is to say, upon time study, and an exact knowledge by the man, and the employers, of how much work can be done.

Differential Rate Piece Work the Ultimate Form of Compensation.—Dr. Taylor's method of compensation, which is acknowledged by all thoroughly grounded in Scientific Management to be the ultimate form of compensation where it can be used, is called Differential Rate Piece Work. It is described in "A Piece Rate System," paragraphs 50 to 52, as follows:—

"This consists, briefly, in paying a higher price per piece, or per unit, or per job, if the work is done in the shortest possible time and without imperfection, than is paid if the work takes a longer time or is imperfectly done. To illustrate—suppose 20 units, or pieces, to be the largest amount of work of a certain kind that can be done in a day. Under the differential rate system, if a workman finishes 20 pieces per day, and all of these pieces are perfect, he receives, say, 15 cents per piece, making his pay for the day 15 times 20 = $3.00. If, however, he works too slowly and turns out only, say 19 pieces, then instead of receiving 15 cents per piece he gets only 12 cents per piece, making his pay for the day 12 × 19 = $2.28, instead of $3.00 per day. If he succeeds in finishing 20 pieces—some of which are imperfect— then he should receive a still lower rate of pay, say 10c or 5c per piece, according to circumstances, making his pay for the day $2.00 or only $1.00, instead of $3.00."

Advantages of This System.—This system is founded upon knowledge that for a large reward men will do a large amount of work. The small compensation for a small amount of work—and under this system the minimum compensation is a little below the regular day's work—may lead men to exert themselves to accomplish more work. This system appeals to the justice of the men, in that it is more nearly an exact ratio of pay to endeavor.

Task Work with a Bonus.—The Task work with Bonus system of compensation, which is the invention of Mr. H. L. Gantt, is explained in "A Bonus System of Rewarding Labor," paper 923, read before the American Society of Mechanical Engineers, December, 1901, by Mr. Gantt. This system is there described as follows:—

"If the man follows his instructions and accomplishes all the work laid out for him as constituting his proper task for the day, he is paid a definite bonus in addition to the day rate which he always gets. If, however, at the end of the day he has failed to accomplish all of the work laid out, he does not get his bonus, but simply his day rate." This system of compensation is explained more fully in Chapter VI of Mr. Gantt's book, "Work, Wages and Profits," where he explains the modification now used by him in the bonus.

Advantages of Task Work with a Bonus.—The psychological advantage of the task with a Bonus is the fact that the worker has the assurance of a living wage while learning, no matter whether he succeeds in winning his bonus or not. In the last analysis, it is "day rate" for the unskilled, and "piece rate" for the skilled, and it naturally leads to a feeling of security in the worker. Mr. Gantt has so admirably explained the advantages, psychological as well as industrial, of his system, that it is unnecessary to go farther, except to emphasize the fine feeling of brotherhood which underlies the idea, and its expression.

The Differential Bonus System.—The Differential Bonus System of Compensation is the invention of Mr. Frederick A. Parkhurst, and is described by him in his book "Applied Methods of Scientific Management."

"The time the job should be done in is first determined by analysis and time study. The bonus is then added above the day work line. No bonus is paid until a definitely determined time is realized. As the time is reduced, the bonus is increased."

Three Rate with Increased Rate System.—The Three Rate System of Compensation is the invention of Mr. Frank B. Gilbreth and consists of day work, i. e., a day rate, or a flat minimum rate, which all who are willing to work receive until they can try themselves out; of a middle rate, which is given to the man when he accomplishes the work with exactness of compliance to prescribed motions, according to the requirements of his instruction card; and of a high rate, which is paid to the man when he not only accomplishes the task in accordance with the instruction card, but also within the set time and of the prescribed quality of finished work.

Advantage of This System.—The advantage of this is, first of all, that the man does not have to look forward so far for some of his reward, as it comes to him just as soon as he has shown himself able to do the prescribed methods required accurately. The first extra reward is naturally a stimulus toward winning the second extra reward. The middle rate is a stimulus to endeavor to perform that method which will enable him easiest to achieve the accomplishment of the task that pays the highest wage. The day rate assures the man of a living wage. The middle rate pays him a bonus for trying to learn. The high rate gives him a piece rate when he is skilled.

Lastly, as the man can increase his output, with continued experience, above that of the task, he receives a differential rate piece on the excess quantity, this simply making an increasing stimulus to exceed his previous best record.

All Task Systems Investigate Loss of Bonus.—Under all these bonus forms of wages, if the bonus is not gained the fact is at once investigated, in order that the blame may rest where it belongs. The blame may rest upon the workers, or it may be due to the material, which may be defective, or different from standard; it may be upon the supervision, or some fault of the management in not supplying the material in the proper quality, or sequence, or a bad condition of tools or machinery; or upon the instruction card. The fact that the missing of the bonus is investigated is an added assurance to the workman that he is getting the "square deal," and enlists his sympathy with these forms of bonus system, and his desire to work under them. The fact that the management will investigate also allows him to concentrate upon output, with no worry as to the necessity of his investigating places where he has fallen short.

Necessity for Workers Bearing This Loss.—In any case, whether the blame for losing the bonus is the worker's fault directly or not, he loses his bonus. This, for two reasons; in the first place, if he did not lose his bonus he would have no incentive to try to discover flaws before delays occurred; he would, otherwise, have an incentive to allow the material to pass through his hands, defective or imperfect as the case might be. This is very closely associated with the second reason, and that is, that the bonus comes from the savings caused by the plan of management, and that it is necessary that the workers as well as the management shall see that everything possible tends to increase the saving. It is only as the worker feels that his bonus is a part of the saving, that he recognizes the justice of his receiving it, that it is in no wise a gift to him, simply his proper share, accorded not by any system of philanthropy, or so-called welfare work, but simply because his own personal work has made it possible for the management to hand back his share to him.

Users of Any Task System Appreciate Other Task Systems.—It is of great importance to the workers that the users of any of these five methods of compensation of Scientific Management are all ready and glad to acknowledge the worth of all these systems. In many works more than one, in some all, of these systems of payment may be in use. Far from this resulting in confusion, it simply leads to the understanding that whatever is best in the particular situation should be used. It also leads to a feeling of stability everywhere, as a man who has worked under any of these systems founded on time study can easily pass to another. There is also a great gain here in the doing away of industrial warfare.

Shorter Hours and Holidays Effective Rewards.—Probably the greatest incentive, next to promotion and more pay, are shorter hours and holidays. In some cases, the shorter hours, or holidays, have proven even more attractive to the worker than the increase of pay. In Shop Management, paragraph 165; Dr. Taylor describes a case where children working were obliged to turn their entire pay envelopes over to their parents. To them, there was no particular incentive in getting more money, but, when the task was assigned, if they were allowed to go as soon as their task was completed, the output was accomplished in a great deal shorter time. Another case where shorter hours were successfully tried, was in an office where the girls were allowed the entire Saturday every two weeks, if the work was accomplished within a set amount of time. This extra time for shopping and matinées proved more attractive than any reasonable amount of extra pay that could be offered.

Desire for Approbation an Incentive.—Under "Individuality" were discussed various devices for developing the individuality of the man, such as his picture over a good output or record. These all act as rewards or incentives. How successful they would be, depends largely upon the temperament of the man and the sort of work that is to be done. In all classes of society, among all sorts of people, there is the type that loves approbation. This type will be appealed to more by a device which allows others to see what has been done than by almost anything else. As to what this device must be, depends on the intelligence of the man.

Necessity of Coöperation a Strong Incentive.—Under Scientific Management, many workers are forced by their coworkers to try to earn their bonuses, as "falling down on" tasks, and therefore schedules, may force them to lose their bonuses also.

The fact that, in many kinds of work, a man falling below his task will prevent his fellows from working, is often a strong incentive to that man to make better speed. For example, on a certain construction job in Canada, the teamsters were shown that, by their work, they were cutting down working opportunities for cart loaders, who could only be hired as the teamsters hauled sufficient loads to keep them busy.

Value of Knowledge Gained an Incentive to a Few Only.—Extra knowledge, and the better method of attack learned under Scientific Management, are rewards that will be appreciated by those of superior intelligence only. They will, in a way, be appreciated by all, because it will be realized that, through what is learned, more pay or promotion is received, but the fact that this extra knowledge, and better method of attack, will enable one to do better in all lines, not simply in the line at which one is working, and will render one's life more full and rich, will be appreciated only by those of a wide experience.

Acquired Professional Standing a Powerful Incentive.—Just as the success of the worker under Scientific Management assures such admiration by his fellow-workers as will serve as an incentive toward further success, so the professional standing attained by success in Scientific Management acts as an incentive to those in more responsible positions.

As soon as it is recognized that Scientific Management furnishes the only real measure of efficiency, its close relationship to professional standing will be recognized, and the reward which it can offer in this line will be more fully appreciated.

Punishments Negative and Positive.—Punishments may be first negative, that is, simply a loss of promised rewards. Such punishments, especially in cases of men who have once had the reward, usually will act as the necessary stimulus to further activity. Punishments may also be positive, such things as fines, assignment to less pleasant work, or as a last resort, discharge.

Fines Never Accrue to the Management.—Fines have been a most successful mode of punishment under Scientific Management. Under many of the old forms of management, the fines were turned back to the management itself, thus raising a spirit of animosity in the men, who felt that everything that they suffered was a gain to those over them. Under Scientific Management all fines are used in some way for the benefit of the men themselves. All fines should be used for some benefit fund, or turned into the insurance fund. The fines, as has been said, are determined solely by the disciplinarian, who is disinterested in the disposition of the funds thus collected. As the fines do not in any way benefit the management, and in fact rather hurt the management in that the men who pay them, no matter where they are applied, must feel more or less discouraged, it is, naturally, for the benefit of the management that there shall be as few fines as possible. Both management and men realize this, which leads to industrial peace, and also leads the managers, the functional foremen, and in fact every one, to eliminate the necessity and cause for fines to as great an extent as is possible.

Assignment to Less Pleasant Work Effective Punishment.—Assignment to less pleasant work is a very effective form of discipline. It has many advantages which do not show on the surface. The man may not really get a cut in pay, though his work be changed, and thus the damage he receives is in no wise to his purse, but simply to his feeling of pride. In the meantime, he is gaining a wider experience of the business, so that even the worst disadvantage has its bright side.

Discharge To Be Avoided Wherever Possible.—Discharge is, of course, available under Scientific Management, as under all other forms, but it is really less used under Scientific Management than under any other sort, because if a man is possibly available, and in any way trained, it is better to do almost anything to teach him, to assign him to different work, to try and find his possibilities, than to let him go, and have all that teaching wasted as far as the organization which has taught it is concerned.

Discharge a Grave Injury to a Worker.—Moreover, Scientific Management realizes that discharge may be a grave injury to a worker. As Mr. James M. Dodge, who has been most successful in Scientific Management and is noted for his good work for his fellowmen, eloquently pleads, in a paper on "The Spirit in Which Scientific Management Should Be Approached," given before the Conference on Scientific Management at Dartmouth College, October, 1911:

"It is a serious thing for a worker who has located his home within reasonable proximity to his place of employment and with proper regard for the schooling of his children, to have to seek other employment and readjust his home affairs, with a loss of time and wages. Proper management takes account not only of this fact, but also of the fact that there is a distinct loss to the employer when an old and experienced employé is replaced by a new man, who must be educated in the methods of the establishment. An old employé has, in his experience, a potential value that should not be lightly disregarded, and there should be in case of dismissal the soundest of reasons, in which personal prejudice or temporary mental condition of the foreman should play no part.

"Constant changing of employés is not wholesome for any establishment, and the sudden discovery by a foreman that a man who has been employed for a year or more is 'no good' is often a reflection on the foreman, and more often still, is wholly untrue. All working men, unless they develop intemperate or dishonest habits, have desirable value in them, and the conserving and increasing of their value is a duty which should be assumed by their superiors."

Punishment Can Never Be Entirely Abolished.—It might be asked why punishments are needed at all under this system; that is, why positive punishments are needed. Why not merely a lack of reward for the slight offenses, and a discharge if it gets too bad? It must be remembered, however, that the punishments are needed to insure a proper appreciation of the reward. If there is no negative side, the beauty of the reward will never be realized; the man who has once suffered by having his pay cut for something which he has done wrong, will be more than ready to keep up to the standard. In the second place, unless individuals are punished, the rights of other individuals will, necessarily, be encroached upon. When it is considered that under Scientific Management the man who gives the punishment is the disinterested disciplinarian, that the punishment is made exactly appropriate to the offense, and that no advantage from it comes to any one except the men themselves, it can be understood that the psychological basis is such as to make a punishment rather an incentive than a detriment.

Direct Incentives Numerous and Powerful.—As for the direct incentives, these are so many that it is possible to enumerate only a few. For example—

This may be simply a result of love of speed, love of play, or love of activity, or it may be, in the case of a man running a machine, not so much for the love of the activity as for a love of seeing things progress rapidly. There is a love of contest which has been thoroughly discussed under "Athletic Contests," which results in racing, and in all the pleasures of competition.

Racing Directed Under Scientific Management.—The psychology of the race under Scientific Management is most interesting. The race is not a device of Scientific Management to speed up the worker, any speed that would be demanded by Scientific Management beyond the task-speed would be an unscientific thing. On the other hand, it is not the scope of Scientific Management to bar out any contests which would not be for the ultimate harm of the workers. Such interference would hamper individuality; would make the workers feel that they were restricted and held down. While the workers are, under Scientific Management, supposed to be under the supervision of some one who can see that the work is only such as they can do and continuously thrive, any such interference as, for example, stopping a harmless race, would at once make them feel that their individual initiative was absolutely destroyed. It is not the desire of Scientific Management to do anything of that sort, but rather to use every possible means to make the worker feel that his initiative is being conserved.

All "Native Reactions" Act as Incentives.—Pride, self-confidence, pugnacity,—all the "native reactions" utilized by teaching serve as direct incentives.

Results of Incentives to the Work.—All incentives in every form of management, tend, from their very nature, to increase output. When Scientific Management is introduced, there is selection of such incentives as will produce greatest amount of specified output, and the results can be predicted.

Results of Incentives to the Worker.—Under Traditional Management the incentives are usually such that the worker is likely to overwork himself if he allows himself to be driven by the incentive. This results in bodily exhaustion. So, also, the anxiety that accompanies an unstandardized incentive leads to mental exhaustion. With the introduction of Transitory Management, danger from both these types of exhaustion is removed. The incentive is so modified that it is instantly subject to judgment as to its ultimate value.

Scientific Management makes the incentives stronger than they are under any other type, partly by removing sources of worry, waste and hesitation, partly by determining the ratio of incentive to output. The worker under such incentives gains in bodily and mental poise and security.

Welfare

••

Definition of Welfare.—"Welfare" means "a state or condition of doing well; prosperous or satisfactory course or relation; exemption from evil;" in other words, well-being. This is the primary meaning of the word. But, to-day, it is used so often as an adjective, to describe work which is being attempted for the good of industrial workers, that any use of the word welfare has that fringe of meaning to it.

"Welfare" Here Includes Two Meanings.—In the discussion of welfare in this chapter, both meanings of the word will be included. "Welfare" under each form of management will be discussed, first, as meaning the outcome to the men of the type of management itself;

and second, as discussing the sort of welfare work which is used under that form of management.

Discussion of First Answers. Three Questions.—A discussion of welfare as the result of work divides itself naturally into three parts, or three questions:

What is the effect upon the physical life?
What is the effect upon the mental life?
What is the effect upon the moral life?

Under Traditional Management No Physical Improvement.— The indefiniteness of Traditional Management manifests itself again in this discussion, it being almost impossible to make any general statement which could not be controverted by particular examples; but it is safe to say that in general, under Traditional Management, there is not a definite physical improvement in the average worker. In the first place, there is no provision for regularity in the work. The planning not being done ahead, the man has absolutely no way of knowing exactly what he will be called upon to do. There being no measure of fatigue, he has no means of knowing whether he can go to work the second part of the day, say, with anything like the efficiency with which he could go to work in the first part of the day. There being no standard, the amount of work which he can turn out must vary according as the tools, machinery and equipment are in proper condition, and the material supplies his needs.

No Good Habits Necessarily Formed.—In the second place, under Traditional Management there are no excellent habits necessarily formed. The man is left to do fairly as he pleases, if only the general outcome be considered sufficient by those over him. There may be a physical development on his part, if the work be of a kind which can develop him, or which he likes to such an extent that he is willing to do enough of it to develop him physically; this liking may come through the play element, or through the love of work, or through the love of contest, or through some other desire for activity, but it is not provided for scientifically, and the outcome cannot be exactly predicted. Therefore, under Traditional Management there is no way of knowing that good health and increased strength will result from the work, and we know that in many cases poor health and depleted strength have been the outcome of the work. We may say then fairly, as far as physical improvement is concerned that, though it might be the outcome of Traditional Management, it was rather in spite of Traditional Management, in the sense at least that the management had nothing to do with it, and had absolutely no way of providing for it. The moment that it was provided for in any systematic way, the Traditional Management vanished.

No Directed Mental Development.—Second, mental development. Here, again, there being no fixed habits, no specially trained habit of attention, no standard, there was no way of knowing that the man's mind was improving. Naturally, all minds improve merely with experience. Experience must be gathered in, and must be embodied into judgment. There is absolutely no way of estimating what the average need in this line would be, it varies so much with the temperament of the man. Again, it would usually be a thing that the man himself was responsible for, and not the management, certainly not the management in any impersonal sense. Some one man over an individual worker might be largely responsible for improving him intellectually. If this were so, it would be because of the temperament of the over-man, or because of his friendly desire to impart a mental stimulus; seldom, if ever, because the management provided for its being imparted. Thus, there was absolutely no way of predicting that wider or deeper interest, or that increased mental capacity, would take place.

Moral Development Doubtful.—As for moral development, in the average Traditional Management it was not only not provided for, but rather doubtful. A man had very little chance to develop real, personal responsibilities, in that there was always some one over him who was watching him, who disciplined him and corrected him, who handed in the reports for him, with the result that he was in a very slight sense a free agent. Only men higher up, the foremen and the superintendents could obtain real development from personal responsibilities. Neither was there much development of responsibility for others, in the sense of being responsible for personal development of others. Having no accurate standards to judge by, there was little or no possibility of appreciation of the relative standing of the men, either by the individual of himself, or by others of his ability. The man could be admired for his strength, or his skill, but not for his real efficiency, as measured in any satisfactory way. The management taught self-control in the most rudimentary way, or not at all. There was no distinct goal for the average man, neither was there any distinct way to arrive at such a goal; it was simply a case, with the man lower down, of making good for any one day and getting that day's pay. In the more enlightened forms of Traditional Management, a chance for promotion was always fairly sure, but the moment that the line of promotion became assured, we may say that Traditional Management had really ceased, and some form of Transitory Management was in operation.

"Square Deal" Lacking.—Perhaps the worst lack under Traditional Management is the lack of the "square deal." In the first place, even the most efficient worker under this form of management was not sure of his place. This not only meant worry on his part, which distracted his attention from what he did, but meant a wrong attitude all along the line. He had absolutely no way of knowing that, even though he did his best, the man over him, in anger, or because of some entirely ulterior thing, might not discharge him, put him in a lower position. So also the custom of spying, the only sort of inspection recognized under Traditional Management of the most elementary form, led to a feeling on the men's part that they were being constantly watched on the sly, and to an inability to concentrate. This brought about an inability to feel really honest, for being constantly under suspicion is enough to poison even one's own opinion of one's integrity. Again, being at the beck and call of a prejudiced foreman who was all-powerful, and having no assured protection from the whims of such a man, the worker was obliged, practically for self-protection, to try to conciliate the foremen by methods of assuming merits that are obvious, on the surface. He ingratiates himself in the favor of the foreman in that way best adapted to the peculiarities of the character of the foreman, sometimes joining societies, or the church of the foreman, sometimes helping him elect some political candidate or relative; at other times, by the more direct method of buying drinks, or taking up a subscription for presenting the foreman with a gold watch, "in appreciation of his fairness to all;" sometimes by consistently losing at cards or other games of chance. When it is considered that this same foreman was probably, at the time, enjoying a brutal feeling of power, it is no wonder that no sense of confidence of the "square deal" could develop. There are countless ways that the brutal enjoyment of power could be exercised by the man in a foreman's position. As has already been said, some men prefer promotion to a position of power more than anything else. Nearly all desire promotion to power for the extra money that it brings, and occasionally, a man will be found who loves the power, although unconsciously, for the pleasure he obtains in lording over other human beings. This quality is present more or less in all human beings. It is particularly strong in the savage, who likes to torture captured human beings and animals, and perhaps the greatest test for high qualifications of character and gentleness is that of having power over other human beings without unnecessarily accenting the difference in the situation. Under Military Management, there is practically no limit to this power, the management being satisfied if the foreman gets the work out of the men, and the men having practically no one to appeal to, and being obliged to receive their punishment always from the hands of a prejudiced party.

Little Possibility of Development of Will.—Being under such influence as this, there is little or no possibility of the development of an intelligent will. The "will to do" becomes stunted, unless the pay is large enough to lead the man to be willing to undergo abuses in order to get the money. There is nothing, moreover, in the aspect of the management itself to lead the man to have a feeling of confidence either in himself, or in the management, and to have that moral poise which will make him wish to advance.

Real Capacity Not Increased.—With the likelihood of suspicion, hate and jealousy arising, and with constant preparations for conflict, of which the average union and employers' association is the embodiment, naturally, real capacity is not increased, but is rather decreased, under this form of management, and we may ascribe this to three faults:

First, to lack of recognition of individuality,—men are handled mostly as gangs, and personality is sunk.

Second, to lack of standardization, and to lack of time study, that fundamental of all standardization, which leads to absolute inability to make a measured, and therefore scientific judgment, and

Third, to the lack of teaching; to the lack of all constructiveness.

These three lacks, then, constitute a strong reason why Traditional Management does not add to the welfare of the men.

Little Systematized Welfare Work Under Traditional Management.—As for welfare work,—that is, work which the employers themselves plan to benefit the men, if under such work be included timely impulses of the management for the men, and the carrying of these out in a more or less systematic way, it will be true to say that such welfare work has existed in all times, and under all forms of management. The kind-hearted man will show his kind heart wherever he is, but it is likewise true to say that little systematic beneficial work is done under what we have defined as Traditional Management.

Definite Statements as to Welfare Under Transitory Management Difficult to Make.—It is almost impossible to give any statement as to the general welfare of workers under Transitory Management, because, from the very nature of the case, Transitory Management is constantly changing. In the discussion of the various chapters, and in showing how individuality, functionalization, measurement, and so on, were introduced, and the psychological effect upon the men of their being introduced, welfare was more or less unsystematically considered. In turning to the discussion under Scientific Management and showing how welfare is the result of Scientific Management and is incorporated in it, much as to its growth will be included.

Welfare Work Under Transitory Management Is Usually Commendable.—As to the welfare work under Transitory Management, much could be said, and much has been said and written. Typical Welfare Work under Transitory Management deserves nothing but praise. It is the result of the dedication of many beautiful lives to a beautiful cause. It consists of such work as building rest rooms for the employés, in providing for amusements, in providing for better working conditions, in helping to better living conditions, in providing for some sort of a welfare worker who can talk with the employés and benefit them in every way, including being their representative in speaking with the management.

An Underlying Flaw Is Apparent.—There can be no doubt that an enormous quantity of good has been done by this welfare work, both positively, to the employés themselves, and indirectly, to the management, through fostering a kinder feeling. There is, however, a flaw to be found in the underlying principles of this welfare work as introduced in Transitory Management, and that is that it takes on more or less the aspect of a charity, and is so regarded both by the employés and by the employer. The employer, naturally, prides himself more or less upon doing something which is good, and the employé naturally resents more or less having something given to him as a sort of charity which he feels his by right.

Its Effect Is Detrimental.—The psychological significance of this is very great. The employer, feeling that he has bestowed a gift, is, naturally, rather chagrined to find it is received either as a right, or with a feeling of resentment. Therefore, he is often led to decrease what he might otherwise do, for it is only an unusual and a very high type of mind that can be satisfied simply with the doing of the good act, without the return of gratitude. On the other hand, the employé, if he be a man of pride, may resent charity even in such a general form as this, and may, with an element of rightness, prefer that the money to be expended be put into his pay envelope, instead. If it is simply a case of better working conditions, something that improves him as an efficient worker for the management, he will feel that this welfare work is in no sense something which he receives as a gift, but rather something which is his right, and which benefits the employer exactly as much, if not more than it benefits him.

Welfare Work Not Self-perpetuating.—Another fault which can be found with the actual administration of the welfare work, is the fact that it often disregards one of the fundamental principles of Scientific Management, in that the welfare workers themselves do not train enough people to follow in their footsteps, and thus make welfare self-perpetuating.

In one case which the writer has in mind, a noble woman is devoting her life to the welfare of a body of employés in an industry which greatly requires such work. The work which she is doing is undoubtedly benefiting these people in every aspect, not only of their business but of their home lives, but it is also true that should she be obliged to give up the work, or be suddenly called away, the work would practically fall to pieces. It is built up upon her personality, and, wonderful as it is, its basis must be recognized as unscientific and temporary.

Scientific Provision for Welfare Under Scientific Management.— Under Scientific Management general welfare is provided for by:—

The effect that the work has on physical improvement. This we shall discuss under three headings—

1. the regularity of the work.
2. habits.
3. physical development.

As for the regularity of the work—we have

   (a) The apportionment of the work and the rest. Under Scientific Management, work time and rest time are scientifically apportioned. This means that the man is able to come to each task with the same amount of strength, and that from his work he gains habits of regularity.

   (b) The laying out of the work. The standards upon which the

instruction cards are based, and the method of preparing
them, assure regularity.

(c) The manner of performing the work. Every time that identical work is done, it is done in an identical manner.

The resulting regularity has an excellent effect upon the physical
welfare of the worker.

2. Habits, under Scientific Management,

(a) are prescribed by standard. The various physical habits of
the man, the motions that are used, having all been timed
and then standardized, the worker acquires physical habits
that are fixed.

(b) are taught;[1] therefore they are not remote but come actually
and promptly into the consciousness and into the action of
the worker.

(c) are retained, because they are standard habits and because
the rewards which are given for using them make it an
object to the worker to retain them.

(d) are reënforced by individuality and functionalization; that
is to say, the worker is considered as an individual, and his
possibilities are studied, before he is put into the work;
therefore, his own individuality and his own particular
function naturally reënforce those habits which he is taught
to form. These habits, being scientifically derived, add to
physical improvement.

3. Physical development

(a) is fostered through the play element, has been scientifically
studied, and is utilized as far as possible; the same is true of
the love of work, which is reënforced by the fact that the
man has been placed where he will have the most love for
his work.

(b) is insured by the love of contest, which is provided for not
only by contest with others, but by the constant contest of
the worker with his own previous records. When he does
exceed these records he utilizes powers which it is for his
good physically, as well as otherwise, to utilize.

Results of Physical Improvement.—This regularity, good habits,
and physical development, result in good health, increased strength
and a better appearance. To these three results all scientific managers
testify. An excellent example of this is found in Mr. Gantt's "Work,

---

[1] H. L. Gantt, *Work, Wages and Profits,* p. 115, p. 121.

Wages and Profits," where the increased health, the better color and the better general appearance of the workers under Scientific Management is commented on as well as the fact that they are inspired by their habits to dress themselves better and in every way to become of a higher type.[2]

Mental Development.—Welfare under Scientific Management is provided for by Mental Development. This we may discuss under habits, and under general mental development.

    1. As for habits we must consider

        (a) Habits of attention. Under Scientific Management, as we have shown, attention must become a habit. Only when it does become a habit, can the work required be properly performed, and the reward received. As only those who show themselves capable of really receiving the reward are considered to be properly placed, ultimately all who remain at work under Scientific Management must attain this habit of attention.

        (b) Habit of method of attack. This not only enables the worker to do the things that he is assigned satisfactorily, but also has the broadening effect of teaching him how to do other things, i. e., showing him the "how" of doing things, and giving him standards which are the outcome of mental habits, and by which he learns to measure.

    2. General mental development is provided for by the experience which the worker gets not only in the general way in which all who work must give experience, but in the set way provided for by Scientific Management. This is so presented to the worker that it becomes actually usable at once. This not only allows him to judge others, but provides for self-knowledge, which is one of the most valuable of all of the outcomes of Scientific Management. He becomes mentally capable of estimating his own powers and predicting what he himself is capable of doing. The outcome of this mental development is

        (a) wider interest.

        (b) deeper interest.

        (c) increased mental capabilities.

The better method of attack would necessarily provide for wider interest. The fact that any subject taken up is in its ultimate final

[2] Pp. 171–172.

unit form, would certainly lead to deeper interest; and the exercise of these two faculties leads to increased mental capabilities.

Moral Development.—Moral development under Scientific Management results from the provisions made for cultivating—

1. personal responsibility.
2. responsibility for others.
3. appreciation of standing.
4. self-control.
5. "squareness."

1. Personal responsibility is developed by

(a) Individual recognition. When the worker was considered merely as one of a gang, it was very easy for him to shift responsibilities upon others. When he knows that he is regarded by the management, and by his mates, as an individual, that what he does will show up in an individual record, and will receive individual reward or punishment, necessarily personal responsibility is developed.

Moreover, this individual recognition is brought to his mind by his being expected to fill out his own instruction card. In this way, his personal responsibility is specifically brought home to him.

(b) The appreciation which comes under Scientific Management. This appreciation takes the form of reward and promotion, and of the regard of his fellow-workers; therefore, being a growing thing, as it is under Scientific Management, it insures that his personal responsibility shall also be a growing thing, and become greater the longer he works under Scientific Management.

2. Responsibility for others is provided for by the inter-relation of all functions. It is not necessary that all workers under Scientific Management should understand all about it. However, many do understand, and the more that they do understand, the more they realize that everybody working under Scientific Management is more or less dependent upon everybody else. Every worker must feel this, more or less, when he realizes that there are eight functional bosses over him, who are closely related to him, on whom he is dependent, and who are more or less dependent upon him. The very fact that the planning is separated from the performing, means that more men are directly interested in any one piece of work; in fact, that every individual piece of work that is done is in some way a bond between a

great number of men, some of whom are planning and some of whom are performing it. This responsibility for others is made even more close in the dependent bonuses which are a part of Scientific Management, a man's pay being dependent upon the work of those who are working under him. Certainly, nothing could bring the fact more closely to the attention of each and every worker under this system, than associating it with the pay envelope.

    3. Appreciation of standing is fostered by

      (a) individual records. Through these the individual himself knows what he has done, his fellows know, and the management knows.

      (b) comparative records, which show even those who might not make the comparison, exactly how each worker stands, with relation to his mates, or with relation to his past records.

This appreciation of standing is well exemplified in the happy phrasing of Mr. Gantt—"There is in every workroom a fashion, or habit of work, and the new worker follows that fashion, for it isn't respectable not to. The man or woman who ignores fashion does not get much pleasure from associating with those that follow it, and the new member consequently tries to fall in with the sentiment of the community.[3] Our chart shows that the stronger the sentiment in favor of industry is, the harder the new member tries and the sooner he succeeds."

    4. Self-control is developed by

      (a) the habits of inhibition fostered by Scientific Management, —that is to say, when the right habits are formed, necessarily many wrong habits are eliminated. It becomes a part of Scientific Management to inhibit all inattention and wrong habits, and to concentrate upon the things desired. This is further aided by

      (b) the distinct goal and the distinct task which Scientific Management gives, which allow the man to hold himself well in control, to keep his poise and to advance steadily.

    5. "Squareness." This squareness is exemplified first of all by the attitude of the management. It provides, in every way, that the men are given a "square deal," in that the tasks assigned are of the proper size, and that the reward that is given is of the proper dimensions, and is assured. This has already been shown to be exemplified in

    [3] H. L. Gantt, *Work, Wages and Profits,* pp. 154–155.

many characteristics of Scientific Management, and more especially in the inspection and in the disciplining.

Moral Development Results in Contentment, Brotherhood and the "Will To Do."—The three results of this moral development are

1. contentment
2. brotherhood
3. a "will to do."

1. Contentment is the outgrowth of the personal responsibility, the appreciation of standing, and the general "squareness" of the entire plan of Scientific Management.

2. The idea of brotherhood is fostered particularly through the responsibility for others, through the feeling that grows up that each man is dependent upon all others, and that it is necessary for every man to train up another man to take his place before he can be advanced. Thus it comes about that the old caste life, which so often grew up under Traditional Management, becomes abolished, and there ensues a feeling that it is possible for any man to grow up into any other man's place. The tug-of-war attitude of the management and men is transformed into the attitude of a band of soldiers scaling a wall. Not only is the worker pulled up, but he is also forced up from the bottom.[4]

3. The "will to do" is so fostered by Scientific Management that not only is the worker given every incentive, but he, personally, becomes inspired with this great desire for activity, which is after all the best and finest thing that any system of work can give to him.

Interrelation of Physical, Mental and Moral Development.—As to the interrelation of physical, mental and moral development, it must never be forgotten that the mind and the body must be studied together,[5] and that this is particularly true in considering the mind in management.[6] For the best results of the mind, the body must be cared for, and provided for, fully as much as must the mind, or the best results from the mind will not, and cannot, be obtained.

Successful management must consider the results of all mental states upon the health, happiness and prosperity of the worker, and the quality, quantity and cost of the output. That is to say, unless the mind is kept in the right state, with the elimination of worry, the

---

[4] F. W. Taylor, *Shop Management*, para. 170, Harper Ed., p. 76.

[5] William James, *Psychology, Advanced Course*, Vol. II, p. 372.

[6] See remarkable work of Dr. A. Imbert, *Evaluation de la Capacite de Travail d'un Ouvrier Avant et Apres un Accident; Les Methodes du Laboratoire appliquees a l'Etude directe et pratique des Questions ouvrieres.*

body cannot do its best work, and, in the same way, unless the body is kept up to the proper standard, the mind cannot develop. Therefore, a really good system of management must consider not only these things separately, but in their interrelation,—and this Scientific Management does.

Result of Physical, Mental and Moral Development Is Increased Capacity.—The ultimate result of all this physical improvement, mental development and moral development is increased capacity, increased capacity not only for work, but for health, and for life in general.

Welfare Work an Integral Part of Scientific Management.— Strictly speaking, under Scientific Management, there should be no necessity for a special department of Welfare Work. It should be so incorporated in Scientific Management that it is not to be distinguished. Here the men are looked out for in such a way under the operation of Scientific Management itself that there is no necessity for a special welfare worker. This is not to say that the value of personality will disappear under Scientific Management, and that it may not be necessary in some cases to provide for nurses, for physical directors, and for advisers. It will, however, be understood that the entire footing of these people is changed under Scientific Management. It is realized under Scientific Management that these people, and their work, benefit the employers as much as the employés. They must go on the regular payroll as a part of the efficiency equipment. The workers must understand that there is absolutely no feeling of charity, or of gift, in having them; that they add to the perfectness of the entire establishment.

SUMMARY

Results of Welfare to the Work.—Because of Welfare Work, of whatever type, more and better work is accomplished, with only such expenditure of effort as is beneficial to the worker. Not only does the amount of work done increase, but it also tends to become constant, after it has reached its standard expected volume.

Result of Welfare Work to the Worker.—This description of welfare of the men under Scientific Management, in every sense of the word welfare, has been very poor and incomplete if from it the reader has not deduced the fact that Scientific Management enables the worker not only to lead a fuller life in his work, but also outside his work; that it furnishes him hours enough free from the work to develop such things as the work cannot develop; that it furnishes him with health and interest enough to go into his leisure hours with a power to develop himself there; that it furnishes him with a broader outlook, and, best of all, with a capacity of judging for himself what he needs most to get. In other words, if Scientific Management is what it claims to be, it leads to the development of a fuller life in every sense of the word, enabling the man to become a better individual in himself, and a better member of his community. If it does not do this it is not truly Scientific Management. Miss Edith Wyatt has said, very beautifully, at the close of her book, "Making Both Ends Meet"[7]: "No finer dream was ever dreamed than that the industry by which the nation lives, should be so managed as to secure for the men and women engaged in it their real prosperity, their best use of their highest powers. How far Scientific Management will go toward realizing the magnificent dream in the future, will be determined by the greatness of spirit and the executive genius with which its principles are sustained by all the people interested in its inauguration, the employers, the workers and the engineers."

We wish to modify the word "dream" to the word "plan." The plan of Scientific Management is right, and, as Miss Wyatt says, is but waiting for us to fulfill the details that are laid out before us.

Conclusion.—The results thus far attained by Scientific Management justify a prediction as to its future. It will accomplish two great works.

1. It will educate the worker to the point where workers will be fitted to work, and to live.

2. It will aid the cause of Industrial Peace.

It will put the great power of knowledge into every man's hands. This it must do, as it is founded on coöperation, and this coöperation demands that all shall know and shall be taught.

With this knowledge will come ability to understand the rights of others as well as one's own. "To know all is to pardon all."

Necessity for coöperation, and trained minds:—These two can but lead to elimination of that most wasteful of all warfare—Industrial Warfare. Such will be the future of Scientific Management, —whether it win universal approval, universal disapproval, or half-hearted advocacy to-day.

When the day shall come that the ultimate benefits of Scientific Management are realized and enjoyed, depends on both the managers

[7] Clark and Wyatt, Macmillan, pp. 269–270.

and the workers of the country; but, in the last analysis, the greatest power towards hastening the day lies in the hands of the workers.

To them Scientific Management would desire to appeal as a road up and out from industrial monotony and industrial turmoil. There are many roads that lead to progress. This road leads straightest and surest,—and we can but hope that the workers of all lands, and of our land in particular, will not wait till necessity drives, but will lead the way to that true "Brotherhood" which may some day come to be.

Index

501

*This book has been set on the Linotype in
11 point Baskerville, leaded 2 points, and
10 point Baskerville, leaded 1 point. Section
numbers are in 24 point Baskerville italics,
and section titles in 18 point Baskerville
italics. Chapter titles are in 24 point Baskerville italics. The size of the type page is
27 by 45 picas.*